THE RISE AND FALL OF THE AMERICAN CENTURY

United States from 1890–2009

William H. Chafe

Duke University

New York   Oxford

OXFORD UNIVERSITY PRESS

2009

Oxford University Press, Inc., publishes works that further Oxford University's
objective of excellence in research, scholarship, and education.

Oxford   New York
Auckland   Cape Town   Dar es Salaam   Hong Kong   Karachi
Kuala Lumpur   Madrid   Melbourne   Mexico City   Nairobi
New Delhi   Shanghai   Taipei   Toronto

With offices in
Argentina   Austria   Brazil   Chile Czech Republic   France   Greece
Guatemala   Hungary   Italy   Japan   Poland   Portugal   Singapore
South Korea   Switzerland   Thailand   Turkey   Ukraine   Vietnam

Published by Oxford University Press, Inc.
198 Madison Avenue, New York, New York 10016
http://www.oup.com

Library of Congress Cataloging-in-Publication Data
Chafe, William Henry.
The rise and fall of the American century : United States from
1890–2009 / William H. Chafe.
   p.   cm
Includes index.
ISBN 978-0-19-538262-4—ISBN 978-0-19-538344-7
1. United States—History—20th century.   2. United States—Politics and
government—20th century.   3. Political culture—United States—
History—20th century.   4. United States—Foreign relations—
20th century.   5. United States—Social conditions—20th century.   I. Title.
E741.C33 2009
973.91—dc22   2008047482

9 8 7 6 5 4 3 2 1
Printed in the United States of America
on acid-free paper

Dedication

To the memory of
Eleanor Roosevelt, Martin Luther
King, Jr., and Robert F. Kennedy
who cared enough to make a
difference

CONTENTS

PREFACE

This is a book about the rise—and potentially the fall—of a nation more powerful, more wealthy, and more dominant than any in human history. It is also about the ongoing challenges that nation has faced—inequalities of race, gender, and income that contradict the country's vision of itself as a community dedicated to equal opportunity. When John Winthrop arrived on the *Arabella* outside Massachusetts Bay in 1630, he talked about creating a new society that would be a "city upon a hill" for the world to look on as a beacon of hope. More than three hundred years later, *Time* magazine founder Henry Luce declared that Winthrop's dream had reached a new stage of fulfillment. This was to be the "American Century," he wrote in 1941, where the greatest exemplar of freedom in the world would carry forward its mandate to lead.

This is the story of how America has struggled, at home and abroad, to realize the promise of what it might become—to fulfill the dreams of Winthrop and Luce. It begins in the late nineteenth century, charting the explosive changes that were already transforming a power once inferior to the great nation-states of Britain, France, Germany, Russia, Japan, and China but now their equal and soon their superior. It traces from the end of Reconstruction, through the era of Populism, into the dawn of Progressivism, then into the Great Depression and New Deal how America did—and did not—engage the ongoing disparities within its midst as well as assuming the growing responsibilities of being the world's greatest economic and military power.

At every stage, tensions—and an inextricable relationship—existed between what was happening at home and what was transpiring in the world. Wars brought new weapons and international responsibilities but also generated dramatic social change and renewed challenges for the country to live up to its ideals. With change came renewed debate over what constituted the basic values of the nation and how, or whether, shifts in population, residential patterns, or immigration would alter the fundamental beliefs that shaped the nation's development. The years after World War II encapsulated those challenges, raising to new heights internal tensions over civil and human rights as well as highlighting the relationship between America's dominant role in world affairs and her ability to make fulfillment of the American Dream a reality at home. By the end of the twentieth century, one huge conflict—the Cold War with the Soviet Union—had ended in triumph, while another—the international challenge of terrorism and revolution—had just begun. No one could be certain of the outcome, or the consequences for America at home, of the ongoing struggle.

The American Century remains a work in progress. It is my hope that this book, and the ideas it puts forth, will help in some way to make more lucid and comprehensible the trajectory of the story and the themes that run through it.

William H. Chafe
Georgetown, Maine

Introduction: The 1890s, a Preview of the Next Century

As America prepared to enter a new century, transformative changes swept the nation. The telephone, the typewriter, and the streetcar revolutionized communications. Industry burgeoned, with huge new steel factories and food plants creating monopolies hitherto unheard of. Cities exploded with people as millions of immigrants started a new life in America, only this time coming from Italy, Hungary, Russia, and China rather than from Britain, Ireland, and Germany.

In the midst of all this, stark inequalities tore at the country's social fabric. Workers launched strikes protesting twelve-hour shifts and below-poverty wages while wealthy entrepreneurs built hitherto undreamed of mansions to memorialize their millions. Racism—the original sin of America's democratic dream—reared its ugly head, blacks and whites in the American South caught in a deadly struggle to see whether the citizenship and justice promised blacks in the Civil War would ever become a reality. Seismic changes were also occurring among America's women. Millions of poor women joined factory sweatshops even as their more well-off sisters entered colleges and sought some way to reconcile their newly found dream of productive independence with society's insistence that they content themselves with being wives and mothers. In the midst of all this, a newly invigorated and muscular nation-state began to assert its power as an international force determined to shape the world outside America's border.

It was not yet clear in which direction all these changes would lead. But the 1890s offered a window onto the new era, defining the tensions, the driving forces, the stark choices that would determine the shape of what would come to be called "the American Century." By looking closely at the transformations that were occurring across the land, one could see the pivotal conflicts that would recur, like points on the compass, in the country's journey over the next one hundred years. At least some would carry over into a new millennium—the twenty-first century—with still unresolved tensions, particularly over issues of racial equality, the role of women, economic disparities, and America's role in the world, dominating the headlines. The 1890s set the stage for all of this—one of the most dramatic epochs in world history.

I. THE ECONOMIC TRANSFORMATION

America's industrial expansion in the years after the Civil War knew no precedent. With the technological and industrial innovations of the war itself as a catalyst, America swiftly became the leading industrial power in the world. Railroads, already with more track miles than any other country in 1865, multiplied nearly sixfold in the three decades thereafter, dwarfing the capacity of all European countries combined. Using its abundant natural resources in coal, oil, and iron, America vaulted ahead in manufacturing, shipping, and marketing. Huge new steel mills shot up in Pittsburgh and Birmingham, with the United States soon producing as much steel as Great Britain and Germany together. One company—U.S. Steel—used an organizational structure called "vertical integration," building and controlling its own rail lines, the raw materials needed to make steel, the manufacturing mills themselves, and the massive capital needed to pay for such expansion. By 1901, this corporation controlled two-thirds of all steel production in the country. Yet it did not stand alone. The Singer sewing machine conglomerate and the Swift meatpacking plants displayed the same impetus to consolidation, while chain grocery stores like A&P (the Atlantic and Pacific Company) and department stores like Woolworth's and Sears and Roebuck nationalized consumer industries. A middle-class family in Athens, Ohio, might share a Sunday-night dinner of pot roast that came from a Swift meatpacking plant, was purchased from an A&P grocery store, cooked on a stove made of U.S. Steel that was bought at a Sears and Roebuck department store, and served on a tablecloth made with a Singer sewing machine, using plates bought at the local Woolworth's. It was a scene inconceivable just a few decades earlier.

A population boom accompanied and energized the sweep of industrialization. From 1870 to 1910, the number of people living in America more than doubled. The West, in particular, became a destination for hundreds of thousands. Some may have come to find gold (the "gold rush" of 1849), but thousands of others—including Asians from Japan and China, and Mexicans from South of the border, as well as whites from the East—flocked to the new Zion to capitalize on the myriad opportunities provided by lush land and a burgeoning commercial economy. Although the famous historian Frederick Jackson Turner declared that the "frontier" had closed by 1890, in reality the West served as a population magnet for generations to come. And although some observers insisted on seeing the West as a peculiarly different part of America, in reality the West, like the rest of the country, experienced the same trials of seeking to figure out the relation of decentralized communities to the state and federal governments, all the while struggling with the pains of sustained, sometimes uncontrollable growth.

Nothing characterized that growth more than the migration of Americans to the ever booming cities that dotted the landscape. While the country's total population had swelled from 40 to 80 million in the thirty years after 1870, the population of the nation's cities tripled. More than 2 out of 5 Americans now lived in urban areas of more than 2,500. Chicago, Philadelphia, and New York each exceeded 1 million people, with New York boasting more than 3.5 million residents. The borough of Manhattan featured the largest density of human beings in the entire world—143 people per acre. More often than not, these urban dwellers clustered into smelly, rat-infested tenements. Structured like dumbbells, with narrow hallways joining two larger rooms at each end, most tenements featured unbearable overcrowding. Ventilation was poor if not nonexistent. Toilets were few. The odors of sewage and garbage were overwhelming. With windows open, tenants were bombarded by the noise of elevated railways in cities like New York and Chicago, trains screeching overhead. The social activist and photographer Jacob Riis took pictures of the immiseration of these slum dwellers, publishing what became a best-selling book and exemplary documentary, *How the Other Half Lives*. In vivid and poignant fashion, Riis brought home the skyrocketing price of industrialism and urbanization in terms of human life, health, and happiness.

Many others of the new generation of urban dwellers, on the other hand, luxuriated in a richer lifestyle. Two- and three-decker homes, with ample porches and wide doorways, sprouted up on the streets of the West Side of Manhattan, Telegraph Hill in San Francisco, Hyde Park in Chicago, and Louisburg Square in Boston. Adventurous architects like Louis Sullivan in Chicago experimented with office buildings that soared into the sky, far above the elevated railways, featuring elegant lobbies, striking ornamental wood-work, and high-ceilinged offices that provided perfect business domiciles for newly rich executives as well as the myriad young women clerical workers who served their every need in the typewriter carrels where they churned out daily communications. As electric trolley lines and subways were introduced in cities like Boston, Chicago, and New York, more and more of the middle class moved uptown or into the "streetcar suburbs" that soon surrounded most major cities. For these people, the ability to combine the comforts of middle-class urban living with the green spaces of Franklin Park in Boston, or Prospect Hill in Brooklyn, amounted to a way of life hitherto inconceivable. In the meantime, the Benjamin and Washington Dukes built their Fifth Avenue townhouses overlooking Manhattan's Central Park, enjoying a life of servants and luxury, with the Metropolitan Museum of Art just down the street, featuring the best that the denizens of high culture could collect.

But the most notable inhabitants of America's teeming cities were the new immigrant classes that flooded the country. America, of course, had always been a nation of newcomers. But these were different. For most of the century, about 200,000 people per year entered the country, most of them Protestants from England, Germany, or Scandinavia or Catholics from Ireland. Now the numbers soared, and the countries of origin shifted. Starting in the 1880s, an average of 500,000 newcomers came each year to the United States, increasing to more than a million a year after 1900. Instead of white-skinned Protestants from northern Europe, they were darker-skinned Jews and Catholics, with Poles, Italians, Russians, Slavs, and Greeks taking over textile mill jobs and garbageman positions on the East Coast and Midwest while Chinese,

Japanese, and Mexican immigrants competed with older-generation whites in the West. Their language was new. So too were the smells, the food, and the religious traditions they brought with them.

Suddenly Yiddish newspapers, Hebrew schools, and restaurants with foreign-sounding names and cuisines dominated the landscape of the North End of Boston and the Lower East Side of New York. The "new" immigrants populated the garment sweatshops of New York, the slaughterhouses of Chicago, the breweries of Wisconsin, the laundries of California. A huge number lived in those dumbbell tenements that Jacob Riis wrote about. They spoke with accents that few second- or third-generation Irish, Scottish, or German Americans understood; constituting America's first underclass— those whose incomes did not come close to the poverty level of six hundred dollars a year—they sometimes seemed, from the point of view of white Anglo-Saxon Protestants, to be "taking over" the country, undermining its historic culture, language, and religion, sabotaging its national morality and values.

At the turn of the century, more than a million immigrants a year flooded into cities like New York. Most were from eastern and southern Europe. Many congregated in areas like this on the Lower East Side of Manhattan, where dumbbell tenements, street peddlers, and sweatshop garment factories dotted the landscape.

Credit: The Granger Collection, New York.

In fact, of course, the new immigrants were adding one more rich patina to the colorful canvas of American life. To be sure, Jews lived in neighborhoods with Jews, Italians with Italians. They ate their own food, shopped at their own groceries, worshipped in their own synagogues and parish churches, read their own newspapers. But these simply constituted the home base from which they moved into the wider world each day, interacting with, changing—and being changed by—those who were from other, more dominant cultures. From their ethnic ghettoes, they derived strength, a sense of community and family identity, and the political smarts to negotiate the larger world. But they brought to this world of mainstream America all the rich talents they had nourished at their home base. David Levinsky, the hero of Abraham Cahan's early-twentieth-century novel about a Jewish immigrant, struggled in the dumbbell tenements of the Lower East Side to piece together a living. He worked in a sweatshop factory, helped with other family members to contribute enough so that the household could survive, and spent his occasional spare moments reading the *Jewish Forward* or studying the Talmud. But then he decided to go to City College, a remarkable experiment in public education that offered newcomers with talent the opportunity for a higher education. And before you knew it, he had become an intellectual as well as a businessman, creating new ideas, new technologies, new approaches to worker productivity that soon made him a kingpin in the garment industry. From a young boy who could barely find his way from Ellis Island to the Lower East Side, he had become an entrepreneur, in his own way reenacting—and validating—the American Dream.

The dream represented the ideological rationale that underpinned America's skyrocketing ascendancy to the top of the capitalist, industrial world. It was supremely expressed in the best-selling novellas of Horatio Alger—books like *Ragged Dick* and *Tom the Bootblack*. Ironically, given the pressures for cultural conformity at the time, Alger was a homosexual who had been expelled from his church due to his "deviant" behavior. But he quickly left behind that humiliation by exalting the norms of social mobility and celebrating the glories of American capitalism. All of his plotlines were the same—a hardworking, industrious young man who shined shoes, sold newspapers, or marketed matchbooks would seize the attention of a wealthy patron, who in turn provided the capital through which the young hero could make the journey from rags to riches. There were actually two lessons to these morality plays. One was that hard work paid off and that anyone could make it to the top. But the other—equally important—was that a form of divine intervention was pivotal to one's success. Only when a rich benefactor interceded did the match boy's fortunes turn around.

In truth, the second lesson proved more accurate than the first. Studies of social mobility in the nineteenth century showed mostly marginal progress upward for immigrant families, usually through combining family wages and being able to secure a piece of property. Biographies like that of Andrew Carnegie, who did move from being a Scottish immigrant telegraph boy to owning the largest steel plant in America at the time, with an annual income of twenty-five million dollars, were few and far between. Nevertheless, the idea that in America anyone could "make it" through hard work and talent propelled generations of young people, immigrants as well as those born in the United States. The corollary of the rags-to-riches myth, of course, was that success or failure rested with each individual, not with inherited privileges based on class, ethnicity, gender, or race. Theoretically at least, success or failure reflected each person's skill and industry. Summed up in the academic theories of William Graham Sumner, a Yale anthropologist, this view quickly became enshrined as Social Darwinism. Whether stated in the aphorism that "the cream always rises to the top" or its companion, "Talent will always tell in the end," the doctrines of Social Darwinism testified in their own way to the kind of "predestination" reflected in Horatio Alger's tales—if you deserved to make it, some larger force would propel you to the top. It was in the cards, it was how the system worked. But on the other side, if you failed to make it, if you had to declare bankruptcy and go to the poorhouse, that too was your individual fault. As Sumner said, "Millionaires are the product of natural selection. They get high wages and live in luxury, but the bargain is a good one for society." Conversely, poor people deserved their poverty because of their flawed character. As the popular minister Reverend Russell Conwell declared, "There is not a poor person in the United States *who was not made poor by his own shortcomings*" (italics added).

According to this social and ideological construct, the American system, through an almost deus ex machina, produced millionaires whose wealth was, in effect, a signal that God had chosen them. On the other hand, America's poor had brought their unfortunate circumstances on themselves. The two doctrines were logically in total contradiction—predestination versus free will—but the result was a social system that appeared to sanction both inequality and the absence of compassion for those least well off. As John D. Rockefeller said, the American Beauty Rose could emerge only "by sacrificing the early buds that grew up around it." Anyone who cared about saving those "early buds"—the countless underpaid workers who toiled in the Rockefeller empire—was reacting against both fate and progress. Besides, it was their own fault.

II. THE UNDERCLASS

Not surprisingly, those on the bottom did not share that conclusion. Workers had little power. Competition for jobs was intense, and even if a 12-hour day, 72-hour week work schedule paid only five hundred dollars a year—20 percent less than what was needed to support a family—at least it was a job. Factory managers, moreover, knew how to play potential troublemakers off each other, dividing and conquering their multiethnic labor force by threatening to bring in more Slavs, or Poles—or blacks—unless the workers quieted down and did their job in peace. There was no such thing as steady work. The vicissitudes of market conditions meant that virtually all workers experienced some layoffs during an average year. There was no opportunity to save money against a rainy day or build up a reserve to sustain a family if workers engaged in labor protest. From coal and silver mines, where safety conditions were nonexistent, to meatpacking plants where workers sometimes fell into boiling vats and were burned alive, to filthy garment industry sweatshops in New York where tuberculosis was a persistent occupational hazard, all most people could do was struggle to survive to the next day, take home a meager paycheck, and hope that enough people in the family—including women and children—were also employed so that the family could eat and pay its rent. God help them if anyone got sick, or someone died, and the family had to pay for a burial.

Yet the hunger for dignity could not be quashed. Rockefeller, Carnegie, and Morgan might wield all the power, but they could not patrol the churches, bars, and street corners where workers met to share their grievances. It was in those "unsteepled place of worship," as British labor historian E. P. Thompson has described English pubs, that workers came together to forge a bond of solidarity and a vision of a better existence based on collective assertion of their human aspirations. Already, in 1877, there had been a national railroad strike to protest a 10 percent wage cut. It was suppressed by federal troops at a cost of 100 lives. But the protest movement did not end. In the 1880s, a national union movement emerged—the Knights of Labor—committed to the idea that all workers who toiled should unite together whatever their skills or leverage. Nearly a million joined. Untimely strikes weakened the Knights, but in the early 1890s, a new militancy among workers developed. At Homestead, Pennsylvania, in a Carnegie steel mill in 1892, workers united to protest a wage cut, and when Carnegie sent in 300 Pinkerton strikebreakers—a private police force hired by industrialists to crush labor—the steelworkers fought back, pouring gasoline on the river by which the Pinkertons were making their way to the plant, setting it afire, and causing the Pinkertons to surrender! Only when the governor sent in 8000 troops were the workers suppressed.

Two years later, George Pullman, the manufacturer of "Pullman cars"— sleeping trains for wealthy patrons who wished to travel long distances in first-class comfort—slashed his workers' wages by 25 percent. They protested and persuaded railway workers in twenty-seven states to join them and go on strike. In sympathy with the workers, and as someone concerned with democratic advancement for all citizens, Illinois Governor John Altgeld refused to call out the troops. For a moment, the workers felt a surge of hope, except that Democratic President Grover Cleveland refused to support Altgeld and at the behest of Pullman and others called out federal troops to smash the strike on the ground that it was interfering with the delivery of the U.S. mail. "If it takes the entire army and navy to deliver a postal card in Chicago," Cleveland declared, "that card will be delivered." The same year more than five hundred thousand veterans threatened to come to Washington to demand a five-hundred-million-dollar federal public works program in response to a four-year-long depression. "We're coming," Coxey's Army, as it was called, declared.

"We're marching on Washington to right the nation's wrong." Once again, Cleveland responded by suppressing the movement and killing this "march on Washington." Still, insurgency was in the air. It would not go away.

Simultaneous with the uprising of workers in the steel and railroad industries, the farmers of America were declaring that they had enough. This time the insurgency took root in the South's cotton fields, then spread west and north to the corn and wheat fields of Kansas, Illinois, and Nebraska. Between 1860 and the turn of the century, the acreage of American farms increased by almost 300 percent, yet the farmers' share of the national wealth had been cut in half. By the end of the 1880s and the beginning of the 1890s, a national protest movement of "Farmers' Alliances" was prepared to lead a grassroots revolt of workers and farmers alike to create a dramatically different governmental regime, where the federal government would step in to protect the basic right of every American who tilled the soil or worked a factory machine to have a chance at true equal opportunity.

It started in the South. When slavery ended with the Civil War, Southern planters had to find a new labor system. There was inadequate capital and currency to finance a true wage system where workers would plant and harvest the fields for an hourly rate. Instead, Southern planters devised dual systems of "sharecropping" or "tenant farming" whereby farm laborers, white or black, would cultivate a portion of a planter's land in return for either the income from a certain "share" of the crop or with the understanding that as a "tenant" they would receive the revenue from the harvest, after expenses such as rent and supplies were deducted. The advantage of the system was that it gave the farm worker some measure of independence, eliminated gang labor, and provided room for gradual improvement over time from the status of a dependent laborer to that of a small landholder. The disadvantage was that it left the sharecropper or tenant farmer totally dependent on the power of the landholder to determine the rent, define the cost of supplies, and establish the rate of debt payments the farmer would owe on the credit that had been advanced.

In the overwhelming majority of cases, the system worked to the detriment of farm laborers. Landlords were often store owners as well. Tenant farmers and sharecroppers had to purchase their seed, equipment, and tools from the same person who owned the land they farmed. Even when that was not the case, close alliances existed between planters and furnishing merchants. Everything was provided on loan, including the food one needed for daily sustenance until the crop came in. No usury laws protected the farmers from being charged outrageous rates of interest on the money they had "borrowed." Nor were farmers in a situation to decide when their crop would go to market or to know at what price it would finally sell. In all too many cases, the result was that instead of slowly accumulating reserves to purchase one's own piece of land, the tenant farmer and sharecropper each year went deeper into debt, their lives—and futures—in effect mortgaged to rich white men with the power to set interest rates as high as 60 percent and to charge inflated prices for food and clothing. The landlords/furnishing merchants had their own problems, of course. They were overextended, risked their wealth on a crop not yet harvested, and suffered all the uncertainties caused by bankers and capital markets in the North, over which they had no control. Not all wished to squeeze their tenants or exploit their sharecroppers. Still, on balance, the system devastated the possibility that farmers could ever get out of the mud hole of debt into which they sank deeper each year.

Yet in a profound tribute to the resiliency of the human spirit, these farmers too refused to succumb. Talking to each other at church or at the local town market on Saturday, they shared stories of how they had been bilked by their landlord. Generating a sense of anger, farmers moved from there to a conversation of how they might work collectively to find a way out. Initially, farmers' alliances started locally, county by county. They combined social events like "covered dish" suppers, where every family brought enough for six people, with political discussions that focused on potential answers to the dilemmas of being powerless and in debt. Then, as word spread, the county alliances became regional and finally state and national. As farmers pooled

As the nation expanded westward, millions of people settled into new lives. Here we see a family of African-Americans in the Oklahoma Territory. Former slaves were welcomed into Native American lands in the aftermath of the Civil War and Emancipation.

Credit: © Corbis

their knowledge, they also came up with new ideas. How about a newspaper to spread word of farmer protests, or a system of lecturers—we would call them "organizers"—who traveled from district to district "preaching" to the farmers' meetings about the causes of their despair and the solutions that the Farmers' Alliances were presenting. Before long, a social movement had developed, combining the intensity of a church revival with the collective discipline of a political campaign in a northern city precinct.

Central to the entire alliance effort was the notion of "cooperation." If farmers could only pool their resources and proceed to do things collectively that hitherto they had done only as individuals, perhaps they could find a way out—purchase supplies in volume at a discount, create "co-ops" that farmers could join, then get food and clothing at a lower rate, perhaps even build warehouses where crops could be stored until maximum market conditions made it profitable to sell.

Quickly, of course, ideas of economic cooperation evolved into political activism. Poor people could not build warehouses without capital. That money, in turn, would have to come from government because it was unlikely that private merchants, bankers, or landlords—the source of the problem—were going to provide a solution. Hence, within a short period of time, the system of lecturers who had set out to educate farmers about the economic realities of their plight turned into political organizers. Soon, Farmers' Alliances were meeting in regional and national conventions that called on state legislatures to provide support for organizing cooperatives and for building warehouses where farmers could store their crops. And they devised a "subtreasury" plan whereby the federal government would give loans to individual farmers with their crops as collateral. Thus the government would become the people's banker, eliminating loan sharks and exploitative furnishing merchants. Prophetically, it was a system remarkably similar to the agriculture support programs that were finally instituted under Franklin D. Roosevelt's New Deal in the 1930s. Except that to make any of this happen, farmers would have to elect congressmen, senators, state legislators—perhaps even a president—to lead the fight.

Hence the emergence from the late 1880s to the early 1890s of a full-blown agrarian revolt—the Populist Party—which in the 1890s sought to fuse economics and politics and take over the government. In 1892, the new political party denounced the "prolific womb of government injustice," proposed a coalition of industrial workers and farmers, called for free silver (an effort to offset the deflationary effect of using only gold as a basis for currency), and in a bold display of political radicalism, demanded not only a subtreasury plan and federal agricultural warehouses but also federal ownership of public utilities like railroads, the telegraph, and the telephone. The platform even called for a graduated income tax, direct election of U.S. senators, and the passage of laws that would allow voters to initiate popular referendums on critical legislative proposals and use petitions to "recall" ineffective officeholders so that they could be revoted on by the citizenry. In short, virtually every innovative proposal that would be discussed in the next four decades was put on the table by the People's Party in the early 1890s. Moreover, there seemed some reason to have confidence that this new coalition of farmers and workers might have an impact. In 1890, politicians who endorsed the gist of the Populist platform had won partial or complete control of twelve state legislatures, half a dozen governorships, and as many as fifty seats in the House of Representatives. Change seemed in the air.

III. RACE

Even on the issue of race—the nation's oldest affront to democracy—the 1880s and early 1890s offered a glimmer of hope. In the decade after the Civil War, black Americans had ridden a roller coaster of surging hopes and plummeting defeats. Initially believing that salvation would come in the form of a radical redistribution of slaveowner lands, thousands of freedmen took possession of the "forty acres and a mule" that the federal Freedmen's Bureau handed out at the end of the war—federally appropriated land, formerly held by slaveowners, and now distributed in areas of Georgia and the islands off North Carolina to former slaves. Except that the government defaulted, and despite the political support of radical Republicans like Congressman Thaddeus Stevens, national leaders decided that all land previously owned by plantation landlords would be returned to them.

Still, hope burned bright. The essence of citizenship, after all, consisted of the right to vote, and when Andrew Johnson sought to return political power to slaveholding whites in the South, Congress struck back, passing the Fourteenth and Fifteenth Amendments, which guaranteed freedmen "equal protection" before the laws and black men the right to vote. Soon blacks, along with whites willing to support the Union, came together in conventions to pass new state constitutions and provide basic guarantees to all citizens. Blacks were elected to state legislatures (along with whites) and helped enact laws that advanced public education as well as mental health care and public services. When white Ku Klux Klan terrorists sought to kill black activists, Washington intervened in 1871, using federal troops to quash vigilante activity. The roller coaster headed downward again when the Republican Party sold out blacks in the South after the presidential election of 1876, agreeing to withdraw all federal troops in the South if Florida, South Carolina, and Louisiana would throw their electoral votes to Rutherford B. Hayes, the Republican candidate, rather than cast them for Samuel Tilden, the Democrat who had won the popular vote. After the deal was struck, black Southerners no longer had blue-uniformed troops from the North to protect their rights.

Even after 1877, however, blacks continued to keep hope alive. As part of the deal Republicans made, Democrats agreed to permit most blacks to continue to hold the franchise. And even though white Democrats, now back in control in the South, could either stuff the ballot boxes in order to win or intimidate black voters, they dared not go too far lest angry white northerners once again intervene. Thus as long as blacks ultimately accepted domination by powerful white Democrats, they could retain some leverage and occasional federal patronage positions from Republicans in Washington. With little other choice, most blacks worked within the system forced upon them. But they also continued to struggle, occasionally with white allies from the old Reconstruction regimes, to create other political alternatives more consistent with the dreams that remained part of their memory of the meaning of Reconstruction.

Thus, in 1879, blacks in Virginia joined with dissident Democrats and former Republicans to form the Readjuster Movement. For four years, the Readjusters helped transform Virginia politics, rejecting racism, including blacks in their social and economic programs, striving to create the better education and more responsive social policies that sought to contain, if not overturn, the domination of rich white planters and merchants. Eventually, in 1884, that alliance succumbed to the power of the old white ruling class but not before it signaled the possibility of a different kind of world if only blacks and whites with shared economic interests could come together in a coalition for progress.

That was precisely what threatened to happen in the Populist movement. Although the Southern Farmers' Alliance, nearly three million strong, was all white, it shared common concerns with black farmers. All were equally the victims of penurious treatment at the hands of planters and merchants; all suffered when unfair interest was added to the money they owed their landlords; all would be equal beneficiaries of federal programs to make loans to farmers or to establish government-financed warehouses for farmers to store their crops. Moreover, like white farmers, blacks organized, with the same system of social events, political lecturers, and eventually a commitment to political action. The Colored Farmers' Alliance, one million strong, met for conventions in the same cities and at the same time as the Southern Farmers' Alliance. With increasing frequency, members of both alliances spoke of the benefits to be gained by combining forces and using their common economic plight as the basis for a united political movement to change the status quo. Even whites who historically had only contempt for blacks saw the wisdom of forging an alliance. As white Populist leader Tom Watson noted, "There is no reason why the black man should not understand that the law that hurts me as a farmer, hurts him as a farmer." With such shared political self-interest, talk spread about the possibilities of a biracial alliance between white and black farmers, where a shared economic agenda could "trump" the issue of race and make possible a vibrant political coalition to topple rich and powerful whites from their position of dominance. The elections of 1892, with their victory for Alliance-endorsed candidates, seemed a signal that such a potential result might be just around the corner.

In North Carolina that harbinger of hope seemed close to realization in 1894. While doing what they had to do in order to survive, black activists there also continued to build their own communities, especially in places like Wilmington, New Bern, Raleigh, and Durham and to assert their rights at every opportunity. In the early 1890s, these activists openly joined a coalition with Populists and Republicans, creating a Fusion Party determined to overthrow Democratic rule. Organizing openly, boldly, and effectively, the Fusionists swept to state power in 1894, winning not only the state legislature but also the governorship. Moreover, two years later, they repeated their triumph. Blacks suddenly held an unprecedented number of public positions, serving as state legislators, district attorneys, and magistrates. One was even elected to the U.S. Congress. And half of the Wilmington police force consisted of African Americans. Blacks owned businesses, worked out shared economic ventures with whites, and to an ever growing degree, replicated the white class structure, with prominent black families having the same kind of elegant coaches and finely detailed furniture as did whites. While Booker T. Washington was proclaiming at the Atlanta Exposition in 1895 that blacks should "cast down their buckets where they were" and forego any attempt at "social equality" with whites, many other blacks were showing on a daily basis their intention to live as equal citizens, in full possession of their citizenship rights.

If nothing else the partial success of the Readjuster movement, the potential of a biracial Populist coalition and the ascendancy of the Fusionists in North Carolina suggested that this was a period of extraordinary volatility. It could as easily produce progress as disaster. With workers ready to fight, farmers eager to claim their just deserts, and African Americans finding the courage to challenge the nation's oldest social inequality, the 1890s seemed a time of possibility.

IV. WOMEN

A final group pivotal to this time of social change was American women. From the beginning, women had played a crucial role in the development of America. Although never allowed to vote and denied the opportunity to pursue careers, own property, or occupy public roles of leadership, women were equal partners in settling the country, shaping its social and religious institutions, and determining its direction in education and social policy. Clearly, differences in class led to a huge disparity in the conditions most women faced on a daily basis. Virtually every woman who was poor or black toiled in the fields or factories to help put food on the table. Virtually every middle- and upper-class white woman, in contrast, was prevented from working outside the home by cultural norms that declared it "unnatural," "improper," and a "violation of God's will" that women serve any role other than that of housewife and mother. Yet women still played a critical part in shaping the public history of the nation, often using their "moral" role in religious and charitable organizations to influence the direction of public institutions. Whether as church reformers during the antislavery movement or as members of women's missionary societies working on the plight of poor and disabled children, women had more to do with creating the social welfare infrastructure of their country than anyone else.

Now, more changes were occurring. In the years after the Civil War a number of women's colleges were created. More and more Americans believed that higher education was essential for those who would rear and shape American children. These were the "mothers of the republic," as historian Linda Kerber has called them. Schools like Vassar, Smith, Bryn Mawr, and Mount Holyoke were founded, admitting the best, brightest, and richest of America's young women. The ostensible purpose of such colleges was to train women in the same liberal arts scholarship as their prospective husbands were learning at Harvard, Yale, and Princeton and then have them carry this learning into their roles as mothers and moral guardians.

But there was a problem. How did you teach a woman that she was an intellectual equal, able to think and act for herself, and then expect that she would accept readily and agreeably the constrained roles that society imposed on her as housewife and mother? If she could debate Greek philosophy and read the natural rights philosophy of John Locke, why could she not vote? If her education prepared her to be a doctor or lawyer, why should she not practice whatever profession most appealed to her? Once the genie was out of the bottle, could it be forced back into the bottle?

Women had first demanded equal rights in the course of the abolitionist movement. They saw no reason they should not sign petitions, speak at rallies, or lobby legislators in the same way that male abolitionists did. When denied that option because they were women, a group led by Elizabeth Cady Stanton and Susan B. Anthony met in 1848 at Seneca Falls, New York, and published a powerful treatise called A Declaration of Rights and Grievances, which asserted the right of women to be accorded the same rights and privileges as men in all arenas of life. Whether in the arenas of morality, professional life, education, or politics, there should be neither "separate spheres" nor double standards. For almost half a century, women activists had agitated for equal rights, fighting especially hard during the post-Civil War era for women as well as former slaves to have the franchise.

The changing conditions of women's lives created a new impetus for change. Especially important was the settlement house, a new institution founded by college-educated women that was committed to improving the living conditions of poor urban dwellers, particularly women and children who were recently arrived foreign immigrants. Victorian-era cultural norms insisted that "respectable women" should remain dedicated exclusively to the "domestic" sphere; hence, many white women college graduates found it difficult to leap the chasm between their prescribed roles as "wives" and "mothers" and that of independent career women. On the other hand, creating a "domestic" environment like a settlement house offered a bridge to realizing the goal of fulfilling their educational potential through public service. It was, after all, a "house," not an office building; and its tasks were helping young children adapt to a new country while teaching their mothers improved standards of hygiene and child-rearing.

Jane Addams personified this movement of well-off nineteenth-century women college graduates into a career of social work. Like nearly half of women's college graduates in the late nineteenth century, she resisted the pervasive pressures of the "family claim" to get married and raise a family. Yet with equal fervor, she rejected the life of being a rich female tourist visiting Paris, London, Rome, and Venice to become cultured in the latest fashions and arts. Desperately seeking a way to employ her education to good ends, she hit upon the British experiment at Toynbee Hall, where people passionately committed to social reform worked to improve the plight of London's slum dwellers. Soon she launched Hull House at Chicago. Located at the edge of the most densely packed urban immigrant ghettoes, Hull House became

Here the social reformer Jane Addams (1860–1935) is shown interacting with children at Hull House, the settlement house she established to address the needs of immigrant families in Chicago. Addams exemplified the decision by many American women to use their education to work for a better society.

Credit: The Granger Collection, New York.

the model of a new option made available to well-off and college-educated women. Founded and largely populated by women—although some men were founders as well—Hull House immediately became a vehicle for women to shape public policy and change the world.

Initially, outreach activities consisted primarily of providing day nurseries for immigrant infants or language classes for their mothers and fathers. But soon workers at the house were drawn to public issues that directly involved the well-being of the larger community. How could a neighborhood be safe if railway crossings were unprotected? How could rampant infectious diseases be stopped if raw sewage in the streets was not eliminated? What could be done to prevent women and children working in factories from losing hands, arms, and fingers to dangerous, unguarded machines?

The residents of Hull House did not begin their work with the intention of becoming political activists, but an inexorable logic linked their feminine, maternal concern with women's and children's health to engagement with public affairs. Only the city council could deal with railroad crossings and only the state legislature with factory safety. Hence women reformers of necessity became political in order to fulfill the roles of nurturance and compassion that they had chosen. Before long, Jane Addams was appearing before municipal commissions lobbying for playgrounds, public sewers, and better schools, while her fellow Hull House founder, Florence Kelley, campaigned for a Factory Safety Law before the Illinois State Legislature. Success produced success, and once the state legislature had acted, it was only natural to ask Florence Kelley to become the state official in charge of regulating factory safety.

Hull House was like a pebble thrown into a stream that then produces endless ripples. Other women in Jane Addams's situation quickly seized on the model of Hull House. Settlement houses were founded in every major city in the country. Even if not ready to dedicate their lives totally to social welfare work, countless other women found inspiration in the new opportunity to become involved in public reform. The General Federation of Women's Clubs, historically a gathering place where genteel women read books together and studied art, suddenly was captured by concern with issues like minimum wages for women, abolition of child labor, and safety legislation that the settlement houses had pioneered. More than doubling in membership, the shift in the General Federation's approach was best summarized by one member who declared, "Dante has been dead for several centuries. I think it is time that we dropped the study of his Inferno and turned attention to our own."

Not surprisingly, the shift toward public engagement based on traditional female roles had an impact on the struggling campaign for woman suffrage. For much of the nineteenth century, advocates for the suffrage had employed a "natural rights" argument: women deserved the vote because they were just like men, born with inalienable rights that by any criteria of justice demanded that they be given the ballot. Now the argument began to shift. In light of the work being done by settlement houses, women's clubs, and other female reform organizations, a new and different emphasis appeared: women deserved the right to vote precisely because they were so different from men. Only when women's "separate sphere" was recognized, and especially women's maternal concern for children, health, and morality, could the government be truly complete. Hence, women deserved the vote, not based on their identity or sameness as citizens with men, but because they brought totally different attributes to bear on the body politic. Just as a family could be complete only when women and men fulfilled their different responsibilities to its well-being, so politics and government could succeed only when women's values were brought to bear to complement those of men.

Thus women joined workers, farmers, blacks, and other marginalized groups in American society to create an era of change, unrest, and volatility. From a time of stability where everyone knew their roles and most people did not dream of challenging the status quo, pressure now mounted from multiple groups to think anew about how people should organize their lives. To be sure, every age experiences similar tensions. But the 1880s and 1890s were different if for no other reason than the seismic shifts that were creating new fissures in the country as a whole. Never had industry expanded more dramatically; immigration multiplied so exponentially; or issues of race, gender, and economic fairness so boldly leaped to the forefront of the national agenda.

Perhaps most important, every issue that demanded attention in the 1890s revolved in some way around state or governmental action. The fate of striking workers depended on how governors and presidents responded. Insurgent farmers had little chance of realizing their goals unless state and national legislatures provided guaranteed loans and government warehouses. African Americans could either advance or fall back depending on the degree to which state and federal authorities were willing to guarantee their citizenship. And nowhere was the role of the government more clear than in determining whether women would gain the right to vote or be able to secure enactment of laws to end child labor and ensure factory safety. In the end, the state—local or federal—became pivotal in determining the direction of the next generation. Whose interests would it serve and with what degree of fairness?

V: THE ROLE OF GOVERNMENT

Whatever choices were made on domestic issues, the state clearly had assumed new, magisterial powers on foreign policy issues. For much of the nineteenth century, with the exception of the Mexican War, diplomacy took second place to domestic developments. Now, at a time when Britain, France, Germany, the Netherlands, Spain, and Portugal were launching crusades throughout Africa and Asia to create a new Age of Empire, the United States boldly asserted its intention to join the rush to colonialism. At least in part, this departure reflected a reassertion of "manliness" in American culture, the notion that character, in the end, depended upon being "tough" and standing aggressively for one's beliefs. Primary among these convictions, certainly, was the belief that no one had a better right than America to spread its values across the globe. It was part of the nation's "manifest destiny"—being a "city on a hill," in John Winthrop's words—divinely ordained and best served by a boisterous nationalism.

The military embodiment of this new nationalism took the form of a highly modernized naval fleet. Built in response to the repeated urging of Admiral Alfred Mahan, what later became known as the White Fleet competed with the naval forces of any other international power and reflected America's contribution to an international arms race. With a new muscularity, the American government confronted Chile after two American sailors were killed in Valparaiso, then invoked the Monroe Doctrine in a border dispute between Britain and Venezuela. The message in both cases: We are in charge in this hemisphere.

With similar assertiveness, the United States imposed its will on Hawaii. There, the invasion of Western populations had wreaked the same epidemiological havoc as the introduction of Englishmen to Native American tribes did in the seventeenth century. Infectious diseases wiped out half the population and the United States took control, negotiating an agreement in 1887 to use Pearl Harbor as a naval base, then dictating economic conditions. When an arrangement for importing Hawaiian sugar duty-free into the United States was revoked in 1890, an insurrection among Hawaiians occurred, deposing Queen Liliuokalani. Reflecting America's attitude during this entire period, the American representative in Honolulu declared, "The Hawaiian pear is now fully ripe and now is the golden hour for the United States to pluck it."

But nowhere was the brusque new American nationalism more on display than in relations with Spain, particularly regarding Cuba and the Philippines. Exerting over Cuba the same kind of dictatorial dominance that America was displaying toward Hawaii, Spain spurred an indigenous rebellion in 1895 by Cubans intent on asserting democracy and their own independence. America's newspapers followed the conflict with avid attention, led by the Pulitzer and Hearst media empires. Committed to what was described as "yellow journalism," papers like the New York *World* and the New York *Journal* (circulations 250,000 and 400,000 daily) used banner headlines and sensational photographs to feed the frenzy of American readers anxious to see a bloody confrontation between the forces of good and evil. Stories of innocent women being captured and ravished by Spanish troops inflamed American public opinion. In February 1898 one of the New York tabloids published a letter from a Spanish diplomat calling President William McKinley "weak and a bidder for the admiration of the crowd." Less than a week later, every paper in the country blazoned the announcement that an American warship, the USS *Maine*, on a visit to Havana, had been blown up and crippled by a spectacular explosion in Havana harbor. Rushing to judgment, the press proclaimed the disaster a direct result of a Spanish attack (later investigations showed it to have been an internal explosion caused by faulty boilers). "You furnish the pictures," publisher William Randolph Hearst told his reporters, "and "I'll furnish the war." "The Whole Country Thrills with War Fever," the New York *Journal* proclaimed. Although McKinley fervently wished to avoid conflict, and the Spanish offered what amounted to a surrender, the clamor of public opinion prevailed and a few days later, McKinley asked Congress to declare war. "Remember the *Maine*," the war cry went, "to Hell with Spain."

No one better exemplified the "macho" new nationalism of the United States than Theodore "Teddy" Roosevelt. A prep-school and Harvard-educated former police commissioner of New York City, TR had been appointed assistant secretary of the navy by McKinley. Using the pre-rogatives of that post, Roosevelt—while his boss, the navy secretary, was away one weekend—cabled the naval commander in the Far East to send the American fleet, with troops, to the Philippines to capture that Spanish colony. Critical of McKinley (TR called him "white-livered [with] no more backbone than a chocolate éclair"), Roosevelt wished nothing more than to savor the taste of battle in his own right. Resigning from the administra-tion, he donned a custom-made Brooks Brothers army uniform and orga-nized a cadre of volunteers—the "Rough Riders," they were dubbed—and with the support of two elite black army regiments, charged up San Juan Hill, screaming frenetically at his Spanish enemies. Personally responsi-ble for killing one Spaniard, TR exulted that his foe had "folded up like a jackrabbit." (A British diplomat, commenting on TR's repeated recount-ings of this episode, declared, "You must remember, [Roosevelt] is only six.") Soon thereafter, the Spanish sued for peace. America had, allegedly, brought democracy to Cuba. The cost—400 American casualties from battle, 5000 from disease. That "splendid little war," as Secretary of State John Hay called it, was over.

The Philippines turned out to be another case entirely. An insurrectionary native force believed that the Americans were as repugnant as the Spaniards and determined to resist. Guerilla fighting, reminiscent of wars to come, soon enveloped American forces. Unable to march to speedy victory as in Cuba, the United States committed 200,000 troops to a four-year struggle. In the process, the United States became a power that acted like the Spanish had acted in Cuba, using concentration camps, executing enemy soldiers without trial—even resorting to what would later be called "waterboarding," a form of water torture where the prisoner was made to believe he was drowning in order to force information from him. This war, unlike the one in Cuba, cost substantial American deaths—over 4,000—but it too ended in victory, though the United States would occupy the Philippines until 1946.

Most important, America had recorded her determination to be a perma-nent imperial presence. "The Philippines are ours forever," Senator Albert Beveridge declared. "And just beyond…are China's illimitable markets. We will not retreat from either…. The power that rules the Pacific is the power that rules the world. That power will forever be the American Republic." Prophetically, Beveridge had forecast the trajectory of America's role in the

Teddy Roosevelt resigned his position of assistant secretary of the navy to go to battle in the Spanish-American War. As commander of the Rough Riders, he became a national hero for leading the charge up San Juan Hill after American troops invaded Cuba. His fame helped him get elected governor of New York, then vice president of the United States. When President William McKinley was assassinated in 1901, TR became president.

Credit: © Bettmann/CORBIS

next century. The American state as a dominant world power had arrived. From America's pronouncement of an "open door" policy toward China in 1900 (no foreign power was to prevent others from investing there) to Woodrow Wilson's Fourteen Points in 1917 to Franklin Roosevelt's Four Freedoms of 1941, America's voice would determine the shape of world politics.

On domestic issues the state played a role of increasing importance as well, though initially in a far more ambiguous and conservative manner. As an acknowledgment of the need to bring some measure of oversight to the out-of-control expansion of industrial empires and transportation networks, Congress had enacted the Interstate Commerce Act of 1887 and the Sherman Anti-Trust Act of 1890. Each represented a benchmark on the federal legislative map, indicating that Congress had taken note that the extraordinary growth of America's economic machine might require that the national government intervene at some point to bring order, fairness, and justice to the sprawling network of new industrial giants roaming the land. Yet these regulatory acts, for the most part, represented more form than substance, a skeletal structure within which more aggressive state intervention *might* take place at a later time but with no indication that the government intended to intrude itself now or anytime soon.

Somewhat more positive forms of intervention took place in specific states, where individual legislatures like those in Illinois, Wisconsin, Oregon, or New York acted in response to demands for regulation. In Illinois, a legislature directly moved by Florence Kelley and her colleagues at Hull House enacted a Factory Safety Law. Other states sought to regulate discriminatory railroad rates and to consider, on a state and municipal level, laws that would establish minimum wages and maximum hours for women and that regulated child labor. Many of these actions took place in direct response to the work of women activists. In still other areas, municipal reformers attacked the precinct-based political structures that had helped sustain urban machines like that led by Boss Tweed in New York. Alternative proposals included either citywide elections that would eliminate the immigrant base of local "bosses" or city-manager forms of government that would bring "scientific management" to the business of running large cities.

On the other hand, there was no evidence of willingness on the part of the federal government to intervene on the side of the least powerful members of society who were aggressively seeking redress of their grievances—industrial workers, poor farmers, or black Americans. To the contrary, the record indicated either indifference to the plight of the poor or active complicity in defending those who benefited from the status quo. As we have already seen, the Cleveland administration helped crush the railroad strike of 1894, and the state government in Pennsylvania had called out eight thousand National Guardsmen to suppress the steel strike at Homestead two years earlier. Established politicians of both major parties endorsed the view that labor activists were reckless visionaries too radical to be trusted. Labor insurgents were more often portrayed as part of foreign, anarchist movements like those who set off the Haymarket riots of 1886 rather than as hardworking citizens toiling for inadequate wages who were denied basic rights to fairness and safety.

Perhaps most devastating, the federal government relinquished all responsibility for the safety and well-being of African Americans in the South. Instead, Congress chose not to pass the Force Bill, introduced by Massachusetts Senator Henry Cabot Lodge, which would have guaranteed black Americans' right to vote and to have the opportunity to build on the gains they had made. At the very time when blacks in places like North Carolina were achieving new heights of political and economic influence, the federal government conveyed to white Southerners the powerful suggestion that it would do nothing to protect black rights if Southern states chose to take them away.

In response to this remarkable cue, white Southern politicians engaged in a systematic, vicious campaign to return blacks to the legalized inferiority of their pre-Reconstruction condition.

The white response came as direct retaliation for the most serious threat wealthy white planters, merchants, and bankers had faced since Reconstruction. By raising the specter of a biracial coalition of blacks and whites, united along class lines, the Populist movement had threatened to topple the rich and powerful. Throughout Southern history, and particularly in the years since the Civil War, rich whites had implicitly played the "race card" whenever they faced such a threat, suggesting that all whites, however different they might be in wealth and education, shared in common the distinction of not being black. Now, faced with a Populist threat to their very base of power, ruling Democrats made the "race card" explicit. Black men, they charged, were threatening the chastity of white women, preparing to rape and pillage white communities. Black voters, the ruling white Democrats charged, were fomenting corruption at the ballot box, preventing true and pure democracy from occurring. Only by "reforming" their constitutions, taking measures to disenfranchise blacks, and enacting laws that would permanently, and legally, separate the two races forever in all areas of public intercourse, would it be possible to cleanse the political process.

Thus, starting with Mississippi in 1890 and proceeding through virtually all the remaining Southern states in the next decade, state legislatures disenfranchised black voters. Poll taxes, literacy tests, a grandfather clause which stated that only people whose grandfathers had voted—that is, prior to slavery's end—automatically had the right to vote, all were used to ensure that virtually every black voter lost his place at the polling booth. By its failure to enact the Force Bill, of course, the Congress had implicitly signaled its willingness to go along with such measures. The ruling whites thus broke the potential class alliance of whites and blacks, demagogically rallied poor white farmers and workers to celebrate their racial superiority with their richer white colleagues, and repudiated forever the prospective stigma of social equality, where whites and blacks might mix together, marry, and lose their racial purity. (Not understood at the time was the degree to which the same laws used to take the vote away from blacks could also be used to take it away from whites—and did so steadily over the next two decades, as poll taxes, literacy tests, and other barriers systematically purged poor whites from the voting rosters as well as poor blacks). It all amounted to the most devastating counterrevolution of modern times, eradicating virtually every gain made by blacks in the aftermath of the Civil War.

Simultaneously, white state legislatures enacted a series of segregation statutes called "Jim Crow" laws, after an old minstrel figure. By passing laws requiring that blacks and whites ride in separate portions of streetcars and trains, attend different schools, be buried in separate cemeteries, not eat in the same restaurants, never sit down together, and never mix in theaters or other public places, the white South sought, legally and institutionally, to forever prevent black children, men, or women from ever "jumping Jim Crow" by crossing the barrier of race. Segregation, per se, had been a predominant social reality in the South since the Civil War. Blacks did not wish to go to church with whites, attend schools with them, or—ordinarily—eat with them or go to the theater together. On the other hand, blacks had consistently and systematically resisted any legal *requirement* that separation occur. The most sensitive area of disagreement came in cases involving first-class seats on trains. Blacks who could afford to purchase a first-class accommodation (and they were increasing in numbers all the time) wished to receive the quality of service they had paid for. In numerous local court cases, judges had agreed, ruling that whoever paid for first-class seats had the right to have them. Now, however, white legislatures insisted that race, and race alone, determined how one would be treated. Whereas before, economic class had "trumped" race when it came to being allowed to sit in a first-class seat, now race had become the only criteria for determining public treatment.

Even the Supreme Court agreed. Seeking to challenge this presumption, Homer Plessy, a well-off New Orleans person of mixed-blood parentage, sued in federal court to protest the fact that he had been thrown out of the first-class coach of an interstate train for which he had paid a first-class fare. Plessy was seven-eighths white. He could have "passed" as white had he chosen to. His case thus highlighted the absurdity of Jim Crow statutes in two ways. It demonstrated what a mockery the law actually was, when someone predominantly white was treated as exclusively black; and it used the historic rule of individual property rights—the notion that one should have what one paid for, based on a person's differential income—to counter the rule of racial essentialism, where individual rights did not matter. When the case reached the Supreme Court, the judges rejected the principle of individual rights for the social custom of segregation. By an 8 to 1 ruling, the highest court in the land decreed that "separate but equal" was the law of the land and declared that the blame for anyone who believed that separate accommodations suggested inferiority must rest with the injured party, who was inventing a feeling of inequality in his own mind. Only Justice John Marshall Harlan dissented, eloquently declaiming that the decision trampled on the Fourteenth Amendment principle of equal protection before the laws.

Harlan was correct. The Supreme Court had constructed what amounted to a "locked box" from which blacks had no way to flee. By sanctioning as constitutionally proper the notion that "separate" did not mean "unequal," the court so narrowed the legal options available to blacks that any protest at all had to begin with the acceptance of the *Plessy* precedent and rely only on the argument that, in a particular instance, the separate facility turned out not to be equal and therefore had to be improved. But for more than half a century, the doctrine that segregation was constitutional could not be directly challenged, and it required decades of case after case proving that separate facilities were in fact unequal before the doctrine itself could be challenged. By its action in *Plessy*, the Supreme Court—and by implication, the federal government of the United States—had unraveled four decades of struggle by African Americans to achieve equal rights under the Constitution.

But it was not just the courts. Some blacks, at least, believed that the Supreme Court decision represented only a temporary setback and that blacks could still hope for the promised day of full freedom to come.

Nowhere was this hope higher than in North Carolina with its Fusion coalition. Black leaders in towns like Raleigh, Durham, New Bern, and Wilmington used their political leverage and economic opportunities to steadily advance. They read their own newspapers published by black editors; they had their own social clubs, varying from upper-class women's clubs to working-class laundress associations; they attended black colleges, conventions of black churches, and political gatherings of black social activists. Many of those who were most well-off believed that the "best" people of both races shared a common agenda. They had cultivated tastes, recognized the need to control the unruly masses, and believed that together, they could unite on issues of class and quality to find a common path forward.

What such black optimists failed to recognize was the degree to which the "best" white people not only shared no sense of a common class identity and purpose but, in a cruel and malicious perversion of the "best" people logic of blacks, actually believed that only by putting all blacks in their "place" could white superiority remain protected and supreme. Thus in North Carolina Josephus Daniels, the publisher and editor of the elite and prestigious Raleigh *News and Observer*, actually led the campaign to destroy black rights and annihilate the Fusion movement. Joined by well-educated and established politicians and educators, Daniels and his colleagues trumpeted their fear of "social equality" and the danger that black men posed to the innocence and chastity of white women. Rallying the white masses on behalf of protecting the white "Southern Lady," they created a campaign of hysteria launched against a caricature of black militancy. During the election of 1898, they conveyed a clear message. "What do you do when you see a black person approach the polls?" white politicians in Wilmington asked. "You shoot them," and you keep on doing so "until the Cape Fear River is full of bodies."

The Wilmington race riot of 1898 was the final step by the state to eradicate black hopes for a better future. In total violation of constitutional rights, blacks were denied their citizenship, had their businesses burned, and were driven from the city. Now, a new government took over in the state as well as the city, one that in the name of "progressivism" immediately set out to enact a barrage of Jim Crow legislation. What the Supreme Court had enunciated as national doctrine, the "best men" of North Carolina now inscribed into civil and social reality. Although the "state" may have proved somewhat responsive to women's concerns in some industrial urban areas and created at least a departure point for future actions with the Interstate Commerce Act and the Sherman Anti-Trust Act, when it came to black people, farmers, and industrial laborers, the record was bleak, the message one of despair.

In national politics, meanwhile, political parties seemed to show little substantive difference. Grover Cleveland brought little executive initiative to either of his two terms in office, the first in the mid-1880s, then, interrupted by four years of Republican rule under Benjamin Harrison, once again from 1892 to 1896. Cleveland's second term of office was best known, on the one hand, for the devastating Panic of 1893 and the four years of depression that followed, and on the other hand, for Cleveland's strident stand against the railroad workers in 1894 and his repudiation of Coxey's Army, with its demand for a massive public works program.

By virtue of the crushing blow to its potential biracial alliance delivered by Southern racists, the Populist threat had evaporated, replaced by the cleverness of Democrats who co-opted a few Populist demands, then failed to follow through. In 1896 that strategy of co-optation came to a peak when the Democrats nominated the young evangelical orator from Nebraska who galvanized the convention with his booming sermon against the gold interests. "You shall not press down upon the brow of labor this crown of thorns," William Jennings Bryan exhorted the delegates. "You shall not crucify mankind upon a cross of gold." Nominated on a free silver platform with some other sops to the Populists thrown in, Bryan received the nomination of both his own party and the Populists. The problem was that the very revivalism that won the hearts of the Democratic delegates alienated the urban Catholic and ethnic constituencies he needed to win. With staid and stoical William McKinley sitting at home on his porch in Ohio, the Republicans seemed the party of stability and reliability. Successfully planting the seed that Bryan was out of control and might well cost urban workers their jobs, McKinley skated to victory with a comfortable margin of nearly one hundred electoral votes.

In reality, one conservative president had simply replaced another, the major difference being the willingness of McKinley to be more aggressive and brazen in his assertion of American power abroad than Cleveland had been. Even there, the disparity was not great, except that it helped set the stage for the most important political development of the decade, the rise of Teddy Roosevelt to national fame and office. Roosevelt so mobilized public opinion with his escapades assaulting the Spaniards at San Juan Hill that he became a national hero. Photogenic with his rimless glasses, his protruding teeth, his buoyant voice, and his charismatic sermonizing, he immediately seized control of the political environment. In the words of one historian, "At a wedding ... [Roosevelt] eclipsed the bride [and] at a funeral the corpse." Returning from Cuba, he quickly became governor of New York State. Then, in a bold move to get him out of that office in order to minimize the damage he might do, New York Republicans succeeded in securing his nomination as vice president in William McKinley's second run for the presidency in 1900. Perceived by most as a brilliant political move almost guaranteed to assure McKinley's reelection, only party boss Marc Hanna had doubts. Prophetically, he observed, "that damned cowboy" was now only one "heartbeat" from the presidency of the United States.

VI. CONCLUSION

To a degree remarkable in the sweep of historical developments, the 1890s framed the major issues of the new century as well as the choices that would have to be made. Literally, the nation was being transformed with huge metropolises sprouting in every region, electrified subways and elevated trains creating transportation links not even conceivable a few decades earlier.

Immigration was skyrocketing, reaching nearly one million new residents per year as the century dawned. These new prospective citizens came from very different kinds of cultures than those who had settled the continent in the first half of the 1800s. Yiddish newspapers, Italian street festivals, Polish folk dances, and Chinese dragon dances now dominated whole areas of cities like New York, Boston, Philadelphia, Chicago, and San Francisco.

Many of these newcomers provided fodder for the industrial machines that were spreading like wildfire around the country. Not only were heavy industries like steel and electricity reaching new heights; so too were consumer industries, the production of ready-made clothes, bakeries with a national market, can and meat products mass-produced for consumers thousands of miles away, transported on new electrified refrigerator cars on railroads—all of this financed by huge financial conglomerates like J. P. Morgan. Magazines, newspapers, and an embryonic motion picture industry circulated information about this nationalizing culture, even as ever new immigrant groups suggested the loss of a national identity and the development of a thousand different island communities of ethnics.

No one knew quite how to deal with the transformative changes. Would local political party bosses remain the most important link between neighborhoods and municipal and state parties? Who would determine whether and how controls were put in place on cleanliness and safety standards? Were business entrepreneurs to be kings of their own empires, freed by the ideology of Social Darwinism to do whatever they wished? Or would the government impose constraints on them, creating order where there had been out-of-control growth? The multimillionaire Cornelius Vanderbilt had one answer. "Law," he declared. "What do I care about the law? Haint I got the power?"

The kinds of changes that were happening knew no parallels. The explosion of entrepreneurship was accompanied by an exponential increase in the size of the American working class, now made up of people from countless nations. How would the new dynamics between workers and bosses be negotiated? Who would frame the discussion and set the terms of negotiation? What would happen with the plight of the farmers, whose numbers had doubled since 1860 but whose income as a share of the national wealth had decreased by half? How would the massive new presence of women in industry be greeted? What about the family and its historic role as a stabilizing force in the community? And how would the newly emancipated educated class of women register their influence on the direction and policies of an ever more powerful country?

A few things were clear as the new century approached. The nation-state had emerged as a powerful presence in international affairs, never again to return to a stance of isolation. Although there would be occasions subsequently when strong voices fought to curtail America's growing role in the world, the 1890s had permanently put that time to rest. In addition, the federal government had made a crucial decision to ignore its oldest, most profound source of social inequality, the issue of race. By sanctioning an apartheid regime in the American South, America left its most oppressed minority bereft of government support.

Like race, issues of women's status would remain an abiding and transcendent theme of twentieth-century America. It might seem that certain patterns were set in stone, but with the expansion of education for women, shifting patterns of sexuality, and changes in family demographics, ripples of change were coursing through the society, with far-reaching implications for everyone.

What remained most unclear was what role the state would play. How might huge corporations be brought under control? When would the government provide support for farmers otherwise drowning in seas of crops that had no viable markets? How would the state deal with working conditions in factories and above all with workers' rights to a decent wage, health care, and living conditions? Above all, what would government's stance become in the clash of workers and employers? At what point, if any, would recognition be given to the rights of workers to have a voice of their own?

In the end, all of these issues came down to three basic questions. How would government bring order and stability to a society rapidly growing out of control? In doing so, how would it treat the efforts of those without power to improve their standing in society? And finally, in pursuing its role as a newly dominant world power, what if any rules or conditions would the government place on its freedom to act as it wished?

None of these questions was simple. But they provided the framework for understanding what was to become the American Century.

2

The Dawn of Progressivism

It quickly became clear as the new century began that reform, not revolution, would characterize the nation's effort to bring stability to a society undergoing dramatic change. The Populist agenda, with its call for public ownership of banks and railroads, federal loans for farmers, and increased government involvement in righting the balance between rich and poor, might have the most systemic response to the transformations at hand, but for the moment, the desire to bring order out of chaos took precedence. Most American politicians seemed to prefer a framework of regulations to bring boundless growth under control rather than to seek grand solutions. The key word was "control"—how to contain within acceptable boundaries changes in acquisition of wealth, consumer consumption, consolidation of industries into trusts, and exploitation of natural resources. Who would speak for the public interest, the "common wealth," as opposed to pursuit of personal aggrandizement? If corrupt politicians threatened to seize the public treasury, who would hold them to account? When gigantic meatpacking plants produced canned chicken that contained rotten ingredients, who would protect the consumer? And when rapacious sweatshop owners sought to maximize profits by employing ten-year-old children for twelve-hour days, who would stand up for the country's rising generation?

I. THE SOCIAL AND INTELLECTUAL CONTEXT

Each of these questions generated its own set of answers. But to a degree unprecedented in earlier decades, the questions captured public attention, at least in part because newspaper reporters and novelists seized reader interest with their exposés of the scandals threatening America's sense of well-being. It might be Henry Demarest Lloyd declaiming against the out-of-control trusts in his book *Wealth Against Commonwealth*, Jacob Riis documenting with dramatic photographs the poverty of slum dwellers, Lincoln Steffens highlighting urban corruption in his "muckraking" magazine articles, Upton Sinclair shocking Americans with stories of bodies falling into huge meat-making vats in Chicago's packing plants, Theodore Dreiser evoking compassion from readers who learned through his novel *Sister Carrie* about the plight of young single poor women drawn into a life of sin, or David Phillips outraging people with his stories of political corruption in "The Treason of the Senate." But whatever the source, middle-class Americans developed a gnawing sense that something was wrong, things were not as they should be, and a response was required.

At the same time, groups of Americans started to organize themselves to act more aggressively on behalf of their concerns. Some groups were professional, others social or personal. Doctors came together in the American Medical Association, lawyers in the American Bar Association. Teachers' associations multiplied. The General Federation of Women's Clubs more than doubled in size. A new group called the National Consumers League was begun by Hull House veteran Florence Kelley to work on behalf of higher consumer standards and better working conditions. People concerned with the environment coalesced in the Sierra Club, dedicated to making sure that

One of Roosevelt's greatest achievements as president was support of the conservation movement. Always drawn to the Western plains and mountains, Roosevelt first discovered California's Yosemite Valley on a trip to Glacier Point with John Muir, founder of the Sierra Club, in 1906.

Credit: The Granger Collection, New York.

the nation's redwoods and mountain waterfalls were not despoiled. A group of women immigrant workers joined together with middle- and upper-class reformers to create the Women's Trade Union League to defend the interests of factory workers. Whatever the immediate cause, in countless cases people took the opportunity to mobilize so that they could work effectively within the body politic. From the National Association of Manufacturers to the Chamber of Commerce, what came to be called "interest group politics" was born.

All of the new constituent groups, whether organized or simply a diffuse assemblage of concerned citizens, shared one conviction in common: the state would have to play a more active role in developing a framework for regulation. For some, that meant municipal reform, as in those who favored city-manager forms of government as opposed to traditional ward bosses. For others, it focused on reforms within state executive and legislative branches, with places like Wisconsin taking the lead under Governor Robert La Follette in forging a partnership between academic researchers and government policymakers to arrive at appropriate means of state intervention. But in most cases attention turned to the federal government. Only national rules, many believed, could bring systematic order to the multiplicity of local regulations, where a hundred different pieces of legislation created chaos for both industry and government, forcing companies to "bargain shop" for those locales where freedom was greatest—at least until the next new piece of regulatory legislation was enacted. If the federal government defined appropriate rules, on the other hand, everyone would have to implement the same practices, enforcement would be predictable, and industries could put into practice uniform behaviors in each plant. Federal rules made more sense, moreover, because it was the interstate commerce clause, and the national government's responsibility to oversee trade between different communities, that provided the constitutional rationale for reform.

All of this, in turn, moved people's attention to the single most important national office as the fulcrum for governmental response. The presidency would, of necessity, become the initiator, the leader—the judge, jury, and referee—charged with reconciling opposing interest groups and speaking on behalf of the public good. For much of the preceding thirty years—really since the Civil War and Reconstruction—the presidency had taken second place to congressional leadership and to developments in industrial expansion, trade, and agriculture. Now, in the face of unbridled growth in all these areas, it was only logical that the one person elected by all the people should sift through their ideas, synthesize their concerns, and find a common ground on which all could agree as the basis from which to create a new order in an otherwise explosively expanding universe.

Historians who have tried to make sense of this transition have come forward with alternative hypotheses to explain the dawning of Progressivism. Seminal as a leader in this debate was the Columbia intellectual and political historian, Richard Hofstadter. With a magisterial overview, he called the Age of Reform—from the Populists through the New Deal—a time of unprecedented governmental innovation. Hofstadter dismissed the Populists as romantics seeking to re-create a golden age of yeoman farmers able to govern themselves and earn a successful living. The Populists, Hofstadter presumed, were drawn to conspiracy theories and solutions—free silver, the subtreasury—and had neither the political skills nor sufficient familiarity with economic realities to succeed. The Progressives, he believed, also suffered from cultural and economic anxiety. These were formerly the professionals—doctors, lawyers, ministers, college professors—who once occupied the top niche in society and now had seen themselves displaced by the nouveau riche, those fast-rising industrialists who had no taste, no sense of community responsibility, no manners. According to Hofstadter, the Progressives suffered from "status anxiety" and sought new forms of regulation to reassert their control in the community. From Hofstadter's perspective, only New Dealers fell within the parameters of normal people. Pragmatists for the most part, they sought practical, specific, well-calibrated legislative responses to specific problems that cried out for solution.

Whatever one's conclusions on Hofstadter's arguments, they set off a whirlwind of debate and counterhypothesis. A number of historians sympathetic to Southern insurgency demonstrated the degree to which the Populists were well grounded in a reality-based politics of community mobilization and pragmatic legislative proposals. Others turned the Hofstadter "status anxiety" thesis on its head and argued that, in fact, the legislative reforms of Progressivism came not from those trying to bring business under control but from business executives themselves who sought to use the centralizing authority of the federal government to make their planning more rational, predictable, and successful. According to this interpretation, Progressive legislation was in fact a tool of big business, not an effort to control it. Still another synthesis found another common denominator—the search for order and for efficiency that was reflected in virtually all progressive legislation, whether in city-manager forms of government, rules on how far trusts could go without violating the law, and how government must assert ultimate responsibility for the health and well-being of women and children. Others asked more critical questions. How could one use the name "progressive reform," they asked, to characterize an age that witnessed the systematic disenfranchisement of virtually every African American man in the South? And what about women's roles, others asked. Were not women really the ones responsible for all the "truly progressive" changes that came about?

Whatever the interpretation, one thing was abundantly clear. A new age of government intervention had emerged. On whose behalf, and with what motivation, remained very much a topic of debate. No one claimed that the "age of reform" constituted a dramatic realigning of the political landscape, with workers, poor people, farmers, and the disenfranchised seizing power that they never before had held. But change was happening and in a way that would shape the debate on state power, and the public interest, for the remainder of the twentieth century.

II. THE ROOSEVELT PRESIDENCY

No individual was better prepared to introduce a more activist presidency than Theodore Roosevelt. The man who charged up Kettle Hill in San Juan, ordered the American fleet into Manila Bay, rounded up cattle and outlaws in the "Wild West," and boasted of fighting Indians and slaying lions made the word "activist" seem like an understatement. Born into aristocracy, educated at private schools and at Harvard, intent on overcoming his fragility as a child through bodybuilding exercises, Roosevelt seemed tracked from birth for a record of unparalleled achievement.

Yet his life was also one of sadness and tragedy. His mother, to whom he was devoted, died prematurely at age 48, her son by her side. Then, less than half a day later, his wife, barely 22, died of kidney failure shortly after giving birth to their daughter. "The light has gone out of my life," Roosevelt said. For most people, such tragedy would have led to months of remorse, religious contemplation, reflection on the meaning of life, inward despair. Roosevelt's response was different. Leaving his newborn daughter in the care of his sister, he struck out for the West. Instead of isolation, he embraced a life of hardship, exploration, and physical conquest. Meditation was not absent—TR read Tolstoy by the campfire at night; nor was intellectual exploration ever far away—he was a Phi Beta Kappa and by age 24 had published the first of more than thirty books he wrote in his lifetime. But Roosevelt's spiritual recovery went hand in hand with physical engagement of a fierce and demanding nature, with his body providing the bravado that spearheaded the forging of his character.

Never one to shun the limelight, on his return to New York Roosevelt immediately ran for mayor. Not surprisingly given his youth, his inexperience, and his recent absence from the city, he lost, but the very act of running underlined his bold and venturesome nature. He quickly moved on to serve as New York City's Civil Service Commissioner for six years—in the eyes of many a "reform" position dedicated to cleaning up the corruption of urban politics—and then, in a role much more simpatico with his image as a crusader for moral reform, Roosevelt became police commissioner for the city. Patrolling the streets at night with rank-and-file officers, he literally gave physical form to his persona as an activist for public safety and morality. It should have been no surprise, then, that when he became assistant secretary of the navy, he both asserted his independence by ordering the Pacific Fleet into action in Manila and became the larger-than-life war hero who tackled the Spaniards head-on and boasted of the bravado of his and his men's victory. No words better summarized TR's approach to politics and life than his verdict on these events: "A just war," he declared, "is in the long run far better for a man's soul than the most prosperous peace." Although thankfully, not all presidents after TR preached the same sermon, it was a message that peculiarly fit both the man and his times. When TR suddenly succeeded to the White House after McKinley was assassinated by an anarchist, he came prepared with a message and a style dramatically different from all before him.

Yet if Roosevelt invented the idea of the White House as a "bully pulpit," he proceeded about his business with a moderation of policy consistent with his upper-class, paternalistic status, acting like a philosopher king watching over his people rather than a rabble-rousing rebel. In the end, TR personified a paradox: the superactivist as centrist reformer, the militant exhorter as someone who preferred to apply palliatives rather than perform radical surgery on the nation's ills. Appropriately, Roosevelt's ability to combine bravado, on the one hand, with incremental reform, on the other, gave him the standing to assure people that something was being done to deal with their most fearsome anxieties, but not enough to provoke unsettling side effects. In a brilliant epigraph, the historian Richard Hofstadter best described TR's secret of success: Roosevelt was, Hofstadter wrote, the "master therapist of the middle class." The president provided daily reassurance that he better than anyone understood the importance of bringing stability and common sense to a world threatening to hurtle out of control, but he would do so in a way that everyone could see was responsible and moderate, not extreme.

Charting that middle ground became the hallmark of the Roosevelt presidency. He chastised the irresponsible but never cut them off at the legs, making sure that the admonition was always greater than the punishment. Nowhere was this better illustrated than in one of his first decisive interventions in the domestic economy, the anthracite coal strike of 1902. It was a classic confrontation between management and workers. The owners of the mines pedantically (and pietistically) proclaimed that the workers' interests would be best left in the hands "of the Christian men to whom God in his infinite wisdom has given the control of property interests of this country." The workers, on the other hand, pleaded for remedial action to address their miniscule wages, exhausting hours, and unsafe working conditions. It was a perfect scenario for TR to step in as the voice of judgment and reason. Issues of justice were involved, he declared, as well as the survival of an economy dependent on coal. Hence, as president, he would have to intervene, representing the voice of the people, and use federal troops to operate the mines if the two sides could not come to an agreement. Quickly, the mine owners and labor leaders agreed to arbitration, which resulted in an agreement that brought substantial improvement in the workers' lives and safety conditions while not destroying the owners' power.

The coal agreement represented the model of national leadership on behalf of the public interest that became Roosevelt's signature as president. In virtually every area, but especially in the fields of corporate authority, consumer rights, and conservation of natural resources, he defined the middle ground. His activities appeared to embody an activist posture—yet they always took the form of incremental improvement rather than radical or structural change. The same year as the coal strike, for example, Roosevelt initiated a major antitrust action against the Northern Securities Company, a J. P. Morgan and James Hill holding company infamous for its consolidated power. Thereby, TR put teeth for the first time into the Sherman Anti-Trust bill enacted twelve years earlier. The Supreme Court upheld his intervention

As factories mushroomed in America's urban areas, they were fueled by nonstop expansion of coal mines in places like Pennsylvania and West Virginia, where safety conditions were often minimal. Here a group of coal miners are preparing to go down into the mines in Hazelton, Pennsylvania.

Credit: © Corbis

two years later. Yet Roosevelt also famously desisted from other major antitrust actions, thereby reassuring business that he would be discriminating—and discrete—in whom he targeted. With other industries, he took a similarly measured stance. Railroads had been all over the landscape with their rates and fares, using their power arbitrarily. Roosevelt thus became a strong proponent of the 1906 Hepburn Act, which abolished long-haul versus short-haul rate differences and created national standards of proper conduct consistent with the Interstate Commerce Act. But railroads actually benefited from the federal legislation because now they had a single standard against which to be measured instead of myriad state and local rules that were often in conflict and led to chaos and inefficiency.

Consumer protection was perhaps the most popular, and notable, of Roosevelt's reforms. After Upton Sinclair published his novel *The Jungle*, the nation rose in outrage at the practices Sinclair described in the meatpacking industry. The scandal was aptly encapsulated in a popular rhyme of the day: "Mary had a little lamb, And when she saw it sicken, She shipped it off to Packingtown, and Now it's labeled Chicken." The Meat Inspection Act performed two functions simultaneously: it reassured desperate homemak-ers that their children were not being poisoned by reckless manufacturers, and it provided the strongest and most work-efficient meatpackers with the regulatory tools to help drive their competitors out of business by allowing them to maximize their appeal as guarantors of product safety.

Roosevelt did perhaps his most important reform work in the one area he also cared most deeply about—conservation of national parklands and forests. Naming environmentalist Gifford Pinchot to head the government's division of Forestry, Roosevelt quickly won the hearts and energies of peo-ple dedicated to preserving the nation's natural resources. Roosevelt went camping with John Muir, the premier conservationist of his time, founder of the Sierra Club, and the person who helped create Yosemite National Park. Returning from his trip, Roosevelt celebrated the glories of the nation's waterfalls and streams, started the long and continuously popular tradition of removing treasured natural forests and streams from private exploitation,

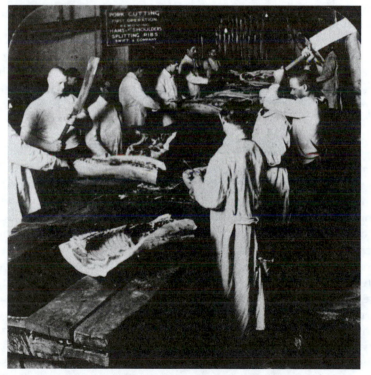

Upton Sinclair's *The Jungle* made infamous the unsafe working conditions in the nation's meatpacking plants. Here butchers are shown carving up beef at one such unsanitary packing house. The Meat Inspection Act of 1906 was a direct response to such revelations.

Credit: The Granger Collection, New York.

and justifiably boosted his credentials as a president who put the nation's public interest ahead of any commercial claims for developing rich natural resources. Before Roosevelt, the president who had set aside the most timberlands for conservation had been Grover Cleveland—25 million acres. By contrast, Roosevelt set aside 150 million acres for national forest reserve, protecting 85 million more in Alaska and the Northwest.

It is difficult to imagine anyone bringing off such a transformation in presidential power and politics more brilliantly. Almost typecast for the part, the once frail, now bullishly healthy physical marvel engaged with poise and reassurance the once incomprehensible eruptions of his age. He simply looked, and acted, as though he knew exactly what should be done. In foreign affairs, he brokered a peace between Russia and Japan in 1905 that earned him the Nobel Peace Prize. In asserting American national self-interest, he thoroughly modernized the Monroe Doctrine, giving America control over its own hemisphere; initiated and supervised the takeover by the breakaway nation of Panama of an isthmus of land from Colombia that would soon become the Panama Canal—under virtually total American control; and presided over final modernization of the American navy—the great White Fleet—which he then sent around the world to signify America's new role as a preeminent world power. In all these ways, Roosevelt created the twentieth-century American presidency—one of independence, supreme power yet cautious moderation, seeking to crystallize and speak on behalf of a maturing people now able to proceed with confidence toward confronting, and controlling, the unprecedented process of modernization sweeping the globe.

III. PROGRESSIVISM, BIG "P" AND SMALL "P"

The history of Progressivism on a national level lends substantial support to those such as Robert Wiebe who have interpreted the "age of reform" as primarily a "search for order" in an era of chaos. Notwithstanding his occasional (and self-projected) pose as an agitator for the public good, Theodore Roosevelt discomfited very few of the rich and powerful. To his enormous credit, he pursued policies that resonated with the concerns of average Americans, proving that he heard their anxiety, understood its focus, and was prepared to take whatever actions were necessary to restore a sense of balance and responsibility to the management of the political sphere. Yet even with the legislative reforms that were enacted, most of his actions could be seen more as symbolic than substantive. The portentous and excessive claims of the Vanderbilts and others that they were beyond the law had now been displaced. No one could afford blatantly to affront public sensibilities or ignore the right of the president, and the national government, to impose a sense of system and stability on the economy. Yet in almost all cases, regulation was consistent with, if not supportive of, the ongoing efficiency of the country's largest industrialists. City managers brought order to municipal government (though taking power away from local, immigrant-dominated precincts), regulations governing railroads limited the unconstrained power of railway magnates but in fact made easier the systematization of the transportation network, and even large trusts welcomed the new oversight of the government because it provided a friendly structure within which to plan just how consolidation could proceed. In all these respects, Progressivism with a capital "P" could thus be seen as moderate intervention by government with the ultimate impact of creating a more reliable, more efficient, more streamlined form of economic production. There was no support for labor radicalism, no movement toward a significant redistribution of wealth or income, no challenge to the ongoing dominance of the rich and powerful. Instead, there was simply a more stable, coherent, and reliable framework within which power as it traditionally had functioned could carry forward.

There was, on the other hand, another form of progressivism that might be labeled small "p" reform. Its concern was less the systematizing and rationalization of industry and government and more the uplifting and enhancement of human possibility. The focus of small "p" progressivism was human beings, particularly those most in need of help and least able to look out for their own interests. Women and children constituted the primary focus of this reform effort, and to a remarkable degree, the programs, legislation, ideas, and values generated by this reform effort were driven by women. This was a gendered progressivism. If men like Theodore Roosevelt wanted to regulate railroads, put brakes on the engorgement of industries into trusts, and bring efficiency to the economy, it was women like Jane Addams and Florence Kelley who worked to end child labor, improve the conditions threatening the health and safety of women in factories, build railroad crossings at inner-city intersections to prevent immigrant children from being hit by trains, and create an infrastructure of recreational and educational institutions that could improve, to however small a degree, the chance that children especially, but also mothers and wives, might improve the quality of their lives.

These too were reforms that began locally but soon became national in scope. Grace and Edith Abbott started their work with children as social settlement house workers in Chicago. They mobilized good government supporters, reached out to churchmen, enlisted friendly journalists—all in the cause of creating a constituency willing and able to work on behalf of young children. Not only did inner-city young people need safe places to play and decent schools to attend. They needed as well the protection of the law so that young children would not become fodder for sweatshop garment industries and could not be put to work on unsafe machinery in large factories. The Abbott sisters achieved striking successes in Illinois, but soon they and their supporters recognized that, just as in the case of consumer protections in the meatpacking industry, children's interests required federal engagement. And so by networking with other reformers from around the country, using their skill at public relations, and mobilizing the "muckraking" journalists of their time, they helped make "children" a national issue and in 1912 succeeded in securing the establishment of the Children's Bureau in the U.S. Department of Labor to look after the interests of the young.

In similar fashion, women reformers sought to provide minimal safeguards for the health and well-being of factory workers. They began with a state-by-state effort to enact maximum hour and minimum wage laws. No one should be forced to work a twelve-hour day, with all the dire consequences for one's health and well-being. Everyone should be paid a minimum wage to make possible the sustenance of life. Factories should be required to introduce safety mechanisms on their machinery so that workers did not lose their limbs. Governments, state and local, should have inspectors to ensure basic levels of health and well-being in the workplace. Illinois passed a Factory Safety Law, and Florence Kelley of Hull House became the state factory inspector charged with enforcing it. Other states followed suit. New York enacted a maximum hour law to keep workers from being exhausted and endangered by too many hours in a row toiling in a bakery or at a machine. Other states passed minimum wage laws. Eventually, as in the case of the Children's Bureau, more and more of these efforts took on a national dimension, especially with regard to finding a way to prohibit child labor.

It is important to note that these reform efforts became more and more gendered, both in sponsorship and in content. All along, it had been women reformers coming out of the settlement house movements who had inexorably moved from neighborhood service into public policy and political activism. But then, as courts started to rule on the new laws passed in various states, it became more and more clear that a specific argument had to be made that women had a special need and interest in legislations explicitly designed to ensure their protection. For decades, the Supreme Court had been moving in a conservative direction. Not only did the *Plessy* case indicate this but so too did a series of industrial suits going back to the *Slaughterhouse* case in 1883. There the Court had ruled that huge corporations could be treated as "individuals" under the Fourteenth Amendment's "equal protection" clause and that they had the same rights as laborers to "equal treatment" and consideration before the law. Now this same reasoning was used to invalidate laws regulating hours of work for men and women.

In the *Lochner* case in 1905, the Supreme Court ruled as unconstitutional, and a violation if the Fourteenth Amendment's Equal Protection clause, a law that established maximum hours of employment for women and men in New York's baking industry. The argument was made by the factory owners that their "equal rights" before the law had been violated by depriving them of the opportunity to negotiate as individuals with their employees to determine their conditions of work. There seemed nowhere to go, no argument to make, to sustain these legislative reforms given the Court's now consensual reading of the Fourteenth Amendment's intent.

This set the stage for one of the more important innovations in twentieth-century political and legislative ideology. Oregon had passed a minimum wage law for women, which, on appeal, went to the Supreme Court for adjudication in 1908. The first breakthrough in the case involved the filing of what has become known as "the Brandeis brief." The defendants in the case successfully argued that the only way the judges could determine the validity of Oregon's law was through the compilation of sociological data that would establish the empirical threat to women's health and safety if they were not protected at the workplace by state legislation. Harvard law professor (and later Supreme Court judge) Louis Brandeis compiled reams of data conclusively proving that women would be endangered by the absence of such legislation. The second breakthrough consisted of the legal argument that followed. Women, the state's brief concluded, constituted a special category under the law, dramatically distinguishing them from men. They were the "childbearers" of the race, whose protection as the guarantors of society's perpetuation represented a pivotal responsibility of the state. Women's peculiarity as those responsible for giving birth to future generations thus placed them in a different category from men and liberated them from the limitations posed by the Equal Protection clause of the Fourteenth Amendment. Hence it was permissible for the court to sanction special legislation designed to protect women because as a different breed of humanity than men, they comprised a distinct category.

The court agreed, upholding Oregon's minimum wage/maximum hour law for women. From that point forward, the survivability of protective social welfare legislation hinged on the particular argument that women were physically inferior to men and depended upon the state for protection if society were to survive. Among other things, such reasoning made it difficult if not impossible to argue that women should be treated in all ways identically to men—the gist of the Equal Rights Amendment of the 1920s and thereafter—and the whole reform argument for social welfare legislation of any kind became tied to an acceptance of women's dependence on the state and the special character of their identity as childbearers. For the next thirty years, until the early1940s, the *Muller v. Oregon* precedent held sway in the Supreme Court, and deep-seated disputes among feminists of various persuasions crystallized around the question of the sameness-versus-difference argument regarding women and men.

One further consequence of the *Muller* case was that it reinforced significantly that side of the woman suffrage argument that insisted women deserved the vote precisely because they were so different from men. Although some still argued vociferously from the natural rights position that all human beings, by definition, were endowed by their Creator with the same inalienable rights, an ever stronger case was now made by those "social feminists" who contended that women occupied a special sphere and brought such different values and perspectives to government that no effective politics could exist without both sexes—so totally different from each other—making a contribution to the body politic.

Clearly, the women's movement had made a decisive contribution to progressivism, especially that small "p" part of the overall movement that focused on human rights, children's future, and the well-being of the childbearers of the race. Often, the two kinds of progressivism—big "P" and small "p"—functioned synergistically, working as much in harmony with each other as in opposition. But a clear difference existed between those whose primary concern was imposing order, stability, and systematization on an economic structure veering out of control and those whose main concern was intervening to protect the humanity and well-being of society's most vulnerable members. The difference said a huge amount about the distinct motivations of those who brought the Progressive era to fruition and about the ongoing tensions that would characterize reform efforts throughout the "progressive era" and into the New Deal three decades later.

IV. THE NEW NATIONALISM AND THE NEW FREEDOM

When Roosevelt was overwhelmingly reelected in 1904, he made the disastrous political mistake of saying he would not be a candidate for reelection in 1908. In effect declaring himself a "lame duck" four years in advance—and before the constitutional amendment limiting a president to two terms (which would not have applied to Roosevelt anyway because he was elected president in his own right only once)—Roosevelt thereby limited his long-range ability to shape Republican Party politics, especially in the years after 1906. Moreover, he made the second mistake of knighting his chosen successor, William Howard Taft, well in advance, building up expectations that Taft would carry on TR's policies while also creating a predisposition to compare the two presidential personalities.

On that score, Taft was foredoomed. Weighing in at more than 350 pounds (jokes had it that he had to be lifted out of the bathtub) and with a singular dislike for backslapping political falderal, he once acknowledged that when he was in the White House, whenever anyone said "Mr. President," he always turned and looked for Roosevelt. Although in many respects Taft was more progressive than "Mr. Progressive," Roosevelt himself, he displayed neither the flair nor rhetoric of his predecessor. In four years, he may have introduced twice as many antitrust suits as Roosevelt had in seven years, yet by contrast with Roosevelt he appeared dull, pedantic, and boring. Moreover, his sense of timing was awful. When Gifford Pinchot, Roosevelt's "darling" of the conservation movement, openly challenged a directive from Taft's secretary of the interior, R. A. Ballinger, Taft fired Pinchot for insubordination. The procedural rationale for Taft's action may have been correct, but the symbolic politics were atrocious, as the issue quickly became one of Taft's commitment to the environment, not his determination to stand up for executive discipline. Instead of carrying forward a reputation as a progressive, he quickly was dubbed a "machine" politician who campaigned for the Payne-Aldrich tariff, the highest ever enacted—usually seen as pro-big business—while seeking to purge insurgents like Wisconsin's Robert La Follette and California's Hiram Johnson from the Senate in 1910. Both efforts were disastrous failures. By the time Teddy Roosevelt returned from his two-year boar and lion hunting safari to Africa in 1910, hordes of Progressives were calling for Taft's hide, and the former president's anointed successor had come to be seen as an apostate rather than a disciple of the progressive mystique.

The stage was thus set for a classic political donnybrook, with Roosevelt, the chest-thumping crusader who personified activist intervention on behalf of the public interest, challenging frontally the Judas who had betrayed his progressive principles. That, at least, was the public presentation by Roosevelt afficionados. Lost in the translation was the degree to which Taft had actually done a good job in pursuing substantive progressive policies on trusts, railroad regulation (the 1910 Mann-Elkins Act), social welfare (the creation of the Children's Bureau), and political reform (congressional passage of both the Sixteenth Amendment, authorizing a federal income tax, and the Seventeenth Amendment, providing for direct election of U.S. senators, both now sent to the states for ratification). Also obscured was the critical degree to which the sitting president, no matter how politically unpopular, still controls the mechanism of the party bureaucracy, including its determination of whose vote will count in a national convention.

Roosevelt came back to the national scene with bombast and vision. Proclaiming his devotion to a "New Nationalism"—a phrase he took from public intellectual Herbert Croly's book *The Promise of American Life*—Roosevelt declared that the time had come to regulate the consolidation of big business and big labor, with big government as the arbiter in between. "Combination and concentration should be, not prohibited, but supervised," Roosevelt declared, "and within reasonable limits, controlled." Completely consistent with his practices as president, the New Nationalism accepted the dramatic changes that had made the American economy the most dynamic in the world but created the role of judge and policeman for the federal government to play, intervening at will on behalf of the moral and social interest of the population as a whole. Moreover, in his New Nationalism campaign of 1911–1912, Roosevelt came close to merging the agendas of big "P" and small "p" progressivism, supporting minimum wages and social insurance for workers as well as women's suffrage—the first time a national candidate had embraced feminist ideas. Initially, at least, Robert La Follette was a powerful contender as well for the Republican Party nomination against Taft. But then he suffered an apparent nervous breakdown and Roosevelt by himself carried the challenge to Taft.

The Republican convention was as close a presidential nominating contest as the most melodramatic playwright could have imagined. Roosevelt had the momentum. By the time the convention met, it all came down to 254 disputed delegates. Had he won only 100 of these, Roosevelt would have been renominated for president on the Republican ticket. Yet it was at precisely that point when Taft's role as party leader came into play. Holding the key cards, the president's lieutenants awarded all but 19 of the 254 delegate votes to Taft. As a consequence, the rotund sitting president rode to renomination, hoping and expecting his former patron to set aside his ego and endorse the party ticket.

But Roosevelt would not so easily be bridled. By now he had become contemptuous of Taft, subsequently referring to him as a "fathead" with the brain of a "guinea pig." (As with all such contests, verbal excesses knew few limits.

Taft called TR a "dangerous egotist" and a demagogue, perhaps not quite so dramatic as TR's descriptions of Taft, but close). With the winds of righteous indignation at his back, Roosevelt and his supporters gathered in convention to create a new third party, the Progressive Party. Jane Addams, the embodiment of small "p" progressivism, placed Roosevelt's name in nomination, together with big business progressives who embraced TR's gospel of a "new nationalism." TR had inspired the delegates with his declaration that he felt "as strong as a bull moose"—a popular song about the new party lyricized "I want to be a Bull Moose, and with the Bull Moose stand, With antlers on my forehead, and Big Stick in my hand." By acclamation, the delegates endorsed TR's bid for election, sending him forth to crusade for the New Nationalism against Taft's far more conventional, though substantively not much different, political philosophy of how to respond to the new industrialism.

The problem, of course, was that there existed a third party as well—the Democrats—one that was ready to compete at every step for the new political constituency that sought government intervention to protect the country and its people from economic abuse.

For three of the previous four Democratic nominating conventions, William Jennings Bryan, the boy orator of the West, had emerged triumphant, with his distinctive brand of populist-style rhetoric. (In 1904, Alton Parker, a conservative Wall Street-backed candidate, had ineffectively opposed TR's reelection). Never, though, had the Democrats chosen someone who represented a more modern, Eastern, urban-based progressivism that might constitute direct competition for Republican progressivism. Having won the 1910 congressional elections, 228–161, the Democrats were now well poised to strike for national victory.

They also hit upon an ideal candidate. Woodrow Wilson was born in the South. A deeply religious man, he brought to his life a stern Presbyterian moralism. Once, when a colleague sought to temper Wilson's penchant to be judgmental by reminding him that there were two sides to every issue, Wilson retorted, "Yes, a right side and a wrong side." That binary way of thinking represented both Wilson's greatest strength and his greatest weakness. It inspired the soaring rhetoric that allowed him to galvanize the American people into waging a "war to save the world for democracy" and also generated the dogmatic determination never to compromise with his political enemies over how to secure the votes necessary to ratify the Treaty of Versailles.

A brilliant student, Wilson soon determined to follow academics as a profession. Wilson was among the first generations of Americans to attend graduate school and receive a doctoral degree. After earning his doctorate at Johns Hopkins University in Baltimore in political science, Wilson became *the* expert in the country on congressional government. Soon he was an award-winning author teaching at one of the nation's elite Ivy League institutions, Princeton University. Although a Southerner by birth, he clearly shared a nationalist political perspective. "Because I love the South," he once said, "I rejoice in the failure of the Confederacy." Advancing steadily in the academy, he was a natural candidate to be selected as president of Princeton, where he brought intellectual panache and political shrewdness to a position that for most people would represent the pinnacle of a professional career.

But consistent with his field of expertise, Wilson also deeply cared about politics and especially the need to bring morality and reform to state and national government. He believed in a strong governorship and a strong presidency, convinced that it was the role of activist leaders to analyze problems, propose solutions, and lead the people forward with policies suitable for resolving the unforeseen dilemmas of modern industrial capitalism. Soon he became the compromise choice to run as Democratic candidate for the governorship of New Jersey in 1910. Decisive and innovative as a reformer in that role, he entered the race for the Democratic nomination as president in 1912. Clear in his platform—he strongly advocated banking reform, a reduction in tariffs, and antitrust legislation—he once again emerged as a compromise candidate, winning nomination on the forty-sixth ballot, largely due to the decisive last-minute support of William Jennings Bryan, who believed that a reformer like Wilson was far preferable to a party regular like Missouri's Champ Clark.

Rarely has a presidential contest featured such intense moralistic rhetoric. Whatever their differences—and on specific policies they were substantial—both Roosevelt and Wilson had Messiah complexes. Each believed that he embodied the truth, held a monopoly on insight into how God would proceed were he present in national politics, and displayed no shyness in claiming the authority to be moral spokesman for Progressivism. Within that similarity, of course, there were approaches to commonly perceived problems that varied dramatically. Whereas Roosevelt repeatedly proclaimed his faith in the doctrines of his beloved New Nationalism—big business, big labor, and an overriding and morally decisive big government—Wilson trumpeted his belief in what he called the New Freedom. Instead of being consolidated, he insisted that trusts should be broken up, the "little man" given new impetus to succeed, and the premises of laissez-faire competition restored to primacy. Despite the apparent divisions in approach, however, the reality was that the exigencies of normal political vote counting would determine the outcome. Of necessity, Roosevelt and Taft would split the Republican tally, and only an abysmal failure on the part of the Democrats would lead to their defeat. Wilson won only a minority of the total popular vote, 6.2 million to a combined 7.5 million for Roosevelt and Taft. But Wilson swept the electoral college with 435 votes because his Republican opponents, in effect, had shot themselves in the foot by running in the same party.

Immediately, Wilson demonstrated the clear-eyed decisiveness that had marked his academic and political careers from the beginning. He set out to do what he said he would do. Only the difference was that in substance, as opposed to rhetoric, his programs were not that distinctive from what Roosevelt would have proposed. Wilson set the tone for his administration with a soaring inaugural address, reminiscent in some ways of one given nearly half a century later by another Ivy Leaguer who had written books, John F. Kennedy. "We have been proud of our industrial achievements," he told his audience, reminding them of the economic forces that had generated the nation's new political agenda, "but we have not hitherto stopped thoughtfully enough to count the human cost"—a clear reference to the concerns of those with a small "p" progressive perspective. "This is not a day of triumph," Wilson declared; "it is a day of dedication. Here muster not the forces of party, but the forces of humanity." With moral conviction providing his steadfast anchor, Wilson thus set forth to deliver on the promises he had made to the American people.

Leaping into action, Wilson convened Congress in special session to pass tariff reform, his number-one campaign pledge. With strong executive leadership, the Congress responded, enacting the Underwood Tariff. Quickly thereafter, he gave substance to the new Seventeenth Amendment by having Congress impose a 1 percent tax on incomes over $4,000 and a 6 percent tax on those with incomes over $500,000, thereby making up for the monies lost by tariff reform. Soon thereafter, as part of his attack on the "triple wall of privilege"—the tariff, banks, and trusts—he secured probably the most important long-lasting structural change of his administration, creation of the Federal Reserve system of national banks, responsible for enacting, then regulating, federal fiscal policy. Finally came the Federal Trade Act of 1914 and the Clayton Anti-Trust Act of 1916, implementing a framework of trust policies to regulate the growth and consolidation of big business. In fact, the Federal Trade Commission acted in a manner much more consistent with TR's attitudes toward trusts than with those earlier articulated in Wilson's New Freedom.

Nor did Wilson stop there. In an effort to undercut the likelihood that large employers would employ child labor, the Keating-Owen Act prohibited shipment across state lines of goods that had been produced by children under age sixteen (it was later invalidated by the Supreme Court), passed the Federal Farm Loan Act of 1916 and the Warehouse Act of 1916 (at least partially delivering on ideas first articulated by the Populists in 1892), and enacted the Workingmen's Compensation Act of 1916 and the Adamson Act, providing for an eight-hour day for workers on United States railroads. It was an impressive list of achievements, giving some credence to Wilson's hope, expressed in 1916, that the future would be a "time of healing because a time of just dealing."

V. CONCLUSION

Whatever one's assessment of the political vectors shaping the direction of Progressivism, one thing was abundantly clear: the state was playing a new and central role never before imagined in American society. In some respects, there was no alternative. The transforming impact of unprecedented industrial expansion, massive urban growth, and explosive immigration had created a country almost spinning out of control. People everywhere, from the middle class to the old professional class to the nouveau riche, yearned for stability and a sense of accountability. The fundamental issues were order versus chaos, control versus nihilism. Were the government not to play the role of policeman and regulator, rampant greed threatened to propel the country into a war of feuding conglomerate interests, all the while leaving the health and safety of average people unattended to and ignored.

There were some who envisioned a more activist, politically left-of-center form of government intervention than that which evolved. The Socialists, renewed in energy by the exploitation that accompanied industrialism, mobilized hitherto unheard of blocs of voters with their ideologically coherent plea for government nationalization of major public utilities and their substitution of commitment to the "common wealth" for the unbridled self-aggrandizement of capitalist entrepreneurs. Invigorated by multiple new immigrants from countries with a much heartier history of left-wing politics, the Socialists, led by Eugene Debs, made a discernible if ultimately unsuccessful impact on the American political scene.

Though less radical ideologically than the Socialists, those who supported Populism also envisioned a new kind of state intervention. Focused on the realm of agriculture, though not oblivious to the condition of industrial workers, Populists wanted the state to even the playing field by providing loans to farmers for their supplies; warehouses to store their crops; an end to usurious interest rates; and public ownership of railroads, the telephone, and the telegraph. This was a form of state interventionism that clearly tilted toward helping those at the bottom of the pile while working to deprive the wealthy and powerful of arbitrary control of those at the other end of the income curve. They too failed to enlist a majority of voters, and at critical moments, the state chose to intervene against those protesting from the bottom, whether workers or farmers, rather than support them. Still, the agenda set forward by the Populists created a benchmark that reformers would return to repeatedly over the next three decades for inspiration as to how to proceed.

In the end, the new form of state power that responded to the specter of uncontrolled growth and selfishness was one which took the most conservative form possible, consistent with the need to do something to keep the society from spiraling into chaos. Theodore Roosevelt exemplified this new approach—using the White House as a bully pulpit from which to preach the urgency of respecting the public interest but resorting in practice to only limited forms of actual regulation and intervention. These were sufficient to give ample warning of what might come were "selfish private interests" not to curtail their greed but not so excessive as to inspire panic in the rich and powerful. This was a form of state intervention that reassured the middle class while avoiding any major redistribution of wealth and influence. The rich might feel unfairly targeted for criticism but not to the point where they had a basis for becoming apoplectic. Ultimately, the forms that state Progressivism developed fit comfortably the theories of both those who saw the entire period as demonstrating simply a "search for order" in the face of potential chaos and those who saw the new institutions of state power as primarily tools used by powerful industrial interests for their own protection. Either way, the result was the same: the status quo continuing as it had been yet now under an umbrella of state regulations that ensured greater predictability, responsibility, and conformity to public standards.

In the end, much of the hullabaloo about "regulation" as opposed to "deregulation" amounted more to verbiage than substance. Notwithstanding the rhetoric about "trust-busting," most of the industrial giants remained as they had been—more attentive perhaps to their need to appear publicly responsible but rarely if ever in fear of being extinguished by a crusading government out to "get the big guys." Thus despite the overblown debate between TR's "New Nationalism," with its commitment to big business consolidation and big government regulation, and Woodrow Wilson's "New Freedom," with its theoretical support of laissez-faire competition, the direction of both presidencies was toward setting rules of conduct that existing structures of capitalism would accept rather than breaking up those structures. Indeed, never would big business achieve greater consolidation and control than under Wilson during World War I (to be discussed in the next chapter).

The real issue for critics of the politics of Progressivism was what happened to human rights during this purported period of reform and democracy. How to explain the paradox whereby the percentage of people who went to the polls declined precipitously between 1890 and 1920? And how to reconcile the brutal contradiction of taking away the right to vote of 95 percent of Southern African Americans at the same time that politicians trumpeted the spread of democracy? Or the stunning hypocrisy of calling this disenfranchisement a "reform"? And what about the initiative, referendum and recall, more often used by well-financed, well-organized private interests to pursue their agendas than by average voters fed up with bad government and seeking to "throw the rascals out of power"? Finally, what about the "efficiency" of city-manager forms of government that in fact provided more a model for making government function like a corporation than a vehicle for making government more accountable to average citizens, many of whom—at least in large immigrant-populated cities—undoubtedly had more power under the old precinct "boss" system of government than under the new municipal reform regimes. In the end, the "Progressive" era provided little voice or power to the poor or disorganized.

The major exception to this generalization consisted of the vastly expanded role that women played in the political process. Though most could not yet vote, women actually—as Suzanne Lebsock has argued—controlled more influence and power by virtue of their role as lobbyists and activists *before* winning the suffrage than afterward. From their settlement houses and women's clubs, women insistently focused on the human side of industrial and urban expansion, working feverishly to secure playgrounds, nursery schools, and recreation centers for the children of the immigrant poor while seeking to protect their parents, and especially their mothers, through brilliant campaigns for minimum wage and maximum hour laws for women and organized consumer boycotts of goods produced under unfair and unhealthy work conditions. This was a side of progressivism that did care about human rights, and even if in the end it achieved only modest successes, at least these provided another benchmark for future generations to heed and to follow.

When all was said and done, therefore, the Progressive era launched a new political entity, the regulatory state. By itself, that was a major development. Given the alternative—capitalist expansion reeling out of control—it may have been the least that could have occurred to sustain and make viable the existing social and economic structure. Yet the creation of the modern, interventionist twentieth- century state provided a departure point for all future discussions of how to achieve a society consistent with the promise of "equal opportunity" decreed by the nation's founders. Even if the primary result of the new Progressive state was to perpetuate and strengthen the power of those already wielding authority in the nation, its very existence provided an instrument to turn to when those who desired social change—including in the area of human rights—sought a vehicle to achieve their ends. In the meantime, that state also became the instrument by which the country assumed a new role in international affairs and became recognized as the most powerful nation on the planet.

3

America and the World

Whatever the new role of the state domestically, the first two decades of the new century proved conclusively that in the domain of world politics the United States intended to speak loudly. McKinley and Roosevelt had started the trend with the Spanish-American War, Roosevelt's sending the U.S. Navy to Manila, and then leading the charge at San Juan Hill. To demonstrate that this was no one-time flexing of muscles, Roosevelt negotiated the Hay-Pauncefote Treaty of 1901, giving the United States the right to build a canal from the Atlantic to the Pacific. He then conspired to support a nationalist revolt that resulted in founding the new country of Panama—under American control—which in turn ended with the construction of the Panama Canal. The Roosevelt Corollary to the Monroe Doctrine extended America's control over her neighbors to the south—a role confirmed when Roosevelt set up a military regime in the Dominican Republic in 1905. William Howard Taft continued the tradition by sending the marines to Nicaragua in 1912 (they stayed until 1933), and his successor, Woodrow Wilson, dispatched marines to Haiti in 1915 (they stayed until 1934) and dispatched American forces to Veracruz over a minor naval dispute with Mexico. Clearly, the United States was experiencing a major infusion of testosterone in its foreign policy, symbolized by the journey of the Great White Fleet around the world in 1906.

But never had the nation's new role as central actor on the world stage been tested as it would be when most of the industrial powers of the world exploded into a massive war in 1914 that killed over nine million people. It was a war that, on the one hand, forecast in stunning fashion a century-long tradition in America of trying to combine balance of power realpolitik with universalist idealism, and on the other, highlighted the contradictions of seeking to impose an American vision on foreign powers proud and independent in their own right. In the process, as would be the case with all other wars in the twentieth century, it illuminated the inextricable connection between what was happening in the world and what was happening at home.

I. WORLD WAR I AND THE CHALLENGE FACING AMERICA

The decades leading up to 1914 had been ones of thriving prosperity and imperial expansion. During the latter half of the nineteenth century, Germany and Italy had achieved national political unification. The British had

America was startled by Germany's decision to sink commercial ocean liners during its war against Britain and France. When the *Lusitania* was torpedoed in 1915, it raised warfare to a new level of intensity and directly affected Americans, some of whom were passengers on the *Lusitania* and lost their lives.

Credit: ullstein bild/The Granger Collection, New York.

continued their colonization of Africa, South Asia, and the Caribbean while France matched its cross-channel competitor with its own ventures into Southeast Asia, Africa, and the Caribbean. The Dutch, Spanish, and Portuguese each boasted empires of their own. Czarist Russia and the Austro-Hungarian empire, ruled over by Franz-Josef from the magisterial Schonbrunn Palace in Vienna, represented, along with Queen Victoria's England, some of the oldest, most established regimes in the world. It was a time, British historian Niall Ferguson has noted, of unprecedented equilibrium, a world bonded together by family alliances and economic partnerships. International tensions could be acted out in areas of colonial expansion, with stability existing along most borders inside of continental Europe. Most governments were well run, their nation-states relatively well off.

Yet just beneath the surface tensions boiled, ready to erupt explosively. Many of these were ethnic—between Italians and Austrians near Trieste, Germans and French around Alsace, and above all between the multiethnic nationalists in the Balkan states gathered together under the rubric of the Austro-Hungarian empire. One of the areas most in dispute was Bosnia—a name that would haunt the end of the twentieth century just as it did the beginning. Slavic nationalists wished to annex Bosnia to Serbia. On a visit to Sarajevo—another name that would resonate with tragedy at both ends of the century—Archduke Franz Ferdinand, expected successor to the throne of the Habsburg monarchy in Vienna, was assassinated by a Serbian nationalist expressing his political outrage at the empire for resisting the Serbian plan for annexation. It was the spark that lit a fire waiting to happen. To retaliate, Austria-Hungary invaded Serbia, which in turn called on Russia for assistance. When the Russians started to mobilize, Germany entered on the side of Austria-Hungary, and then the French came in on the side of Russia. On August 4, barely five weeks after the assassination, the British finally entered in, eventually to be joined by Italy, then Japan.

A single bullet ended up detonating a world war, with millions mobilized overnight to kill each other in fighting, the brutishness of which had never before been seen, except perhaps in the American Civil War—and all because of tensions surrounding ethnic nationalism. In one 24-hour period, 20,000 British soldiers were killed at the Battle of Somme with another 40,000 wounded. Overall, France lost 1.7 million men, Germany 1 million, England 1 million, Austria-Hungary 1.5 million, and Russia 1.7 million. The war decimated a generation in a kind of trench warfare so intense and cruel that no one who experienced it would ever be able to forget. It was like the face-to-face combat of gladiators, only this time suffused with the inhumanity of poison gas, the sudden appearance of planes overhead dropping bombs on targets only a hundred yards away, and the endless fatigue of being huddled together within shouting distance of the enemy waiting for the moment of engagement to come. And for what purpose?

Notwithstanding their own increasingly bold forays into the world, most Americans had no answer to the question. The world war seemed an inexplicable battle between old-guard nations with competing self-interests. No one articulated a rationale for fighting and dying that appealed to global or supranational values. Complicating America's response even further was the fact that one-third of the United States consisted of first- or second-generation immigrants from Europe. More than eight million citizens of the United States were of German origin, with another four million from Ireland. On the other side were countless descendants of English lineage. Where ethnic loyalties played such a critical role, how could the United States take sides?

Appropriately, in this context, President Woodrow Wilson enjoined his fellow citizens to be "neutral" in spirit as well as in deed. Americans should use whatever moral and political influence they had to encourage negotiation and bring the parties to an armistice. But they should not intervene on either side.

Such a high-toned, dispassionate response became more complicated, however, when Germany started to pursue a policy of sinking commercial ships that might be carrying munitions as well as people to the United Kingdom and France. Brilliantly deploying the new and terrifying weapon of submarine warfare, the Germans quickly struck fear into the heart of every

When Woodrow Wilson set aside his earlier plea for Americans to be neutral in World War I, he sought to galvanize the nation on behalf of the "war to make the world safe for democracy" throuch mass propaganda and parades such as this one on behalf of the Red Cross.

Credit: © Bettmann/CORBIS

foreign traveler. In May 1915, less than nine months after the start of the war, German U-boats sank the passenger liner the *Lusitania*. Over 1,000 innocent civilians fell victim to the German torpedoes, including 128 Americans. The world, and America especially, was horrified. Just a few months later a second vessel, the *Arabic*, went down, with the loss of two more Americans. Although in response to diplomatic protests Germany promised henceforth to give warning before firing on such vessels, she once again violated her word when German submarines torpedoed the *Sussex* in March 1916, barely ten months after the sinking of the *Lusitania*.

In the face of such brazen behavior—contemptuous of the world's richest and potentially most powerful nation—Wilson now took the bold step of confronting Germany with an ultimatum. It was imperative, he told his counterparts in Berlin, that Germany issue an unconditional pledge that it would never fire on passenger vessels without ample advance warning and the opportunity for innocent civilians to escape. The Germans capitulated to Wilson's brinkmanship tactics, issued the pledge, and thereby reduced the clear possibility that America would be drawn into the conflict on the opposite side from Germany simply as a means of protecting her own citizens. (Wilson, in the meantime, was ratcheting up the U.S. armed forces to more than three hundred thousand, but this was still a pittance compared with the armies destroying each other on the battlefields of Europe).

For the moment, at least, Wilson appeared to have scored a major diplomatic victory. By playing his trump card, he had extracted the *Sussex* Pledge from Germany. On that basis, he ran for reelection to the presidency in 1916, using as his major argument (besides his domestic reforms) the galvanizing claim, "He Kept Us Out of War." The "peace" issue in all likelihood explained Wilson's subsequent narrow victory over Charles Evans Hughes—the popular vote difference was 600,000 votes, with only a 23-vote margin, 277–254, in the electoral college. But to secure his victory, Wilson had engaged in the riskiest diplomatic venture imaginable, pinning all his plans on the hope that the Germans would never abandon their pledge. The very nature of his ultimatum gave him no "wiggle room" were the Germans to default because by his own words, there would be only one place to go if Germany once again fired on passenger vessels without warning. By his demand for the *Sussex* Pledge, Wilson had played virtually his last diplomatic card, thereby ceding all control over the future to the German chancellor.

II. AMERICA ENTERS THE WAR

Nevertheless, Wilson concluded that his reelection on a platform of seeking peace placed him in an ideal position to break the military stalemate now besieging the warring parties. He would offer to mediate a settlement. As more and more thousands of lives were eaten up on the battlefields of Europe, with demoralization and despair spreading from the war scene back to troubled domestic populations, Wilson concluded that the time was ripe for his intervention. Hence in early January 1917 he sounded the tocsin of what would become his distinctive rallying cry from thence forward. It was time for warfare to end, he declared on January 2, and for the nations of the world to proceed to a "peace without victory." As if called in almost a religious sense to transcend the rhetoric and reality of power politics, Wilson asked the warring parties to set aside their nationalistic ambitions and cleave to a higher, more noble purpose—placing the ideals of peace, respect for democratic self-determination, and collective mediation ahead of militarist aggression.

Yet neither Germany nor France and Britain responded. Trapped in their own mental prisons, neither side could envision a world where there were neither victors nor losers. Thus, rather than provide the diplomatic space that might have allowed Wilson to attempt a breakthrough, both sides schemed to find a military means to dissolve the existing logjam. Germany moved first, taking a massive and decisive risk. Discarding the *Sussex* Pledge, Berlin announced on January 31—just four weeks after Wilson's effort at peaceful intervention—that it would embark on unrestricted submarine warfare against any and all ships in the war zone, including civilian passenger vessels. It was a bold gamble, based on two huge assumptions: first, that the breathtakingly radical nature of the new military strategy would intimidate the United States into quiescence, and second, that the submarine warfare would itself take such a toll that even if America did eventually pursue military intervention, the war in Europe would have ended, with Germany the undisputed victor.

Neither assumption proved valid. Immediately, Wilson asked Congress to arm merchant vessels and to provide navel escorts for ships traveling into the war zone. As a result of such steps, the tonnage of allied vessels sunk in the North Atlantic decreased nearly two-thirds in nine months, from 900,000 tons in April 1917 to 350,000 tons in December 1917. More to the point, rather than being intimidated, the United States military machine roared back with a mobilization unprecedented up to that time. Using a military draft, the armed forces vaulted from 300,000 to more than 4 million within a year.

Although millions of Americans still opposed war, the effectiveness of their opposition declined in the face of further evidence of German chicanery. As part of their bold decision to confront the United States, Germany had also sent an urgent diplomatic communiqué to Mexico in February proposing a German-Mexican military alliance, with the proposition that defeat of the United States might well lead to a return to Mexico of lands previously annexed by their northern neighbor. But the British intercepted the note and made sure it reached Washington. When Wilson announced the intended plan, the American populace reacted with fury. Then on March 17, the Russian czardom collapsed, making the war more than ever before a fight between democracies on the one hand, and authoritarian regimes on the other. When Germany then sank four American merchant vessels, Wilson on April 2 went before the Congress to ask for a declaration of war. Wilson had lost his gamble that the *Sussex* Pledge would allow America to remain out of war, but Germany had lost its wager that the announcement of unrestricted submarine warfare would bring a quick victory and foreclose American intervention.

Perhaps the most important part of Wilson's presentation to the American people was the moral idealism that accompanied his call to arms. Drawing on the same spiritual vision that had informed his January attempt to bring the warring parties to the peace table, Wilson declared that this would be a different war than any before it—not a battle for military or economic supremacy of one nation over another but rather a "war to end all wars," a global struggle that would usher in an era of peaceful relations among all peoples functioning under a new understanding of how nations of all backgrounds should relate to each other. This was not a war for plunder or conquest of lands, Wilson declared, but rather a war "to make the world safe for democracy." Consistent with that prophetic aim, Wilson outlined the "Fourteen Points" that should define the "peace without victory" that would occur when the Allies triumphed. There would be freedom of the seas, he announced, self-determination of sovereign peoples in all nations, no secret treaties between governments run from the top down, a movement toward ending colonial domination of subject peoples. Finally, to make all this happen and to supervise and mediate tensions in the postwar world, a new international organization would be created—the League of Nations—which through reason and a shared commitment to the values of the Fourteen Points would adjudicate disputes between countries and provide an unprecedented experience in collective security.

No president had ever justified the nation's entry into war in such terms. Patriotism, national pride, the righteous zeal of manifest destiny—all these had repeatedly been used in the past to rationalize committing the nation's resources to battle. But now, Wilson presented war as a selfless, universalist crusade, almost messianic in nature, to realize ideals of democracy, self-determination, and collective security that would solve forever the instinct of nations to do battle with each other. Clearly, America had a vested interest in an Allied victory. American banks had invested billions of dollars in loans and munitions for Britain and France. Notwithstanding anti-English sentiment among Germans and the Irish, most Americans felt a closer affiliation with British institutions. Ties of trade and finance were stronger than with Germany. American banks had loaned $2 billion to the Allies, only $27 million to the Central Powers. Yet while not denying the existence of such arguments of self-interest, Wilson soared to new heights of rhetoric in presenting the war as a moral crusade—one so utopian in its aspirations that it would take almost a miracle to realize its promises. Perhaps he felt that only such a majestic vision of a postwar world could justify his own ambivalence about engaging in war. But whatever the case, the President had inspired the American people to believe that what was at stake in this struggle was literally the creation of a world as close to perfection as humans could imagine. It was a transforming vision—yet one that contained seeds of self-destruction and disappointment as well as dreams of a safer and better world.

Soon enough, the American contribution to the war started to make a difference. Germany had lost its gamble. Rallying to the cause, Americans purchased Liberty Bonds to fund the war to the tune of $23 billion. Sharply increased taxes generated another $10 billion. Whereas a few years earlier the federal budget in toto reached only $1 billion, now it exceeded $32 billion. Factories that had mass-produced consumer goods changed overnight into war machines, producing a range of tanks, airplanes, ships, and other war materiel that quickly altered the balance of military power on the battlefield, even before American troops could be deployed. In the meantime, the more than three million men who joined the armed forces prepared speedily, and methodically, to take on their assignment as foot soldiers for Wilson's "peace without victory." Young male college students left their campuses for basic training and deployment on troopships to France while young women nurses put on army uniforms and rushed to the front to offer desperately needed medical assistance to the wounded.

Before long, the tide of battle turned in the Allies' favor, with Americans playing a critical role in several decisive battles. At first, Americans simply served under Allied command as part of multinational units. In May 1918 they made a pivotal contribution to the Allied victory over German troops at Chateau-Thierry. GIs played an even more critical role two months later in the second battle of the Marne, which triggered the decision by German commanders to start the retreat that led inexorably to the determination to sue for peace. By the end of the summer, Americans constituted 1.2 million of the Allied troops taking part in the Meuse-Argonne offensive. In the course of that campaign, more than 120,000 Americans suffered casualties. Their numbers might pale beside the numbers of dead and wounded in the ranks of the German, French, British, and Russian armies, but they came at a critical time. Literally, America's intervention had altered the balance of power in the world and on the battlefield. Recognized by all as now the wealthiest, strongest, and most powerful nation in the world, America had assumed a role on the world stage that transformed international politics for the remainder of the twentieth century. By November, the Germans knew they had lost their wager. Unrestricted submarine warfare had not worked. Now Wilson's pledge to give birth to a "peace without victory" became their last best hope, and on November 14, only eighteen months after America's entry, they negotiated the Armistice that ended World War I.

III. THE WAR AT HOME

Inevitably, a national expedition as massive as World War I exerted a dramatic influence on events at home as well as abroad. Perhaps no military event could have as immediate and dramatic an impact on social relations as the Civil War did. But World War I, like the Civil War, set in motion conflicting patterns of change affecting the economy, urbanization, government involvement on issues of labor and social welfare, and the fate of underrepresented or oppressed segments of the population. It also generated an enormous exercise in propaganda production, illustrating the extraordinary influence the government could have on people's thoughts and behavior, even as it highlighted the dangers of violating freedom of thought and expression among those Americans who dissented from the government's policies. In all these respects, World War I provided a model of events at home that would accompany each major military conflict the United States has waged throughout the twentieth century and into the twenty-first.

For those Americans intrigued by the possibility that a new role for the state could advance social progress in the workplace and the cause of a more just society, the war brought impressive evidence of positive change. From the beginning, the government pursued a role as arbiter of those practices that created maximum effectiveness in the production of food, munitions, and social services, with the collective good of the nation as a whole taking precedence over individual competition or aggrandizement. Thus the War Industries Board took over regulation of the economy in order to ensure that companies cooperated in producing as quickly and efficiently as possible the goods needed to win the war. With Bernard Baruch at its helm, the WIB demonstrated brilliantly the positive effect that government intervention could have on economic innovation and production. In similar fashion, the War Labor Board ensured that workers in critical industries received fair treatment in wages, working conditions, and benefits. The WLB protected the right of labor unions to effectively represent workers (unions reached new heights of membership during the war), made sure that labor disputes did not interrupt the effective flow of wartime production, and created new limits on the freedom of both labor and capital to pursue their own selfish interests. For these reasons as well as others, many intellectuals and policy-makers saw the war on the home front as the highest embodiment of Progressivism, proving conclusively what the state could do to move the society forward in the interests of the collective well-being of the nation.

Many reformers also saw the war as an ideal framework for advancing the rights of women. The woman suffrage movement had achieved incremental gains during the early years of the Progressive period, but only with the war did a massive mobilization of support for women's right to vote develop. Due to the work of settlement house reformers, the federal government had already established a Children's Bureau. Now, with the recruitment of large numbers of women to the workforce to take the place of men gone to war, the Department of Labor created a Women's Bureau. Equally important, women's contribution to the war efforts gave new cachet to the argument that women had earned the right to vote by virtue of their selfless service to the nation in time of crisis. Although some women pacifists like Jane Addams opposed the war, and other more militant feminists in the Congressional Union chained themselves to the White House fence (and went to jail) on behalf of women's rights, most suffragists followed the lead of Carrie Chapman Catt and the National American Woman Suffrage Association by working within the system and lobbying political leaders to give women their just due. Woodrow Wilson joined the fray in 1918, endorsing the suffrage amendment as a "war" measure that would repay women for their sacrifice. "The executive tasks of this war rest upon me," he told Congress." I ask that you lighten them and place in my hands instruments…which I sorely need, and which I have daily to apologize for not being able to employ.…" Wilson's subject: woman suffrage. Its enactment, he declared, was "vital to winning the war." Within months, the Nineteenth Amendment had passed Congress and by 1920 had been ratified by three-quarters of the states. Woman suffrage represented another example of the progressive reforms that war could help make possible.

Black Americans also saw this as a moment of opportunity. Blacks constituted more than three hundred thousand of the soldiers drafted to serve in the war effort. Although they suffered massive discrimination and were not allowed to fight alongside their white compatriots, they also experienced a heightened consciousness of the rights they had earned and in their encounters with Europeans witnessed a more cosmopolitan, tolerant, and non-judgmental attitude toward race. W. E. B. DuBois, a founder of the NAACP (National Association for the Advancement of Colored People) and the editor of the NAACP journal *The Crisis*, exhorted African Americans to seize the moment and to "Close Ranks" with Woodrow Wilson and the United States government in the cause of making the world "safe for democracy." Taking Wilson at his word, DuBois saw the crusade of fighting for a new

As they had so often in the past, black Americans demonstrated their patriotism by volunteering in large numbers to serve in World War I. Here one wounded black veteran joins his comrades in being honored at a victory parade on Fifth Avenue. Yet within a year, race riots and violent repression of black rights dominated the headlines.

Credit: The Granger Collection, New York.

international order as instrumental to the struggle of black Americans to win their freedom at home.

Just as important, more than four hundred thousand black Americans moved north to pursue new job opportunities made possible by the fact that the draft had taken hundreds of thousands of workers into the army. Although employment mobility was far more limited than blacks had hoped, it nevertheless remained true that in the North wages were better, some industrial jobs became open, and those who journeyed north escaped the legal prison of Jim Crow. They could ride the subways and trolleys as equals; they could go to the movie theater and sit in the same seats available to whites; and perhaps most important, they could vote. Soon cities like Chicago and New York had major black political machines helping to elect blacks to city councils and to Congress. This was the beginning of the Great Migration, which by the 1930s had brought nearly two million black Americans to the North. In 1918 it was by no means clear where all this would lead, but the evidence suggested there was at least the possibility that for black Americans, as well as for women, the war might bring the opportunity for progress.

However, there was another side to the war at home, one where the power of the federal government to mobilize public opinion and pass legislation of social control threatened some of the basic human rights fundamental to any democratic society. As part of the effort to galvanize the American people in support of his crusade for democracy, Woodrow Wilson appointed George Creel to head the Committee on Public Information. Using the enormous powers conferred upon him, Creel mobilized intense public opinion drives in support of the war. His efforts helped sell all those Liberty Bonds, rally the American people to zealous displays of patriotism, and raise loyalty to the American cause to the level of religious fervor. The downside, tragically, was the sanction Creel and his colleagues conferred on systematic efforts to demean German Americans and quell any form of dissent. The Creel committee circulated films such as *To Hell With the Kaiser*; insisted that "sauerkraut" be renamed "liberty cabbage"; and urged that German books, and titles by German authors, be purged from library shelves. One German American was shot dead when he refused to stand for the singing of the national anthem. Others were fired. Furthermore, the Supreme Court—theoretically the defender of civil liberties—determined in the *Shenck* decision of 1919 that censorship was legal under the doctrine that a "clear and present danger" justified rules restricting human freedoms.

Congress, meanwhile, did its part as well. In a rush to judgment similar to coercive moments in other wars before and subsequent to World War I, lawmakers enacted the Espionage Act of 1917, the Sabotage Act of 1918, and the Sedition Act of 1918. Each of these measures made legal the suppression of dissent. Any person who criticized the war committed a crime. Moreover, federal prosecutors seized the power given them by such acts to go after any and all dissidents. Magazines were taken off the newsstands for publishing articles critical of the administration. Members of the Socialist Party and the International Workers of the World were harassed. Eugene Debs, the leader of the Socialist Party in America, was hustled into jail for seven years for speaking critically of the war. All told, more than eleven thousand citizens were arrested for the crime of raising questions about the wisdom of the war.

If a new more activist role for the state on issues of labor, economic regulation, and issues like woman suffrage represented a positive, enlightened side of government power enhanced by wartime mobilization, clearly a monolithic patriotism that defamed all those who belonged to the wrong ethnic or political group represented a very different consequence of the war at home. Although many saw the "positive" effects of wartime regulation as demonstrating the vast potential of Progressivism for social advancement, others feared that the same state power would eviscerate the very human rights for which the war was allegedly being fought and propel the United States into an age of repression. If it were true that there were two paths on the home front to the future, it was by no means clear which one would prevail.

IV. FAILURE AT VERSAILLES

Consistent with the boldness of his Fourteen Points and his plea for "peace without victory," Wilson greeted the Armistice with an unprecedented decision: he, the President of the United States, would personally travel to Paris to lead the American delegation to the peace conference at Versailles. No president in office had ever crossed the Atlantic Ocean before. Certainly no one had even contemplated spending six months away from the nation's capital to engage in the highest-level diplomacy with world leaders. With courage and vision, Wilson had put himself and his political legacy on the line. One more time he had raised the stakes, this time risking his entire presidency on the success or failure of the Versailles Treaty he was about to negotiate.

Simultaneously, Wilson committed one of the most egregious political errors any statesman had ever contemplated. Rather than take senior representatives of the opposition party with him to Paris to share the burden of negotiating the treaty, and therefore also the responsibility for defending it, Wilson excluded all prominent Republicans from the delegation. Making the dangers of his course even more perilous, he had recently politicized the entire process by defining the 1918 congressional election as a referendum on his war policy, exhorting the American people to assist the peace process by voting in a Democratic majority. The not-so-implicit message: if the voters selected Republicans, they would be operating in a nonpatriotic manner and undercutting the war effort. It was a horrible mistake. The voters elected a Republican majority, and Wilson had burned the bridges he most needed if he were to construct a bipartisan coalition in support of his peace plan. Only someone possessed of righteous self-confidence in the inviolability of his personal crusade could have committed to these two courses of action. And although the first enabled him to exercise the maximum possible leverage on the peace negotiations, the second placed him in the precarious position of alienating the very people whose support he most needed in order to achieve his objectives.

It soon became clear that Wilson needed to be in Paris to defend his idealistic peace proposals. Neither French premier Clemenceau nor the British prime minister, Lloyd George, took kindly to the idea of not punishing

Germany for the war. They expected billions of dollars in reparations and sought to impose a harsh and bitter set of conditions on the German people for all the suffering, material and personal, that the war had occasioned. Tenacious, obsessed with pursuing national interest first and world peace second, and determined to exact a heavy price from those they had defeated, the British and French resisted at every turn Wilson's effort to return the focus to deliberation on his Fourteen Points. Still, Wilson stubbornly persisted. He believed mightily in the righteousness—indeed the holiness—of his cause. Back and forth, back and forth the deliberations went. In the end, Wilson could not claim total victory for his side. Certainly the Germans believed they had been misled into an Armistice based on Wilson's Fourteen Points, when in fact, Wilson was able to deliver on so few of them. But the one huge victory he did emerge with from the Versailles conference was the agreement to establish a League of Nations. With at least the centerpiece of his Fourteen Points salvaged, Wilson could still argue that the world had been turned in a new direction, and henceforth, an international deliberative body would be able to prevent any future conflagration of the dimensions just witnessed.

Now Wilson had to sell the package he had just accepted to the American people, and more important, the American Congress. Having committed his heart and soul to the cause he now was committed to defending before the American people, Wilson had committed his third egregious error He absolutely resisted any request for compromise or amendments. In some ways, the very fact that he had worked so tirelessly for the half a pie he returned from Paris with, and against such intense opposition from his Allied partners, made the president even more dedicated to defending to the bitter end his achievement. Anything less, he believed, would mark a dismal failure for all he had risked his life and presidency to secure.

With his own form of blind fanaticism, therefore, Wilson refused even to consider "reservations" offered by Republicans to be attached to the treaty. Wilson displayed self-righteous contempt for his foes. Henry Cabot Lodge, the senior senator from Massachusetts and the powerhouse on the Senate Foreign Relations Committee, became the special object of Wilson's fury. It was as if every time Lodge opened his mouth, Wilson hardened his position further, literally despising the person who more than any other held the secret to any compromise that might be struck. The two were of totally different temperament, Wilson the steely-minded intellectual with values of a supermoralist, Lodge the Brahmin aristocrat whom one critic said had a mind like that of the New England soil where he was reared, "naturally barren but highly cultivated." If Wilson detested Lodge, the feelings were reciprocated. "I never thought I could hate a man as I hate Wilson," Lodge declared. The setting was not one conducive to negotiation.

Facing what he quickly perceived to be a stone wall of opposition, Wilson then ratcheted up the debate one step further, determining to go to the American people directly to galvanize their rage against the obstreperous Republicans in Congress. By dint of an outpouring of public support, Wilson believed, he could force through ratification of the treaty. Setting off by train

Woodrow Wilson had staked his life and presidency on his Fourteen Points, and the Treaty of Versailles, with its commitment to establish a League of Nations to ensure international stability. Here he defends the peace treaty. When Congress failed to ratify the Treaty of Versailles, Wilson saw all his dreams for world peace turn into ashes.

Credit: Hulton | Archive by Getty Images

from the nation's capital, Wilson took his passionate, missionary message of a holy crusade across the country, seeking to fire up his audiences to write their senators in support of Wilson's treaty. The more he traveled, the more passionate he became, literally captive to a mission that he saw as almost divine in nature. Although physically and mentally exhausted, Wilson insisted on continuing the voyage, convinced that only this kind of total commitment could make a difference. Then, at the end of his rope, Wilson suffered a devastating stroke on October 2, 1919, near Pueblo, Colorado. Partially paralyzed and unable to speak clearly, he was rushed back to Washington, where he remained an invalid in the White House for the remainder of his term.

Although Wilson gradually recovered some of his facilities, his wife ran the White House for the duration of his presidency and conveyed Wilson's decisions. True to his vision, the president would not compromise, and so when the Republican version of the Versailles Treaty was brought before the Senate with its myriad "reservations," Wilson ordered the Democrats to vote no, thereby depriving the Republicans of the two-thirds majority necessary to ratify their modification of the treaty. When the Democrats, in turn, sought to pass the original treaty, with none of the reservations suggested by the Republicans, it too failed to garner the two-thirds majority needed for ratification. At any step along the way, some compromise version of the two alternatives could have secured the necessary votes. But Wilson refused to even entertain such a possibility. In a holy war, with good on one side and evil on the other, the idea of compromise of any kind became a sin in its own right. When he left office, only three years after having announced the most utopian vision of a peaceful world that any American had ever articulated, Woodrow Wilson saw his dream turn to ashes and the nation that he had foreseen as playing the major role in an international League of Nations forswear the possibility of even joining the organization as a member. The dimensions of the tragedy could not be overstated, nor the degree to which one man bore the responsibility for making it happen.

On the home front as well, things fell apart. To be sure, women had won the vote, and in 1920, both political parties fell over themselves trying to persuade women that they would pass the kind of legislation that women supposedly wanted—like maternity and infancy health legislation—and ensure that women played a major role in party councils. But in some respects, this was the only positive social change to survive the end of the war. With the encouragement of the WLB, unions had achieved a new level of popularity and organization, with millions of workers intent on capitalizing on the gains made during wartime when it came to negotiating contracts in the postwar world. But notwithstanding the success of the WIB in managing the most successful economy in the world during the war, once the fighting ceased the economy collapsed. The GNP (Gross National Product) fell by 10 percent, inflation soared to 15 percent, nearly 5 million workers lost their jobs, and a massive malaise seized the country. Workers newly intent on standing up for themselves launched a series of strikes virtually unprecedented in the twentieth century. More than 350,000 steelworkers walked off the job; a general strike, triggered by shipyard workers, paralyzed the state of Washington; and a riot led by workers devastated Gary, Indiana. More than three thousand strikes occurred in 1919 and almost as many the next year. But this time, the state did not intervene on behalf of labor. On the contrary, in most cases, government sided with management. And in the most dramatic confrontation of all, when police in Boston walked off the job demanding recognition of their rights, the governor of Massachusetts, Calvin Coolidge, became a national hero when he declared, "There is no right to strike against the public safety by anybody, anywhere, anytime." Instead of support, a national wave of antilabor sentiment spread across the land.

With similar rapidity, the hopes of black Americans for a better life after the war were shattered. Black veterans returning from the war convinced that their sacrifice would now lead to expanded citizenship rights met instead the fury of white resistance and the terrorism of Ku Klux Klan violence. Lynchings skyrocketed in the South, reaching a total of seventy in 1919 alone. Race riots erupted throughout the nation. Tulsa, Oklahoma, blew up as whites chased blacks from trolley cars and pummeled them with stones and bricks. In Chicago, a black swimmer who had accidentally drifted into the white area drowned after being stoned. All in all, 120 black Americans were killed by the racial violence of the summer of 1919, and all the hopes envisioned by W. E. B. DuBois and every other civil rights proponent who had supported his "Close Ranks" editorial came crashing down.

Symptomatic of every other loss that occurred was the destructive assault on civil liberties that occurred in 1919–1920. In the aftermath of the Bolshevik revolution in Russia in 1917, many Americans became deeply suspicious of an effort to spread Communist doctrine to the West. Anarchists still existed in the country as well. In April 1919, the post office uncovered scores of parcels addressed to businessmen in different cities that contained bombs. After explosions on Wall Street and elsewhere, hysteria grew, and states throughout the country enacted antisedition laws. A national Red Scare swept the land. A new agency in the Justice Department headed by J. Edgar Hoover, a young anti-communist firebrand, specifically targeted immigrants from eastern European countries who were feared to be infected by radical political ideas. Starting in November 1919, and culminating on January 2, 1920, federal agents swooped down on groups of immigrants who had done nothing criminal, arrested them without search warrants, and proceeded to deport them from the country. On January 2 alone, in what became known as the Palmer Raids (after Attorney General Mitchell Palmer) five thousand people were arrested in the most extreme assault on civil liberties ever seen in the country. For those who had hoped that the new role of government in domestic affairs might bring social justice, the news was not good.

V. CONCLUSION

In any assessment of the new role of the state in twentieth-century American history, World War I clearly constituted a searing as well as pivotal event. Never before had the power, energy, and exuberant domination of the United States on the world stage been so clearly manifest. However reluctant the country and its people had been to enter the war, once it had made the choice to intervene, the stakes changed dramatically, with America's presence decisively shifting the course of events. In a tit-for-tat exchange of bold gambles, Germany and the United States sparred with each other to seize control of a struggle otherwise locked in paralysis. First Germany took the risk of launching unrestricted submarine warfare, hoping with break-neck speed and efficiency to end the war before America could do a thing to stop it. But then the United States responded, demonstrating the capacity of an economic and military giant to awake from its slumber, mobilize rapidly, and make its power and will felt long before the German military break-through could take its toll. If measured solely in terms of power shifts on the geopolitical scene, the war represented a tectonic rearrangement of world economic and political dominance. The United States, on sheer military and economic capacity alone, now had become the unquestioned giant on the stage of world power.

Underneath that transformation, however, rested another of almost equal importance: America sought to impose a new vision of world governance on all its sister nations. It was a vision grounded in idealism, based on democratic values of self-determination, and premised on the rule of reason shaping collective security through a new international forum, the League of Nations. The vision certainly had connections to the ideas of "manifest destiny" that had been used to rationalize the Mexican-American War in 1848 and the Spanish-American War in 1898. But now it became more inclu-sive, more universalist, with the United States putting forth the argument that all nations, including America, should be governed by rules and values greater than those of any single power. For the first but not the last time, the United States would face the need to reconcile an international politics of self-interest and national security priorities with an international rhetoric of selfless commitment to universal values of democracy and human rights that knew no national boundaries.

In all of this, one man played a critical role. Woodrow Wilson in prac-tice used the power of the United States in the same manner that Theodore Roosevelt might have used it—to shape an international settlement consis-tent with American wishes. Only Wilson went beyond this more narrowly scripted notion of America's role to subscribe to a utopian vision of world governance that had never before been contemplated. Perhaps he did so as a way of finding an overarching—almost religious—justification for pursuing a war he had so long avoided. Perhaps it was a posture so consistent with his own moralistic, religious background that anything more pragmatic and flexible would have been a betrayal of character. Whatever the case, once embarked on his crusade, Wilson could not psychologically, or politically, step back and recalibrate. Instead, the measure of his commitment seemed to compel an ever more dogmatic and judgmental denunciation of compro-mise. The very terms of the debate became polarizing, excluding the possi-bility for negotiation, driving the opposing sides into positions irrevocably frozen in time. Hence Wilson's tactics in the 1918 election, making peace a partisan issue; then the intensity of his insistence on the Treaty of Versailles being ratified *as written* rather than be subject to amendment. As a result, the moral vision that helped make American involvement in World War I so different and transcendent became the moralistic dogmatism that smashed all Wilson's hopes to smithereens and destroyed the very foundations of the world order he had striven so mightily to bring into being.

All of this—the energy, the power, the moral absolutism, the new and pivotal role of the state—reflected the dramatic changes that the Progressive Era brought to America. There was an upside. Factory safety legislation, the state as moral arbiter of labor-management disputes, the recognition that a third party must step in to regulate the otherwise uncontrolled expansion of economic entrepreneurs, the victories achieved in women's rights and children's rights—all of these exemplified the constructive, positive dimension of envisioning a new role for government in a society being transformed. But there was a downside as well—as when the same state that extended human rights for women also denied them to blacks and refused to intervene when racist riots occurred; or engaged in the suppression of dissent, arrested people illegally, and pursued purges based on suspected radicalism of citizens simply engaging in freedom of political expression.

In the end, World War I did not resolve these tensions. Rather, it crystallized the choices that had to be made. Perhaps most important, it helped to create the agenda of national issues that would define the conflicts of the next generation.

4

The Roaring (?) Twenties

After Wilson's idealistic fervor had shattered into acrimony over the Versailles Treaty, people yearned for a return to what Warren Harding, Wilson's successor, called "normalcy." The country had seen enough soaring rhetoric. Now was the time to enjoy life, buy a new washing machine, listen to a comedy on the radio, and have a good time. Before long, a booming economy lifted millions of people to a new level of comfort. National chain stores like Sears and Roebuck and Montgomery Ward marketed mass-produced clothes and vacuum cleaners to every corner of the nation. Moviegoers from Boston to Sacramento thrilled to the *Jazz Singer*, the first motion picture with sound. Young people from Evanston to Mobile danced to the music of the Paul Whiteman Orchestra. With nearly thirty million cars on the road, Americans from coast to coast expanded their vacation plans to include trips to amusement parks they had never seen before. Americans seemed happy to put aside the visionary calls for change of the Progressive Era and let the good times roll. These were the "Roaring Twenties." Or were they?

Just beneath the surface of good times lay a gnawing sense of anxiety. Nothing seemed certain anymore. In physics, Albert Einstein had come forward with his theory of relativity, Eisenberg his principle of uncertainty—there were no constants, nothing was "for sure," everything was contingent. But it wasn't just science. "The world has been convulsed . . . and every field of thought and action has been disturbed," one religious magazine proclaimed. What was the definition of Americanism at a time when more than a third of the workforce consisted of immigrants from southern and eastern Europe, or Asia and Mexico? How could a young man plan on a traditional family when so many young women flaunted their independence, wore scandalously short skirts, and talked about birth control? What did it mean to believe in God and his creation if in fact all human beings evolved from monkeys?

The 1920s did roar, but not with a constant voice, or a clearly defined message. Beneath a surface of "normalcy," there existed countless competing currents. Contradiction rather than consistency defined the era. It was as much a time to come to grips with polarizing forces dividing the society as to celebrate the new homogenizing influence of the mass media and consumer goods. Thus, despite the appearance of collective enjoyment, the decade was basically a time of trying to find a new direction, a new set of shared values and beliefs. Ironically, none of that would happen until a crisis totally out of sync with the image of galloping prosperity startled the country into a new awareness of its collective fate—the Great Depression.

I. THE ECONOMY

The foundation for all else that happened during the 1920s was economic growth. The two years after the war had witnessed significant unemployment due to demobilization and the conversion of factories from wartime to domestic production. Labor strife accelerated the sense of things being out of control. But the dislocation proved temporary and in 1920 there began a sustained boom that some people believed would never end. Incomes rose during the decade by an average of 30 percent; despite occasional blips, inflation remained under control; and perhaps most important, industrial production shot up by nearly 60 percent.

As might have been expected, automobiles spearheaded the surge. Henry Ford set out to "democratize the automobile" and succeeded brilliantly. When he first produced the Model T in 1908, production was relatively slow and the cost nearly half of an average year's income for a white-collar clerk—$850. By the 1920s, in contrast, production had become so streamlined that a new car came off the Rouge River assembly line every ten seconds. Equally important, the price had plummeted to under $300, less than one-sixth of an average worker's annual income. The results were stunning. By 1920 more than eight million cars were registered, and by 1930, almost four times that number. Nearly one American family in five boasted of owning a car—a sign of having "made it" in America. They ranged from factory workers in Toledo to a black former tenant farmer in Alabama named Ned Cobb. No longer was this symbol of middle-class status out of reach for average citizens.

Facilitating this record level of acquisition was an ethos of consumerism that made buying new products almost the sine qua non of being a "good American." Advertising seduced customers in every home. Slick magazines from *McCall's* to *Good Housekeeping* glorified the new household goods that were available—washing machines, vacuum cleaners, and Frigidaires—while popular writers like Bruce Barton made heroes out of those spreading the word about buying bigger and better things, even claiming that Jesus himself was the model of a "super salesman." The new Gospel was buying on credit—making a down payment, then completing one's purchase through installments over time. "Possess today, pay tomorrow" was the motto. In this world, sin was redefined. As one economist declared, "People may ruin themselves by saving instead of spending."

Radio and movies helped bring all segments of the country together through an immersion in a national popular culture. Families gathered around the fireplace at night to listen to their favorite programs: "Hi-Yo Silver," the radio blasted to the *William Tell Overture*. "Return with us now to those thrilling days of yesteryear....The Lone Ranger rides again!" Many of the standards were Westerns—Tom Mix, Gene Autry. Others were detectives—"Mr.

Keene, Tracer of Lost Persons." And then there were the comedies, *Amos 'n' Andy* with its minstrel show exploitation of black stereotypes, Will Rogers and his homespun humor, George Burns and Gracie Allen. By the mid-twenties, there were five hundred radio stations broadcasting network programming and nearly three million receivers. By 1930, virtually every household in the land could tune in. Meanwhile, more and more families were going to the movies at least once a week. From Charlie Chaplin to Al Jolson, new national heroes and heroines became a familiar part of America's weekly entertainment schedule. It cost only a nickel; starting in 1927 there was sound as well as pictures (no more player pianos to accompany the silent films), and

New forms of entertainment dominated recreational life in the 1920s. None proved more popular than the motion picture, with families going to the movies on an average of once a week. Here is a New York City theater showing a film starring Buster Keaton.

Credit: The Granger Collection, New York.

attendance soared still further. In 1930 almost 100 million people per week were going to their favorite local cinema—up from 40 million in 1922—to see the most recent Movietone newsreel; the latest installment of their local theater's serial thriller (a new episode every week); and then the feature presentation, a Jolson musical or a cowboy or gangster shoot-out. Life was fun, and you could call your best friend on the next block by telephone—there were now twenty-five million phones in the country—to make a date.

Part of the new boom economy rested on the growth of urban areas. By the Roaring Twenties, more than half of all Americans lived in cities of more than 2,500 people, and the number of cities with more than 100,000 people had leaped from nineteen in 1880 to more than fifty by 1920. The larger cities dominated the news—Chicago, Boston, New York, Philadelphia, Los Angeles. Clusters of ethnic enclaves, most of these cities exemplified the degree to which America was following a pluralist rather than an assimilationist model of interaction. Jews lived with Jews, Poles with Poles, Italians with Italians, Chinese with Chinese. One neighborhood might be cheek by jowl with another, but each had its own churches, synagogues, ethnic food stores, and clubs. Everyone rode together on the subways and buses, and in large factories or offices, worked together in the same buildings. But daily life consisted of going back and forth to a home base, ethnically defined. Although everyone might be exposed to the nationalizing influence of mass culture, it was the "home country" folks who defined a person's basic identity. Still, the rapidly growing cities in the country provided the energy, the consumers, and entrepreneurship—witness the garment industry in New York—that helped fuel economic growth.

In smaller towns and larger midwestern cities, of course, ethnic diversity played far less an important role. "Main Street," U.S.A., looked more Protestant and Anglo-Saxon than Philadelphia, Boston, or Los Angeles. White-steepled churches dominated the landscape, with more parks and green space. Rotary Clubs and Kiwanis gatherings served the same function that the Knights of Columbus and ethnic clubs offered in Eastern metropolises. Department stores were smaller, green parks more frequent. Still, every small city had at least one—and usually three or four—movie theaters. A Sears Roebuck or Montgomery Ward store served as the consumer outlet for nationally marketed goods. And in small cities as well as large, people used the new system of buying on credit to expand their worldly goods.

The agricultural sector also experienced its own form of economic growth. Mechanization vastly expanded the productivity of the land. Between 1920 and 1930, the number of gasoline-driven tractors exploded by 400 percent. Land that had hitherto seemed beyond reach of cultivation suddenly became accessible to these giant machines, with the result that more than thirty million new acres were added to the nation's productive agricultural sector. At the same time, this burgeoning growth created serious problems. As surpluses mounted, prices declined, and farmers became ever more concerned with putting in place government guarantees of a secure income—a demand that went back eventually to the Populists. Now the focus was on enacting legislation—called the McNary-Haugen bill—that would keep prices at the same level relative to other sectors of the economy that had prevailed in the period 1909–1914, with the government purchasing agricultural surpluses and selling them abroad as a means of protecting farmers.

Still another downside of the agricultural boom was its impact on the poorest farmers who could not afford expensive machinery and whose labor was gradually being displaced by the same tractors they were unable to buy. Black sharecroppers and tenant farmers in the South were particularly vulnerable. Partly as a result of such pressures, more than three million people who had been engaged in farming as a vocation in 1920 had left the fields by 1930, most often moving to the cities where more opportunity existed.

Even in the factories, there was a significant downside to the economic boom of the 1920s. Labor unions had been crushed by the repressive response to widespread walkouts in 1919–1920. Shrewdly, industrial giants like Henry Ford stepped into the breach with a substitute, company unions, and what came to be called welfare capitalism. Rather than negotiate with independent labor unions chosen by the workers to act on their behalf, companies like Ford created their own set of benefits—paid annual vacations, a limited work week, and "company" gatherings where some work issues could be discussed. But these were totally under management control, with anyone daring to question the arrangement being immediately fired. As a result, membership in organized and independent labor unions had fallen from five million in 1919 to less than three million ten years later. Perhaps even more important, the new arrangements helped keep labor from getting its proportionate share of the economic prosperity of the 1920s. Although manufacturing wages increased by 30 percent in the decade, the gains were very unevenly distributed. Even in the midst of what was then the most prosperous decade in history, half of America's workers earned less than $1,500 per year—$300 below what experts stated was the minimum necessary for a decent standard of living.

Clearly, America was experiencing an extraordinary surge of growth and economic success. Never before had so many people been able to buy dresses, shirts, household appliances, radios, cars, and telephones or have access to such a variety of public entertainment. Never before had national companies been able so successfully to manufacture and market goods to the entire country. Never before had credit been so accessible, or advertising so effective in persuading customers to engage in installment buying. Yet just beneath the surface lay nagging fissures—the absence of wage increases for workers parallel to the profit margins of manufacturing companies; a growing inequality of income; the disruption of rural life for those forced off the land; and perhaps most important, the degree to which economic prosperity rested on the precarious, and ultimately flawed, institution of buying on credit, with no guarantee that resources would be available to pay the bill. It was a time of inconceivable change—so rapid in fact that warning lights of caution should have been flashing.

II. WOMEN

No group more dramatically highlighted the paradox of the 1920s than women. For more than seventy years —ever since the Women's Rights convention in Seneca Falls in 1848—women activists had crusaded for the vote and an end to second-class treatment. Now, in 1920, they cast their ballots in national elections for the first time, signaling, in the eyes of many, a revolution. "At last, after centuries of disabilities and discrimination," Margaret Drier Robins told the Women's Trade Union League, "women are coming into the labor and festival of life on equal terms with men." Politicians cowered before the feared new "woman's bloc," feverishly trying to align themselves with issues women cared about, like health care for infants. Commentators noted the number of middle-class girls "pour[ing] out of schools and colleges into all manner of occupations." Sinclair Lewis observed in his 1920 novel *Main Street* that "even the girls who knew that they were going to be married pretended to be considering important business positions." The census offered evidence in support—eight million women in 1920 worked in 437 different occupations, from preachers to secretaries to lawyers to fur trappers and bankers. If the magazines were to be believed, a "revolution in manners and morals" was sweeping the country, with women in the forefront. It was the "Jazz Age" with the "new woman"—wearing rolled hose, bobbed hair, and short skirts—leading the way. A cigarette in one hand, a

Depicted here is a fashion show featuring the latest fashions.
Credit: © Hulton-Deutsch Collection/CORBIS

cocktail in the other, she danced the night away, setting tongues a-wagging with her flirtatious manner. "Who put the sin into syncopation," asked one women's magazine, humorously commenting on the intersection of the new morality and the new music.

The "flapper" was at the heart of this discourse about "the new woman." The *New York Times* pronounced in 1929 that "by sheer force of violence [*sic*] [the flapper] has established the feminine right to equal representation in such hitherto masculine fields...as smoking and drinking, swearing, petting and upsetting the community peace." Though hyperbolic, the description contained more than a kernel of truth. In style at least, the flapper represented a profound departure from the previous generation. "I mean to do what I like...undeterred by convention," one short story heroine commented. "Freedom—that is the modern essential. To live one's life in one's own way." When sociologists Helen and Robert Lynd wrote their path-breaking 1920s study of "Middletown"—(Muncie, Indiana),—they noted how thoroughly the new generation of women appeared to depart from the norms of their parents and how readily they challenged the idea of "dainty femininity."

Clearly, something important was going on, and in no sphere did it resonate more loudly than that of sexuality. One analysis of popular literature concluded that "between 1915 and 1925, taboos associated with sex in general and marital infidelity in particular were lifted from the middle class mind in America." Articles on prostitution, birth control, and divorce soared. F. Scott Fitzgerald made "petting parties" a set piece of his novels on contemporary America, observing that Victorian mothers "had [no] idea of how casually their daughters were accustomed to be kissed."

Where there was smoke, there was also fire. One student of sexuality found that although among women born between 1890 and 1900, 74 percent were virgins when they married, among those born after 1910 the figure plummeted to 31.7 percent. Nor was he alone. The famous sexologist Alfred Kinsey confirmed women born after the turn of the century were two times as likely to have experienced premarital sex as those born before, with the critical change happening among those born in the decade 1900–1910. Not surprisingly, breakthroughs in birth control occurred at the same time. With activist Margaret Sanger in the lead, birth control leagues sprouted in every major city in the country between 1914 and 1917, and the American Birth Control League came into existence in 1921. Among middle- and upper-class white women in particular, contraception became conventional and widely used. In all of the twentieth century, there were only two decades when norms regarding sexuality significantly changed, and the twenties were one of them (the period 1965–1975 was the other).

But did the flapper or the sexual revolution really signify an era of "emancipation" for women? On that score, the evidence was dubious. First of all, as F. Scott Fitzgerald observed, the Jazz Age was in fact jazzy for only "the upper tenth of the nation." Young women with resources in New York, Chicago, Boston, and San Francisco might dance the night away in speakeasies; and obviously, a shift occurred in premarital and extramarital sexual practices. But the high life that preoccupied so many popular magazines was limited primarily to urban white women in cosmopolitan areas, and while reflecting some underlying shifts in behavior and outlook, did not by any means characterize a daily or weekly part of the lives of most young women in the country. Second, and perhaps more important, the rebellion symbolized by the flapper was primarily one of style, not substance. "Petting" or wearing short skirts and dancing with reckless abandon in no way altered the structure of male-female relationships. Even if she smoked, drank cocktails, and had an extramarital affair, the average white middle-class woman—even in the Roaring Twenties"—was still a housewife and mother. The percentage of women who married, especially from the middle class, did not diminish, nor did the division of labor between male breadwinners and female homemakers alter in any significant way. Girls were still taught to sew and to cook, boys to play sports and to tinker with automobiles. The Lynds observed that in "Middletown," social occasions were marked by men clustering in one part of the room to discuss business and sports, women on the other side to talk about children and household products. The local women's club in "Middletown" boasted a motto that said it all: "Men are God's trees; women are his flowers," and the Lynds found little evidence that either husbands or wives disagreed.

Sinclair Lewis's portrayal of the rebellious Carol Kennecott in his novel *Main Street* conveyed the same message. Carol initially refused to accept the constraints of woman's traditional "place." "She was a woman with a working brain and no work," Lewis wrote. But when she broke with tradition and tried to engage men in discussions of social issues, or women in conversation about challenging convention, she was ostracized. After she had a son, the antagonism diminished, but Carol still found herself restless, yearning for a "conscious life" of individuality, not just a housewife's boring routine of "drudging and sleeping and dying." So she went to Washington briefly to work as a government clerk. But Carol found that too not fulfilling and returned to "Gopher Prairie," resigned to never being able to build a "room of [her] own." The moral of the tale: it was difficult to chart a new path in life without social support, particularly from other women who also believed in change and were prepared to fight for it.

In the end, the primary lesson of the 1920s was that most women were not prepared to fight for shifting the traditional division of labor between the sexes. Even in the area of employment there was less change than initially seemed likely. Despite the vaunted breakthroughs of the World War I years that led Woodrow Wilson to endorse woman suffrage, the gains made were, in the words of one student of the time, only a "brief interlude." Women were still sex-typed—primarily concentrated in "women's work" as telephone operators, textile mill workers, secretaries—and excluded from 60 percent of all civil service examinations, especially those for scientific and professional positions. Unequal pay rates persisted—a Treasury Department official ordered that no woman in its employ receive more than twelve hundred dollars a year. As reformer Mary Van Kleeck wrote, "When the immediate dangers [of war]...were passed, the [old] prejudices came to life once more." During the Roaring Twenties, the actual proportion of women who held jobs increased by only 1 percent, and virtually all white women workers were young, single, and poor. As a general rule, older married women remained out of the work force unless they were black or poor. Indeed, as late as 1930, nearly 60 percent of employed women were either African American or foreign-born whites.

Theoretically, college-educated women with career aspirations were supposed to be the chief beneficiaries of the new age of emancipation. But in fact, the number of women pursuing professions declined during the 1920s. Virginia Gildersleeve of Barnard College observed that her female students of the twenties were characterized by "blasé indifference, self-indulgence, and irresponsibility" rather than tenacious ambition. By the 1920s, sociologist Jessie Bernard noted, "the éclat of the earlier years had spent itself, and all of a sudden...the increase in the percentage of academic personnel who were women slowed down." The primary reason was that marriage remained the sine qua non of success for women, and an independent career seemed fundamentally at odds with the prospect of finding a mate. In 1920, only 12.2 percent of all professional women were married. Cultural anthropologist Margaret Mead crisply stated the dilemma. A woman had two choices, she noted: either she proclaimed herself "a *woman* and therefore less an achieving individual, or an *achieving individual* and therefore less a woman." If she chose the first option, she maximized her opportunity to become "a loved object, the kind of girl whom men will woo and boast of, toast and marry," but if she chose the second option, she might lose forever "as a woman, her chance for the kind of love she wants." Not surprisingly in such a climate, increasing numbers of college women chose marriage. In a newspaper poll of Vassar women in 1923, 90 percent of the students wished to be wed, with fewer than 8 percent expressing interest in a business career or professional position. The *Ladies' Home Journal* summarized the ethos of the time. "The creation and fulfillment of a successful home," the magazine wrote, "is a bit of craftsmanship that compares favorably with building a beautiful cathedral."

Perhaps appropriately, politics—the area where the greatest breakthroughs had been anticipated—reflected the strongest persistence of traditional patterns. Leaders of both political parties were terrified that women might form a new third party—a woman's bloc—devoted to an agenda shaped by their special interests as women. Hence, they rushed to embrace ideas that they believed would make them attractive to the new voters and in 1921 enacted the Sheppard-Towner Act, a program of maternal and infancy health legislation that various women's groups had propounded. By mid-decade, however, the specter of a separate "woman's" party had disappeared. It became clear first of all that women did not vote in the same proportions as did men, and second, that when women did vote, they ordinarily cast their ballots for the same candidates as their fathers or husbands. In short, they voted according to their class, ethnicity, or regional identity, not according to their gender. A number of women continued to lobby effectively for social reform through their membership in groups like the League of Women Voters, the National Consumers League, or the Women's Trade Union League. Others, such as Eleanor Roosevelt, played a major role in both reform groups and party politics, working inside the existing political apparatus to galvanize support for their priorities. But no longer was there widespread fear on the part of male politicians that they might lose control of their parties. For the most part, women were accorded the same second-class treatment in politics that they received in wages, salaries, and career opportunities. It was not until 1932, with the ascendancy of Eleanor and Franklin Roosevelt to the White House, that women began to gain partial recognition for all that they were contributing.

In the end, therefore, the experience of women underlined the degree to which the Roaring Twenties represented a time of contradiction. The decade started with the impression that a revolution in women's status was in progress. The "new woman," according to pundits, was bold, risqué, ambitious, and outspoken. She would turn the world of politics, sexuality, and male-female relations upside down. In part that was true. A significant shift had occurred in female (and male) sexuality. Women were charting dramatic new forms of social behavior, from their dress styles, to their drinking, their courtship patterns and their speech. Yet in the end, the fundamental structures of male-female relationships remained the same. Most of the dramatic changes were more superficial than substantive, with only a small proportion of largely white, middle-, and upper-class women actually experiencing the "liberation" so widely discussed. In jobs, career patterns, and the choices of the highly educated, the pattern of traditional sexual spheres persisted. Men were expected to be family breadwinners, focusing on the world outside the home, engaging in their own "masculine" obsessions with sports and cars; women, on the other hand, were expected to view marriage and motherhood as the essence of success. Even if significant changes in style happened for some—and these largely excluded black Americans, the poor, and recent immigrants—the structure of sex roles remained largely intact. Never before had women been depicted as so central to the changes of an era, but in fact, what they embodied was the degree to which contradiction—as well as change—represented the "bottom line" of the twenties.

III. POLARIZATION

Another way of conceptualizing the 1920s is to see them as a period of systematic polarization. Profoundly antagonistic cultural forces engaged in mortal combat to determine who would control the future of the nation. Would it be Protestants or Catholics? Immigrants born in alien, distant lands or third-, fourth- and fifth-generation "natives" who dominated the country in the late nineteenth century? People who lived in multiethnic, cosmopolitan urban areas or those who resided in small-town, rural America? Those who viewed ethnic, political, and cultural dissent as healthy barometers of democracy or those who believed in suppressing difference in support of moralistic homogeneity? Religious fundamentalists or those who embraced "free thinking?" Conventional patriots or dissenting critics? In many ways, during the 1920s the nation was pulled to and fro between competing visions of what it meant to be an American. No set of questions would prove more important to the future of the country.

Immigration encapsulated almost all these tensions, dividing the nation in the 1920s as it does today and posing a critical test of what the country aspired to be. Throughout the first two decades of the century, more than one million immigrants per year entered America. Most of the new immigrants came from southern and eastern Europe, then from Mexico and Asia. Their skins were darker. Unlike the Germans, Swedes, Finns, English, and Irish who preceded them in the nineteenth century, they looked "different"—less white, less "Anglo-Saxon." From the perspective of older Americans, the newcomers appeared alien, eating foods that were "smelly," speaking polyglot languages. Too many were Jewish. And too many looked like they might be "radical," sympathetic to the Bolsheviks who had taken over Russia in 1917 and wished to export their revolution around the world. Hence, when the Red Scare swept the country in 1919, most of its victims were immigrants suspected of being Communists, swept up in raids where up to six thousand people were arrested, with many of the recent immigrants deported immediately back to their native lands.

Now, a surging political movement sought to restrict immigration and to regulate who would or would not be welcome to "the land of the free." The target of this nativist movement was clear—the *new* immigrants who had taken over so much of the industrial workforce in the country's largest cities. As a start, Congress passed an act in 1921 limiting immigration from any given country annually to 3 percent of the number of people from any given country living in the United States in 1910. But that was not "clear" enough, so in 1924, they expanded the legislation. The National Origins Act limited the annual figure to 2 percent of a given country's past immigrants. More important, the legislation changed the foundational date for comparison from 1910 to 1890, thereby privileging northern Europeans who dominated migration prior to 1890 and punishing the southern and eastern Europeans who had flooded the nation's borders thereafter. To wrap it all up, Congress placed a national ceiling of 150,000 on total immigration allowed per year starting in 1929—approximately 15 percent of the annual immigration totals for the first decade of the century—and excluded entirely people who were Chinese. Never had a more restrictive, xenophobic, or punitive set of laws been enacted on immigration.

Totally consistent with such nativism, the Ku Klux Klan experienced a startling resurgence. In 1915, a group of white activists gathered at Stone Mountain, Georgia, to resurrect the Klan. It was the same year that D. W. Griffith's incendiary film *Birth of a Nation* premiered, depicting black Reconstruction as a horrific time of repression for white Southerners. (The movie premiered at the Wilson White House.) The same year Leo Frank, a Georgia Jew, was lynched for allegedly raping a white woman co-worker. This time, though, the Klan found its primary audience in the Midwest with Kokomo, Indiana, its capital, and animus toward Jews, Catholics, and immigrants its primary focus for action. America was not a melting pot, Klan leader William J. Simmons exhorted his followers. Rather, it was a "garbage can.... When the hordes of aliens walk to the ballot box and their votes outnumber yours, then the alien horde has got you by the throat." Rallying millions of members, the Klan seized cultural control of large segments of the country based on its message of racial purity and contempt for all those who were not white Protestant patriots. Only a scandalous exposé, which showed that the new Klan's leadership had absconded with millions of dollars of membership dues, helped stem the reactionary flood tide.

Not surprisingly, fundamentalist religious views reached a new height of influence at the same time that the Klan revived and anti-immigrant fervor peaked. Profoundly distressed by the apparent fragmentation of traditional American values, millions of God-fearing Americans flocked to a literal interpretation of the Bible, denouncing all those who embraced "free thinking" and dissident mores. Fundamentalists endorsed Prohibition as an appropriate means to eliminate the sin of alcohol, supported repression of the radicalism of socialists and anarchists, and sought to stifle those mavericks who challenged traditional values. In state after state—particularly in the Midwest and South—legislators introduced bills to ban the teaching of evolution in the schools.

Tennessee was one of those where fundamentalists succeeded. The stage was thereby set for an intentional confrontation of the issue. A young biology teacher named Scopes invited arrest for brazenly violating the law by teaching the science of Darwin. Immediately, the case became a national cause celebre, with famous civil liberties lawyer Clarence Darrow arguing for the defense and three-time presidential candidate William Jennings Bryan representing the prosecution. With a conservative judge denying Darrow's ability to put most of his evidence before the court, the stage was set for a bizarre conclusion to the trial. Darrow then called Bryan as a witness, and before a national radio audience, made him an object of ridicule for insisting that, according to the literal word of the Bible, a "great fish" had really swallowed Jonah. In the end Scopes was convicted (a Tennessee appellate court rescinded his hundred-dollar fine), but fundamentalism suffered by being made a laughingstock before the country.

As would happen again in the late 1940s and 1980s, these fundamentalists often burst through the banality of most political discourse in the 1920s to dominate the national news. The persecution of those thought to be tainted by their radical political views offered the most flagrant testimony to this phenomenon. Nowhere was it more clear than in the case of Nicola Sacco, a worker in a shoe factory, and Bartolomeo Vanzetti, a fruit peddler. Two Italian immigrants, they were accused of robbery and murder in 1920 in Massachusetts. Having participated in some radical political causes, they

Despite the new consumerism, America was torn during the 1920s by fundamental cultural fissures over religion, drinking, and immigration. No conflict was more sensational than that over belief in evolution. Here Clarence Darrow, defense attorney for a young biology teacher indicated in Tennessee for teaching evolutionism, raises his fist at the infamous Scopes trial.

Credit: © Bettmann/CORBIS

were denounced in the midst of their trial in Massachusetts as "anarchist bastards." The judge was a Boston Brahmin. From the point of view of many, including large numbers of people from Harvard, Sacco and Vanzetti were victims of a rush to judgment based less on the evidence of their guilt or innocence than on their origin as southern European immigrants and the coloration of their political views. The country became polarized over their trial, and its subsequent guilty verdict, up until their execution in1927.

Through all of this, a sense existed of two Americas being cast against each other in a deathly struggle to determine which way of life would prevail. Would it be that of the polyglot, sophisticated, politically progressive, Catholic, urban America or that of the homogeneous, Protestant, rural, parochial, and moralistic America? Was this the country of flappers flitting about in their rolled hose and talking about free love or that of the *Main Street* moms who compelled Carol Kennecott to give up her dreams of independence and return to a life of total middle-class conformity where fulfillment came in the form of wifely subservience? Repeatedly during the decade, these diametrically opposite cultural forces clashed with each other. In most cases, it appeared that the conservative side came out on top. Immigration slowed to a trickle. Radicalism was suppressed. Prohibition prevailed. Evangelical fundamentalism proved much more resilient than tepid Unitarianism. Yet even in the face of repeated setbacks, observers could not ignore the degree to which energy and innovation resided more in the ranks of the challengers than those of the defenders of the status quo.

IV. POLITICS

To a remarkable degree, politics seemed far removed from the cultural clashes dividing evolutionists from fundamentalists, flappers from "Main Street" housewives, and gin-imbibing urban Catholics from Prohibitionist rural Protestants. Yet in their own way, the presidents of the 1920s did represent the times. They provided a veneer of complacency—surely true of the general atmosphere—beneath which conflicts roiling the underlying coherence of American society played themselves out. In that sense, the 1920s were akin to the 1950s. Both decades seemed a time of affluence and conformity while turbulence that would soon engulf the larger society gathered strength beneath the surface.

Rarely has a person of less ability or distinction occupied the presidency than Warren Gamaliel Harding, the former Republican senator from Ohio. "I am a man of limited talents from a small town," he confessed. "I don't seem to grasp that I am President." Yet in many ways Harding was exactly what the country wanted. His simplicity, superficiality, and shallowness offered the perfect contrast to the intellectualism, passion, and gravity of Wilson. Harding himself brilliantly posed the issue before the American people. "America's present need," he declared, "is not heroics, but healing; not nostrums but normalcy; not revolution, but restoration...not experiment but equipoise." Facing off against Governor James Cox of Ohio and his running mate, Assistant Secretary of the Navy Franklin Delano Roosevelt, Harding and his running mate, Massachusetts Governor Calvin Coolidge ("Silent Cal," he was called) were thrilled to make the presidential contest a referendum on the League of Nations. In a stunning victory, they crushed their opponents almost 2–1—16 million votes for Harding, 9 million for Cox. Succinctly summarizing the election, commentator William Allen White pronounced that Americans were "tired of issues, sick at heart of ideals, and weary of being noble."

Harding proceeded to manifest the best and worst sides of his personality. As someone who understood his own shortcomings, he appointed talented people to the cabinet positions with the heaviest agenda of national policy concerns. The distinguished governor and future Supreme Court Justice Charles Evans Hughes became secretary of state, pioneering a disarmament conference that significantly reduced the naval arms race among the United States, Japan, Great Britain, and France. As secretary of the treasury, Harding appointed Andrew W. Mellon, the multimillionaire wizard who immediately set out to liberate investment capitalists by reducing taxes and government regulation. Mellon was joined as economic mastermind by perhaps the most talented government official of the decade, Herbert Hoover, who had brilliantly coordinated war relief under Wilson and as secretary of commerce developed coordinated trade and economic policies that made America the most prosperous country on the planet.

On the other hand, Harding gave vent to his petty and greedy side when he appointed one crony, Ohio machine boss Harry Daugherty, to be attorney general, and another, Albert Fall, to head the Department of the Interior. This was the side of Harding more consistent with his true self. A man who loved to play poker, drink heavily, and on more than one occasion carry on extramarital affairs, Harding, in effect, provided a role model for those who sought to use their positions of political privilege for outrageous personal gain. A longtime influence peddler, Daugherty thought nothing of selling his authority within government to the highest bidder. He was joined by Fall, who leased valuable Wyoming oil tracts to companies without any bidding process. What was in it for him? A $400,000 "loan." What quickly became known as the Teapot Dome scandal—that was the site of the Wyoming oil tract—quickly catapulted the Republican Party into scandalous disrepute. Yet before he faced the full political price of his recklessness, Harding fell victim to a devastating heart attack on a trip to the West Coast and soon thereafter died. He was mourned by the entire country (his more mendacious side had yet to be fully disclosed) and left behind as his chief legacy, a Supreme Court to which he had named four members and which overturned child labor legislation as well as minimum wages for women.

Appropriately, "Silent Cal" Coolidge continued his predecessor's policies on the economy, even as he became a "sphinxlike" embodiment of fiscal and governmental integrity. Coolidge had achieved national fame by staring down the police in Boston when they went on strike in 1919 and declaring that no public employee ever had the right to shirk his public duties. His laconic personality made him almost a caricature for humorists. Allegedly, one White House guest told the president that he had made a wager with a friend that he would be able to get Coolidge to say more than two words. "You lose," was Coolidge's supposed response. The new president attempted no new bold initiatives, instead continuing the trend started under Harding to reduce the role of government. Under Secretary of the Treasury Mellon, income taxes were reduced still further, so that the top rate fell from 65 percent to 20 percent. A person with $1 million in income paid $633,000 in taxes in 1920 but only $200,000 by the end of the decade. When the Democrats met to gather their forces in 1924 to oppose Coolidge, they were in total disarray, taking more than one hundred ballots to choose John Davis, their compromise candidate, who stood no chance at all. When the Socialists and labor put forth Wisconsin's Robert La Follette as a third-party "Progressive" candidate, Coolidge simply denounced him as an agent of a "communistic and socialistic state" and soared to victory with 54 percent of the total vote. If Harding had been most known for cronyism and superficiality, Coolidge left as his legacy a philosophy of indifference to the idea of government as an active agent of change. "[He] slept more than any other president," satirist H. L. Mencken observed, "whether by day or night. Nero fiddled, but Coolidge only snored."

Having already renounced a second term, Coolidge was succeeded by Herbert Hoover, perhaps the most well-prepared and widely admired politician in the entire country. (At the end of World War I, Franklin Delano Roosevelt had noted that the nation would be well served if Hoover became president).

Notwithstanding the fratricide of their 1924 convention, two events from that gathering symbolized a new direction that party would soon take. New York Governor Al Smith's name was placed in nomination at Madison Square Garden by an ebullient Franklin Delano Roosevelt, who struggled manfully to the podium—on crutches, assisted by his sons—to register, in one of the most dramatic nominating speeches ever made, both his own gutsy return from being paralyzed by polio in 1921 and his confidence in the new direction he hoped the Democratic Party would take under Smith. Although the more than one hundred ballots that then ensued exemplified the tectonic battle within the party between urban, Catholic, anti-Prohibition Smith and William McAdoo, the favorite of Southerners and Westerners, the stage was set for Smith's subsequent nomination in 1928.

Against Hoover, Smith stood barely a chance. Hoover took credit for all the prosperity of the 1920s, pledged to cut taxes for the poor as well as the rich, and seized on his own popularity (and Smith's "negatives") to present himself as the "All-American" candidate whose presidency would mean "a chicken in every pot and a car in every garage." Cultural conservatives through the South and Midwest balked at Smith's anti-Prohibition stance and the fact that he was a Roman Catholic. The solid Democratic South split in half, Smith winning only six states. Overall, Hoover won 21 million votes to only 15 million for Smith.

Still, 1928 was an election that signaled the beginning of a new party alignment. Smith had increased the Democratic vote by 100 percent over four years earlier, and for the first time, Democrats triumphed decisively in the nation's urban areas. At the time there seemed no question that the Republicans were totally in charge. They boasted a national leader who more than almost any other public servant deserved credit for the prosperity that was now sweeping the country and who seemed to speak for the best values of the Republican Party. Yet in retrospect—and particularly in light of events about to unfold—1928 justifiably warranted the label historians subsequently bestowed upon it as a "critical election" that shifted the direction of national politics because of the new urban majorities for Democrats.

V. HOOVER AND THE GREAT DEPRESSION

Few presidents have been more sorely victimized by historical circumstance than Herbert Hoover. Not only had he played a major positive role in facilitating the prosperity sweeping the country but he also sought to extend those benefits to the least advantaged and to reach out to others marginalized by past history. By targeting his tax cuts to the poor, he hoped to bring America "nearer to the final triumph over poverty than ever before in the history of any land." Unlike some of his more conservative party colleagues, moreover, Hoover discouraged hysteria about the "Red Menace," supported the Agricultural Marketing Act with a loan fund for agricultural cooperatives (a la the Populist platform of the 1890s), and—at least in a relative sense—took a more progressive stance toward black Americans. He proposed larger amounts of federal support for the all-black Howard University in Washington, D.C., while his wife invited black Americans, for the first time since Theodore Roosevelt, to the White House for social affairs.

At the beginning of Hoover's term, things could not have been rosier. At the end of 1927, the stock market started upward at a more rapid pace than before, then in February 1928 it skyrocketed. In the eighteen months from February 1928 to September, 1929, the Dow Jones average rose by 40 percent, an unheard of rate of increase. Suddenly, everyone thought they could become millionaires. Speculation surged, investors plowing their profits back into investments in stocks rather than into productive capacity in the manufacturing sector. Encouraging the feverish surge still further was the fact that investors could purchase stocks "on margin," putting up only 10 percent of the purchase price in hard cash and borrowing the rest from brokerage houses. As long as stocks continued to move forward, of course, the "margin" strategy posed no problems. But once the market started to slide, investors suddenly owed up to 90 percent of their original purchase price to banks and brokerage houses. What had gone up like a rocket could suddenly plummet downward with the same velocity.

That was what occurred on October 29, 1929—Black Tuesday—when an overinflated market, having already begun a process of self-correction, suddenly plunged into panic. On that one day, seized by hysteria, investors sold sixteen million shares of stock. Instead of a gradual and acceptable decline, the Dow Jones average fell overnight by 13 percent, wiping out months of gains. Within days, losses on the stock exchange had mounted to 37 percent. As margin loans were called in to salvage the solvency of banks and brokerage houses, bankruptcies exploded. Hundreds, then thousands, of financial institutions were forced to close their doors. Investor accounts were wiped out. Home owners lost their mortgages. In a scenario that represented everyone's worst fears of a domino effect, one piece of bad news produced another. Just as the fever of speculation had created a dream world where everything good seemed possible, the epidemic of depression created a nightmare of one failure after another. What had once seemed an economy that guaranteed permanent prosperity had suddenly, overnight, become a scene of wreckage and despair.

As failure followed failure, the infrastructure of the entire economy fell apart. Consumers no longer had the resources to buy new commodities like washing machines and vacuum cleaners for their homes. With inventories growing and goods unsold, factories laid off employees. What had been a

As the nation reeled from the stock market crash of 1929, millions of people lost their jobs, homes, and savings. The banking industry plummeted into crisis as people rushed to salvage their savings. Here depositors are lined up outside the closed doors of the Union Bank of New York City.

Credit: © Bettmann/CORBIS

boom became a bust. Obviously, the loss of jobs meant a further decline in consumption. In a downward spiral that seemed to have no bottom, despair mounted. By 1930, thirteen million people were out of work. As banks closed, hundreds of thousands of average citizens lost their savings. When there was no money to pay for the mortgage, housing loans were foreclosed. Families whose homes were taken away either doubled up with parents and relatives or joined the thousands riding the rails, hoping that somehow, somewhere, there would be a place they could find respite. Villages of cardboard or tented shelters cropped up across the country. Called "Hoovervilles," many featured a "Hoover flag"—an empty bucket turned upside down.

Clearly, part of the cause of the Crash was the jerry-built, unsound financial system that funded the orgy of speculation leading up to Black Tuesday. "Buying on margin" proved to be a disaster. So too did a banking system that opted for speculation rather than solid investment as a way to spend depositors' resources. In a version of the "hedge fund" scandals that would occur seven decades later, too much floating money was risked in huge bets that a given enterprise would flourish rather than falter, and when investments turned bad, everything came crashing down. Perhaps more important, channeling money into speculation meant that it could not go into developing further the productive infrastructure of the country; generating new products; creating new jobs; and reinforcing the cycle of higher wages, higher production, and higher consumption that was the foundation of genuine prosperity.

On balance, however, it was the flawed nature of the underlying economy that provides the best explanation for the Great Depression. To be sure unsound investment policies triggered the Crash, which in turn led to the Depression. But even without the Crash, there was trouble ahead. Too much of the economy's boom depended on a couple of industries. Too little diversification existed. Thus when the pivotal industries suffered a slowdown, everything else threatened to come to a halt. Construction—one of these key industries—experienced a dramatic decline in the late 1920s, falling 20 percent from 1926 to 1929. Automobile production also stopped growing, and in 1929, automobile sales plummeted by 33 percent. The fact that the bottom fell out of the consumer market helps explain both the decline in construction and in car sales, but that trend in turn reflected the degree to which financial profits were going into speculation rather than manufacturing and wages, which might have generated more jobs and consumer potential.

Even more basic was the fact that workers' wages failed to keep pace with the ascending spiral of the economy in the 1920s. A huge imbalance existed between the salaries of the well-off and the wages of their employees. Much like the glaring income disparity of the 1990s and 2000s, the gap in spending potential between average consumers and their employers created the possibility that at some point, there would be no capacity among consumers to continue buying—even on installment plans—the goods that were being manufactured for their purchase. While the top 5 percent of the population garnered 33 percent of the total income, nearly half the rest of the nation took home less than what was defined as necessary for subsistence. All along, too much of the prosperity had been based on optimism and credit-buying. Once the optimism turned sour, and the credit-buying became impossible because of plummeting employment and bank failures, there was nowhere to go but down. Not surprisingly, personal incomes fell by half from 1929 to 1932 (from $82 million to $40 million), while unemployment soared from 3 percent to 25 percent. As reckless as Wall Street money practices might have been, the underlying problem was the absence of purchasing power in a working population that did not receive its fair share of the economic resources that accompanied the 1920s boom.

Although Hoover may have been better trained than most to address these realities, his responses were too little and too late. For too long, he insisted to the American people—and perhaps to himself—that "the fundamental business of this country...is on a sound and prosperous basis." Viewing the problem as primarily psychological, a matter of confidence and morale, he sought to use the power of positive thinking to turn people's spirits around, all the while failing to take action on escalating homelessness, climbing suicide rates among the jobless, and the spread of "Hoovervilles." In the meantime, the crisis was compounded by the spread of the Depression to Europe. No longer could Germany repay its reparations to France and Great Britain, which in turn meant that they could not repay loans to the United States. In fact, Hoover's trade policies made the situation worse, with the Smoot-Hawley tariff—the highest in recent history—making it even more difficult for European products to be exported to the United States.

In fairness, when the full dimensions of the Depression became clear, Hoover pursued more activist policies than any of his predecessors in a similar context. The Agricultural Marketing Act in 1929 sought to help suffering farmers; the Glass-Steagall Act of 1932 provided federal support for commercial loans for companies threatened with failure, and the Federal Home Loan Act of 1932 tried to help home owners threatened with foreclosure. But unlike what was to come, these efforts were too "top down" and bureaucratic while not putting the suffering of the "have nots" at center stage. Even Hoover's boldest move, the Reconstruction Finance Act of 1932, offered government guarantees for declining manufacturing industries months if not years too late to make a difference. Worst of all, perhaps, Hoover appeared reluctant to embrace bold initiatives, arguing that he did not wish to undermine the fundamental values of independence and individuality among Americans. If the nation were enveloped in a massive Depression, Hoover as president seemed paralyzed in response, almost as depressed personally as the country was economically.

Such was the political climate in 1932 as the nation prepared for its quadrennial exercise of choosing a president. More than five hundred thousand people had lost their farms or homes. Millions of banking accounts were at risk. Unemployment exceeded 25 percent. And Hoover, whatever his talent, offered no persuasive answers. His Democratic opponent, it turned out, also provided no clear-cut formula for how to proceed. But Franklin Delano Roosevelt did inject into the political equation a powerful new ingredient. Roosevelt, elected governor of New York to replace Al Smith in 1928, pledged to act boldly and quickly to address the nation's ills. He might have no comprehensive ideology, no pat answers to revitalizing the economy. But what he did have was a resilient spirit dedicated to trying anything that might work. Coming from a decade-long struggle to overcome the debilitating paralysis of polio, and with a solid record of innovation on relief measures in New York, Roosevelt was like a breath of fresh air imparting new life to a political process that seemed close to rigor mortis. Roosevelt even had the nerve—the Yiddish word *chutzpah* is more appropriate—to make his campaign theme song "Happy Days Are Here Again."

VI. CONCLUSION

Justifiably, it was a decade called the "Roaring Twenties," the "Jazz Age," the era of the "flapper." Young people danced the night away, women used language never before heard in proper circles, sexuality was upfront and pervasive, and Prohibition was known more for "speakeasies" where alcohol flowed freely than for sobriety. Just as in physics, in society also everything seemed "relative." Novelists wrote about a "lost generation" searching for a "new life." All the certitudes of the past seemed open to question, everything was in flux. Novelists and poets like Ernest Hemingway, Ezra Pound, T. S. Eliot, and Gertrude Stein became expatriates in Paris, seeking a "place" or a "meaning" that seemed to elude them in the United States, while those who stayed home—like F. Scott Fitzgerald and Sinclair Lewis—bemoaned the failure to reconcile growing superficial affluence with deeper personal meaning.

It was above all a time of division between differing cultural perspectives. While the Klan, fundamentalist opponents of evolution, and xenophobic nativists sought to restore the country to its Anglo-Saxon white roots and to oppose all foreign influence—culinary as well as intellectual—the avant-garde in New York, Chicago, and Paris crusaded for a different way of life, more multicultural, sophisticated, and diverse. Reflecting such condescension, Sinclair Lewis denounced the "emptiness" that besieged the people who occupied "Main Street"—"a savorless people, gulping tasteless food, and sitting afterward, coatless and thoughtless, in rocking chairs prickly with inane decorations, listening to mechanical music, saying mechanical things about the excellence of Ford automobiles, and viewing themselves as the greatest race in the world." The gap could hardly have been greater. While Southern white racists lynched black dissidents in Alabama and Mississippi, Langston Hughes, Zora Neale Hurston, and Claude McKay pioneered a black renaissance in Harlem, celebrating the "soul" and African-laden poetry and literature of black culture. In the meantime, Marcus Garvey and his United Negro Improvement Association plotted freedom from the hegemony of white culture and a return to black Africa, while W. E. B. DuBois spearheaded his own campaign for a Pan-African movement that would end all white colonialism.

At bottom, this was an era that was more like a kaleidoscope of clashing lifestyles than one of monochromatic consistency. Conflict was the motif. But it was not just a conflict of cultures. It was also a conflict of material circumstance, the rich getting far richer than they had ever been before, the average worker lagging behind, and nearly half the people still living in conditions of poverty. That conflict created the structural preconditions for the depression that started to sweep the country in 1929. Average consumers had run out of the wherewithal to buy more products, even with the credit system that seduced people into purchasing what they could ill afford. In their own version of installment buying, stock market speculators purchased Wall Street shares with only a 10 percent down payment. When the house of cards collapsed, it took everything with it. Speculators had put their money into stocks rather than manufacturing production, which would have hired workers. Once the market imploded, financial resources evaporated. With consumers out of money, factories stopped hiring, unemployment skyrocketed, and the Depression was on.

From all this two things were clear about the Roaring Twenties. The cultural divisions would not go away. They would persist and reappear with regularity in the '40s, '50s, '60s, and beyond. Yet even in the face of that persistence, energy was more on the side of those supporting ethnic diversity, urban lifestyles, and intellectual breakthroughs than on those defending the status quo. The cultural wars would go on, but within that tradition, the campaign of Al Smith in 1928 constituted a turning point that also provided the key link between the cultural dynamics of the era and the political history that transpired. Even if the age of Harding and Coolidge provided a veneer of conformity, just beneath the surface complacency a massive struggle was transpiring, with both a cultural and an economic dimension. In 1929, the economic dimension vaulted to the forefront, paving the way for a new political paradigm to take control in America. The age of the New Deal coalition was about to begin.

5

FDR and the New Deal

I n the fall of 1932 the American people were on the edge of despair. More than nine thousand banks had closed. Millions of Americans had lost their life savings. The unemployment rate skyrocketed. So did foreclosures, leaving countless Americans with neither a home to live in nor an income to support themselves. Nature itself seemed intent on making Americans suffer. A huge drought spread throughout the land, from Midland, Texas, to Bismarck, North Dakota, creating a "dust bowl" that caused hundreds of thousands to flee in search of salvation, usually to California. State and municipal relief budgets collapsed, with even the most well-off cities in the country paying $2.39 per week to support whole families. The automobile industry was a wreck, with General Motors stock falling from $73 a share in 1929 to $8 in the fall of 1932. No one could afford to buy consumer goods. The new department store giants of the Roaring Twenties collapsed from lack of customers. Montgomery Ward's share prices declined from $138 to $4. By the fall, the steel industry was producing at 12 percent of capacity and had no full-time employees. Nothing was working. It was time either to give up, or somehow, someway, find a new way to proceed, maybe even with a whole set of new answers.

I. THE ROOSEVELTS

The person who assumed this massive burden was Franklin Delano Roosevelt. Former assistant secretary of the navy under Woodrow Wilson during World War I, then vice-presidential candidate for the Democratic Party in 1920, Roosevelt had been elected governor of New York to succeed Al Smith in 1928. There he had a better record than most in combating the Depression. He inaugurated a statewide system of unemployment relief, initiated public power projects, pioneered conservation efforts, and with geniality as well as compassion, spoke of the need to fight for the "forgotten man" in America. One potential sign of Roosevelt's willingness to act boldly was his decision to take the unprecedented step of flying in an airplane to accept his nomination at the Democratic convention. No one ever before had been so daring.

Still, Roosevelt was all over the place in his campaign. At one point he talked favorably about greater government planning in running the economy, at another of being dedicated to conservative laissez-faire policies. On alternate days he embraced the idea of spending more government money on relief payments, and then, reversing himself, talked of the need for greater reductions in the federal budget. At no point did he mention massive deficit spending or the idea of a huge federal works program to aid the unemployed. In truth, he seemed not to know where he was going. As the pundit Walter Lippman observed, Roosevelt seemed "a pleasant man...without any important qualifications for the office [of president]."

What Roosevelt did have was a set of life experiences that helped make him uniquely qualified to lead the nation during its period of greatest desperation. Born into the aristocracy, Roosevelt grew up in comfort and privilege, though with a domineering mother who provided him little opportunity to express his real feelings. Still, with the grace expected of one "to the manor born," Roosevelt charmed his way through prep school, Harvard College, and Columbia Law School and then embarked on a public career as state assemblyman in New York from Dutchess County, where the family estate at Hyde Park was located. At ease with rural farmers and city bosses alike, he proceeded up the political ladder in Albany until recruited to go to Washington in the same subcabinet-level office that his distant Cousin Teddy had held twenty years earlier. Smooth and gregarious, Franklin was known more for his affability than for his gravitas.

Until one summer day in 1921 when his world came apart at Campobello Island, the Roosevelt summer retreat off the coast of Maine and Canada. There, after a day of swimming in the icy depths of the Gulf of Newfoundland, Roosevelt was engulfed by fever, chills, and an aching body. By morning, he could not move his legs. A few days later, a Boston specialist gave him the awful news: he had infantile paralysis—polio—a disease from which no recovery was possible and that in nearly every instance led to a life as an invalid, consigned to a wheelchair, prevented in any way from participating actively in the world of business or politics. In the horrific moments following his diagnosis, Roosevelt responded with stunning calm, perhaps displaying the stoic character expected of someone born to power. But what was really going on was an internal debate over how he should proceed, and the decision was not long in coming. Roosevelt decided then and there that he would not succumb to polio. He would fight back. He would do all he could to find a therapy that would return him to a life of activism. He would try anything, pursue the most experimental treatment, rule nothing out of bounds—all with the certainty that he would, and that he could, find the resources to move forward into a role as a public and active citizen.

Within three years, Roosevelt had achieved his goal. After months of pursuing multiple therapies—swimming in the hot spring pools of Warm Springs, Georgia, struggling with braces to wend his way down a driveway—Roosevelt came to Madison Square Garden in New York to place Al Smith's name before the Democratic Party as a candidate for its nomination for the presidency of the United States. Outwardly, Roosevelt's son James said, "[Father] was beaming, seemingly...unconcerned...but his...fingers dug into my arms like pincers—I doubt that he knew how hard he was gripping me. His face was covered with perspiration." Geoffrey Ward describes the scene:

Franklin Delano Roosevelt was struck down by polio in 1921. Refusing to accept the life of a retired invalid, FDR experimented with repeated therapies and regained enough strength to walk, with the help of braces and his two sons, to the podium of Madison Square Garden in 1924 to nominate Al Smith for president. Most Americans were unaware that their president used a wheelchair.

Credit: Associated Press

> He began moving slowly toward the podium alone, sweat beading his brow, jaw grimly set, eyes on the floor....It seemed to take an age, but when he finally stood at the podium, unable even to wave for fear of falling, but grinning broadly, head thrown back and shoulders high, in the exaggerated gesture that would now become his trademark, the delegates rose to their feet and cheered for three minutes, and as they did so the sun broke through the clouds above the Garden skylight and poured down upon him.

Roosevelt was back, but now with an inner strength of character that made him uniquely capable of engaging the crisis he was soon to confront.

In that task, he was strengthened further by his helpmate, Eleanor Roosevelt. Although also born into the aristocracy, Eleanor—unlike Franklin—could not have had a more tragic childhood. Both her parents had died by the time she was ten. Her father—the person with whom she lived a "dream life"—was an alcoholic who abandoned her when it came to a choice between being a father and having a drink. "It was the grimmest childhood I have ever known," her cousin Corinne remarked. "Who did she have? Nobody." But somehow she pulled herself together. Attending Allenswood, a private girls school in England, she found a role model, the headmistress Mlle. Marie Souvestre, who taught her intellectual independence and the importance of serving others. Thus even as she came back to the United States to marry her cousin Franklin—a man, like her father, who charmed her completely and with whom she thought she could once again live a "dream life"—she devoted days at a time to settlement house work on the Lower East Side of New York, seeking to help those with few resources and skills to live a better life. Significantly, when World War I came, she continued such efforts through her work with army recruits and mental health victims in Washington, D.C., even as she raised four children.

Eleanor suffered further unhappiness when she discovered that her husband, Franklin, was carrying on an extended love affair with Eleanor's private secretary, Lucy Mercer. Crushed, she offered Franklin a divorce. But they remained together, and during the years of helping Franklin to wage war against polio, she expanded still further her own life of political activism. She headed up the women's Democratic national campaign committee, worked hand in hand with the League of Women Voters, walked the picket lines with her colleagues from the Women's Trade Union League, and became a singular leader of women's social reform efforts. Although she and Franklin never recovered the magic of their early romance, they became political partners, each bringing to their common enterprise strengths that maximized their effectiveness, at first in Albany, then in the White House.

In virtually every way, both Franklin and Eleanor became indispensable to the creation of what soon would become known as the New Deal. Franklin Roosevelt brought buoyancy, poise, and a deep self-confidence rooted in his struggle with polio to the task of devising new solutions to the economic crisis. Furthermore, his experience trying endless therapies to aid his polio recovery translated into a ready willingness to engage in "bold, persistent experimentation" to address the dilemmas of the Depression. Eleanor, in turn, provided the conscience of the White House team. Replicating her role of the 1920s, she served as Franklin's eyes and ears in repeated tours of the country to learn from the experiences of average citizens. She combined that participant/observer intelligence gathering with a deep commitment to social justice, constantly reminding her husband of the needs of those most marginalized by society—black Americans, tenant farmers, the poor and displaced. Using her prerogatives as White House hostess, she would seat next to Franklin those whose causes most needed to get his attention. That teamwork did not always feature affection or joie de vivre. But it created a complementarity of perspectives without which the New Deal could never have achieved what it did.

II. THE EARLY NEW DEAL

Consistent with the eclectic programmatic suggestions of his campaign for the presidency, Roosevelt started his presidency with extraordinary energy but pursued multiple directions. No coherent themes shaped his legislative agenda. Rather, he addressed each emergency as it arose, seeking pragmatically to bring to each particular problem an approach, or series of approaches, that might make a difference. If Roosevelt had a ground rule it was "Try one thing, and if it does not work, try another, until you hit pay dirt." The rule might have come directly from his experience with polio therapies.

The banking crisis provided a model for all that would follow. By the time of FDR's inauguration, banks had totally closed in thirty-eight states. The stock market had shut down. A sense of foreboding was universal. After telling the American people in his inaugural address that "the only thing we have to fear is fear itself," Roosevelt put muscle behind his rhetoric. He immediately declared a bank holiday, taking decisive action to stem the tide of panic. He then sent to Congress the Emergency Banking Act, which provided for federal oversight of all banks before they could reopen. Reassured that the government was now involved, people responded to Roosevelt's plea that they trust their savings institutions. Just a few short days after he had become president, 75 percent of all banks had opened their doors once again, and instead of withdrawing money, average citizens deposited more than one billion dollars. Quickly following up his initial bold action, FDR secured quick passage of the Economy Act, offering further reassurance that he intended to provide fiscal responsibility. Just two months later, he closed the circle of building community trust by signing the Glass-Steagall Act, which placed government controls over speculative investments by banks—one of the causes of the stock market crash—and created the Federal Deposit Insurance Corporation, which provided a government guarantee of all deposits up to twenty-five hundred dollars. Each step of the way made sense, while together, Roosevelt's actions created a new aura of confidence that the federal government would protect the savings of the American people and ensure that financial institutions behaved responsibly.

During the first one hundred days of the Roosevelt administration, each week spawned a new example of problem-oriented legislation that engaged directly a crisis in the economy, put in place a practical solution, and gave the American people hope that the government was acting on their behalf and things were now under control.

Agriculture was a top priority on Roosevelt's list. Hundreds of thousands of farmers had lost their land. Thirteen million bales of cotton sat unused, rotting away. A new Farm Holiday Association had formed, threatening to declare a farm holiday. In response, FDR introduced the Agricultural Adjustment Act. Drawing ultimately on the ideas of the Populists in the 1890s, the AAA allowed the government to take over the production and regulation of agriculture. Federal officials determined how much land could be effectively put into production and how many pigs, cows, and sheep were needed to feed the people. The government then paid farmers to plow under millions of acres of cotton, corn, and wheat, thereby providing a foundation for a stable farm income. More than six million pigs were slaughtered; with government regulation and subsidy, the market for food was stabilized; and within three years, farm income increased by 50 percent.

Getting industry back online proved a more substantial challenge. Yet once again—with the philosophy that every player should get something in the bargain—FDR crafted a response that, temporarily at least, seemed to provide relief. Restarting a moribund manufacturing sector posed a huge dilemma. First, business needed to believe it had the freedom to proceed at minimum risk. So FDR proposed that antitrust rules be suspended and companies be allowed to collude to set prices and manufacturing quotas. To help make consumers more amenable to buying consumer goods, the National Recovery Administration used a badge, the Blue Eagle, to legitimize products made under the new plan and urge customers to buy such goods as a matter of patriotism. Labor unions were brought on board by Section 7(a) of the NIRA (National Industrial Recovery Act), which specifically authorized them to organize in factories. Average workers, in turn, were offered pivotal improvements at the workplace: a federal minimum wage, a maximum work week (forty hours), an end to child labor. In the meantime, the same omnibus bill allocated $3.3 billion for work relief—a provision that helped provide jobs for more than two million unemployed workers. In many respects, the bill lacked cohesion. In the eyes of its critics, it amounted to a patchwork mélange. But to the various constituencies it touched, the NIRA seemed a responsive, pragmatic means of speaking to diverse concerns, all of which revolved around the necessity of reenergizing the workplace.

Perhaps the boldest expression of state intervention came with the Tennessee Valley Authority bill in the spring of 1933. Involving a whole region of the country, the Tennessee Valley extended through several states, no single one of which could handle the multiple problems of creating damns, providing electricity, encouraging agricultural productivity, or ensuring flood control. Clearly, this was a job that only the largest state—the federal government—could undertake successfully. In what became the closest thing to socialism, or state capitalism, that the United States had ever seen, the TVA enabled the federal government to transform an entire region, making it one of the most productive, streamlined, and coordinated economic and social enterprises ever attempted. More than six huge dams were under construction by 1936, electricity for the first time became available to hundreds of thousands of families, and perhaps most important, a stable plan existed for economic and social development in the future—all through the coordination of a federal agency.

Clearly, the state had become a daily presence in millions of lives. An array of federal work projects put millions of the unemployed back to work while building a domestic infrastructure of facilities, roads, post offices, and parks that benefited the entire populace. Although the Public Works Administration under the NIRA was slow to spend its resources, it soon was superseded by the Federal Emergency Relief Administration (FERA), which funded public construction of more than 5,000 public buildings and 7,000 bridges. Starting in the fall of 1933, the Civil Works Administration (CWA) put 4 million people to work building or improving more than 1,000 airports, 40,000 schools, and countless sewer systems. It then was succeeded in 1935 by the Works Progress Administration, which eventually helped as many as 9 million Americans. The WPA not only helped refine and modernize the nation's infrastructure but also, through extraordinary inventiveness, helped provide federal funding for the Federal Writers Project and the Federal Arts Project, which made it possible for thousands of artists to contribute their creativity to the public sector through community histories, wall murals inside post offices, and plays performed for local audiences.

In many respects, the genius of the early New Deal was that it provided something for nearly everyone. Big business and big agriculture found new stability through the support the government provided in the NIRA and AAA. Social reformers were thrilled to see Washington intervene to end child labor and establish maximum hours and minimum wages. Labor felt, at least initially, empowered to organize unions without fearing employer repression. Average citizens now knew that their banking system was safe, while investors appreciated the reforms that had occurred through the Truth in Securities Act and the creation of the Securities and Exchange Commission. The millions of unemployed now felt that at least someone cared enough to provide the chance for meaningful work, and those countless Americans who longed to be liberated from the restraints of Prohibition and enjoy a glass of beer were thrilled by the 1933 Volstead Act, which legalized 3.2 beer and set in motion the process of repealing the Eighteenth Amendment. The list of laws enacted dwarfed anything that had ever been attempted before in American history. Now, the new role of the state promised during the reforms of the Progressive Era had come to fruition. Even if there was no grand blueprint or thematic unity to the myriad proposals that emerged from the Roosevelt White House, one thing was clear: the government was now an imminent and intimate part of every citizen's daily life.

In truth, the early New Deal experience—whatever its heterogeneity—did have an earlier model to emulate. As William E. Leuchtenburg has shown, the antecedent most important to understanding the thrust of New Deal activism was the nation's experience in World War I. Whatever the aspirations of Populists and Progressives, World War I involved a degree of massive federal intervention in the economy never before imagined. The War Industries Board imposed government edicts and set production goals; the War Labor Board defended enforced equal pay for women and stood up for union rights; the intellectuals and "dollar a year" executives who flocked to

Washington placed service to a national goal ahead of any private agendas. During the war, a sense of national purpose took precedence, the good of the whole becoming paramount. Understandably, Leuchtenburg asserts, it was the wartime experience to which Roosevelt and his aides turned for guidance as they sought a path to recovery. The same personalities returned to run New Deal agencies who had managed wartime boards. Indeed, the summer of 1933 was like a reunion where colleagues from 1917 came together one more time to put in place the same kinds of programmatic response they had devised sixteen years earlier.

The imagery of war prevailed everywhere. Washington, the *New York Times'* Arthur Krock noted, was "like a beleaguered capital in war time." FDR embraced the same imagery. The country, he declared, must move "as a trained and loyal army willing to sacrifice for the good of a common discipline." Elaborating, he declared that he would seek from Congress "broad executive power to wage a war against the emergency, as great as the power that would be given to me if we were in fact invaded by a foreign foe." Constantly invoking the metaphor of the fight against depression as a patriotic crusade, he sought to transcend partisanship and create a national coalition of people concerned with a higher good than simply their own self-interest. Hence the use of the Blue Eagle as a patriotic symbol for national commitment to the NIRA; the presence of marching bands to celebrate the inauguration of the NIRA; the conscious way in which legislation like TVA was modeled on World War I public resource precedents like the Muscle Shoals power development initiative; the use of the army as a model for the Civilian Conservation Corps. In all these ways—appropriately—Roosevelt raised the crisis of the Great Depression to the same level of national emergency that had existed in 1917, seeking in the process to cast a rubric of patriotic loyalty around mobilizing support for his multiple initiatives. There may not have been ideological coherence in the legislation passed; but there was the unifying notion that all these varied endeavors were part of a common crusade to take on a crisis as devastating as war.

III. THE COALITION COMES APART

Yet the Depression was not war. Real economic and political forces, with divergent agendas, fought for recognition and domination. Countless undercurrents roiled the political waters. For only so long would antagonistic factions subsume their partisan interests in deference to a call for unity. Early New Deal legislation possessed as many flaws as cure-alls. NIRA codes were poorly written. How and why did big businesses get the authority to make the rules on marketing and pricing? Why should big farmers—subsequently called "agribusiness"—get huge subsidies while small farmers and sharecroppers got the short end of the stick? And if you believed in capitalism as a market ideology, how did the government get the right to tell you what to do, set the wages of your workers, and determine the distribution of your products? Although the rhetoric of wartime patriotism and nonpartisan coalitions might prevail during the period of immediate crisis following the election and the bank holiday, before long partisan vendettas began to puncture that veneer of unity and expose anew the underlying fault lines dividing America.

The right launched the first direct attack. Starting in the summer of 1934, a group called the Liberty League attacked the New Deal as a concerted effort to undermine traditional American liberties. Led by prominent industrialists such as John Raskob and the DuPont family, as well as centrist politicians like Al Smith, the Liberty League accused the Roosevelt administration of statism that amounted to near socialism. Roosevelt was portrayed as the archenemy of capitalism, an upper-class aristocrat who had betrayed his own class. The NIRA became a favorite Liberty League target, with league leaders and their lawyers mounting concerted attacks on the NIRA both in the courts and in the political arena. Typical was the name right-wing dissidents gave to the President: "Stalin Delano Roosevelt."

The Left was not far behind. From all over the country, radical intellectuals, maverick church leaders, and ambitious populist politicians lambasted Roosevelt for halfway measures that never addressed the fundamental inequalities in American society. Why, during a time of suffering for average working-class people, the critics asked, should the government "get into bed" with millionaire industrialists? What was the justification for helping those who owned huge farms while doing nothing for their tenants? How could Roosevelt justify defending the capitalist status quo when as much as 40 percent of the country lived in poverty?

Huey Long, former governor of Louisiana and now a U.S. senator, was one of those spearheading dissent from the Left. Known for mobilizing the poor in Louisiana against entrenched greed, Long had built roads, bridges, and schools in his state—one of the poorest in the South—while socking it to the wealthy. Now he brought to the American people a national campaign— "Share the Wealth—which claimed 7.5 million subscribers and pledged to seize the wealth of the rich and redistribute it to every citizen. Under Long's proposal, every American would own a home worth $5,000 and receive an annual income of $2,500.

Long's allies on the Left boasted similar ideas. Dr. Francis Townsend, a physician from California, organized a group called "Old Age Revolving Pensions," which focused on the immiseration of senior citizens. If the government would pay each senior citizen two hundred dollars per month, Townsend declared, money would be injected into the economy, older citizens would be able to escape poverty, and the entire society would benefit. Townsend claimed over ten million supporters. Father Charles Coughlin of Detroit brought an equally powerful message to his weekly radio audience. A demagogue, Coughlin railed against privilege, clamored for redistributing wealth, and vilified Roosevelt and others as traitors to the people. Couglin's "National Union for Social Justice" conveyed perhaps the harshest message from the Left: Coughlin demonized his political enemies, sowed hatred among his followers, and threatened the kind of fascist/totalitarian mass movement that only recently had brought Adolf Hitler to power in Germany.

In the labor movement, meanwhile, radicalism of a different sort was taking root. Notwithstanding Section 7(a) of the NIRA, labor had not been able successfully to organize workers, nor did the federal government provide the kind of protection for such efforts that initially seemed likely. The AF of L (American Federation of Labor) remained focused on skilled industries, and although in 1933 they signed up one hundred thousand industrial workers, a year later only 6 percent remained dues-paying members.

More radical instincts soon took over. John L. Lewis helped pioneer a more militant form of unionism and expanded the membership of the United Mine Workers from 150,000 in 1933 to 500,000 in 1934. That year, strikes broke out across the country. Taxi drivers walked out in New York and Philadelphia, teamsters in Minnesota, textile workers throughout the South, and longshoremen in California. Meanwhile, Communist activists became more involved in a series of incipient industrial unions (labor groups that organized by industry rather than by skill group) in steel, automobiles, rubber, and the electrical industry. With each passing day it became more likely that workers might engage in open rebellion—despite, or perhaps because of, the fact that the new administration seemed more sympathetic to the cause of labor. Meanwhile, the 1934 elections produced a Congress also more left of center, with nine new Democratic senators, and a host of congressmen ready to move forward energetically on a bold agenda of change.

Faced with the disintegration of the cherished "warlike" coalition he had put together, Roosevelt knew it was time to take sides. Whatever his devotion to the cause of saving capitalism, Roosevelt was infuriated by the Liberty League's dismissal of his efforts. In the first eighteen months, he had been conservative on labor issues, more often than not siding with big business. But faced with a growing revolt on his left, he now decided to cast his lot with those seeking more progressive social programs. To offset the growing strength of the Townsend movement, he demanded in June of 1935 that Congress enact the Social Security Act—a measure that each month would pay retired American workers a pension as well as provide unemployment compensation for those out of work and relief support for mothers with dependent children. In reality, the Social Security measure was deeply conservative. Instead of coming from general tax revenues, it was paid for by regressive taxes. Workers had money withdrawn each week from their paychecks and deposited into a trust fund. Only many years later, when they retired, would they receive their pensions from the fund. Nor were many of the most needy included in the plan, including domestic servants and sharecroppers. Still, it was a measure that seemed responsive to the crisis among senior citizens that Townsend had articulated.

The same month, FDR brought to Congress the Holding Company Act. In direct contrast to the NIRA, which suspended antitrust laws and allowed big businesses to collude on price and market conditions, the Holding

Company Act set out to dismantle the interlocking directorates that permitted utility companies to get away with exactly the kind of cooperation FDR had encouraged with NIRA. Correctly, the legislation was perceived as anti-big business. As if to ensure that the public got the message, Roosevelt the same summer introduced a new tax measure. Quickly dubbed a "soak the rich" bill, the Revenue Act of 1935 escalated taxes on those with incomes of more than fifty thousand dollars, hiked the rate on wealthy estates and gifts, and conveyed the clear intention that those with the greatest personal wealth must pay the largest share of those programs dedicated to the common wealth. Randolph Hearst denounced the measure as "essentially communism," and although the label bore no relationship to reality (in fact, the "Soak the Rich Tax" led to no redistribution of income), it helped cement in the public's mind the image of Roosevelt taking on "the big boys" and committing himself to the "forgotten man."

Paradoxically, the most important progressive measure passed by Congress during this flurry of activism took effect without Roosevelt's participation or endorsement. The Wagner Act was correctly dubbed in later years as the "Magna Charta" of labor. Introduced by New York's activist liberal senator, it provided the government protection for labor organizers that, ostensibly, Section 7(a) of the NIRA was supposed to offer. Only now the guarantees were solid, with federal officials and a new National Labor Relations Board overseeing labor's right to go into factories, enlist workers in union campaigns, and not suffer retribution. Roosevelt never supported the measure—nor was he ever "friendly" to labor in the way union leaders wished—but seeing the handwriting on the wall, neither did he oppose the measure. This time, labor and liberals had the votes and the Wagner Act became law.

The effect of labor's "Magna Charta" was immediate. In October 1935, the CIO (Congress of Industrial Organizations) under John Lewis's leadership established an independent union dedicated to industrial unionism. Fifteen months later, autoworkers in Flint, Michigan, showed what it meant to organize an industry as a whole with the assurance that government would not intervene on management's side. A group of workers in a Flint, Michigan, General Motors plant sat down at their workplace and refused to leave. Occupying the factory, they refused to leave until the company recognized their union and sanctioned an election. In the past, management had enlisted the support of governors and police forces to suppress such labor militancy. But Governor Frank Murphy of Michigan refused management's appeal to send troops. In the absence of government support on management's side, labor vaulted to success, with the United Auto Workers becoming a signature leader in the crusade for mobilizing assembly line workers. Within a year, workers in steel, rubber, and the electric industry followed the example set at Flint. In 1937 there were more than forty-seven hundred strikes across America, and unions won 80 percent of the battles. No legislation enacted at any time during the 1930s had a greater impact. Whereas in 1932 labor unions had a membership of only 3 million, by 1940 their ranks had soared to 10 million.

The American labor movement was transformed in early 1935 when workers at a Flint, Michigan, General Motors plant sat down at the job and refused to leave. Their tenacity forced the auto giant to negotiate a labor agreement with the newly formed United Auto Workers and led to the massive expansion of union membership in other industries as well.

Credit: © Bettmann/CORBIS

Whether by design (as with Social Security, the Holding Company Act, and the Revenue Act) or by accident (the Wagner Act), the Roosevelt administration had boldly departed from the nonpartisan, nationalist model of 1933 and 1934. As politics polarized, FDR knew instinctively which side he was on. The product of his change were the two most important measures of the New Deal—Social Security and the Wagner Act. Both would constitute a legacy that any president might boast of, and each, in its own way, pointed to the themes that would dominate the presidential election of 1936.

IV. THE 1936 ELECTION

By virtue of aligning himself with the forces of change rather than those of reaction, Roosevelt made the election of 1936 a referendum, not on coming together in a wartime-like coalition but on moving forward toward a liberal definition of America's mission in the future. To be sure, Roosevelt boasted of his achievements on behalf of all the country. He was proud of the fact that his administration had created six million jobs, that the nation had pulled itself out of a downward spiral, and that national income had increased 50 percent. During FDR's first term, industrial output had increased 100 percent, with the business index up to one hundred for the first time since 1930. But the thrust of the campaign was on celebrating the new departures of the previous eighteen months and on exhorting America's voters to join the crusade to realize the promise of American democracy.

In his new role as champion of the disenfranchised and maltreated, Roosevelt was aided by both fate and his own actions. No one had threatened Roosevelt more from the left than Huey Long. His bombastic (and persuasive) call to "Share Our Wealth" had resonated with voters all over America. But in the fall of 1935, Long fell victim to an assassin's bullet. Social Security had appeased many of the followers of Charles Townsend, and Father Coughlin's demagoguery (and anti-Semitism) had seriously undermined his credibility. Working-class voters were not necessarily aware that FDR had not championed the Wagner Act, and as long as he did not interfere with its enforcement, they would be for him. Even black Americans, increasing numbers of whom lived in the North, where they had migrated since World War I, now abandoned the party of Lincoln. Here too, FDR was not a partisan of equal rights. He failed to support an antilynching bill and worked closely with white Southern legislators. Yet New Deal relief programs benefited blacks as well as whites. More than 30 percent of African Americans received federal aid. Roosevelt had a "Negro cabinet" consisting of white (and black) officials sympathetic to civil rights. The WPA had no quotas restricting blacks from participation. And the First Lady was known for her support of Negro rights.

As a consequence, Roosevelt became the first Democratic presidential candidate to ever secure black support. Whereas in 1932, FDR earned only 23 percent of the Chicago Negro vote, in 1936 he took a majority. In Cleveland, every black ward was recorded in the Roosevelt column. As one black journalist told his readers, "My friends, go home and turn Lincoln's picture to the wall. That debt has been paid in full."

In the meantime, the Republican Party had no place to go. Its nominee, Kansas Governor Alf Landon, would ordinarily have been seen as a moderate to liberal representative of his party (as had been Herbert Hoover). Landon had no quarrel with the need for government to do more to aid the defeated and depressed; his own record was solid. But in the face of the sea change wrought by the Depression and the dramatic new initiatives pursued by Roosevelt, Landon seemed caught in a backwater, neither relevant nor competitive in the debates shaping the electorate's decisions about the nation's future.

With prescience, Roosevelt cast the campaign not as a battle between traditional parties but as a choice of fundamental directions. He ran as a liberal crusader, proud to have in his stable of supporters "independent" midwestern

No First Lady in history had exerted a stronger public presence than Eleanor Roosevelt. An activist and social reformer in her own right, she was the president's eyes and ears as she journeyed around he country visiting New Deal project. Here she is shown handing out Christmas gifts at a school for boys in New York that sought to rehabilitate children under the age of twelve had been identified as delinquent or neglected.

Credit: © Bettmann/CORBIS

progressives (known for being mavericks) like Robert La Follette, Hiram Johnson, and Frank Norris. Only three times during his campaign did he mention the words "Democratic Party." The Roosevelt message was strikingly populist, even radical. He denounced the "economic royalists" who fought against him. They might be "unanimous in their hate for me," he declared, *"[but] I welcome their hatred"* (italics added). Even in his milder statements, FDR accentuated the issue of division in the country. Proudly, he contrasted his own record of leading a government animated by a "spirit of charity" as opposed to the philosophy supported by his opponents, one "frozen in the ice of its own indifference." By election day, the verdict could not have been clearer. More than 60 percent of the American people chose Roosevelt for a second term. Landon won only two states. The statistics on who voted for whom were stark. More than 80 percent of those with incomes under $1,000 chose Roosevelt, 79 percent of those with incomes from $1,000–$2,000. By contrast, Landon won 54 percent of those with incomes of more than $5,000.

The "forgotten Americans" now had chosen a leader, and this time one not simply pledged to create a national government of unity and compassion, but one dedicated to speaking on behalf of those for too long underrepresented. As FDR said in his inaugural address in January 1937, "I see one third of a nation ill-housed, ill-clothed, ill-fed," and he gave every indication of his intention to do something about it. The questions was, could he deliver?

V. THE DECLINE OF THE NEW DEAL

Never before had there existed greater reason to believe that America could move to eliminate the gross inequalities that scarred the nation. A president had been reelected on a platform of uplifting the downtrodden. He carried with him majorities in the House and Senate hitherto unheard of, with more than two-thirds of both bodies committed (in theory at least) to Roosevelt. Now was the ideal time to put together legislation specifically targeted to correcting the worst inequities plaguing the nation—structural unemployment, urban poverty, perhaps even racism.

Yet it was not to be. Perhaps even the size of Roosevelt's victory was a harbinger of ill fortune. In 1937, as would happen repeatedly throughout the rest of the century, a president overwhelmingly elected to a second term encountered fragmentation and discord rather than acclamation and progress. It was a scenario full of irony, complexity, and failed optimism, with lessons hard to learn and even harder to correct.

The pivotal moment in the months after FDR's reelection came when he presented a plan to enlarge the United States Supreme Court from nine to fifteen. Allegedly, Roosevelt sought to "reform" the court and help it to deal with the twin problems of aging judges and a growing caseload. Nothing could have been further from the truth. As everyone knew, the Court was a bone in Roosevelt's throat. Repeatedly, it had thwarted his wishes, holding unconstitutional critical New Deal laws and threatening to do the same to many more. By the time of Roosevelt's second inaugural, the Court had ruled against him in seven out of nine cases it had heard. The heart of New Deal legislation consisted of the NIRA and AAA. By 1936, the Court had invalidated both. Soon cases on Social Security and the Wagner Act would come before it. As one token of the Court's conservatism, it had even ruled unconstitutional a New York State law establishing minimum wages for women workers. Clearly, Roosevelt and his allies had ample reason to feel at war with this "third branch" of government and to fear its intention to destroy everything that had been or might be accomplished.

Yet Roosevelt erred profoundly in thinking he could get away with the charade of calling "reform" what everyone knew to be "court packing." It was a transparent case of hypocritical political "spin." Everyone knew the real reason for the plan, and most took umbrage at the hubris of a chief executive seeking to manipulate the truth and deceive the people. As the *New York World-Telegram* said, it was "too clever, too damn clever."

More to the point, Roosevelt had violated one of the most sacred tenets of American political etiquette: it was wrong to tamper with the American Constitution. The foundational document of the nation was not a rough draft to be edited and revised at will. The checks and balances that Madison and his colleagues had spent months negotiating existed for a purpose—to prevent any one of the delicately separated units of government from trampling on or invading the domain of the others. Despite Roosevelt's more than two-thirds majority in Congress, senators and congressmen of both parties shrank from the implications of what Roosevelt intended. This was beyond the pale, an act of heresy, breaking the pact of America's civil religion—the nation's devotion to the Constitution as a sacrosanct document. Although Democratic leaders in the House and Senate gave Roosevelt nominal support, there was no fire in the belly. Everyone understood, almost instinctively, that this was going too far, giving off the odor of executive tyranny, more analogous to something Hitler or Mussolini might try than to reform impulses imbedded in the American political tradition.

At the same time, the Supreme Court itself preempted Roosevelt's fundamental argument for passage of the court-packing plan by reversing itself midstream. In a case virtually identical to the New York State minimum wage case, the Court now upheld a minimum wage law for women in Washington State. Owen Roberts, a "swing" vote on the court in many cases, had simply jumped the fence to join the other side. It was, pundits pontificated, the "switch in time that saved nine." Shortly thereafter—and consistent with Roberts's shift—the Court upheld both the Wagner Act and Social Security. In the meantime, one of the most conservative court members retired, and Roosevelt was able to replace him with Senator Hugo Black, a dedicated New Dealer who would become one of the Court's longest-lasting liberal and influential jurists. The combination of events spelled the death knell of Roosevelt's "reform" plan to alter the composition of the Court. With minimal support from the beginning, the Court's reversal on cases central to the New Deal's concerns now sapped any enthusiasm that existed on Capitol Hill for Roosevelt's plan, and after months of debate, it met its demise.

Yet the impact of the court-packing fight proved long lasting and devastating. Any chance that Roosevelt had of presenting a new "one hundred days" of reform legislation to a Congress primed to act was now gone. All the momentum of the liberal triumph of 1936 had dissipated. Drained of energy and the collective will to act by the controversy Roosevelt had stirred up, the Democratic Party became factionalized. Congressional leadership became more resistant to executive prodding, almost as though the court-packing plan had been an inoculation that created antibodies in Congress to any form of deference to White House initiatives. Within eight months after Roosevelt's stunning reelection victory, Roosevelt had become sorely weakened. "The whole New Deal really went up in smoke as a result of the Supreme Court fight," Secretary of Agriculture Henry Wallace declared. Not only did Congress now react with immediate skepticism to new ventures Roosevelt proposed; in addition, an undertow developed within the Democratic Party itself, with scores of Southern Democrats finding themselves in common cause with Northern Republicans. A new "conservative coalition" sprang up in the House, with a counterpart in the Senate. In a startling example of political paradox, it seemed that the larger the majority that Roosevelt achieved, the less his actual power.

As if this were not enough, in 1937 the country descended into a new and deep recession. Never having fully adopted the view that government spending was critical to "priming the pump" of the economy on a consistent basis, FDR started to cut back federal programs when it appeared that the country was coming out of the Depression. At the same time, of course, new taxes—including two billion dollars in new Social Security deductions—were sucking money out of the economy. A dramatic slowdown followed. The business index fell from 110 in August to 85 in December; steel production dropped by two-thirds; and four million citizens lost their jobs. In Detroit alone, WPA work relief roles skyrocketed 434 percent. When the downturn finally bottomed out in March of 1938, the country was in almost as bad condition as it had been six years earlier. Belatedly recognizing the need for spending on a continuing basis, Roosevelt resumed heavy deficit spending, with the WPA in the lead, hiring the recently unemployed. Another lesson had been learned. Yet it would not be until World War II that sufficient government resources were injected into the economy to end the Depression.

In the meantime, Roosevelt took another bold gamble. Rather than passively accept the new conservative coalition that had flowered in response to his court-packing plan, Roosevelt set out in 1938 to "purge" the Congress of some of its more conservative Democratic members. Targeting Southern senators like Walter George, "Cotton" Ed Smith, and Millard Tydings, Roosevelt hoped that new, more liberal Democrats could take over. Instead, as with the court-packing plan, Roosevelt vastly underestimated the power of the status quo. He won in a couple of races—Claude Pepper in Florida, Lister Hill in Alabama—but overall the "purge" attempt was a dismal failure. More important, the Republicans surged to an impressive victory, gaining eighty-one seats in the House and strengthening significantly the already existing conservative coalition.

The New Deal was not completely over. Propelled by a growing distrust of big business, antitrust advocates initiated investigations of the ongoing tendency of American business to end up in monopolies. Thurmond Arnold, as assistant attorney general, revitalized the antitrust division of the Justice Department. After an extended battle, the White House finally persuaded Congress to enact the Fair Labor Standards Act, which re-created the minimum wages and maximum hours standards that the Supreme Court's had invalidated in the NIRA. More than twelve million employed Americans benefited and in the end, the Supreme Court upheld the right of the Congress to legislate on behalf of both sexes—a significant breakthrough. Congress also made a tentative start toward supporting the construction of Public Housing, a benchmark initiative that provided at least a foundation for further action in subsequent years.

Yet on balance, it was clear that all the dreams of transformation that had accompanied the Democratic rout in 1936 had largely vanished into thin air. Now, the energy field existed on the right, dominated by Republicans and their conservative Democratic allies. A new focus on anticommunism sprouted vigorously in Congress, with a House Committee on Un-American Activities holding hearings to suggest that New Dealers were conscious or unconscious agents of Marxism. "Stalin baited his hook with a 'progressive' worm," committee chair Martin Dies declared, "and New Deal suckers swallowed [it] hook, line and sinker." In the lives of so many of those filled with hope three years earlier, the ensuing period had turned into a staccato series of bitter defeats. Many were self-inflicted. Some reflected underlying trends, including the growing willingness of conservative Southern Democrats to show their true colors. But whatever the cause, those who in 1936 boldly hoped to be able to act on behalf of the "one third of a nation" that was ill-housed and ill-clothed now tasted the bitter ashes of defeat. In the meantime, the nation's attention re-focused on another crisis, even larger than that of the Great Depression—the oncoming reality of world conflagration.

VI. PREPARATION FOR WAR

From the beginning of his presidency, Roosevelt brought a keen sensitivity to issues of foreign policy. Although international affairs clearly ranked second to domestic despair as a focal point for presidential energy, Roosevelt showed a willingness to break with precedent in that domain as well. Recognizing that part of the world Depression was tied to outmoded fiscal practices, FDR took America off the "gold standard" in 1933 to facilitate trade. Of equal or greater importance, he ended America's sixteen-year refusal to acknowledge, diplomatically, the existence of the Soviet Union. Starting in 1933, the United States "recognized" the USSR, and an exchange of ambassadors ensued. The president also determined to alter the nature of America's relations with her South American neighbors. Setting out to withdraw American military forces from various Latin American countries to which they had been assigned over the previous two decades, Roosevelt proclaimed a new "Good Neighbor" policy. "No state has the right to intervene in the internal or external affairs of another," the United States now affirmed.

But it was developments in Europe and Asia that most dominated Roosevelt's attention. Instinctively and presciently, Roosevelt recognized the mortal threat to world stability posed by the ascendancy of Adolf Hitler to power in Germany. FDR saw the bully-like arrogance of Hitler, his reliance on demagoguery, his insatiable appetite for power and land. Well before most people, Roosevelt perceived the dangers of an alliance between Hitler and Italian fascist dictator Benito Mussolini. He also understood the geopolitical implications of Japan's seemingly unconstrained appetite for greater power in Asia. Tokyo's earlier invasion of Manchuria and its subsequent move into

China signaled the likelihood of having to confront in Asia the same kind of territorial hubris that was likely to happen with Germany in Europe.

Significantly, Roosevelt's freedom to deal with all this was severely hampered by ongoing isolationism at home, compounded by ever widening belief that American intervention in World War I had been a mistake, propelled by bankers and the munitions industry. Congressional hearings in the early 1930s raised the specter—largely unfounded—that the United States had been "tricked" into joining the war against Germany by profiteering industrialists. Partly in response, Congress enacted a Neutrality Act in 1935 prohibiting the United States from intervening in foreign conflicts and prohibiting the sale of arms to either side. Initially prompted by the likelihood that Mussolini's Italy would soon invade Ethiopia, the Neutrality Act became a millstone around the neck of American foreign policy, denying the president any flexibility in dealing with what loomed as a series of pending international crises. This became particularly true when the Spanish Civil War started in 1936–1937 with pro-Fascist forces under Generalissimo Francisco Franco seeking to topple the democratically elected Republican government in Madrid. Almost a rehearsal by surrogates of the underlying philosophical confrontation between democracy and fascism that would soon transfix all of Europe, the Spanish Civil War aroused deep passions among many in America, leading to the formation of the "Abraham Lincoln" brigade of American volunteers to go to Spain to fight against Franco. Ernest Hemingway's *For Whom the Bell Tolls* and *The Sun Also Rises* memorialized those passions for generations of subsequent American readers. Yet the United States could do nothing to help the Spanish Republican government because it was prohibited from selling arms by the Neutrality Act.

At various times, Roosevelt sought to shift the terms of debate and facilitate a more rational basis on which to build a policy of responsible engagement with the world conflicts that were emerging. After Japan extended its aggression into China, becoming increasingly bellicose in both rhetoric and action, Roosevelt delivered what became known as his "Quarantine" speech. Using the homely metaphors he had employed so effectively in his "fireside chats" on radio to the American people during the New Deal, Roosevelt suggested that the world community was like a local neighborhood. When a contagious disease broke out in a community, he told his audience, it often became necessary to "quarantine" the home where the disease was located until it could be brought under control. Only then could normal interactions resume. By implication, Roosevelt suggested, when a nation threatened the world community by its policies of aggression, the international community should act collectively to isolate that nation and have no further dealings with it until it reformed and merited reentry into the fellowship of nations. Yet, although brilliantly conceptualized, Roosevelt's appeal fell on deaf ears. Deeply fearful of being trapped once again in a foreign venture, Americans protested loudly against Roosevelt's suggested course of action, and the president soon retreated. Although he never ceased his vigilance toward the threat he knew to be imminent, he became less direct in his efforts to prepare the American people for what was coming. Rather than frontally talk about the threat of fascism, he focused instead on trying to educate the public about how alien fascist ideology was to America's core values: freedom of speech, freedom of religion, freedom to develop one's talents in the workplace and have laborers' rights respected.

Roosevelt's efforts in this direction were more than vindicated by the outright course of aggression now pursued by both Germany and Japan. With brazen disregard for international law, Hitler marched into Austria in 1938, declaring the two nations now a single entity. Soon, he was claiming the right to Sudetenland, a German-speaking province in Czechoslovakia, which then led to the infamous Munich meeting in September 1938 where the British and French prime ministers agreed to one final territorial acquisition by Germany as a price worth paying for "peace in our time." Hitler, of course, had no intention of halting his march to world domination. Occupying the rest of Czechoslovakia by the spring of 1939, he then mounted threats against Poland, even though both Britain and France said they would go to war if Poland were attacked. Cleverly avoiding the possibility that the Soviet Union and the West might combine forces against him, Hitler then signed a nonaggression pact with the USSR and proceeded on September 1 with the wanton invasion of Poland. World War II in Europe had begun. Although the Neutrality Act prohibited the United States from taking any immediate action, FDR declared, unlike Wilson a quarter of a century earlier, "I cannot ask that every American remain neutral in thought."

In Asia, meanwhile, Japan persisted in expanding her empire. Intent at last on making that expansion more difficult, the United States chose to deny Japan the oil and steel purchases from America that Japan needed to fuel her imperialism. Faced with growing U.S. intransigence, Japan had to make a choice between either giving up her territorial ambitions or finding new supplies of the goods she needed. Now under the control of an aggressive military regime, the Japanese government chose to expand its aggression into Southeast Asia, seizing the capital of Vietnam and preparing to conquer the Dutch East Indies. In response, FDR imposed U.S. control over all Japanese assets in the United States and awaited the next fateful step.

In Europe, Hitler ended the six-month "phony war" that ensued after his takeover of Poland and launched the blitzkrieg that swept across Belgium, Holland, and into France. The Western Allies, as if fighting the last war, had devoted their resources to reinforcing the "Maginot Line," the battlefield Germany had chosen in 1914. This time, German tanks and troops sped around the Maginot Line, circumventing Allied defenses, routing the opposition, and preparing to occupy Paris even before the Allies knew what had happened. In what was literally a "miracle," British troops and equipment managed to escape across the channel from Dunkirk in thousands of boats and sailing vessels manned by volunteers from England who came to the rescue. But there then followed the nightly horror of German bombing attacks on London, testing as they had never been tested before the English people's resolve to endure, survive, and fight back. With CBS News reporter Edward

R. Murrow reporting by radio each night from a London under incessant attack, the American people began to have an immediate sense of how close this war was to their own lives and future.

Faced with what he had long known would become a reality, Roosevelt responded with courage, imagination, and genius. He met with the new British prime minister, Winston Churchill, on a destroyer off the coast of Newfoundland to chart strategy for the alliance they knew was soon to come. Sailors from the two countries worshipped together on deck on Sunday morning as the choirs from two countries separated by three thousand miles sang hymns from their common religious tradition, as if to highlight the values shared by two countries born of the same family. Churchill and Roosevelt announced to the world the results of their deliberations in the Atlantic Charter, a resonant call to ideological arms, pledging both nations to fight for the universal values that each espoused and that were hallowed in the Magna Charta and the Declaration of Independence: freedom of speech, religion, and economic opportunity. Dedicated to a new world order, precisely of the kind FDR had talked about in his Quarantine speech, the two leaders presumed what was yet to happen: that they would stand side by side in a war to preserve all the most cherished values of the Western world against the tyranny of Nazi aggression.

To add substance to rhetoric, FDR now employed his legendary political skill to get aid to the British. Again using his homely analogies, he told the American people that when a neighbor's house burst into flames, and the neighbor had no fire hose, the only right thing to do was to lend him a hose until the fire was out and then take the hose back. Similarly, Roosevelt declared, when Britain (and soon Russia, which Hitler chose to invade in the summer of 1941) desperately needed the wherewithal to survive, it was only fair for her neighbor, the United States, to "lend and lease" the food, munitions, ships, and planes needed to carry on the battle. With the Neutrality Act no longer in effect (it had been repealed), Congress endorsed the "lend/lease" plan resoundingly. Soon thereafter, Roosevelt proposed "trading" the right to use various British bases in Bermuda and the Caribbean for sending more than fifty destroyers to England to help the British defend their country.

In the meantime, FDR did whatever he could to force the Germans into an outright military confrontation. American naval vessels were assigned to escort the lend/lease convoys sending American munitions to England and Russia. The American ships were ordered to fire on any German vessels attacking the convoys. Systematically, American destroyers dropped depth charges on suspected German submarines lurking in the sea channels waiting to ambush the lend/lease merchant vessels. The war may not have been declared yet, but it was clearly only a battle away.

As fate would have it, the armed attack that triggered full-scale war came not in the Atlantic but in the Pacific. The United States had long since determined that conflict with Japan was inevitable as long as Japanese aggression continued. But virtually every American military person believed that the

Japanese would first launch a military assault on Southeast Asia. No one imagined that Japan either could, or would, dream of launching an assault on the American naval base in Hawaii. But the Japanese, emboldened by their success, struck on the brilliant idea that if they could destroy American naval power in the Pacific with one mighty blow, the United States would never choose, or be able, to intervene militarily to prevent Japan's imperial ambitions. (It was, in effect, the same kind of gamble Germany had undertaken when it embarked on unrestricted submarine warfare in 1917.) Hence, the secret plans to send thousands of Japanese airplanes over the Pacific to drop their lethal bomb loads on Pearl Harbor. Caught totally unaware, with American planes lined up side by side like ducks in a shooting gallery, the Japanese bombers arrived over Pearl Harbor at dawn on December 7, 1941, and pulverized the American ships and planes. More than three thousand lives were lost, virtually every ship sunk or seriously damaged, the entire fleet of planes devastated. Only the fact that several aircraft carriers had left port prevented the complete annihilation of the Pacific Fleet.

By early afternoon on Sunday, the nation faced a world totally new and terrifying. What Roosevelt long had feared had finally become a reality not just for him but for all those millions of American citizens who had been reluctant to face the prospect of renewed world conflagration. Japan and Germany had earlier signed a pact to join in common cause. When FDR went before Congress to ask for a declaration of war against Japan for the Pearl Harbor attack—"a day that will live in infamy"—he knew that within hours, the country would be involved in war with Germany and Italy as well.

It was a moment he had long believed would come to pass. And it posed a test to his leadership even greater than that represented by the Great Depression.

VII. CONCLUSION

Franklin Roosevelt's New Deal represented the culmination of the Progressive Era's new focus on the state as a pivotal presence in national life. Using the "analogue" of being in a situation parallel to war, the president established for the federal government the right to become a central player in regulating the nation's industrial, commercial, and agricultural life. Because of that dramatic intervention, the New Deal also created the foundation for all subsequent efforts in the twentieth century to improve the social welfare infrastructure of the country—efforts that led to Medicare, federal aid to education, the war on poverty, and civil rights legislation. Because of those innovations, some historians have concluded that FDR's New Deal represented a "revolution" in American politics.

More on target is the assertion by New Deal historian William E. Leuchtenburg that the New Deal was at best a "halfway revolution." Always based on a capitalist framework—and dedicated to preserving the free enterprise system—the New Deal sought not the redistribution of wealth and resources among the American people but stability for the status quo. Under FDR, the federal government became a "broker state," balancing competing interests but focusing more on regulation than reform. Big business, big agriculture, and big banking benefited the most from New Deal intervention. The poor and disenfranchised received greater recognition than in the past, including welfare payments and government jobs—but they did not receive a larger share of the national wealth or greater influence over the nation's political agenda. Under Roosevelt, the state was a "parallelogram of pressure groups"—those who already had power achieved sustained acknowledgment of that power, but those with neither economic resources nor political clout continued to struggle to be seen.

Only in the case of organized labor did a substantive shift in power occur. Based on a powerful grassroots insurgency within industries like automobiles, rubber, steel, and textiles, a new militancy emerged in protest against the staid, crafts/guild structure of the American Federation of Labor. The Wagner Act of 1935 provided the federal protection that made it possible for that militancy to prevail, enabled the Congress of Industrial Organizations (CIO) to be created, and opened the door for a politically progressive and powerful labor presence to join the "parallelogram of pressure groups." But FDR had no part in the passage of that legislation, except to acquiesce in its enactment once it became clear that there was no choice.

Most New Deal legislation, on the other hand, did not materially alter the condition of that "one third of the nation" who were ill-housed, ill-clothed, and ill-fed. Despite the PWA (Public Works Administration), CWA, and WPA, only a portion of the unemployed received work assistance. At least in part because of the AAA's focus on helping the largest farmers, sharecroppers and tenant farmers actually suffered during the New Deal, millions being forced off the land because the AAA paid big farmers to take their land out of production. Meanwhile, the greatest defenders of sharecroppers were fired from their jobs in the AAA for advocating too strenuously for the poor. The vaunted "Soak the Rich Tax," which allegedly sought to take money from the rich to give to the poor, produced nothing in the way of income redistribution. The Home Owners Loan Corporation, theoretically designed to protect citizens' homes from foreclosure, offered no protection to the unemployed. Social Security—by any measurement surely one of the most important New Deal achievements—nevertheless was based on a regressive form of taxation and left uncovered those in the poorest jobs such as farm laborers, domestics, and the self-employed.

The experience of blacks and of women suggested the degree to which the New Deal was more a time of partial reform than far-reaching substantive change. African Americans constituted a disproportionate number of the sharecroppers and tenant farmers forced off the land by the AAA. Although the New Deal boasted a "black cabinet" of African Americans and white sympathizers who sought to look out for the interests of blacks, New Deal programs like the TVA and the CCC (Civilian Conservation Corps) practiced clear racial discrimination, the Federal Housing Authority failed to back up mortgages of blacks if they lived in white neighborhoods, and the federal government did nothing to intervene in repeated episodes of violence against blacks in the South. FDR refused even to endorse a federal antilynching law because of his fear of alienating powerful Southerners who chaired most of the major committees in Congress. Clearly, there were many reasons that, starting in 1934, black Americans shifted their allegiance to the Democratic Party. Thirty percent were receiving some form of federal relief; blacks had strong allies in the administration, including the First Lady—who in 1939 intervened when the Daughters of the American Revolution refused to permit black opera star Marian Anderson to sing in Constitution Hall and arranged for her instead to sing at the Lincoln Memorial—and for the first time, issues of civil rights were not simply ignored at the White House. But progress in some areas did not amount to transformation.

Women experienced similarly mixed results. With Eleanor Roosevelt in the lead, women reformers flocked to Washington to take on important government positions. Departments like Labor, the National Youth Administration, and the WPA featured women in critical roles. Mary Anderson,

Racism remained a dominant presence in American life during the 1930s, typified by the refusal of the Daughters of the American Revolution to grant permission for opera star Marian Anderson to perform at the DAR's Constitution Hall. Outraged Americans, black and white, protested, and Eleanor Roosevelt, the First Lady, arranged for Anderson to perform at the Lincoln Memorial instead.

Credit: Associated Press

director of the Women's Bureau, commented that whereas in the past, women government officials in Washington needed only a small room for a meeting, now they required an auditorium. The First Lady held special press conferences for women reporters only, became the president's eyes and ears as she traveled the country to assess the effectiveness of New Deal programs, and wrote a daily newspaper column ("My Day") that highlighted her views on all the issues of the day, political as well as familial. Aligning herself visibly with women garment workers, female reformers, and petitioners for black civil rights, ER created a powerful presence for women and activists inside the inner circle of the White House.

Yet despite this, women continued to be persistent victims of official discrimination. Little was done to puncture the myth that women were working for "pin money," not family subsistence. From 1933 forward, a federal civil service regulation made it illegal for a husband and wife both to be employees of the federal government—a regulation that virtually always meant it was the woman who lost her job. More than 75 percent of all school districts fired a woman if she got married. Women recipients of federal relief jobs worked for less pay than men, were forced into sex-segregated and stereotyped types of work, and received less than their fair share of available positions. The very presence of some change highlighted, ironically, the persistence of a far larger pattern of discrimination.

In all of this, the gains of the "halfway revolution" were important to acknowledge. Never before had issues of women's rights, racial inequality, and recognition of workers' just demands received so much attention from a national administration. Comparing the policies and philosophical outlook of the Grover Cleveland and Franklin Roosevelt administrations was like contrasting night and day. Whatever advances Theodore Roosevelt and Woodrow Wilson had made in aligning themselves with a more progressive role for the state in regulating social welfare and the economy were eclipsed entirely by the New Deal. A brand-new policy paradigm had come into play: henceforth, government would be a central *and overt* actor in all that happened in the economy. There was also a new political paradigm, the New Deal coalition, where labor, immigrants, farmers, workers, urbanites, and intellectuals would forge common bonds based on what each could bring to a winning combination.

At the center of all these changes was Franklin Delano Roosevelt. With a personality forged by both the charm of his upbringing and the suffering of his struggle with polio, Roosevelt shared an empathy with his fellow citizens uniquely suited to the time and place in which they found each other. Few have ever demonstrated such political skill or emotional sensitivity. Roosevelt knew what to say and when to say it. He united the country behind the early New Deal by persuading everyone that this was a crisis as profound as war, requiring a similar response of patriotism and sacrifice. When that time had passed, with equal skill he took up the banner of reform, portraying himself as a crusading advocate for justice against the "malefactors of wealth" and the "economic royalists." Although—atypically—he failed abysmally in turning his electoral victory in 1936 into a policy triumph in the second term because of his court-packing faux pas, Roosevelt was a consummate practitioner of the *politics of gesture*. His rhetoric conveyed an image of change, which—for many of his listeners—became conflated with the belief that the substance of change had occurred as well. That skill helped explain why so many Americans assumed that the country had been transformed by the New Deal, even though in structural ways, almost nothing had changed at all: the Depression did not end until World War II, there was no "shift" in income or wealth, and the "parallelogram of interest groups" remained largely intact.

But a "halfway revolution" was far better than none, and as the nation approached a crisis even more severe than the one it had just endured, the American people also were prepared to do something they had never even contemplated before—elect a president for a third term. Franklin Roosevelt had now made himself almost indistinguishable from the nation he led. And so, despite the conflicts of his second term, and recent conservative victories, when Franklin Roosevelt determined that he would offer to lead the country through its next moment of truth, the verdict was a resounding yes. The question was whether Roosevelt could lead the country through its most profound international crisis with the same success and fortitude he had demonstrated responding to the Great Depression.

6

World War II: 1941–1945

N ever before had America mobilized so totally. In what became, from today's perspective, the nation's "last good war," millions of citizens bought war bonds, volunteered for civilian defense, donated blood, rushed to enlist in the armed forces, and enthusiastically dedicated virtually every waking hour to helping defeat the Axis powers. The Japanese attack on Pearl Harbor galvanized people of all political persuasions; ended the debate on national preparedness; and set in motion changes in the nation's economy, social relations, and geopolitical presence that can only be described as seismic. Much of what was to come in the next half century could be traced back to the war: the Cold War, unprecedented affluence, the transformative struggle for black civil rights, massive demographic and educational changes, a revolution in sex roles. It was the beginning of a new nation.

I. THE MILITARY STRUGGLE

The Japanese attack on Pearl Harbor left America's military forces devastated. Against sometimes overwhelming opposition, Franklin Roosevelt had systematically sought larger military appropriations and a stronger army, knowing that at some point it would be necessary to do battle with fascist tyranny. By only one vote had reinstatement of the military draft passed Congress. Now the nation understood the reasons for the commander in chief's concern. Two-thirds of the Pacific Fleet was gone, over two thousand sailors and soldiers killed, the American air force decimated by the Japanese raids. Within weeks, Thailand, Singapore, Guam, Hong Kong, and Borneo had fallen to Japanese forces, and by the end of December, General Douglas MacArthur—vowing "I shall return"—had been forced to evacuate Manila and the Philippines. Never in the history of America had there been such a staccato series of defeats. The Japanese ruled East Asia, from Rangoon west to British India, south to the waters surrounding Australia. With brilliant air, naval, and marine attacks, Emperor Hirohito seemed in command.

In the European theater, meanwhile, German fortunes continued to soar. By dint of their courage and genius, the British had managed to save their army by evacuating soldiers across the English Channel from Dunkirk after they were surrounded by German forces. But bombing raids continued to scar London and other population sites on a nightly basis, and when German troops captured Tobruk in North Africa in June 1942, fears escalated that Egypt would soon fall, opening the way for German forces to go all the way to India. Russia, meanwhile, was enduring savage attacks. German troops surrounded Stalingrad, causing hundreds of thousands of deaths by starvation—just a small portion of the eventual Soviet toll of more than twenty million dead, by far the largest sacrifice of any Allied power.

But then, in both theaters of war, the tide started to turn, a product both of the huge military machine the United States had mobilized and of exquisite planning by commanders in the field. In the Pacific, the Japanese chose— unwisely—not to consolidate their victories but rather to extend their attacks and try to complete their decimation of the American navy. This bold ambition soon turned sour. Admiral Nimitz's carrier-based planes destroyed four Japanese warships in the Battle of Midway in June 1942, forcing the Japanese navy to withdraw; soon thereafter, American marines landed at Guadalcanal. After seven major naval battles and countless casualties, the Japanese finally evacuated Guadalcanal in February 1943. The allies had proven they could stand up to, and overcome, the once invincible Japanese army and navy. No longer on the defensive, America's armed forces now embarked on their long journey northward toward Tokyo.

The European theater proved more complicated. Sensitive to the desperate plight of the Soviet army, FDR favored a cross-channel invasion of France in 1942, which would force Hitler to divert troops from the Soviet front. But Churchill, ever conscious of the huge losses of British soldiers in France during World War I, persuaded Roosevelt that a safer option was to invade North Africa. And so in late October, Allied forces under the overall direction of General Dwight D. Eisenhower invaded Oran, Algiers, and Casablanca while General Sir Bernard Montgomery led British troops against Rommel. The pro-Fascist Vichy regime quickly negotiated a surrender. By the time Churchill and Roosevelt met in Casablanca in early 1943 to plan the next stages of the war, Egypt had been saved, the Mediterranean was no longer Mussolini's backyard, and the Russians had turned the tide at the decisive battle of Stalingrad. In the long history of human warfare, Stalingrad would take its place alongside Gettysburg and Waterloo as a decisive turning point as well as a testament to human suffering.

By May 1943, Rommel's forces in Tunisia had been cornered, and 275,000 German troops surrendered to the Allies. North Africa was cleared of the enemy, the spliced lifeline of the British Empire to India through the Suez Canal made it possible to reinforce Russia via the Persian Gulf, and the way was open at last for a strike at what Churchill mistakenly called the "soft underbelly" of Europe. Within two months, a quarter of a million troops had invaded Sicily, dismaying the 350,000 Italian and German defenders, who by August 17 had retreated to the mainland. There, however, German troops resisted mightily, giving the lie to Churchill's notion of a "soft underbelly." In the mud and frost of that miserable campaign, wrote the war correspondent Ernie Pyle, GIs "lived like men of prehistoric times, and a club would have become them more than a machine gun." It took nearly a year, until June 4, 1944, before the Fifth Army entered Rome.

In the meantime, Britain and the United States were laying the groundwork for the long-promised second front in France. By 1944 more than 14 million people were in the armed forces—3 out of every 4 men ages 18–32 served in the military during the war. The industrial output of America was twice that of all the Axis nations, a tribute to the phenomenal capacity of the American war machine. In 1939 America's airplane industry had employed fewer than 47,000 people and produced fewer than 6,000 planes. Five years later, the industry employed 2,102,000 workers and rolled out more than 96,000 planes. With a group of "dollar-a-year" economic "czars" presiding over key industries like oil and rubber, the Office of War Mobilization transformed the American economy into a smooth-running, powerfully organized military machine capable of producing enough planes, tanks, and ships to defeat any power on earth.

By making significant progress in the Battle of the Atlantic, American planes and ships enabled all that military hardware to reach its destination. During the first eleven months of 1941, German vessels sank over 3.6 million tons of supplies, and in 1942 nearly two hundred ships were destroyed between January and April, some as close as thirty miles to New York City. But by 1943 the tide had turned. New radar and sonar technology made it easier to identify U-boats, and despite massive new deployments of German subs, a larger and larger number of convoys successfully completed their voyages to Britain and the Soviet Union. Meanwhile, English and American airplanes bombarded German positions in France and Germany. An incendiary bomb attack against Hamburg in the summer of 1943 wiped out over half the city, killing almost forty-three thousand people, while deployment of hundreds of planes shipped from America helped give the Allies a thirty-to-one superiority over the German air force. The stage was set for D day.

Never before in modern times had an invading army crossed the English Channel against opposition. Hitler's coastal defenses were formidable: underwater obstacles, artillery emplacements, wire entanglements and land mines—all backed up by 58 German divisions. Yet the Allies had reason for confidence. Allied planes had smashed roads and bridges. Thirty-nine divisions and 11,000 planes were ready for the initial landings, supported by a naval fleet overwhelmingly superior to anything the Germans could deploy. More than 600 warships, with 176,000 troops from a dozen different ports, set sail for the Norman coast, ready at long last to fulfill America's promise to Russia for a second front.

The first assault troops touched down at 6:30 in the morning, achieving tactical surprise. Others, such as those who landed at Omaha Beach, encountered a maze of mined underwater obstacles, with hundreds drowning or caught in a vicious cross fire from German concrete pillboxes. But all in all, the D day assault was a brilliant success. In a single week the Allies landed 326,000 men, 50,000 vehicles, and over 100,000 tons of supplies. "The history of war," Stalin declared, "does not know any undertaking so broad in conception, so grandiose in scale, and so masterly in execution." Within three months, Paris had been liberated, and General Charles de Gaulle—leader of

No moment better typified the courage, mass mobilization, and logistical effectiveness of Allied troops in World War II than D Day. Here Allied troops are depicted advancing on a beach in Normandy, France, on June 6, 1944. Within a year, Nazi Germany had surrendered.

Credit: © dpa/Corbis

the Free French government in exile—triumphantly entered the city. By the end of October, all France had been cleared of the enemy and Allied armies stood poised for their advance into Germany.

Although Hitler mounted a desperate counteroffensive through the Ardennes Forest in December 1944, by January Allied forces had resumed their advance toward the Rhine, while the Russians, moving on a thousand-mile front, swept toward Germany in a gigantic pincer movement that inflicted over a million German casualties. As the Allied armies drove deep into Germany, Austria, and Poland, they came upon one concentration camp after another—Buchenwald, Dachau, Belsen, Auschwitz—which sickened all who saw them. There, Hitler had exterminated six million Jews, engaging with scientific calculation in a campaign of genocide that constituted the greatest crime against humanity ever committed. Nothing crystallized more clearly the reason the war against fascism had to be fought.

Now victory was in sight. From the west, British and French troops rolled unopposed to the Elbe, while from the east, the Russians thrust toward Berlin. On April 25, in a deep bunker, Adolf Hitler took a gun, killed his mistress, and then shot himself. Two weeks later, the Germans signed an unconditional surrender, and General Eisenhower called his boss, General Omar Bradley with the news: "D day plus 335," Bradley wrote. "I walked to the window....Outside the sun was climbing into the sky. The war in Europe had ended."

Events in the Pacific moved less quickly yet culminated in an explosion that forever changed the world. After MacArthur fulfilled his pledge to return to the Philippines in October 1944, the Japanese risked everything in one last naval battle, sending their entire fleet into Leyte Gulf. Despite an enormous toll in casualties in the ensuing struggle, the Americans annihilated a naval force ten times larger than their own. Soon thereafter came the marine landing on Iwo Jima in February 1945, then the launching of nonstop bombing raids on the Japanese mainland, and finally the invasion of Okinawa. In this war of attrition, however, American generals feared it might take eighteen more months of battle and one hundred thousand casualties before victory was finally achieved.

That apprehension highlighted the pivotal importance of research that had begun four years earlier on a secret new weapon. In 1939 a group of scientists headed by Albert Einstein—all political refugees from Nazi tyranny—warned Roosevelt that the Germans were moving full speed ahead on using atomic fission to develop a nuclear chain reaction that would create an atom bomb. Quickly, FDR set up a scientific team to promote the "Manhattan Project," with a special laboratory in Los Alamos, New Mexico, headed by physicist J. Robert Oppenheimer. Working at a feverish pace, the scientists perfected a weapon that was tested for the first time in the New Mexico desert on July 16, 1945. A blinding flash illuminated the desert, and an enormous fireball, changing colors from deep purple to orange to "unearthly green" erupted skyward, followed by a huge column of smoke rising from the ground in the form of a mushroom-shaped cloud. In awed silence at what he had helped create, Oppenheimer recalled the words of the Bhagavad-Gita: "I am become Death, the shatterer of worlds." Another scientist commented, "This was the nearest to doomsday one can possibly imagine. I am sure that at the end of the world—in the last millisecond of the earth's existence—the last man will see something very similar to what we have seen."

Within days, American leaders determined to use the bomb against Japan, short-circuiting the war of attrition the generals had predicted. On August 6, the *Enola Gay*, a B-29 bomber, dropped the atom bomb on Hiroshima. Pilots and crewmen witnessed the same horrific display of light, heat, and destruction Oppenheimer had seen three weeks earlier. More than 60,000 people were killed immediately. Dreadfully burned survivors moved silently through the city, holding their arms out before them to prevent the burned surfaces from touching, hoping desperately that someone could ease their pain. Three days later, a second atomic bomb was exploded over Nagasaki, killing 36,000 more Japanese. Together, the two explosions altered irretrievably the present and future of every nation's diplomacy and military planning. Five days after Nagasaki, Emperor Hirohito announced he would accept the Allies' demand for Japan's unconditional surrender. World War II had come to an end.

II. THE WARTIME ECONOMY

In 1939, the United States remained mired in Depression. Nearly 20 percent of the workforce was unemployed. Despite the New Deal's success in creating massive new programs of unemployment insurance, Social Security, supports for agriculture, and protection for labor, the national economy appeared paralyzed, unable either to use the entrepreneurial energies of capitalism or the newly active role of government intervention to rebound into prosperity. No consensus existed on how best to proceed—spend more or balance the budget, give the government greater power, or curtail its excesses? Despite seven years of experimentation with alternative public policies, nothing was guaranteed to work. Indeed, the recession of 1938 hurled the country into a state of insecurity and instability as bad as that which existed when Roosevelt had first taken office.

Now all that changed. The defense crisis, like jumper cables on a dead battery, kick-started a moribund economy with new energy, resources, and creativity surging through the workforce. Even before America entered the war, military spending skyrocketed, reaching almost seventy-five million dollars a day by the time of Pearl Harbor. Unemployment disappeared as workers flocked to new wartime jobs. With the government offering contracts that guaranteed profits, companies poured money into research and technology, creating new methods of mechanization that increased worker productivity at a rate far in excess of what would normally have been anticipated.

The shipbuilding industry exemplified the transformation. The genius of ship construction, Henry J. Kaiser, trimmed the time for turning out merchant ships from 105 days to 46, then to 29, then to 14. By the end of 1942, Kaiser's Richmond, California, shipyard launched the *Robert E. Peary* in 4 days, 15.5 hours. Merchant shipping construction that had amounted to 1 million tons in 1941 surpassed 19 million tons by 1943.

In a full-employment economy, paychecks went through the same upward spiral as production. Salaries and wages more than doubled between 1939 and 1944, with average incomes in Hartford going from $2,207 to $5,208 and in Los Angeles from $2,031 to $3,469. As a result of increased wages, purchasing power skyrocketed, with average sales at department stores leaping fivefold. Taking advantage of the government's focus on a stable workforce, trade unions seized the initiative in organizing more workers, with membership in organized labor jumping by 50 percent from 10 million workers in 1941 to 15 million in 1945. These changes, in turn, led to two other critical developments. Personal savings increased dramatically, growing by nearly 300 percent in four years and providing the resources that would be critical to the postwar economic boom, when refrigerators, automobiles, and washing machines were once again available. And for the first time in the twentieth century, there was a move toward greater equity in income distribution, with the top 5 percent of the nation declining in its share of the national income (from 22 to 17 percent) while the bottom 40 percent increased their share of the economic pie.

In all of this, government played an ever increasing role. To pay the wartime bills, taxation grew dramatically. Before the war, fewer than four million Americans paid individual income taxes. Now, three years later, that figure exploded tenfold. For the first time a system of federal withholding taxes came into being, and tax rates for the richest Americans increased to 94 percent of total net income. The War Labor Board helped ensure unions would continue to grow, while the Office of War Mobilization, under former Supreme Court Judge James F. Byrnes, helped regulate economic production, making sure that pivotal industries such as oil and rubber could function effectively. In 1942, FDR created the Office of Price Administration (OPA), which, in effect, dictated what Americans could buy at the store. From coffee to gasoline to the amount of rubber used in undergarments, rationing became the rule of the day with American consumers told exactly how much of which product they would be allowed to purchase. Newspaper advertisements testified to the degree to which these kinds of government controls had entered the broader culture: "No girdle required for this dress of tobacco brown spun rayon," one ad declared, "with no fastenings (zippers gone to war)...." To help matters along, the government's Office of War Information helped mold public opinion in support of the struggle, using films, posters, and radio broadcasts to mobilize the home front. Lest anyone get grumpy about unnecessary sacrifices, there was always the film showing a wounded GI pleading with his family not to waste food. "We haven't had anything but a little horsemeat and rice for days," the soldier says, "and kitchen fats mom. Don't waste any. Kitchen fats make glycerin and glycerin makes explosives. Two pounds of fat can fire five anti-tank shells." With such reminders, how could civilians not decry selfishness and sign up to buy another war bond?

Never had an economic and political machine functioned with such efficiency. The nation had been transformed from economic paralysis to lean, streamlined, record-shattering productivity. Everyone had a job, every job had a purpose, and every paycheck created purchasing power that would fuel a consumer explosion once normality had returned. It was a world totally different from that which existed in 1939. And the war had made that happen.

III. SOCIAL CHANGE

During the heart of the Great Depression, the federal government passed a law requiring that if two spouses worked in civil service jobs, one had to resign. Implicit, though never stated, was the assumption this would be the wife. Three-quarters of all school districts in the nation required that a woman resign her job as a teacher if she married. According to a Gallup Poll, the vast majority of Americans, male and female, agreed that married women should not work because their employment might take jobs away from men—the traditional "breadwinners." In short, a national consensus seemed to exist: a fundamental inconsistency existed between women's "natural" role—that of housewife and mother—and pursuit of a job or career.

World War II changed all that too—at least for the moment. The government that a few years earlier had discouraged women from employment now loudly proclaimed it was a "patriotic duty" for women to join the war effort. "Men are needed at the battlefront," an Office of War Information filmstrip declared. "Women are needed at the home front...with attention for their work undivided." "Rosie the Riveter" became a new national heroine. In response to the wartime crisis, more than 6.5 million women took jobs for the first time, increasing the female labor force by 57 percent. Most important, more than 75 percent of these women were married, and 60 percent were over thirty-five years of age and from the middle class—a direct contradiction to the previous ethos that women who worked were young, single, and poor.

Once more, the shipbuilding industry highlighted the contrast. In late 1939, only 36 women worked in shipyards. Two years later, that figure reached into the stratosphere—160,000 women welding hatches, riveting gun emplacements, binding keels on the ships that were to carry the arsenal

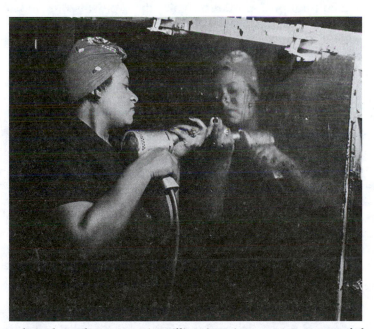

In unprecedented numbers, over six million American women answered the call to serve their country during World War II by entering the labor force. Many became munitions workers, including the widely acclaimed "Rosie the Riveter." Here we see a woman riveter in Nashville, Tennessee in 1942.

Credit: The Granger Collection, New York.

of democracy. In the long years ahead, Erwin Canham of the *Christian Science Monitor* observed, "we will remember these short years of ordeal as a period when women rose to full stature."

It was too soon to declare a revolution, however. Even as women's entry into the labor force dramatically altered past patterns, traditional forms of discrimination persisted with astonishing strength. Notwithstanding the number of women breaking into new jobs like building airplanes, huge numbers continued to occupy sex-segregated positions. Thousands became clerical workers for the government. Moreover, women were still being described in stereotypical language. "Women excel at processes of a painstaking or repetitive nature," Mary Anderson of the Women's Bureau declared, "those requiring finger dexterity—the ability to stick at a tedious job without flagging." Despite the War Labor Board's endorsement of equal pay for women, most women continued to receive less than men, employers using such devices as substituting "heavy" and "light" for "male" and "female." In 1945, as five years earlier, women in manufacturing earned only 65 percent of what men earned.

Nor did the federal government act decisively on the central issue of childcare centers and community services for women workers. Surveys showed that as many as 25 percent of the new female war workers had at least one child needing care during the workday. But providing such care violated deeply held cultural presumptions. Again, the Women's Bureau itself reinforced such views. "In this time of crisis," the bureau declared, "mothers of young children can make no finer contribution to the strength of the nation than to assure their children the security of the home, individual care and affection." In the end, the Lanham Act provided some federal funds to build daycare centers in 1943, but at its most effective, the program offered care to only 10 percent of those needing it.

In the end, therefore, a profound tension existed between apparently transformative changes on the one hand and deeply imbedded patterns of discrimination on the other. Millions of women found that they enjoyed the experience of working and wanted to continue after the war. "Women must get it out of their heads [that they belong in the home]," one government advisor said. "We are in the throes of a stupendous social revolution. Because of their work in the war, [women] will come to feel that they are socially useful. They will want to continue that feeling of independence." Yet the perpetuation of sex stereotyping, the clustering of women in "women only" jobs, and the absence of equal pay cast doubt on the permanence of the changes that had occurred. "Legal equality...between the sexes is not possible," Secretary of Labor Frances Perkins commented, "because men and women are not identical in physical structure or social function, and therefore their needs cannot be identical." A dramatic revision of sex roles had started. But would it continue?

The experience of black Americans during the war revealed a similar pattern: radical changes on the one hand and an ongoing pervasiveness of demeaning racism on the other. For generations after *Plessy v. Ferguson*, when segregation became the law of the land, blacks had struggled to inch their way forward against stupendous odds. Deprived of their right to vote; denied any jobs other than domestic servant or common laborer (except in the black community); systematically humiliated by paying at the front of the bus, then having to enter through the back door, blacks in the South nevertheless continued to strengthen their own institutions, go the extra mile to send their children to school, fight back—in whatever way they safely could—the meanness of whites. The New Deal had helped, primarily by making blacks eligible for relief payments. In addition, Eleanor Roosevelt had become an ally in the equal rights struggle, an informal "black cabinet" came into existence in Washington, and groups like the NAACP and the National Negro Congress redoubled their efforts to mount a black protest movement. Still, with 75 percent of the black population living in the South, primarily in rural areas, progress was often hard to discern.

Now the war intervened, jolting the racial status quo in ways that laid the foundation for the civil rights struggle. Hundreds of thousands of Southern blacks moved either to cities in the South or to the North and West to seek new jobs—two million in all by 1950. Women might be the first called to serve in industrial jobs to meet the wartime crisis, but blacks were not far behind. Everyone was needed, and suddenly, the desperate shortage of labor opened up the possibility that blacks could be considered for jobs other than that of janitor in war factories. The possibility fused brilliantly with a newfound militancy among black protest organizations. A. Philip Randolph, head of the all black Brotherhood of Sleeping Car Porters Union, mobilized an all-black coalition to demand that the federal government mandate a policy of nondiscrimination in hiring defense workers. Invoking Roosevelt's rhetoric about fighting a war for freedom and against tyranny, Randolph created a March on Washington Movement (MOWM), declaring, "WE LOYAL NEGRO AMERICANS DEMAND THE RIGHT TO WORK AND FIGHT FOR OUR COUNTRY." Threatening to bring as many as fifty thousand blacks to demonstrate in the nation's capital if his protests were not answered, Randolph mobilized his allies in the Roosevelt administration. Under the pressure of Eleanor Roosevelt and her friends, the president acquiesced and in June 1941 issued Executive Order 8802 creating the President's Committee on Fair Employment Practices to ensure that "there shall be no discrimination in the employment of workers in defense industries or government because of race, creed, color, or national origin."

Although the FEPC often proved less effective than Randolph wished, the combination of federal policy and wartime needs transformed the employment situation, opening new jobs for blacks in industrial occupations as well as helping others, such as Mexican Americans, get new jobs in factories in Los Angeles and shipyards in Galveston. Overall, the number of Negroes employed in manufacturing more than doubled, from 500,000 to 1.2 million. In iron and steel, blacks grew to more than 25 percent of the workforce. The number of Negro federal employees leaped 333 percent, to 200,000. Nearly half a million women who had been domestic servants left their jobs to take new positions in the wartime economy, with the proportion of employed black women who were servants falling from 72 to 48 percent. Black membership in trade unions doubled during the war, as did the number of Negroes who now worked as skilled craftsmen or foremen. On the other hand, racism persisted in most situations. Blacks were denied positions as conductors and trolley operators in Washington, D.C.—with the FEPC doing nothing about it. Blacks in industry were still primarily hired at lower-level positions, with whites often erupting in protest if employers made an effort to upgrade their positions. Many unions continued to exclude Negroes. Nevertheless, for the first time in half a century some change of a positive nature was happening.

That chemistry of seismic shifts occurring in the midst of persistent prejudice characterized every area of race relations, nowhere more clearly than in the armed forces. Although blacks enlisted in the war for democracy at a rate 60 percent higher than their proportion of the population, they virtually always encountered discrimination. "This is a white man's country," one Southern draft board declared, "the Negro had nothing to do with the settling of America." Everything was segregated, from church services to blood plasma. Army officials in the South were infamous for the meanness of their treatment of Negro soldiers, denying blacks access to sports and recreation facilities used by whites, standing silently by in Montgomery, Alabama, when a black army nurse was beaten up by whites for refusing to take a Jim Crow seat on a local bus. One episode in Salinas, Kansas, crystallized the absurdity blacks confronted each day. When Negro troops tried to enter a lunchroom, the manager said, "You boys know we don't serve colored here." So they stood inside the door, "staring at...German prisoners of war...having lunch at the counter." As one of the soldiers observed, "It was no jive talk. The people of Salinas served these enemy soldiers and turned away black American GIs."

Even in the army, though, some progress took place. Over time, more and more blacks were trained for combat positions—something that had been totally denied them at the beginning—and by 1944, black soldiers were distinguishing themselves, often in the company of whites, in lengthy battles with the Japanese and Germans. More and more black officers were trained, including the famous Tuskegee Air Corps, a segment of black pilots whose élan and battle accomplishments made them a national source of pride for black Americans. By the end of the war, black soldiers who might have experienced brutal racism in Southern training camps were serving in Britain, France, Germany, and Hawaii, where they were treated as equal citizens, honored for their participation in the common battle, and celebrated for their service. White officers might resist when black soldiers were invited by local whites to dances in British and French towns. But the black soldiers went, and tasted, often for the first time, what life without prejudice could be like.

The combination of America's idealistic rhetoric in the war for freedom and democracy and the tenacity of traditional racism helped fuel the black protest movement. The NAACP, which had done so much to fight racial injustice in the courts, had never enjoyed much success as a grassroots organization, largely because of the use of white terrorism to discourage black membership. Now the organization grew tenfold, from 50,000 to 500,000, as blacks felt newly empowered to claim openly their freedoms. "Negroes are organizing all over [North Carolina] to secure their rights," Roy Wilkins declared. "They are not frightened." The black press took on a new militancy as well. Led by journals like the *Pittsburgh Courier* and the *Chicago Defender*, black papers proclaimed their commitment to the "Double V" campaign—victory at home as well as victory abroad. With their circulation growing by 40 percent, these papers drove home the inextricable connection between defeating racist tyranny in Germany and assaulting racist tyranny in Mississippi. "We die together," one group of black protestors said, "Let's eat together." For the first time, black leaders openly talked about taking on the whole segregationist system. "We are fundamentally opposed to the principle and practice of compulsory segregation in our American society," an assemblage of black leaders declared in Durham, North Carolina. A new day was coming.

Highlighting the tensions created by this cauldron of change was the Detroit race riot of 1943. As much as anyplace in America, Detroit embodied the contradictions of ascending black aspirations and abiding white racism. Thousands of blacks migrated to the Motor City to take jobs. Housing was impossible to find. Whites exploded in protest when blacks, who in the North could vote and fully express themselves, were given promotions or better housing. Suddenly on a hot summer day it all came apart. Whites hurled rocks at a black swimmer at a local park who wandered into "white" waters. Rumors of racial murders spread like wildfire and a full-scale riot erupted, with seventy people dying and hundreds more suffering serious injury. In a nation where race had always been the festering contradiction separating democratic ideals and social practice, the Detroit riot heralded how difficult finding a way forward would be.

Thus, for blacks as for women, the war unleashed possibilities hitherto unimaginable, even as it drove home the endurance of abiding inequities. Victories were palpable—new jobs, the Tuskegee airmen, an FEPC, black congressmen, a new surge of protest organizations. But so too were defeats, from segregated blood supplies to the shooting of a black soldier in Durham, North Carolina, for daring to ask for courteous treatment on a bus, to being denied food at a restaurant that was serving German POWs. The irony was encapsulated by a slogan black draftees popularized about the epitaph that might accompany a fatally wounded black soldier: "Here lies a black man killed fighting a yellow man for the glory of the white man." Whether such bitter wisdom could inspire a movement for lasting racial justice was yet to be seen.

Other minority groups in America fared less well, notwithstanding the rhetoric of human rights that so infused wartime propaganda. In one of the most ignominious acts of the country's entire history, FDR issued Executive Order 9066 in February 1942 ordering the relocation of all Japanese Americans to areas far removed from any potential military target. The act reflected three interrelated causes: the ongoing racism against Asian Americans that had been part of America's history for more than half a century; the hysteria of a few politicians, panicked at the possibility of future Pearl Harbors; and the willingness of millions of average citizens to scapegoat a visibly distinctive minority in their midst rather than deal with the complexity of treating people as individuals. One general conflated all three. "A Jap is a Jap is a Jap," he declared. "It makes no difference whether he is an American citizen or not....I don't want any of them....There is no way to determine their loyalty."

As a result, more than one hundred thousand Japanese Americans, virtually all from the West Coast, were forcibly removed from their homes, lost their businesses and possessions, and were clustered in internment centers—America's concentration camps—hundreds of miles away from home. People who had fished the Pacific or farmed California's green belt now found themselves in dusty, barren barracks—no private toilets, no family dining spaces. Ironically, in the multiracial climate of Hawaii, where the Japanese assault took place, no such action occurred, and Japanese Americans continued to live with their neighbors as they always had. Eventually, a corps of Nisei Japanese Americans joined the American army and fought with heroic distinction in the war—just as did segregated groups of African Americans. But their countrymen and women huddled in internment camps, victims of what Justice Frank Murphy of the U.S. Supreme Court called a "legalization of racism." Only after the war did the Supreme Court finally rule that the incarceration of Japanese Americans had violated the Constitution of the United States. It was one of the most ignominious moments in all of American history.

Equally shameful was the ongoing presence of anti-Semitism in America. Magazines like *Fortune* continued to talk of Jewish "klannishness" and racist politicians declared that the entire war was a Jewish plot. But most distressing were the failures of the American government to act decisively to help the millions of Jews in Europe who were seeking escape. Knowledge of Hitler's "final solution" to the Jewish "problem" in the concentration camps of Auschwitz and Buchenwald had become widespread by 1942. Jewish groups held rallies seeking redress; rabbis and church leaders pleaded with people like Eleanor Roosevelt to intervene. And there were ways to help. In 1943, Romania agreed to evacuate seventy thousand Jews to the United States in return for a bribe of $170,000. But there was no will or commitment on the American side. State Department officials, some with a record of anti-Semitic remarks, obstructed the issuance of visas. Those in the department who protested found themselves transferred to other posts. As a result, hundreds of thousands of people who might potentially have been rescued were sent to their deaths instead. Appropriately, the State Department's internal investigation of what had occurred was entitled "Report to the Secretary on the Acquiescence of This Government in the Murder of the Jews."

Mexican Americans also experienced, on balance, more negative than positive consequences from the war. Given the shortage of agricultural labor in California (partly caused by the Japanese American internments),

One of America's most shameful acts during World War II was to round up and place in internment camps over one hundred thousand citizens of Japanese descent. Here we see a line of Japanese American internees preparing to have lunch in a prisonlike dining facility in the state of Washington.

Credit: Seattle Post-Intelligencer Collection; Museum of History and Industry/CORBIS

two hundred thousand Mexicans were brought to the country under the so-called bracero program. (As many as two million Mexicans, by contrast, were deported during the 1930s in order to make more jobs available to whites). With increased crowding and tensions in Mexican American neighborhoods in Los Angeles, riots broke out. American sailors attacked young Mexican Americans dressed in zoot suits, a distinctive form of dress adopted by young males called pachucos. The riots highlighted the nativism of many whites, particularly when a minority group like the pachucos visibly promoted their ethnic identity and pride by the clothes they wore. Like blacks, Mexican Americans bore a disproportionate share of the military burden— 25 percent of those on the Bataan death march were of Hispanic origin—yet their advances on human rights issues failed to reflect that reality.

Native Americans participated actively in the war as well, both in factories and in the military, but as a body of people they lost more than they gained. Hundreds of thousands of acres from their reservations were appropriated for bombing ranges while other reservations became the new homes for one-quarter of the Japanese American detainees.

Any event as momentous as a world war inevitably dislocates the status quo and puts into play multiple options for recasting relations between different groups of people. Aside from its extraordinary military and economic impact, World War II exercised perhaps its greatest influence on the behavior and aspirations of women and blacks, especially the latter. There could be no understating the dimension of the changes that had taken place—new economic and social roles for millions upon millions of women, a chance for African Americans to leave the prison of the South, challenge directly the horror of segregation, and feel the surge of empowerment that comes from occupying new space in a society that for so long had insisted that the only place for black Americans was at the bottom. There could be no gainsaying the tenacious commitment of millions to old patterns of prejudice or the burden of the tensions that came with changed aspirations and realities. But something had started that would in the end become one of the war's most precious and important legacies.

IV. THE POLITICAL SCENE

No less than in other spheres, politics in America conveyed two messages during the war years. Clearly, the state had become omnipresent, with government regulation extending to areas hitherto unknown. From the FEPC to the Office of War Information and the War Labor Board, Uncle Sam shaped the nation's thought and action more than ever before. Unions thrived, government propaganda films trumpeted the importance of racial tolerance, and national leaders such as Vice President Henry Wallace talked about the war as an opportunity to carry forward the struggle for social justice. The administration, one newspaper columnist wrote, was "trying to do two things at the same time—carry on a social revolution and conduct a war." As government expenditures increased—the country spent more in the war years than in its entire previous 154-year history—many saw an ongoing prospect of expanded social programs dedicated to making real the nation's commitment to be an equal opportunity society for all people.

Yet there was much to discomfort liberals, who were already in disarray after the defeat of Roosevelt's court-packing plan in 1937 and his failure to purge the Congress of conservatives in 1938. Not only did FDR announce the retirement of "Dr. New Deal" in favor of "Dr. Win-the-War." Those New Deal agencies that had been in the vanguard of social progressivism disappeared into oblivion: the Works Progress Administration, the Civilian Conservations Corps, the Farm Security Administration, which had done so much to help poor farmers, and the National Youth Administration, which had trained thousands of white and black young people in basic skills. Arguably, some of these programs were no longer needed in a full-employment economy. Still, their demise suggested a pattern of retrenchment from New Deal liberalism.

Consistent with that interpretation was the triumph of Republicans in the 1942 congressional elections, with forty new GOP seats in the House and five in the Senate. There followed the Smith-Connally bill, which authorized the president to seize plants if strikes interfered with wartime production, and increasingly strident conservative attacks on the Office of War Information for its liberal propaganda about social justice and on the National Resource Planning Board for its focus on increased expenditures for education and health care. The NRPB's agenda, the *Wall Street Journal* editorialized, represented a "totalitarian plan" to use the war as an instrument for achieving socialism. A new generation of "border state" Democrats, political scientist Samuel Lubell observed, were now in the ascendancy, a transition embodied in the replacement of liberal idealist Henry Wallace on the 1944 Democratic Party ticket as the party's vice-presidential nominee by Missouri Senator Harry S Truman, the personification of moderation.

The critical unknown, of course, was where Franklin Roosevelt wished to go. One straw in the wind was FDR's adoption of a liberal rhetoric reminiscent of his 1936 campaign. Roosevelt denounced a 1943 tax bill for "providing relief not to the needy, but for the greedy," exhorted Congress to pass substantially enhanced Social Security, unemployment, and educational benefits for veterans (what eventually became the GI Bill), and in 1944 urged Congress to enact a "second bill of rights under which a new basis for security and prosperity can be established for all." The 1944 presidential campaign mirrored the aggressiveness of this liberal legislative agenda. A heart attack, and the isolationism of most Republicans, forced "one-worlder" Wendell Wilkie from the race for the Republican nomination. New York "moderate" Thomas Dewey took his place but proved to be a colorless candidate. Meanwhile, FDR campaigned on a platform calling for an economy with sixty million jobs, a permanent FEPC, more hospitals, and better health care while excoriating Republicans as all clones of Herbert Hoover. Sweeping thirty-six states with 55 percent of the vote, Roosevelt also carried twenty-two new Democrats to the House. For the moment, at least, liberalism appeared to be robust and determined, healthier than at any time since the 1936 election. Everything would depend on what happened in the new administration.

V. AMERICA AT WAR'S END

It had been a tumultuous time—a devastating military attack followed by mass mobilization; a vigorous rebuilding of the nation's military; and finally, through bold invasions of Normandy, Okinawa, and Iwo Jima, a decisive thrust toward victory; an economy nearly paralyzed at the end of a decade of depression suddenly transformed into a wonder of efficiency, technological innovation, and unprecedented productivity that provided not only the "arsenal" for the world's democracies but also an economic infrastructure capable of manufacturing enough radios, washing machines, and automobiles to satisfy the long-deferred appetites of even the most avaricious consumers; a society mired in traditional social attitudes toward race and gender almost instantaneously engaged in new initiatives toward greater economic opportunities for blacks and women; massive migrations that created new social and political possibilities; and the beginnings of a public discourse that introduced for the first time in decades debate about sex and race equality.

So much change had occurred. Yet so many uncertainties remained. Would the isolationism of America in the 1920s and 1930s return once Germany and Japan were defeated? What would be the impact of the United States holding an exclusive monopoly on the horrific power of nuclear weapons? Would America seek to dominate the world based on its unilateral strength, or would it pursue a policy of multilateralism in concert with other nations around the world? What would happen to women workers? At the beginning of the war, most anticipated returning to domesticity as soon as the conflict ended. But now, three out of four declared that they wanted to stay in the workplace, seeming to corroborate the *Saturday Evening Post*'s conclusion that "millions of the sex are going to sniff at postwar bromides about women's place." And what about blacks? Surely the new militancy reflected in the Double V campaign and the tenfold increase in NAACP membership was not going to disappear. As Eleanor Roosevelt noted, "A wind [is] rising throughout the world of free men everywhere, and they will not be kept in bondage." What would happen when black veterans returned from France, Britain, and the Pacific, where they had experienced a different kind of acceptance and respect? Would their aspirations be acknowledged and gratified, or would whites—and the federal government—seek to suppress their quest for dignity, as had happened after World War I? Finally, what about the average worker? The war had produced full employment, but could the economy sustain the return of twelve million veterans? With memories of the Depression still vivid, 70 percent of Americans worried that their families would be worse off after the war's end, and fewer than four in ten believed that their children would have a better life than their parents had enjoyed. Which direction would the country take? How would the people of the nation, and their leaders, arrive at a consensus on all the questions that now came rushing to the fore?

For more than twelve years, critical guidance on how to answer such fundamental questions had come from one person—Franklin D. Roosevelt. Like a masterful Broadway director, Roosevelt called on different actors on the national stage to come forward with solutions for the problems the nation faced. Often, he intentionally set people with different views in opposition to each other, pooling their disparate points of view while never disclosing his own preferences. Wily and shrewd, Roosevelt always kept his own counsel, never sharing with even his most intimate aides or family members the directions or policies he wished to pursue. Thus, for example, almost no one knew ahead of time about FDR's court-packing plan, which played such a critical role in triggering the conservative coalition in Congress in 1937 that stalled other New Deal initiatives.

Roosevelt's penchant for stealth made his intentions in the foreign policy and military arenas particularly enigmatic. With much justification, FDR possessed total faith in his ability to develop personal relations with foreign leaders that would make possible alliances beyond the ability of the State Department to comprehend. Thus, he believed that he and he alone could "work with" Stalin, developing an understanding that would permit the two men to carve out agreements on the postwar world that otherwise would elude bureaucrats. "I know you will not mind my being brutally frank," he told Churchill in 1942, "when I tell you [that] I think I can personally handle Stalin better than either your Foreign Office or my State Department." Yet FDR shared none of his ideas about the shape of the postwar world with his diplomatic advisors. Similarly, he held to himself any ideas about how to deal with postwar competition over nuclear technology—should America share or jealously defend her nuclear monopoly? And although his political rhetoric in 1944 resonated with his diatribes in 1936 against "economy royalists" and in support of progressive government initiatives that would improve the status of that "one-third of a nation" that was "ill-clothed, ill-housed, and ill-fed," the specific programs FDR had in mind remained a mystery.

Thus, when FDR died on April 12 in Warm Springs, Georgia, he not only took from the American people the cherished leader they had followed through depression and war but also left them deprived of the ideas of the one person who more than anyone else held the key to planning for the future. Roosevelt knew he was living on borrowed time. With an enlarged heart and advanced arteriosclerosis, he no longer possessed the physical reserves to cope with all the pressures that surrounded him. When he returned from his Yalta meeting with Churchill and Stalin, he was exhausted and for the first time addressed Congress from his wheelchair rather than stand at the podium. Seeking respite, he journeyed to his beloved Warm Springs, where he could relax among friends and begin work on his speech for the first convening of the United Nations, where he would outline his vision for a postwar international order. There, while his portrait was being painted, he suffered a massive cerebral hemorrhage and died. Across the nation, people mourned as though they had lost their father or brother. "He was the only president I ever knew," one woman said. The same thought was shared by millions of her fellow citizens. Stalin held the hand of the American ambassador for thirty seconds in silence when he heard the news. People everywhere in the world had lost a friend. The American people also had lost the one person best able to chart the ship of state through the treacherous shoals that lay ahead.

As the war came to a close in August 1945, therefore, Americans faced a bewildering array of choices. How to act in a world where the United States alone wielded decisive economic and military power? What to do at home in a society roiled by fundamental challenges to long held assumptions about the appropriate "place" for women and blacks? How to handle the profound impact of demobilization and the return to a peacetime economy? And which political direction to pursue in a country torn between the bold vision of Roosevelt's 1944 campaign and the narrow conservatism of the Seventy-eighth Congress. "Americans suddenly seemed to stand," the historian Allen Nevins wrote, "beholding a new heaven and a new earth...." But which way to go? That was the challenge of the immediate postwar years—in its own way as enormous a test as had been posed by the Great Depression or World War II itself.

7

The Cold War and the Politics of Anti-Communism: 1945–1952

T he new president knew little about the intricacies of foreign policy. Early in the war, after the German invasion of Russia, Harry Truman had declared that if the Russians were winning we should pull for the Germans, and if the Germans were winning, for the Russians. Now he presided over the world's most powerful nation. Although he had been vice president for three months, he knew nothing of the atomic bomb—he had not even been briefed on its existence; nor had Roosevelt shared any of his strategic thinking about how to mold the postwar world or cope with the geopolitics of conflict among the British, Chinese, French, or Russians. What Truman did understand was how important it was that the world see him as strong, decisive, and tenacious.

From day one of his presidency, therefore, and even before he knew of the atomic bomb, Harry Truman was determined to prove himself a strong president who would brook no nonsense from any foreign power. Because he could not benefit from Roosevelt's private thoughts, he looked to his diplomatic advisors for their perspective. There he encountered a growing distrust of the Soviet Union. The day after he entered the White House, he told his secretary of state, "We must stand up to the Russians and not be easy on them." At his first meeting with Soviet Foreign Secretary Vladimir Molotov a few weeks later, he discarded diplomatic niceties and chewed out the Russians for not keeping their pledges. "I have never been talked to like that in my life," a stunned Molotov told the president. "Carry out your agreements," Truman responded, "and you won't get talked to like that [again]!" In fateful ways, the die had been cast.

I. ORIGINS OF THE COLD WAR

For decades, historians have debated whether it had to be so. Were there options to the ratcheting escalation of antagonistic words and actions of the Cold War? Was it all inevitable, based on a fundamental incompatibility between democracy and dictatorship, capitalism and communism? Or did a middle ground exist, of accommodation, adjustment, mutual recognition of priorities, and respect for national interests? How much did personality play a part? Was it all just a testosterone-driven contest for domination? Or could shrewd politicians with a tolerance for ambiguity negotiate ground rules that would contain the impulse toward open conflict?

There are no simple answers, yet it is critical to recognize the historical origins of the tensions. From the mid-nineteenth century forward, Americans had detested Communism. During the Red Scare of 1919, thousands of purported Communists were arrested in a Justice Department effort to ensure that the Bolshevik revolution of 1917 would never spread to America. During the 1920s, conservatives fearful of social reform drew up a "Spider Web" chart linking women reformers who favored expanded child care and social services to members of the Soviet Politburo. It took sixteen years before the United States finally granted diplomatic recognition to the Soviet Union in 1933, and for years thereafter, a group of "Moscow hands" led by George Kennan and Charles Bohlen sent back to the State Department detailed stories of Soviet torture and manipulation. To be sure, the war helped make the tyrant Stalin into "Uncle Joe," but the tides of anti-Soviet feeling ran deep, just as, from a Soviet perspective, did the view that American capitalism remained the source of all evil and injustice in the world.

Even the war itself proved a source of conflict. The Soviets suffered sixty times the casualties of the United States. The suffering experienced during the siege of Stalingrad was unspeakable. Stalin desperately sought relief from the United States, insisting that Britain and France launch a second front by invading France, thereby diverting German divisions from Soviet territory so that they could defend their conquests in western Europe. Roosevelt understood Stalin's needs and embraced the strategy of a second front. But Churchill resisted, arguing that the casualties would be too high and the invasion too risky. Instead, he proposed a North African invasion, then the assault on Italy. Reluctantly, FDR went along, all the while recognizing the legitimacy of Soviet unhappiness with not securing more direct and immediate relief from the crushing burden Russia was experiencing.

Four other issues compounded these tensions as the war drew to a close. The first—and most overarching—involved fundamental principles about how the postwar world would be governed. Both the United States and the Soviet Union operated from motivations of national self-interest. But the United States also devoted extraordinary rhetorical energy to the defense of universal principles such as self-determination. The Soviet Union, on the other hand, insisted that the world be divided into spheres of influence. The Monroe Doctrine, of course, served as a primary example of such a "sphere of influence," and Russia saw no reason it should not exercise the same control over Eastern Europe that the United States exerted over Latin and South America. But ever since Roosevelt and Churchill had met off the coast of Newfoundland in 1941 to discuss wartime aims (even before the United States entered the war), the Western Allies had been committed to open trade, popular elections, freedom of worship and expression, and an end to traditional balance-of-power diplomacy. The Atlantic Charter, as the Churchill-Roosevelt declaration was called, made self-government the nonnegotiable core of the postwar world. A new United Nations, representing governments throughout the world, would provide a forum for negotiating world conflicts. Notwithstanding FDR's willingness to "strike a deal" with Russia over issues of paramount national interest to the Soviets, a world of difference separated the apparent postwar objectives of the two superpowers.

Nothing highlighted the depth of this difference more than the issue of Poland—and Eastern Europe more generally. Three times in the past century, Russia had been a victim of a military invasion through the Polish corridor. No single wartime objective ranked higher for Stalin than domination over any future Polish government. Yet the Western Allies had declared war over Germany's violation of Polish sovereignty in the fall of 1939. For them the future status of Poland symbolized all that the war had been fought for. Not to have a representative government in Poland would be a betrayal of every ideal for which the Atlantic Charter stood. The same argument applied with almost equal force to such other Eastern European countries as Romania, Czechoslovakia, and Hungary. Moreover, the decisions on how these nations would be governed had to be made immediately. They could not be postponed while an international process of dispute resolution evolved.

The future of Germany constituted a second postwar source of tension. Everyone agreed that never again should Germany have the capacity to wage world war. "We either have to castrate the German people," FDR declared, "or you have got to treat them in such a manner so they can't just go on reproducing people who want to continue the way they have in the past." Stalin and FDR agreed that one practical means of disabling German strength was through dividing the country into different sectors "as small and weak as possible." FDR also supported eliminating all heavy industry from Germany and transforming the country into a pastoral landscape of small farms. Yet such consensus quickly evaporated in the face of immediate clashes of self-interest. Russia demanded at least ten billion dollars in reparations from Germany, which required maintaining a strong industrial base. The United States also quickly retreated from supporting pastoralization, recognizing that an economically vibrant Germany constituted a powerful counterbalance to the Soviet Union. The parties clashed over who would be assigned which districts of postwar Germany to govern and how they would interact. Before the war had even ended, chaos rather than consistency had come to characterize postwar planning for Germany.

The German issue reflected, in turn, the third large area of contention—how to organize Europe's postwar economy. The Atlantic Charter had envisioned an open, capitalist world order based on free trade, entrepreneurship, and equal access to raw materials and capital. To that end, the United States had helped launch the World Bank in 1944 and an International Monetary Fund, each capitalized at over seven billion dollars, which was provided mostly by the United States. But the entire concept ran counter to Soviet notions of a separate socialist bloc, functioning as a sphere of influence under tight control of the Soviet state—no free trade, no open access, no individual entrepreneurship. As with all the other Cold War tensions, the issue of Europe's future economic development hinged on free choice and a Western capitalist model rather than state control and socialist constraints.

The final source of conflict also proved one of the most politically and emotionally powerful—who would control access to nuclear weapons? From the beginning, the world's physicists understood that scientific research knew no national boundaries; and even though they insisted that the United States leap to the fore in nuclear research, they recognized as well that ensuring a monopoly on nuclear technology was scientifically and politically impossible. Partially in recognition of that principle, FDR in 1943 agreed to a "full exchange of information" about the bomb with Great Britain but with no one else. The nuclear physicist Neils Bohr, and many of his colleagues, immediately challenged Roosevelt's decision. In his typical fashion, FDR agreed that "contact with the Soviet Union should be tried" but at the same time placed Bohr under surveillance while reaffirming U.S. bonds with Britain and keeping to himself any long-range shift in strategy, perhaps in the hope that future sharing of nuclear information could occur as part of a larger quid pro quo with the Soviets on postwar arrangements. Ironically, a meeting to discuss the subject was scheduled for FDR the day he was to return from Warm Springs in April 1945. In the meantime, his vice president knew nothing, not only about research on the bomb but also about the hostility among scientists toward the idea of a nuclear monopoly.

As we now know, the Soviets were fully aware, via their own spy network at Los Alamos, about America's progress on a nuclear weapon. They also understood what a British official noted at the time, that the bomb "would be a terrific factor in the postwar world...giving an absolute control to whatever country possessed the secret." There were two ways to go: develop a mechanism for sharing research and control over this terrible weapon of annihilation, or engage in an all-out contest for nuclear domination. The first approach fit nicely a pattern of establishing bona fides of cooperation and trust between world powers; the second undermined such a prospect completely. In perhaps a final paradox, this was the one issue where the United States seemed dedicated to standing foursquare against the principle of free exchange and open access, preferring instead, at least for the moment, a more Soviet-like stance of maintaining tight control over one's own sphere of power.

Even in the midst of such tensions, there were countervailing indications that perhaps some modes of accommodation might be possible. Whatever his predilection for grandiloquent Wilsonian principles, FDR was always ready to strike a deal, recognizing compelling Soviet needs for security in her own backyard. Hence, notwithstanding his devotion to universalist doctrines of free government and self-determination, Roosevelt authorized Churchill to speak for him when he went to Moscow in 1944 and in a one-on-one meeting with Stalin specifically agreed to spheres of influence between Russia and the West: the Soviets would have 90 percent control of Romania, the West would exercise the same domination over Greece, East and West would share fifty-fifty in determining the future of Hungary and Yugoslavia. Poland was not even mentioned, suggesting Churchill's recognition that this was mostly a Russian sphere. Meanwhile, Roosevelt had told Stalin at Tehran in 1943 that the Soviets could control the Baltic states, as long as Stalin made some public commitment to future elections to satisfy FDR's constituents at home. Even in Poland, Roosevelt acknowledged that the Russians needed to have a "friendly" government, hoping—perhaps naively—that a gesture of including non-Communist Poles in a postwar regime would be enough to create at least the appearance of representative government.

At bottom, Roosevelt understood that political control came with having troops on the ground. It had been that way when the United States and Britain made their decisions vis-à-vis negotiating with Admiral Darlan in North Africa and with the Badoglio regime in Italy—over Soviet objections; and it would be that way in Eastern Europe. "The occupying forces had the power in the area where their arms were present," FDR said, "and each knew that the other could not force things to an issue." Based on such realpolitik, there seemed some basis for thinking that a peaceful resolution of abiding differences between East and West might be found. At Yalta, FDR celebrated his good relationship with Stalin and their ability to find common ground. "I believe we are going to get along very well with him and the Russian people," FDR said. "I would call [Stalin] something like me...a realist." It was perhaps from that framework of understanding that Roosevelt focused his hopes on the United Nations as the future arbiter of international understanding, not necessarily through the General Assembly, where each nation would exercise a vote, but rather through the Security Council, where the "Four Policemen" of the world—Russia, China, Great Britain, and the United States—could govern the world. "We are faced with the pre-eminent fact," FDR wrote just before he died, "that, if civilization is to survive, we must cultivate the science of human relationships—the ability of all people, of all kinds, to live together and work together in the same world, at peace." Through his own peculiar combination of "realism" and universalist principles, FDR believed he might have the formula to make his dream come true.

II. THE COLD WAR BEGINS

Alas, it was not to be. No one else was privy to Roosevelt's "formula." He alone held the cards he intended to play and told none of his colleagues or partners where and how he intended to use them. To a degree remarkable in the history of America's chief executives, Franklin Roosevelt confided in virtually no one; although he encouraged voices from contentious parties to argue against each other, he always held his own counsel. It was hardly surprising that Harry Truman turned to those who knew most about the difficult issues confronting him to ask what Roosevelt's policies had been. They could not answer that question but they could volunteer their own thoughts, and to a surprising extent, they came forward with the same answer: be tough, call Stalin to account, use the power of your military might to demand that the Soviets comply with their agreements. Hence, the Truman conversation with Molotov, taking him, and those he represented, to the White House woodshed for a much deserved spanking.

Poland once again encapsulated all the issues. Roosevelt had sought to "ameliorate the situation," asking Stalin at Yalta to make some concession to the Polish government in exile in London, which justifiably indicted the Soviets for having murdered thousands of Polish officers in the Katyn forest and for having permitted the courageous Warsaw underground fighters to be slaughtered by the Nazis in the spring of 1945 when nearby Soviet forces could have come to their aid. Initially, Stalin seemed responsive to Roosevelt, promising some voice for the London Poles in the new government and giving lip service to "free and unfettered elections." But by the time of FDR's death, Stalin had fallen back. A number of the Poles from the Warsaw underground were arrested, and the Soviets imposed iron control on the country that more than any other symbolized for both sides the meaning of World War II. Truman's outrage toward Molotov reflected the pivotal breakdown that had occurred in the supposed understanding Roosevelt had struck with Stalin.

Soon thereafter, the consensus over how to deal with Germany came apart as well. Roosevelt had already retreated from pastoralization. "No one wants to make Germany a wholly agricultural nation again," he declared. But then

Periodically during World War II, Allied leaders gathered for "summit" meetings to plot strategy for both the war and the postwar world. The last of these that FDR attended was Yalta. Now Harry Truman took his place, joining Generalissimo Josef Stalin and Prime Minister Winston Churchill at Potsdam to consider plans for defeating Japan and arranging peace.

Credit: © Bettmann/CORBIS

the Allied agreement to treat Germany as a single economic unit, with each occupied sector—the French, British, American, and Russian zones—sending reparations from one zone to the other in a coordinated fashion, fell victim to sharply divergent practices. The Soviets stripped their zone and made heavy demands for factories, power plants, rolling stock, and tools in the British and American zones. The West, however, wished Germany to revive economically—not become a wasteland—and within a year completely halted delivery of reparations to the Soviet zone, creating an open break with the Russians. Stalin was offended that his country was being denied assistance in its own economic reconstruction when the Soviets had paid the heaviest price in war casualties while the United States prospered. Yet from a Western perspective, Stalin was breaking the rules he had agreed to, creating a totalitarian Communist state in the Soviet zone and threatening to leave Germany economically destitute. In response, Secretary of State James Byrnes announced a new Truman "get tough" policy in September 1946. The British and American zones became one on January 1, 1947, creating a total division of the country between East and West, and the United States committed itself to a wholesale revival of a thriving capitalist economy in the West—precisely what Stalin most feared.

Not surprisingly, growing fissures between Moscow and Washington soon appeared as well in debates over how to establish international control over atomic weapons. Truman wished to retain America's monopoly over nuclear weapons yet also move toward some sharing of information on atomic energy, always with the proviso that the United States would exercise a dominant voice. Part of his plan—presented to the United Nations Atomic Energy Commission by U.S. representative Bernard Baruch in June 1946—provided for international control over such raw materials as uranium, international custody of all atomic weapons, and rigid international inspection to prohibit the illegal manufacture of atomic bombs. No veto power would exist to block such inspections. If such a plan were adopted, the United States stood ready to destroy its stock of atom bombs and share its scientific knowledge with the rest of the world.

From an American perspective, this represented a generous offer. Yet for the Russians, it suggested a one-way deal that would allow Westerners to inspect their scientific laboratories, take away their veto power, and give the United States the ongoing advantage of knowing how to make an atomic bomb while restricting experimentation by others. Gromyko proposed instead the immediate destruction of all atom bombs and the prohibition of any further manufacture of nuclear weapons. But this was clearly unacceptable to the West because it would require the United States to sacrifice its advantage while eliminating the inspection process, which was the only assurance that the Russians would not proceed secretly to build their own weapons.

Like virtually every issue discussed between 1945 and 1947, the debate over atomic weapons highlighted the profound clash of perspectives between two global giants who brought totally different worldviews to bear on every dispute. Although each country began with a sense of its own national interest, the rationales each deployed soon evolved into a battleground of ideologies, with almost no ground left for striking a deal based on the actual issues.

There were in fact areas of potential conflict where accommodation took place. The Soviets withdrew from Hungary after free elections there; they permitted a Western-style parliament to rule Czechoslovakia and allowed a coalition government there; they made some concessions in Romania; and they took their troops out of Azerbaijan, under considerable pressure, leaving that oil-rich Iranian province free of outside domination. Yet all the momentum was primarily toward confrontation, not peaceful resolution. In February 1946, Stalin declared that war was inevitable as long as capitalism survived—an address that Supreme Court Justice William Douglas called a "Declaration of World War III." One month later, Winston Churchill arrived in the United States to give a commencement address in Fulton, Missouri. With Truman at his side, he told the audience that "from Stetting in the Baltic to Trieste in the Adriatic, an iron curtain has descended across the [European] continent." America and Britain must stand side by side, Churchill declared, in a "fraternal association of the English speaking people," maintaining their monopoly over nuclear weapons and waging war against their common foe.

Articulating the new geopolitical strategy that soon would dominate Washington, Soviet expert George Kennan drafted an eight-thousand-word word telegram. Kennan elaborated what soon came to be known as the "containment" policy, arguing that it must be made clear to the Soviets that expansion beyond a given perimeter was unacceptable and would be met by force. The United States, Kennan noted, faced a "political force committed fanatically to the belief that [with the] United States there could be no permanent *modus vivendi*, that it is desirable and necessary that the internal harmony of our society be broken if Soviet power is to be secure." Faced with a world divided irreconcilably into communist and capitalist camps, Kennan concluded, it was incumbent upon America to exert sufficient military and diplomatic pressure to cause "either the breakup or the gradual mellowing of Soviet policy." Within such a construct, no room existed for "striking a deal" or buying time for the rebuilding of trust. If conflict were inevitable, only a hard-line position made any sense. As Truman told his secretary of state a year earlier, "I'm tired of babying the Soviets. They [must be] faced with an iron fist and strong language....Only one language do they understand—how many divisions have you?"

By March 1947, Truman was ready to go public with a declaration of a Cold War, defining the world as divided into two incompatible forces of good and evil. The precipitating event was Britain's determination that it could no longer economically afford the military and financial aid necessary to sustain the stability of Greece and Turkey. Greece, in particular, faced a bitter civil insurrection by forces directly tied to Communists in Yugoslavia and Bulgaria. Faced with the unacceptable option of leaving two pivotal nations vulnerable to a Communist takeover, Truman determined that the United

States must provide four hundred million dollars immediately in military and economic aid to Greece and Turkey.

In their initial approach to congressional leaders, Truman's aides made their case on grounds of self-interest. The nation could not afford financial and political chaos, they argued, and America must help. But such arguments "made the whole thing sound like an investment prospectus," according to one observer. The Republicans wanted to cut the budget, not expand it, and the arguments of Truman's aides were falling on deaf ears. Sensing imminent defeat, Dean Acheson, then assistant secretary of state, seized the moment to speak. "This was my crisis," he later wrote. "For a week I had nurtured it." Now, taking the floor, Acheson redefined the battle as one involving Soviet determination to capture Western Europe and take over three continents. "Like apples in a barrel infected by the corruption of one rotten one, the corruption of Greece would infect Iran and alter the Middle East,... Africa,... Italy and France." No struggle was more pivotal to the cause of freedom. "Not since Rome and Carthage has there been such polarization of power on this earth," Acheson concluded. "We and we alone are in a position to break up [the Soviet quest for world domination]." Suddenly the atmosphere in the room changed. *That* argument, Senator Arthur Vandenberg told the president, made sense. If Truman wanted his aid package, Vandenberg said, he would have to "scare the hell" out of the American people.

The exchange played a critical role in the presentation of the Truman Doctrine and its definition of a holy war between God-fearing democracy and atheistic communism. No longer relying on arguments of self-interest, Truman posed the issue as one of containing the spread of tyrannical communism. The question before Congress, the president said, was not simply ensuring the military and political stability of two countries. Rather it was a choice "between alternative ways of life." One was democratic, open, dedicated to "representative government, free elections, guarantees of individual liberty, and freedom of speech and religion," the other a system of "tyranny" that utilized "terror and oppression," controlled its press, denied people the right to worship, and undermined personal freedom. In this war between good and evil, Truman concluded, "it must be the policy of the United States to support free peoples who are resisting attempted subjugation by armed minorities." Truman had learned the lesson that Acheson had taught him: defining the struggle as one between freedom and tyranny left little room for equivocation or debate. "There is precious little we can do except say yes," Senator Vandenberg concluded. One month later, Truman's aid package passed Congress by overwhelming margins.

Almost all the pieces of the Cold War strategy were now in place. Shortly after enactment of the Truman Doctrine, Secretary of State George Marshall told a commencement audience at Harvard that it was incumbent upon America to finance the economic reconstruction of Europe. His proposals led directly to enactment by Congress of the Marshall Plan in April 1948—the most effective aid program mounted in the course of modern history and the savior of capitalism in Western Europe. In the meantime, the Soviets responded by taking control of the government in Hungary and ending the coalition regime in Czechoslovakia, thereby almost confirming the inevitability of perpetual conflict. One year later, the final piece of the Cold War jigsaw puzzle was put in place. The North Atlantic Treaty Organization (NATO) was founded to defend Western Europe and create a mighty military alliance against any Soviet effort to mount aggression against a Western power. The confrontation that had seemed potentially avoidable just a few years ago was now set in stone.

III. THE POLITICS OF ANTI-COMMUNISM

It would have been impossible for such a decisive stance in foreign policy to leave unaffected the course of politics at home. For much of the first twenty months of the Truman administration, America had sought a new consensus about how to proceed in domestic policy. Was the New Deal dead or simply in hibernation awaiting a new awakening in the postwar world? How would the country deal with demobilization, the conversion of munitions factories into automobile assembly lines, the demand for new houses and consumer goods, the return to industrial and white-collar jobs of twelve million soldiers? What would happen with the incipient social changes among women and blacks? How would Americans respond to their new international role? When Truman ascended to the White House, he and other politicians from both parties struggled—often unsuccessfully—with finding answers to such questions. But by 1948, the country began to come together around a new consensus, partly rooted in an ongoing commitment to social reforms for those most in need of assistance, but above all shaped by the pervasiveness of the fight against communism—a fight that played as large a role in defining domestic politics as it did in molding the nation's foreign policy.

In the early months of his presidency, Harry Truman oscillated between a commitment to carry forward the New Deal liberalism of FDR and an angry, sometimes petulant impatience at the demands of organized labor for higher wages and the frustrating presence of persistent inflation. Reconversion proved easier than many had feared, with government playing a major role in smoothing the transition. Government spending increased to four times what it had been before the war. Pent-up consumer demand sparked a postwar boom. As much as any other single piece of legislation in American history, the GI Bill of Rights, with its provision of loans for veterans to buy houses and tuition payments for returning soldiers to go to college, helped propel a generation of prosperity. More than twelve million veterans took advantage of it. One result of such government support was that by 1950 half of all families in the country earned more than three thousand dollars per year compared with only 6 percent fifteen years earlier. Truman supported a Full Employment bill in 1945, giving the government a major new role in shaping the economy through a new Council of Economic Advisors, an increase in the minimum wage, and national housing legislation.

Yet in the end, much of the liberal legislation he initiated was truncated or stalled. After a number of months, key New Dealers like Harold Ickes left the cabinet, more moderate and conservative friends of Truman replaced them, and liberal disillusionment mushroomed. "The path Franklin Roosevelt charted," his son Elliott proclaimed, "has been grievously—and deliberately—forsaken."

In the meantime, Truman grappled with the infuriating problems of rampant inflation and labor insurrection. Manufacturers and farmers, who had bridled at wartime price controls, wanted to exploit a sellers' market, while consumers, bursting with wartime savings, wanted to rush automobile showrooms and appliance stores. When Truman sided with a conservative banker whom he had named director of the Office of War Mobilization against Chester Bowles, the liberal OPA administrator who represented the consumer, he alienated New Deal liberals who wished to keep a tight control on prices. Then, after Truman finally took a strong stand against inflation in wages, he had a head-on conflict with organized labor, which demanded increased compensation to make up for the loss of overtime pay. Within a month after victory over Japan, half a million workers were out on strike, and 1946 saw a loss of 116 million man-days of work. On April 1, 1946, John L. Lewis led 400,000 coal miners out of the pits, and for forty days the strike cut off the nation's supply of fuel and threatened European recovery. In the midst of the coal crisis, rail workers also walked off the job, marooning 90,000 passengers and stopping 25,000 freight cars, many of them loaded with perishables such as food. Five weeks later, price control legislation ended, and prices surged 25 percent.

As a result of labor unrest and consumer frustration, Truman's political stock plummeted. At the peak of his popularity, 87 percent of the American people supported the president. By October, that figure had plunged to 32 percent. Although many of Truman's political problems could be traced to the conservative congressional coalition that had come into power in 1938, the president's apparent vacillation on traditional New Deal policies was also to blame. "To err is Truman," became the stock joke of Truman detractors. When the voters went to the polls in 1946, the Democrats sustained a devastating rebuke. For the first time since 1930, Republicans won Congress, 246 to 188 in the House, 51 to 45 in the Senate. Among the new senators was Joseph McCarthy, who toppled the La Follette dynasty in Wisconsin, while newly elected to the House were Richard Milhous Nixon of California and John F. Kennedy of Massachusetts. Reading the election returns, Arkansas Senator J. William Fulbright urged Truman to name a Republican successor and resign. With a quick retort, Truman called his nemesis Senator "Halfbright" and vowed to continue to continue his Fair Deal agenda. But only a political fool could fail to acknowledge the depth of the Democratic defeat.

Almost immediately, the new Republican Congress focused its energies on organized labor, passing the Taft-Harley Act of 1947. Significantly curtailing the wide-open endorsement that the Wagner Act of 1935 had provided unions in 1935, Taft-Harley outlawed the closed shop and secondary boycott, required a 60-day cooling off period for strikes, authorized an 80-day injunction against labor stoppages that might affect national health or safety, forbade political contributions from unions, and required labor leaders to take a non-Communist oath. When Truman vetoed the bill, Congress reenacted it by thumping majorities. By that action, Congress almost overnight drove organized labor back into Truman's arms, but it had also severely weakened the trade union movement at a critical moment in its history.

Among the more positive achievements of the Eightieth Congress were a series of laws modernizing the administrative structure of the federal government. Congress sent to the states for ratification the Twenty-second Amendment limiting presidents to two terms of office; authored a Presidential Succession Act delineating who, after the vice president, should be next in line of presidential succession (the Speaker of the House and the president pro tem of the Senate); unified the army, navy, and air force under a secretary of defense; gave legal status to the Joint Chiefs of Staff; and created a National Security Council, the Central Intelligence Agency, and the Atomic Energy Commission. Clearly, each of the last series of acts directly reflected the new role of America in the world and the powerful impact of the Cold War.

By 1947–1948, in turn, the domestic politics of anti-Communism had become pervasive and controlling. Operating in tandem, foreign and domestic policy reinforced each other, shaping a set of constraints that not only prohibited any dissent on America's foreign policy of opposing the USSR but also ruled out of bounds any domestic initiative that could be characterized as "left of center." From health insurance to child-care centers to proposals for civil rights or income redistribution, the greatest obstacle to significant reform was the allegation that the change would promote socialist practices and be seen as "soft on communism." Only measures totally insulated from such characterization stood a chance of enactment. The politics of moderation reigned supreme in domestic matters.

The centerpiece for anti-Communism was the House Committee on Un-American Activities (popularly known as HUAC). Established in 1938, it quickly became known for the intimidating tactics of its chairman, Martin Dies, and the speed with which it called witnesses who might be vulnerable to prosecution under the 1940 Smith Act, which made membership in the Communist Party, or advocacy of Communist doctrines, a federal crime. In the aftermath of World War II, HUAC—working closely with FBI Director J. Edgar Hoover—sought to "ferret out" Communist sympathizers in the federal government, movie stars or directors who were suspected of insinuating Communist doctrines into Hollywood movies, or even ministers who were pacifists. With people like Mississippi's John Rankin playing a leading role (he claimed that World War II had been started by "a little group of our international Jewish brethren"), the committee called witnesses who at some point might have been a member of a group on the attorney general's subversive activities group, for example, a Soviet-American Friendship Society during World War II. Once a person answered a single question, they were compelled to answer all the questions that followed lest they face contempt charges, including who their colleagues were who also were members of the group under examination. If they took the Fifth Amendment, refusing to answer on constitutional grounds, witnesses ran the risk of being portrayed in the news media as "fellow travelers" or "com-symps" and might subsequently lose their jobs. A number of Hollywood directors and actors, for example, found themselves on a "blacklist" and were barred from employment. So seriously did Hollywood take the threat that the president of the Motion Picture Association declared that no jobs would be given to anyone who did not cooperate with the HUAC.

There were legitimate reasons for concern about Communist spying. In June 1945 government agents entered the office of *Amerasia*, a magazine sympathetic to Chinese Communists, and unearthed a series of classified government documents. In early 1946, a Canadian atomic spy ring with direct American connections was revealed. We also know from recently disclosed Soviet documents (the Verona project), declassified after the demise of communism, that the Russians had an extensive network of spies throughout the scientific community working on the atom bomb as well as highly placed Communists operating undercover in the federal government.

None of these was more prominent or more widely defended than Alger Hiss, a former undersecretary of state who had been with Roosevelt at Yalta. In a bizarre set of exchanges, Whitaker Chambers, a former Communist and by the late 1940s prominent *Time* magazine editor, accused Hiss of secretly purloining government documents for transmission to the Soviet Union. When Hiss indignantly denied the charges—supported by "establishment" Easterners from both parties, including John Foster Dulles and Dean Acheson—most HUAC members were ready to desist. But Richard Nixon, elected to Congress in 1946 at least in part because he smeared his opponent as a "lip service American" who "fronted for un-American elements," would not let go of the issue and by dint of effective sleuth work discovered that Hiss and Chambers did know each other, had collaborated, and that Hiss had perjured himself. After extensive controversy, Hiss was convicted and sent to jail—the Verona project subsequently confirmed that Hiss was a spy—and Richard Nixon's career as a leading anti-Communist was launched.

But far too often, little or no evidence existed for the reckless charges brought against individuals. When David Lilienthal, former head of the Tennessee Valley Authority and a leading advisor to the president on nuclear matters, was nominated to become chairman of the Atomic Energy Commission, members of Congress questioned his loyalty, one senator arguing that Lilienthal's family had come from a part of Austria-Hungary that later was incorporated into Czechoslovakia, and after all Czechoslovakia was now a Communist country. Leland Olds was denied reappointment to the Federal Power Commission because in 1922, a column he had written was republished in the *Daily Worker*, a Communist paper, as well as in a variety of other papers friendly to labor. Famous playwrights had to use pseudonyms to get their work produced because they had refused to "name names" before the HUAC.

Significantly, the Truman administration played a crucial role in legitimizing such tactics. In the end, it also used the tactics itself in order to secure political success. Within two weeks of proclaiming the Truman Doctrine, which defined the Cold War as a holy crusade between good and evil, Truman also promulgated Executive Order 9835, which created a federal employment loyalty program that had the authority to screen two million federal employees for any indication of political deviance. With dramatic disregard for civil liberties, the first president of the Loyalty Review Board declared that "the government is entitled to discharge any employee without extending to such employee any hearing whatsoever." In fact, he declared, any "suspicion of disloyalty...however remote," justified such dismissal. Not to be outdone by Nixon or Rankin, Truman's attorney general, J. Howard McGrath, charged that Communists "are everywhere—in factories, offices, butcher stores, on street corners, and private business. And each carries in himself the death of our society."

If anyone doubted the power of the new politics of anti-Communism, the presidential election of 1948 offered a decisive rebuttal. Notwithstanding his feisty and combative personality, everyone expected Truman to be swamped. In addition to his own unpopularity, reflected in the 1946 elections, two splinter sections of the Democratic Party threatened to reduce the president's share of the total vote to less than a third. Henry Wallace, fired from the cabinet when he questioned Truman's foreign policy, headed a new Progressive Party. Wallace championed progressive New Deal policies on welfare and race while supporting a policy of détente with the Soviet Union. Potentially, he might attract as much as 20 percent of the overall vote. Meanwhile, Southern segregationists bolted when the Democratic platform endorsed a strong civil rights plank. South Carolina's Strom Thurmond headed up a new States Rights, or Dixiecrat, party that promised to weaken Truman substantially in the South. Almost smug with optimism, the Republicans nominated the bland Thomas E. Dewey, governor of New York. "Dewey doesn't seem to walk," one reporter noted, "he coasts out like a man who has been mounted on casters and given a tremendous shove from behind." Another commentator declared that Dewey looked like the bridegroom on a wedding cake, charming but lifeless. It did not matter, most Republicans believed. He was a shoo-in.

But it was not to be. Truman's aide Clark Clifford had developed a campaign strategy destined to transform everyone's expectations: cultivate liberals, maximize the party's strengths in urban areas and among minorities, and, in the event of a Wallace candidacy, "identify him and isolate him in the public mind with the communists." A quick study, Truman wasted no time implementing Clifford's strategy. By vetoing the Taft-Harley Act he had already gone a huge distance to winning back labor's vote. Then he endorsed a set of progressive civil rights proposals, weakening Wallace's claim to be the only candidate supporting Negroes. Finally, he zeroed in on Wallace's left-wing credentials. "I do not want," he declared, "and [I] will not accept the political support of Henry Wallace *and his communists*....These are days of high prices for anything, but any price for Wallace and his communists is too much for me" (italics added). If that commentary seemed calculated, even stronger was the indictment of Wallace by Hubert Humphrey, the liberal mayor of Minneapolis, who had electrified the 1948 Democratic convention with his endorsement of civil rights. "If I have to choose between being called a Red-baiter and a traitor," Humphrey said, "I'll be a Red-baiter." Within weeks, Wallace's support in the Gallup Poll fell from 15 to 4 percent. In the South, meanwhile, Truman ignored Thurmond while pulling out all the stops to appeal to traditional Democratic loyalties.

Whistle-stopping by train across the country, Truman denounced the "do-nothing" Eightieth Congress; mocked the Republicans as staid and lifeless; and galvanized the Democratic mainstream with his hard-talking, colorful attacks on conservative Republicans and Communist-like progressives. Throughout the year he fired a series of messages to Congress calling for specific reforms, and that summer he called Congress back into special session the day turnips are planted in Missouri. When the "turnip Congress" did nothing, Truman was well on his way to making the issue of the campaign the "good for nothing" Eightieth Congress. Election day suddenly became the "miracle of 1948," a stunning victory pieced together with blue-collar votes, liberal supporters who rejected Wallace as a "dupe of the Communists," traditional Southern Democrats, and most critical of all, a solid bloc of black votes. The politics of anti-Communism had triumphed, providing an anchor for a new consensus at work in the American body politic.

IV. SOCIAL CHANGE IN POSTWAR AMERICA

Some of the most important developments in postwar America—negative as well as positive—occurred among those groups most affected by the war. Despite the desire of 75–80 percent of women who had taken jobs during the war to remain in the paid labor force, the drive for demobilization, and a resurgence of antifeminist propaganda, forced many of them to return to the home. "The old theory that a woman's place is in the home no longer exists," one woman steelworker said. "Those days are gone forever." But she was wrong. One U.S. senator said that Congress should compel "wives and mothers to [go back] to the kitchen." Magazine advertisements glorified housework, exhorting women to return to the job they "like best." A new best seller, *Modern Woman: The Lost Sex*, concluded that women who wished careers were victims of a feminist neurosis. "The independent woman," it proclaimed, "is a contradiction in terms." Medical schools refused to admit more than 5 percent women in their entering classes, and 70 percent of all hospitals rejected women interns.

Interestingly, despite these pressures, millions of women returned to work after a brief period of demobilization. Although 3.25 million women lost their jobs in the year after Japan's defeat, another 2.75 million were hired. But now they were taking jobs in less well-paying industries that offered little prospect for promotion—work as waitresses, service workers, or maids rather than as assembly line workers in a steel plant or aircraft factory. When the war ended, women in manufacturing earned 66 percent of what men earned. Five years later that figure had fallen to 53 percent. Thus there were two stories existing side by side: by 1950, the proportion of women at work had increased from 27 percent in 1940 to 32 percent, with the greatest increase coming among the 45- to 54-year-olds who had been most committed to staying in the workforce after the war—clearly a structural change with long-term significance for the future; but on the other hand, most of these women held low-paying jobs, were denied access to high prestige professions, and worked within a culture that continued to presume that women's "place" was in the home and that their work was worth considerably less than that of men.

The experience of black Americans suggested the most immediate and long-lasting impact of the war. The explosion in NAACP memberships and the popularity of the Double V campaign carried over immediately into the postwar world. Veterans like Mississippi's Medgar Evers and Amzie Moore came back from the war determined that if they were going to fight for American democracy abroad, they would insist on the right to vote at home. Civil rights groups lobbied for a permanent FEPC, abolition of the poll tax, and a commitment by the federal government to support desegregation. The NAACP brought repeated cases to end segregation in law schools while pushing vigorously for equality in public school education. Voter registration campaigns in Georgia, North Carolina, and Tennessee helped increase the number of blacks who could vote in the South from 2 percent in 1940 to 12 percent in 1947.

Not surprisingly, racist repression accelerated in direct proportion to black demands for change. The stories were horrific. A black veteran named Isaac Woodward, still wearing his uniform, demanded to be treated with respect on a public bus. He was taken off the bus, beaten viciously, and had his eyes poked out by a bully club. In Georgia, one black who dared to vote was shot to death in his front yard. "No Negro will vote in Georgia for the next four years," Governor Eugene Talmadge declared. When Medgar Evers and four fellow veterans went to try to vote, they were driven away by men with pistols. In one Georgia county, whites shot and killed two blacks trying to register and when one of the wives of the victims recognized his assailant, the wives of the two men were murdered as well. In Columbia, Tennessee, where black veterans came back insisting on a "new deal" in their hometown, whites led a race riot that burned down sections of the black community and left scores wounded or killed. Mississippi Senator Theodore Bilbo crystallized the response of most powerful whites to the new insurgency. "You know and I know what is the best way to keep the nigger from voting," he told a political rally. "You do it the night before the election. I don't have to tell you any more than that. Red-blooded men know what I mean."

Yet black protestors fought back. Following the Columbia race riot and countless examples of voter intimidation, black leaders led pickets outside the White House carrying signs screaming, **"SPEAK, SPEAK**

World War II helped trigger a massive increase in the number of American blacks who joined the NAACP, fought in the armed forces, competed for better jobs, and insisted on recognition of their citizenship rights. Here black Americans in Atlanta, Georgia, are registering to vote in 1944, reflecting this new determination.

Credit: Associated Press

MR. PRESIDENT." More than fifteen thousand blacks demonstrated before the Lincoln Memorial for an end to the Ku Klux Klan. When Truman finally agreed to meet members of the newly formed National Committee Against Violence, he showed a new level of sympathy to the group., "My God," he observed, "I had no idea it was as terrible as that. We have to do something."

The president responded by creating a Committee on Civil Rights in December 1946. Consisting of nationally distinguished business, education, and political leaders—including Frank Porter Graham, president of the University of North Carolina, and Franklin D. Roosevelt, Jr.—the committee wasted no time in issuing a call to action. "To Secure These Rights," its official report, demanded desegregation of the armed forces, antilynching legislation, enactment of a permanent FEPC, abolition of the poll tax, an end to segregated housing, and the creation of a permanent Commission on Civil Rights.

Truman not only endorsed the proposals but also became the first president to address the NAACP. "There is a serious gap between our ideals and some of our practices," Truman said, and "this gap must be closed."

Although Truman's follow-through proved less than might have been desired, he issued an executive order calling for desegregation of the armed forces, pushed for a permanent FEPC, and belatedly endorsed a bold civil rights platform at the Democratic convention in 1948 that Hubert Humphrey had proposed. For the first time since Reconstruction, an American president had aligned himself with the aspirations of black Americans. His actions often fell short of his rhetoric. But they were sufficient to turn out the black vote in the 1948 election—the decisive factor in Truman's victory—and successfully reinforced the already powerful grassroots insurgency sweeping black America that would eventually create the civil rights movement of the 1950s and 1960s.

Mexican Americans, although significantly different in background, culture, and appearance than African Americans, nevertheless suffered discriminatory treatment remarkably similar to that of blacks. Throughout the twentieth century, Mexican American children received on average only two-thirds as much schooling as whites. When factories and large farmers in the Southwest and California needed cheap labor, the border with Mexico suddenly opened wide; yet when depression hit, the border closed precipitously. During the 1930s hundreds of thousands of Mexican Americans were deported; roundups of undocumented workers occurred whenever the American economy was in trouble and whites needed employment. Schools throughout the Southwest were segregated, with Latinos going to school with other Latinos, even though most identified themselves as white. The major Mexican American civil rights organization, LULAC (League of United Latin American Citizens), argued that Latinos as a race were in fact Caucasian. Both politically and through litigation, they fought for that designation. LULAC was in many respects the NAACP of the Hispanic population.

Nevertheless, Latinos were targeted for the same kind of second-class treatment as blacks. During the 1980s and 1990s, three different propositions in California specifically proposed that only English be taught in the schools, that undocumented immigrants be prohibited from receiving public health and educational services, and that no affirmative action programs be instituted for any residents of the state. Although many Mexican Americans continued to think of themselves as significantly different from (and better than) blacks, the fortunes of the two groups as well as their struggle for freedom bore remarkable similarities, from school segregation to instances of poverty, low wages, and discrimination in the workplace. The war had brought both persistent discrimination and some advances for Mexican Americans, whose long-term future would more than anything else be affected by the determination of the nation as a whole to deal fairly with its minorities. The issue of discrimination against Latino immigrants would not soon go away.

The final group that had experienced massive positive change during the war years was organized labor. Here, as with women, the verdict of the postwar years was mixed, if not ultimately negative. By 1945, union membership had soared to fifteen million—a fivefold increase over 1933. CIO leaders in particular approached the end of the war with ambitious plans to create an "industrial democracy"—sharing with business leaders decisions about the future directions of the economy. More open to women and minorities than the AFL and less tied to the tenets of "business unionism," with its focus solely on wages and benefits, the CIO envisioned ever growing ranks of organized workers and new access to decision-making power. Business, of course, found such ideas profoundly threatening. Equally unacceptable was the CIO's ambition to wield greater influence over politics, particularly in the area of national health insurance, civil rights, and government support for full employment.

In the context of postwar politics, it was business that ended up with the upper hand. Faced with an almost unprecedented upsurge of labor militancy, automobile, steel, and railroad executives responded with a hard line: labor would receive no access to the decision-making process, and the most that strikers would secure was higher wages and pensions, precisely the focus on "business unionism" that the CIO was seeking to transcend. Moreover, the president seemed to side more with business than with unions. He took over the coal mines in May 1946 to curtail the severe shortage in the nation's supply of fuel, seized the railroads shortly thereafter to try to abort a railroad strike, and suggested by each of his actions a deep unwillingness to let CIO unions control his political or economic agenda. Although Truman vetoed the Taft-Hartley Act, ensuring labor's support for him in the 1948 presidential election, he could not prevent the harsh antilabor restrictions contained in the act—many of which he had supported himself—from coming into effect after the bill was passed over his veto.

Labor proved particularly vulnerable to the politics of anti-Communism. Members of the Communist Party, or people close to them, had played a major role in some of the most aggressive CIO unions. Committed to organizing women and minorities, they bore a large share of the credit for the CIO's success in the electrical, steel, rubber, and textile industries. Now, the Taft-Hartley act required that all labor leaders sign a pledge that they had no relationship to the Communist Party. Caught in an impossible dilemma given the fever pitch of anti-Communism, most labor leaders supported the oath, purged their unions or those with a pronounced "leftist" past, and accepted as orthodoxy a set of moderate political beliefs that substantially eroded the radical vision so visible in the labor movement just a few years earlier.

As a result, by 1950 labor was severely diminished in both its political and economic horizons. Defeated by business in its quest for sharing power with management, it also trimmed its sails in the political sphere. Now tied to a philosophy of "business unionism," and inextricably linked to the Democratic administration in power, it ceased to be an independent spur for political and social change. National health insurance, one of its highest-priority items, fell by the wayside in the Eighty-first Congress, a direct casualty of the newly triumphant politics of anti-Communism. Providing federal support to health insurance, Republicans and the American Medical Association insisted, was tantamount to "socialized medicine," a direct step toward imitating the Soviet system. Although Truman succeeded in raising minimum wages, extending Social Security, and passing a National Housing Act that provided for the construction of 810,000 subsidized low-income housing units over the next six years, he failed in his bid to secure a permanent FEPC, provide federal aid to education, or extend the TVA principle to the Columbia and Missouri river valleys. Instead, he found himself fighting a rearguard action against those who wished to repeal the New Deal, all the while struggling to find a way to preserve the integrity of the party in the face of a pervasive anti-Communism that both controlled the rhetoric and the reality of domestic politics and caused the nation to embark on an undeclared war in a part of the world that most of the country had never heard of or considered.

V. THE KOREAN WAR

When the North Korean Army invaded South Korea in June 1950, it was simply the latest in a series of reversals the United States had experienced in the Cold War. By mid-1948, the Red Army had clamped an iron grip on Hungary, Czechoslovakia, and Poland. In Berlin, Soviet troops mounted a blockade around the city barring Western Allies from resupplying West Berlin via railroad. In response, the United States launched a massive airlift that heroically provided all the materials Berliners needed to survive, an airlift that proved so effective that within a year the Russians had lifted their blockade. But in 1949, perhaps the most devastating blows of the Cold War thus far were landed. The Soviet Union successfully exploded an atomic bomb, years before the United States believed they could; and Communist troops under the leadership of Mao Zedong drove the Chinese nationalist army under Chiang Kai Shek from the mainland of China onto the island of Formosa. The latter two events not only stunned Western leaders but also accelerated, almost geometrically, the paranoia in the West that Communists had successfully infiltrated Western governments and were engaged in a systematic effort of subversion. Clearly, Soviet success in exploding a nuclear weapon owed a great deal to the presence of Soviet spies in Los Alamos. And as soon as China fell, the first, reflexive question was, "Who lost China?" as if Americans had caused Chiang's defeat and the Chinese had nothing to do with it. It was in the midst of these shocking developments, and the wave of doubt and suspicion that surrounded them, that North Korea suddenly put America, and Harry Truman, on the spot.

The "loss" of China had already transformed American policy toward the Far East. Together with the Soviet Union, the Communist Chinese now held the balance of power in Asia. As a result, the United States, once committed only to democratization in Japan, came to view their conquered foe as a military and economic counterweight to China. This became even more the case when North Korean troops suddenly crossed the thirty-eighth parallel and sped their way toward Seoul, the South Korean capital. "If this was allowed to go unchallenged," Truman observed, "it would mean a third world war." Truman immediately announced that he was sending American troops to defend South Korea, then succeeded in getting the United Nations to commit to repel aggression there (the USSR was boycotting the Security Council and hence failed to veto the resolution).

In the face of unrelenting aggression, South Korean and American troops initially retreated steadily southward. Then, in one of the most daring and risky military responses ever conceived, the troops of General Douglas MacArthur, the Allied commander in the Far East, carried out a bold amphibious landing at Inchon, north of Seoul. Within weeks, the South Korean capital had been recaptured and Allied forces were pounding on the North Korean border.

At that point, all the geopolitics of the Cold War came together. As we now know, Stalin had given approval to the North Korean invasion, although he went to great lengths to disguise his complicity. China was not involved in the planning but felt immediately threatened by the presence of United States troops on its border, particularly in light of America's rhetorical commitment to "liberate" China and return Chiang Kai Shek to control. Deeply worried about Chinese intervention, Truman flew to Wake Island, where MacArthur assured him there was no chance of a Chinese military response. He was wrong. Even as Truman and MacArthur spoke, masses of Chinese soldiers were streaming across the Yalu River into North Korea. An army of more than a quarter million Chinese drove MacArthur's forces out of all the territory they had won and sent them reeling back to the thirty-eighth parallel. It was one of the cruelest, most difficult winters ever faced by American forces, with shocking cold and blinding storms, a rugged terrain of jagged mountains, treacherous swamps, and unbridged streams, with an enemy who gave no quarter. When MacArthur then publicly urged that America bomb China, blockade the coastline, and unleash Chiang Kai Shek's army to invade the mainland, he had gone too far. With the support of the Joint Chiefs of Staff as well as the entire Pentagon, Truman relieved MacArthur of his command.

It had been an unpopular and unhappy war. Congress was never asked for a Declaration of War—hence there was no political "buy-in" to the conflict. As casualties mounted (nearly forty thousand Americans died) and hardships intensified, little will existed to carry the conflict any further. Thus when the Soviet ambassador proposed an armistice in June 1951 with mutual withdrawal behind the thirty-eighth parallel, Washington welcomed the initiative. But negotiations dragged on interminably, moving toward the 1952 presidential elections with no end in sight. On the positive side, desegregation in the armed forces advanced dramatically during the Korean conflict— Korea, in fact, was the real occasion for desegregation to take place. But on the negative side, the president lost virtually all his political capital, and the nation had aligned itself more closely with the interests of Chiang in Formosa and the French in Indochina, thereby moving the country a fateful step toward further disasters in Southeast Asia. Perhaps most disturbing of all, the war brought to fever pitch a period of xenophobia that ultimately rivaled the Red Scare of 1919. For in the same year the country went to war in Korea, a young senator from Wisconsin named Joe McCarthy started dominating

Within five years of the end of World War II, Americans once again found themselves at war, this time in Korea, in opposition to a Communist regime in the North that was seeking to take South Korea. Although fighting a war that displayed none of the fervor or idealism that accompanied World War II, American GIs still battled courageously. Here they are shown marching toward the thirty-eighth parallel, the dividing line between North and South Korea.

Credit: © Bettmann/CORBIS

the national airwaves with a new sensational cry. "I have here in my hand the names of 57 (or was it 207?) card-carrying Communists" in the State Department, McCarthy shouted. The spies were selling America down the road to Communist domination, he claimed, and no barriers should stand in the way of ferreting them out.

VI. CONCLUSION

McCarthyism represented the culmination of a political era. When World War II ended, it was by no means clear that there would be a Cold War or a Red Scare to accompany it. Roosevelt still believed that he could find a way to deal with Stalin and that recognizing the Soviet leader's national interest in having a secure sphere of influence on the borders of his country would provide the foundation for working out international rules of governance that might simultaneously accommodate a nation's security priorities and also show proper respect for universal human rights. Although some possibility of such an arrangement remained alive between 1945 and 1947, by the time of the Truman Doctrine a state of perpetual conflict between the United States and the Soviet Union had become a foregone conclusion. Once that decision had been made, it was almost inevitable that each nation would rely on the hyperbole of holy war rhetoric to justify to its people the sacrifices that would be required. No longer could policy be made on the basis of "practical arithmetic," as Stalin called it. Now the struggle was between good and evil, God-fearing democracy and atheistic communism.

Inexorably, framing foreign policy in such a manner seeped into the ways in which domestic issues were conceived. When the politics of anti-Communism became the anchor of all political discourse, it was no longer possible to talk about social measures such as national health insurance or a new sharing of economic power with labor. Such ideas were ruled automatically out of bounds because they were "leftist" or "pro-Communist." Instead, social reforms had to be advanced as part of the effort to strengthen democracy in its war with Communist tyranny. Thus the civil rights movement moved much more carefully in its political approach, focusing on litigation and incremental advances within the existing social and political structure rather than far-reaching systemic change. Similarly, organized labor—and particularly the CIO—had to pull back from the idea of industrial democracy that had so animated the labor movement at the end of World War II and instead satisfy itself with more narrow goals such as enhanced wages and better pension plans. Unlike Europe and Scandinavia, a politics of the Left could not exist in the United States. All that could be envisioned was incremental reform.

The British journalist Godfrey Hodgson has dubbed this new political framework America's "liberal consensus." It was, according to Hodgson, based on a series of axioms: (a) capitalism was the best economic system in the world; (b) democracy was the best political system in the world; (c) democracy and capitalism were inextricably linked, just as were tyranny and communism; (d) despite occasional problems, there was nothing structurally or organically wrong with the American system; (e) whatever problems did exist could be dealt with through economic growth and incremental reforms; (f) all of this, in turn, hinged on a national consensus to fight communism anywhere and everywhere it appeared: there could be no dissent, no debate. This was a bipartisan commitment.

Although historians might quarrel with the simplicity of Hodgson's diagnosis, it provided an important model for understanding the centrist thrust of American politics over the ensuing years and the degree to which Democrats and Republicans—however different their partisan perspectives—nevertheless shared these common assumptions. The direct product of the political struggles that had evolved from 1945 forward, this new consensus, rooted in anti-Communism, would shape the course of American politics for the next four decades.

8

Ike and the Affluent Society: An Age of Contradictions

Rarely has a decade of American history appeared so full of contentment and progress. A booming economy made the Great Depression look like a bad dream of the distant past. The population grew like wildflowers in the summer sun; suburbs sprouted in ever widening circles around American cities; televisions, automobiles, and outside barbecue grills became fixtures in countless American households; and a new generation of teenagers learned to "rock and roll." The nation was at peace despite periodic crises caused by Cold War tensions. The question that most engaged millions of people was not whether, or when, they would find a job to support their family but who would win the *$64,000 Question* and how long it would take Lucille Ball of *I Love Lucy* to have her baby born on television.

Yet just beneath the surface, stress fractures that would eventually lead to open breaks with the past were visible to the discerning eye. Despite a pervasive image of women as homemakers luxuriating in their domestic and suburban bliss, an incipient sense of dissatisfaction started to grow, indicated by an increasing divorce rate, an accelerated use of tranquilizers, and a haunting if still quiet question: "Is this all there is?" Young people, supposedly captive to a hegemonic conformity of striving for better grades in order to sooner enter the world of the "gray flannel suit" executive class also began to ask questions about the meaning of life, the persistence of social injustice, and the value of upward mobility as an end in itself. Above all, millions of African Americans persisted in challenging their country to live up to its ideals, manifesting by their actions a determination never again to accept "no" for an answer to their struggle for freedom.

Presiding over all of this was a venerated war hero and national symbol of America's most cherished values. Perceived at the time as a great unifier who would bring peace and stability to a society desperately in need of a respite from war and depression, Dwight David Eisenhower was also a farsighted, shrewd, and talented politician who understood well the forces that were transforming America both at home and in her role in the world. Although on many critical issues he would fall short—most glaringly in his response to race, the greatest domestic challenge he faced—Eisenhower also provided the pivotal leadership that helped consolidate the political consensus that had grown out of the postwar era and guided the country through potentially catastrophic international crises with wisdom and poise.

I. THE EISENHOWER PRESIDENCY

The secret to Ike's effectiveness was his personality. "He has this power of drawing the hearts of men towards him," British Field Marshal Bernard Montgomery observed, "as a magnet attracts the bits of metal. He has merely to smile at you, and you trust him at once." Direct, honest, strong, Eisenhower conveyed who he was from first contact. "There was one feature of his face impossible to forget," another colleague stated, "the blue eyes of a force and intensity singularly deep, almost disturbing, above all commanding." Neither academically brilliant nor economically well off, Eisenhower grew up in Abilene, Kansas, then went to West Point, where he finished 61 in a class of more than 150. But in the 1920s he went to the Command and General Staff School at Fort Leavenworth, where he graduated first in his class, and began the long upward climb in the military ranks, working with MacArthur in Washington and the Philippines, then with Marshall in the War Office before being assigned to be supreme commander in Europe. There he impressed everyone with his diplomatic skill—the ability to bring order out of chaos and reconcile military egos as diverse as Patton and Montgomery—but above all by his cool decision-making skills. Alone, and faced with dire possibilities of weather disasters on D day, he made the decision to launch the invasion. His troops understood Ike's honesty, warmth, and courage. They loved and trusted him like a father—as soon would be the case with the American people as a whole.

Ever since the war ended, politicians from both parties had sought his support and potential candidacy for national office. Ike avowed his political neutrality, claimed he had no further ambitions—"I think I pretty well hit my peak in history when I accepted the German surrender in 1945," he said—and seemed content with his postwar roles as president of Columbia University and then commander of NATO in Europe. But the politicians kept knocking, and finally in 1952 Ike answered when Republicans from the Eastern, internationalist wing of the party beseeched him to carry the banner for moderation against the isolationist and conservative candidacy of Ohio Senator Robert Taft. Perhaps he had always wanted to be president and simply needed to be persuaded he was indispensable ("Ike wants to be president so badly you can taste it," General George Patton noted in 1943). Or perhaps it was his sense of duty and fear of what would happen if Taft—"he has no intellectual ability nor any comprehension of the issues of the world," Ike said—were to become the Republic nominee.

In any event, Ike finally permitted his name to be entered in the New Hampshire Republican primary. With a stunning victory there (he did not even campaign), he rapidly garnered mainstream party support and defeated Bob Taft, "Mr. Republican," for the nomination. He then overpowered Democratic nominee Governor Adlai Stevenson, waging a vigorous campaign against the Democrats and their K1, C2 record—Korea, Communism, and Corruption—and promising, "I shall go to Korea" to end the war. The only hitch in his campaign occurred when it was revealed that his vice-presidential nominee, Richard Nixon, had received a campaign slush fund to pay for expenses not covered by his congressional allowance. Ike wanted to dump Nixon, but the vice-presidential candidate shrewdly bought half an hour of network TV time and made his famous "Checkers" speech—my children, he said, received a gift cocker spaniel that they named Checkers and adored. Surely, the American people would not want them to give the dog back because of some legalistic campaign finance regulations. Overwhelmingly the people supported Nixon and he stayed on the ticket. With that blip behind him, however, Ike steadily built momentum and was overwhelmingly elected president of the United States.

The most notable feature of the Eisenhower administration was its continuity with the Truman administration before it. To be sure, Ike appointed a cabinet of businessmen—three were from General Motors, and Charles Wilson, secretary of defense, became infamous for his comment that "what's good for the country is good for General Motors and vice versa." Moreover, on a variety of issues Ike took a position different from that which Truman would have followed: jettisoning plans for federally controlled dams on a TVA model (Ike called the TVA "creeping socialism"), releasing federal rights over offshore oil deposits to seaboard states, eliminating the Reconstruction Finance Corporation, and vetoing a school construction bill. Still, the many Republicans who hoped for a complete reversal of Democratic policies were sorely disappointed. The core of Eisenhower's political philosophy was distilled in a letter he sent to his conservative brother Edgar. "Should any political party attempt to abolish Social Security, unemployment insurance, and eliminate labor laws and farm programs," he warned, "you would not hear of that party again in our political history." Far from wishing to dismantle the New Deal legacy, Ike saw his major responsibility as seeking to consolidate and make more effective the social welfare legacy Roosevelt and Truman had bequeathed him. He expanded Social Security, extended the minimum wage to thousands of new workers not previously covered, created a Department of Health, Education and Welfare as a cabinet-level position, and created a federally financed new interstate highway system. Although he clearly was not a bully pulpit reformer a la Teddy Roosevelt, Eisenhower accepted and expanded the social welfare role government had assumed during the Depression and war.

In a similar fashion, Eisenhower modified and refined the domestic anti-Communist policies pursued by Truman while for the most part continuing their thrust. Personally, Eisenhower was repelled by McCarthy, just as Truman was. McCarthy infuriated Eisenhower when he attacked Ike's hero, General George C. Marshall, as "soft on communism" and considered opposing his appointment of Walter Bedell Smith, Eisenhower's chief of staff in the army, as undersecretary of state. But Ike refused to challenge McCarthy directly. "I will not get into the gutter with that guy," he told a friend. "I just won't get into a pissing contest with that skunk." Instead, Eisenhower avoided open criticism of McCarthy, even deleting a portion of a speech where he praised Marshall, and preferred instead to work quietly to defuse his attacks.

In the end, of course, McCarthy overreached and brought on his own destruction by taking on the United States Army and accusing generals of undermining American security. This time he had gone too far, and in the televised Army-McCarthy hearings that followed, the garrulous McCarthy dug his own grave. When for no apparent reason he launched a public attack on a young associate of the army's counsel, Joseph Welch, who was not even involved in the case, accusing him of Communist sympathies, Welch galvanized the Senate—and the country, which was watching. "Little did I dream you could be so cruel," Welch said. "Let us not assassinate this lad further, Senator. You have done enough. Have you no sense of decency, sir, at long last? Have you left no sense of decency." Within six months, the Senate had responded by censuring McCarthy.

From one perspective, Ike demonstrated his political shrewdness by refusing to "get into the gutter" with McCarthy. Eventually, the senator's reckless disregard for truth, manners, and collegial responsibility caused him to commit political hari-kari. By permitting McCarthy to walk out on a limb all by himself, without becoming publicly engaged, Ike both preserved his own dignity and denied McCarthy his ultimate weapon—being able to attack the president of the United States from his own party as being "soft on communism." On the other hand, Eisenhower also displayed temerity. It was TV commentator Edward R. Murrow who became a "profile in courage," daring to take on McCarthy by featuring his words and actions on national TV and challenging the American people to stand up for decency and fairness. Ike, by contrast, offered a "profile of detachment," absenting himself from the battle.

Yet in all this, Ike embodied the style that would identify his administration from start to finish—moderation. Reluctant to take positions that were divisive or that would tarnish the standing of the presidency, Eisenhower chose instead to remain a centrist, a "modern Republican," as he described himself. He would support government's responsibility to provide a safety net for those most in need. "The legitimate aim of government," Ike used to quote Abraham Lincoln as saying, "is to do for a community of people whatever they need to have done, but cannot do...for themselves....[But] government ought not to interfere...in all that the people can individually do... for themselves." It was the kind of political philosophy that could make a young conservative like Barry Goldwater accuse Ike of running a "Dime Store New Deal." But it was also a philosophy that most Americans heartily endorsed, reflecting that "liberal consensus" that Godfrey Hodgson perceived as constituting the foundation of American politics after 1948. With anti-Communism, economic growth, and commitment to government's responsibility for basic social welfare as common ground, the center would hold and prosper in American politics. As if to reflect the popularity of such a centrist posture, Ike was overwhelmingly reelected to the presidency in 1956.

Ike also continued with success the policy of containment toward Communism that constituted the anchor of mainstream American politics.

Although President Dwight David Eisenhower was shrewd, bright, and very much on top of national policy, he had a persona as a father figure who benevolently watched over the country while enjoying card games and golf. Here he is shown engaging in his favorite pastime.

Credit: © Bettmann/CORBIS

Following his trip to Korea after being elected, Ike vigorously pursued the effort to achieve a permanent armistice in the two Koreas. Bolstered by an implicit threat to use far more powerful weapons if negotiations proved unsuccessful, the North Koreans agreed to an armistice in June 1953. With John Foster Dulles as his secretary of state, Eisenhower chose a public posture of aggressive anti-Communism. (Although some accused Ike of being lazy and delegating his authority to others, he was always in charge and informed.) The United States strongly supported French interests in Vietnam and bankrolled most of the war against the Vietminh, largely as a means of securing French cooperation against Communism in Europe. When the French defeat at Dien Bien Phu prompted an international conference at Geneva to arrange terms of peace, Dulles refused to shake hands with the Chinese foreign minister because "one does not shake hands with the devil," and the United States persistently resisted efforts to unify Vietnam under a Communist regime. The United States also continually used the Cold War as its principal raison d'etre for determining which countries would receive American foreign aid. Nations like India or Egypt risked losing support if they declared themselves neutral in the Cold War. Meanwhile, the CIA took on a life of its own under Allen Dulles (John Foster Dulles's brother), initiating coups d'etat in Iran and in Guatemala to depose regimes that threatened American interests. An Iranian coup deposed the nationalist Prime Minster Mussadegh because he wished to nationalize oil reserves and imposed instead a pro-American, Shah Reza Pahlevi—an act that would have consequences that lasted well into the twenty-first century.

To back up this interventionist stance, the Eisenhower administration announced a military policy of "massive retaliation" in January 1954 against any country that threatened the United States. In the face of vastly greater numbers of Soviet troops, the United States would rely on its superior nuclear-strike capacity, which would be deployed "by means, and at places of our choosing." Putting all America's military eggs in one basket, the doctrine was intended to secure "more basic security at less cost," making it possible for the United States to avoid the expense of drafting and training massive numbers of ground troops while utilizing to maximum advantage its incredible air strength—more than 1,700 planes capable of dropping nuclear weapons by 1955, ten times the comparable number of Soviet aircraft. By the end of the Eisenhower administration, America had 6,000 nuclear weapons, four times more than it possessed in 1953.

The advantage of Ike's "more bang for the buck" strategy was that it allowed America's military budget to decline. "Every gun that is made," Eisenhower said in 1953, "every warship launched, every rocket fired, signifies, in the final sense, a theft from those who hunger and are not fed, those who are cold and not clothed." Sometimes the threat of massive retaliation worked, causing the Communist Chinese, for example, to be cautious in their periodic harassment of Quemoy and Matsu, islands that the Chinese Nationalists claimed, off the Chinese mainland. On the other hand, it proved useless when the Soviet Union's armored divisions brutally invaded Hungary in 1956 to quell anti-Communist dissidents. Despite its propagandistic rhetoric about supporting the "liberation of Eastern Europe," the United States was not really prepared to start World War III over an Eastern European country already in the Soviet sphere.

In retrospect, Eisenhower's restraint in the foreign policy arena stands forth as one of his most notable accomplishments and as singular testimony to "moderation" as the leitmotif of his presidency. When the French faced imminent defeat at Dien Bien Phu, for example, prominent American officials, including Vice President Richard Nixon and the air force chief of staff, urged dropping tactical nuclear weapons on North Vietnamese troops. Ike's response: "You boys must be crazy. We can't use those awful things against Asians for the second time in less than ten years. My God." Similarly, he rejected the use of tactical nuclear weapons against China over Quemoy and Matsu, though he let the Chinese think such strikes were still in the realm of possibility. In 1956, when Israel attacked Egypt in concert with Britain and France after Egyptian nationalist Gamal Abdal Nasser had seized control of the Suez Canal, Ike went to the United Nations and secured a resolution demanding an end to the fighting. Alienating three of America's closest allies, Eisenhower also threatened to intervene if the Russians got involved.

But in the end, and largely due to Eisenhower's careful negotiation of the issues, the crisis was resolved peacefully.

Eisenhower's greatest hopes and bitterest disappointments centered on his quest for nuclear arms control and a reduction in tensions with the Soviet Union. With an insight not usually associated with generals, Eisenhower keenly understood the danger of military machines that were unconstrained by a sense of a larger responsibility to the country's well-being—hence his plea for reduced military budgets to help feed those who were hungry. Eisenhower missed his golden chance to cut the Gordian knot of the Cold War when Stalin died in 1953 and the new Soviet leadership seemed ready to take a fresh look at the entrenched antagonism between the two superpowers. But at the very beginning of his administration, and with Dulles insisting on a hard line, Eisenhower failed to act. Still, in the summer of 1955, at the first summit conference since 1945 at Potsdam, world leaders met in Geneva to discuss world tensions. There, Eisenhower seized the world's attention by proposing an "Open Skies" program whereby each superpower would open its military resources for inspection. Nikita Khrushchev rejected the idea as a propaganda ploy (which in truth it was), arguing that everyone already knew about U.S. strength, and only the West would gain by finding out Soviet secrets. Still, a seed had been planted. Khrushchev, for all his impetuous behavior, represented a breath of fresh air. In February 1956 he startled the world by denouncing Stalin as a tyrannical psychopath and called for de-Stalinization of both Russia and Eastern Europe. For a moment, there was hope. But then came the Hungarian revolution in the summer of 1956, brutal repression by Soviet troops, and renewed conflict with the West.

One more opportunity presented itself. After John Foster Dulles's death from cancer in 1958, Eisenhower became a much more open and ardent advocate of détente. Assured by intelligence overflights of the Soviet Union conducted by high-flying U-2 aircraft that America had decisive military superiority over the Soviets, Ike prepared a new peace initiative. The United States suspended atmospheric testing of nuclear weapons in late 1958 (after completing a lengthy series of explosions), and the Soviets reciprocated. Tensions over Berlin seemed to calm down after the Soviets let a deadline pass for signing a separate peace treaty with East Germany. Ike pursued discussions with Russia and lambasted alarmists in America who demanded more money for the military. "I'm getting awfully sick of the lobbies by the munitions [industry]," he said. "You begin to see this thing isn't wholly the defense of the country, but only more money for some who are already fat cats." A final summit conference with Khrushchev was now scheduled for Paris in the spring of 1960, perhaps the final chance Ike could realize his dream.

But then a U-2 spy plane piloted by Gary Powers was shot down over the Soviet Union. Initially, the United States disclaimed knowledge of the event, assuming that Powers had used his suicide kit to kill himself. Now Khrushchev revealed that, no, Powers was alive and spilled the beans publicly about America's spy missions (which, of course, the Soviets already knew about). The United States looked both stupid and foolish. Eisenhower took responsibility for the spy planes and went to Paris hoping to salvage something positive from the disaster. But Khrushchev was on a tear, and seizing the momentary propaganda advantage he had, blustered at the United States, seeking to humiliate his adversary. All he accomplished was to subvert the summit and torpedo the final opportunity he would have with Eisenhower to find a way out of the dark dungeon of the Cold War.

In the end, Dwight David Eisenhower ranks as one of the more successful twentieth-century presidents. Always brighter than people gave him credit for being, he also had a keen political intelligence. Ike wrote clearly and elegantly but occasionally fudged his verbal comments—intentionally—to befuddle people. Thus, when his press secretary James Haggerty worried about Ike being challenged on Quemoy and Matsu by the press, Eisenhower said, "Don't worry Jim, I'll just confuse them." Neither detached nor aloof, he knew what he was doing at all times. Nothing mattered more to him than appearing to be above the fray, preserving his popularity, and maintaining the dignity of the presidency. One result of such a predilection was Ike's dismal failure to take a strong stance against McCarthyism or, as we shall see later, to act energetically in support of racial equality. A second result, however, was to pursue policies of moderation on virtually all issues. By doing so, Ike exemplified the politics of continuity and consensus that had grown out of the immediate postwar years. He would neither recklessly attack the New Deal nor militantly go after the Soviet Union.

Peace was Eisenhower's ultimate goal, and nowhere did he articulate his commitment to that objective more than in his farewell address to the nation. There he eloquently warned against "the acquisition of unwarranted influence...by the military-industrial complex." Eisenhower had striven for eight years to bring peace. Disarmament, he declared, "is a continuing imperative. Together we must learn how to compose differences, not with arms, but with intellect and decent purpose." To that end, it was imperative, Eisenhower declared, to "never let the weight of this [military-industrial] combination endanger our liberties or democratic processes." It was a fitting farewell for one who had struggled so insistently to find the path to world harmony.

II. BOOM TIME IN AMERICA

The extraordinary prosperity of America in the postwar years facilitated enormously the success of Eisenhower's pursuit of moderation. Ironically for a free-enterprise economy, it was government spending that helped propel the nation's newfound affluence. The pump priming by Uncle Sam had begun in the war, with billions of dollars flowing into the modernization of the industrial infrastructure. What had been tank factories soon were producing automobiles. Military fighter production lines quickly were transformed into Boeing, Lockheed, and McDonnell-Douglas factories producing commercial prop planes, then jets. The Research and Development (R&D) money injected into chemical and electrical companies now helped produce a new generation of plastics, transistor radios, and television sets. In what historian Richard Hofstadter dubbed "military Keynesianism," the government enabled private industry to leap forward with technological innovations that, literally, made for a new world.

Nor did infusion of government resources end with the war. The GI Bill provided tuition and stipends for hundreds of thousands to get a higher education, and the Veterans Administration offered loans that made it possible for millions to afford a down payment on a new house. Government-financed technology breakthroughs made possible heightened levels of productivity through laborsaving devices—a 200 percent increase between 1947 and 1956 alone—and the new emphasis on theoretical knowledge helped more than double the number of American workers engaged in professional and technical occupations. As just one indication of how federal dollars made a difference, in 1929 federal expenditures accounted for 1 percent of the Gross National Product; in 1955, 17 percent—all this while the GNP itself was increasing dramatically, from $355.3 billion in 1950 to $487.7 billion in 1960, a rise of 37 percent. The number of citizens receiving Social Security payments leaped five times in the 1950s, and the total paid out grew from $960 million per year in 1950 to $10.7 billion a decade later.

As the economy grew, dramatic changes took place as well in the workforce. Laborsaving devices and technological wizardry meant fewer assembly line jobs. In 1956, the nation passed a milestone: for the first time white-collar employees outnumbered blue-collar workers. The office with a thousand little cubicles housing office staff superseded the assembly line as the dominant image of the American workplace; clerical employees increased at a rate of 23 percent between 1947 and 1957 while factory operatives declined by 4 percent. To be sure, manufacturing jobs still grew. Labor unions represented eighteen million people, or 34.7 percent of the nonagricultural workforce. But unions now focused more on bread-and-butter issues, the national leadership became more conservative, and union chieftains acted and looked a lot more like their business executive counterparts than rivals in class conflict. In the meantime, the new jobs being created were in offices, department stores, and automobile showrooms, places where shirts, ties, and skirts took the place of blue factory work shirts.

Propelling the new economy as much as government dollars was the burgeoning consumer power of citizens seemingly caught in a marathon race to see who could spend the most money the fastest. Credit cards made their national appearance. People went into hock as they never had before, with private indebtedness growing 150 percent in the 1950s, from $104.8 billion to $263.3 billion. People who had never imagined having a washing machine or a television went wild with the new opportunities for adding household appliances like air conditioners or outdoor barbecue grills to their homes. Television, in particular, became the medium of the new consumer culture. Within a decade, ownership of the new instrument of popular entertainment went from 172,000 to nearly 100 million. Children rushed home from school to watch *Howdy Doody,* and adults made a weekly ritual of watching Milton Berle or Sid Caesar's *Show of Shows*. Advertisers, meanwhile, used the new medium to sell more of their wares to the general public.

Partly as a result of the new world being introduced to people via TV, millions of Americans now traveled out of state on vacation, staying at another new phenomenon of the 1950s—Holiday Inns—and eating at fast-food franchises like McDonald's, which soon swept the countryside. They got there in their new, tail-finned cars, trading in their old models if they had one—4.5 millions old cars per year were replaced—or buying a car for the first time. More than 8 million cars per year were sold by the end of the decade; 80 percent of all American families owned one (and 15 percent owned two), and nearly 75 million cars were registered, compared with only 40 million a decade earlier. And it was a good thing because Americans needed those cars to drive to their new homes in suburbia. No single development changed the face of America in the 1950s more than the orgy of home-building that occurred in the ever growing crescents of housing developments that emerged outside the nation's cities. The move to suburbia was equivalent to the mass European migration to America from abroad in the first decade of the century, when an average of 1.2 million people came to this country every year. Now the same number moved each year to the suburbs, with 18 million people making the transfer in one decade. Easy housing loans from the VA and Federal Housing Authority provided the capital for people to start with. Huge, massively efficient building contractors provided the housing stock. Levittowns in New York and Pennsylvania were carefully planned, symmetrical neighborhoods, with four- to five-room houses of twelve hundred square feet lined up on quarter-acre lots on slightly curving streets, block after block, for as far as the eye could see. For under twenty thousand dollars (and no money down due to federal loans) a family who had never before been able to even dream of owning their own home could now move into middle-class comfort, with an electric range and refrigerator, central heating, a backyard big enough for a picnic table and grill, and a "family"/living room with a couch, two easy chairs, and a fourteen-inch TV. Between 1950 and 1960, thirteen million homes were built in the United States. Eleven million of those were in suburbia. By the end of the decade, 25 percent of the entire population lived there.

Once again, the government helped to make it all happen. In addition to the loans and mortgage assistance, Washington helped link all those suburbs to the industrial and commercial centers of the country by constructing a massive new interstate highway system. Starting in 1956, Congress appropriated more than thirty billion dollars to build over forty thousand miles of roads. The Long Island Expressway took people from New York City to Merrick, Levittown, and Freeport. The New York Thruway went to White Plains and Albany. Los Angeles blossomed, with intricate ties of highways from the Santa Monica Freeway to U.S. 101, linking people together in a seemingly never-ending nerve system of connectedness (featuring among other things a never-ending traffic jam). As the new roads were finished, gigantic

The migration to suburbia in the late 1940s and 1950s matched and even exceeded the massive movement of the foreign born to America in the early 1900s. More than eighteen million Americans joined the ranks of suburbia in the 1950s, living in new developments like this one in Fairfax, Delaware.

Credit: © Bettmann/CORBIS

shopping malls appeared at the exits from the interstate, featuring all the name-brand department stores like Macy's and Marshall Field's, once found only in downtown cities but now spreading their wings near and far to wherever people could drive from their suburban homes. Where once a town drugstore or a neighborhood juke joint was the "hangout" spot for teenagers, now it was the Yonkers or Palo Alto mall with its countless appliance stores and fast-food franchises.

Clearly, suburbia altered dramatically the culture of America—how people related to each other; what they did with their spare time; how and with whom they communicated about politics, religion, marital dilemmas, family illnesses. In the city, children on the same street might play with each other. But more often than not, intimate friendships were few, with adults exchanging greetings on the stoop or at the elevator. Now, everyone on a suburban street could observe who was coming and going into other people's houses. Playtime was a group experience, not only for children but for parents—usually mothers—as well. Neighborhood children gathered either on the street or in someone's backyard, and their mothers congregated also, exchanging gossip, talking about local schools, new neighbors, cliques in and around town, the careers of their husbands, the latest scandal or noteworthy national event.

The wonderful part of such interaction was its ready availability—indeed ubiquity. It was difficult to be lonely. But the terrible part was the sense of being forced to join, to conform, to get into the rhythm of saying and doing what everyone else was saying or doing in what the critic Lewis Mumford called "a multitude of uniform, unidentifiable houses, lined up inflexibly, at uniform distances, on uniform roads, in a treeless, communal wasteland, inhabited by people of the same class, the same income, the same age group." What at first appeared to be a gift of togetherness could easily become a prison denying its inmates any possibility for individuality, free expression, or rebellion. Hence the appearance of a series of scathing books denouncing the stultifying conformity of suburbia: *The Lonely Crowd, The Split-Level Trap, The Crack in the Picture Window*. One satirical song summarized the growing critique:

> They all play on the golf course
> And drink their martinis dry
> And they all have pretty children
> And their children go to school,
> And the children go to summer camp
> And then to the university,
> Where they are put into boxes
> And they come out just the same.

In reality, of course, such an assessment represented a caricature. Most people inhabiting the new suburbs exulted in the freedom they had achieved, the new opportunities that had opened to them, the opportunities they and their children now enjoyed for a qualitatively different and better life than they had experienced before. Although in some instances community might seemed forced and tyrannical, in most cases people welcomed the opportunity to share friendship, provide and receive emotional support, and develop a network of solidarity to withstand the tensions that accompanied modern living. Still, the critique pointed to a darker side of life in the 1950s that, even if only rarely present, nevertheless spoke to a potential for more far-reaching discontent.

III. THE ORGANIZATION MAN

Reflecting the confluence of suburban lifestyles and corporate culture was the emergence of a new business icon, the "organization man." With his button-down shirt, gray flannel suit, silk rep tie, and gregarious personality, the organization man, as author William Whyte dubbed him, brought to his business responsibilities the same "social ethic" that prevailed in his suburban village: to get along, one had to go along; success came not from making waves but from making friends; following the opinions of others proved more productive than being a maverick and standing alone. From grade school through college, the "organization man" learned that "fitting in" and working well with others was indispensable to being "one of the boys," and "being one of the boys" was the first and most critical step to rising up the corporate ladder. Executives prided themselves on the positive relationships they cultivated with their management "teams." Like a smooth machine, the corporation functioned most effectively when all its component parts interacted smoothly, lubricated by an ethos of togetherness and harmony.

Such a paradigm dramatically clashed with the traditional image of the CEO entrepreneur as a hard-driving, take-no-prisoners tough guy who made decisive calls on his own and cared not a whit whether colleagues liked or disliked what he had done. In at least the popular image of traditional executive leadership, individualism prevailed, the president of the company followed his own inner voice, and the test of a commander's mettle was his ability to make a tough call despite competing pressures. Now, it seemed, the group was in charge, with conformity to its customs the key to advancement and success. An individual who disregarded his peers or acted without attentive consultation with his "team" about the appropriate course of action would be marginalized, not celebrated. It was imperative for everyone to be on board and for executive action to reflect the ethos of the corporate team.

Both paradigms, of course, were caricatures, but the "organization man" pointed to the ascendancy of a new cultural model. In one of the most perceptive analyses written during the 1950s, Harvard sociologist David Riesman argued that the "inner-directed" personality of nineteenth- and early twentieth-century America had been replaced by a new "other-directed" personality. The inner-directed man was a strong individualist who took his marching orders from an inner voice. With a strong ego and superego, he was a person of character who had a sure sense of direction and could be counted upon not to sacrifice his convictions or compromise his integrity. He was Gary Cooper in the movie *High Noon*, who knew that as sheriff, he must stand up to the ruthless gunslinger who threatened his town because that was his duty, and he must be true to himself. The other-directed personality, by contrast, took his cues from the attitudes of others around him. With sensitive antennae, he quickly picked up on signals others were giving, modifying his behavior to conform to their expectations and acting in a manner they would find congenial. Whether or not the other-directed personality had an inner voice, it would be subordinate to the course being charted by others, and it was their attitudes and preferences that would finally guide him. In the one instance, a person would do whatever the inner self said to do; in the other, whatever the group decided was preferable. In perhaps the greatest irony of Riesman's analysis, the "other-directed" personality was acting in a much more classically "feminine" way, showing sensitivity to others and seeking to resolve conflict rather than barging full steam ahead in a more classically "masculine" manner. And although there were almost no "organization *women,"* it appeared that the organization *man* was more and more emulating his suburban partner back home.

What made all of this so intriguing was the way in which the new managerial culture reinforced and replicated the social lifestyle of the suburbs, and how both, in turn, mirrored the conformity that had so infused the political system. Vociferous dissent in any of the three spheres—the corporation, the suburb, and politics—was verboten. The person on Elm Street who painted her house pink while all the others were gray and blue could count on being ostracized as "weird." So could the homemaker who preferred reading Plato or Kierkegaard to going to the neighborhood kaffeeklatsch. The middle-level executive who argued against his co-managers' desire for a change in advertising policy could count the days until his demotion. So too could the maverick who refused to join the company bowling league and displayed his contempt for such boring entertainments. Such individuals would quickly join in retirement the politician who dared to claim that America should reexamine her instinctive anti-Communist stance and consider supporting democratic insurgents against fascist but anti-Communist dictators in Spain and Portugal. To an unusual degree, the different worlds of business, home, and politics thus constituted an interlocking system of shared assumptions, at the heart of which was a powerful new sense of group-centeredness and conformity.

Not surprisingly, the worlds of education and religion reflected some of the same tendencies. Grade schools and high schools have always been testing grounds of popularity. No fear is greater for a young person than that of being unpopular or "different"—a fifth- or tenth-grader who no one plays with at recess or who walks home alone after school rather than with a large group. But the focus on "getting along" appeared to increase during the 1950s, with more and more emphasis on being well adjusted, not being a loner, becoming an integral part of the peer group. At the same time, youngsters had drilled into them the degree to which they should fear communism and rally to the American flag. School principals warned students to be aware of people spouting "foreign" ideas and to tell their teachers or parents if anyone uttered unpatriotic ideas. Students regularly engaged in "air-raid" drills, huddling under their desks to practice what they would do in the event of a Soviet nuclear attack. School assemblies sang military songs—"From the Halls of Montezuma," the marine hymn, or "Anchors Aweigh," the navy anthem—while teachers imparted lessons on how students should be loyal to each other and to their community.

Churches also joined in the chorus of conformism. Starting in 1954, the words one nation "under God" were inserted into the Pledge of Allegiance— which school pupils collectively uttered each morning. Congress, in turn, ordered that "In God We Trust" be inscribed on the national currency. Evangelists like Billy Graham and Oral Roberts galvanized a new evangelical following, and overall the number of people who were "churched" increased from 49 percent in 1940 to 69 percent in 1959, with 110 million people attending Sunday services and 97 percent declaring that they believed in God.

Religion and anticommunism went hand in hand, Billy Graham calling communism "a great sinister anti-Christian movement masterminded by Satan." Children left school each week to attend religious education classes at their local church, and everyone was expected to join in the ritual celebration of God and country together.

Most notable was the focus in suburban churches on the ethic of togetherness. Churches became veritable country clubs, with each night devoted to a different group activity for couples, a men's group, a bowling league, a youth forum, or a women's arts and crafts group. The commentator Lionel Trilling commented acerbically: "Religion nowadays has the appearance of what the ideal modern house has been called: a machine for living." Gone from many churches were the more traditional, stark declarations of faith focusing on individual dedication—wherever God chooses to go, I will follow—and the substitution of messages that offered comfort to the group as a whole. The sociologist GibsonWinter noted that "in place of the sacraments we have the committee meeting, in place of the confession, the bazaar...in place of a community, a collection of functions....Every church activity seems to lead further into a maze of superficiality which is stultifying the middle class community." The suburban minister was more a Scout leader than a prophet, measuring his success less by the fervor of his congregation's faith than by their participation in a plethora of group activities focused on collective fellowship.

In all of this, the underlying theme of postwar suburban culture was the juxtaposition of unprecedented prosperity and the emergence of a new emphasis on group conformity. More than ever before, people were buying the same cars, watching the same television shows, sharing the same religious and social values, and becoming socialized in an ethic of togetherness that discouraged individual dissent or behavior that challenged the hegemony of anticommunism and middle-class conventionality. It has been said that every historical moment produces a social system that can reproduce itself through the institutions it creates. The consumer culture of suburbia and of massive affluence suggests the degree to which Americans in the 1950s had created such a social system.

IV. THE TENSIONS BENEATH THE SURFACE

Yet even as commentators focused on the pervasiveness of conformity, it was not necessary to dig very deep to see fracture lines virtually everywhere, from sex roles to religion to education to politics. The "organization man" might exemplify the conventional and gregarious lifestyle that inhabited so many of the middle- and upper-class suburbs of the nation, but his wife might be asking, "Is this all there is?" His children might be contemplating rebellion, both in their musical taste and in their attitude toward conventional behavior, and at least some in his church and in the political sphere were raising searching questions about a higher calling that could produce more fulfillment than just climbing the corporate ladder.

From most perspectives, it appeared that middle class-women were luxuriating in their roles as suburban matrons. The baby boom created a population explosion that gave most women little if any time to consider anything but raising a family and caring for a spouse. The fertility rate went up 50 percent, from 80 in 1940 to 123 in 1957. Women married earlier—60 percent of eighteen- to twenty-four-year-olds had husbands in 1950 versus only 42 percent in 1940—had their first child soon thereafter, and then another, and then another. The birthrate for third children doubled between 1940 and 1960. Life in suburbia was full to overflowing—church clubs, PTAs, playgroups, volunteer associations—not to mention nonstop chauffeuring. As Betty Friedan wrote in *The Feminine Mystique,* most of these women were living out the dream prescribed for them by women's magazines and psychiatrists. The *Ladies' Home Journal* described women as supremely happy "in a world of bedroom, kitchen, sex, babies and home." A happy woman, the psychiatrist Helene Deutsch preached, suppressed any masculine strivings she might have and lived through her husband and children, finding therein the fulfillment of "normal femininity." "What modern woman has to recapture," a prominent social commentator declared, "is [that] just being a woman is her central task and her greatest honor.... Women must boldly announce that no job is more exacting, more necessary, or more rewarding than that of housewife and mother."

It was all a bit much, as if women had to be reassured that everything was all right. Why, in that case, did a 1946 *Fortune* magazine poll show that one in four women would rather be men if they had a chance (as opposed to only 3.3 percent of men who would rather be women)? *Life* magazine answered in 1947 that women had a dilemma—many wished to do something more than learn to be gourmet cooks and superb mothers. They were also tired of "playing dumb" in front of men in order to make them feel good when they knew they had as many brains as any male executive. Toward the end of the 1950s, more of these women started talking about their dissatisfaction, although they could not give it a label—hence Friedan's description of "the problem that has no name."

Moreover, millions of such women were breaking away from the role prescribed for them and taking jobs. They were not pursuing careers or competing with men. But they were helping to make a middle-class life possible for their families (especially after their children were in school). More and more of them came from homes where their husband earned $7,000–$10,000 a year (25 percent of women worked in such households in 1960 versus 7 percent in 1950), and increasing numbers of them were college graduates (53 percent of college graduates were employed versus 36 percent of high school graduates). In short, the picture was more confusing than clear. Indeed, by 1960, both husband and wife worked in more than ten million homes—surely not what women's magazine editors had in minds when they declared that the only path to fulfillment as women

The 1950s were the height of the "baby boom," with the average family having four children. As later depicted by feminist author Betty Friedan, this was also the age of the "feminine mystique," where magazines portrayed women as lyrically happy with their lives as mothers and housewives. This picture captures that portrayal.

Credit: © H. Armstrong Roberts/CORBIS

was full-time devotion to their roles as housewives and mothers. TV situation dramas like *Father Knows Best* might continue to trumpet the message that women who pursued careers were depriving themselves of their only chance for happiness. But the situation in reality seemed a bit more complicated, with some women, at least, no longer totally captive to the "feminine mystique."

Nothing confounded traditional stereotypes more than the Kinsey report on American sexuality. If ever Americans believed that women remained virgins until marriage, that couples did not cheat on each other, and that virtually every man and woman in the country was a dyed-in-the-wool heterosexual, the research of Alfred Kinsey and his associates exploded their preconceptions. Half of women and probably three-quarters of men experienced premarital intercourse. A quarter of women and half of all men engaged in extramarital sex. And in the greatest shocker of all, 13 percent of women and 37 percent of men reported at least one homosexual encounter, with 10 percent of men practicing an ongoing homosexual lifestyle. The Kinsey findings suggested that more than the "feminine mystique" was being questioned in the real-life behavior of most American citizens.

Young people, meanwhile, started to live to the beat of a different drummer—namely, rock 'n' roll—epitomized by the skyrocketing success of merica's new sex symbol, Elvis Presley. In contrast to the button-down lifestyle that prevailed among their parents, rock 'n' roll viscerally pleaded with the young to let go of their inhibitions, discover their bodies, and rock around the clock. In this, as in so much of popular culture, black Americans paved the way with their rhythm and blues and jazz. But white "covers" of black music soon came to dominate mainstream radio stations, with even some black musicians like Fats Domino, Chuck Berry, and Little Richard "crossing over." The titles of the new music told the story. "Be-Bop-a-Lula, That's My Baby"; "Sha-na-na-na, Sha-na-na-na-na." White disc jockey Dick Clark started a TV show, *American Bandstand,* which captured the heartland as teenagers danced to music each day that captivated a generation. But nothing matched the impact of a young singer from Tennessee named Elvis Presley, who actually sounded "black" and who sensationalized the art of pelvic gyrations to the point where when he appeared on the nation's premier Sunday-night TV entertainment, the *Ed Sullivan Show,* cameras were instructed to show only the top half of his body as he sang "Don't Be Cruel" and "You Ain't Nothing But a Hound-dog." Teenage girls swooned and screamed hysterically, in alternating cycles, while teenage boys desperately tried to emulate Elvis's hairdo so they could be more attractive to their female classmates.

The rebelliousness symbolized by Presley found its movie counterpart in the sultry pensiveness of James Dean. The romantic hero of *Rebel Without a Cause,* Dean symbolized those adolescents, however small in number, who felt uncomfortable with their pietistic parents and sought some outlet, whether it be raucous music, playing "chicken" in their cars—racing toward each other head-on, until one or the other veered away—or becoming juvenile delinquents, where they could differentiate themselves from the conformist tastes of TV's *Ozzie and Harriet.* Young people who felt disdain for conventional manners found a role model for their cultural skepticism in Holden Caulfield, the hero of J. D. Salinger's *Catcher in the Rye,* who displayed only contempt for the hypocrites and "phonies" he encountered in the adult world. College students who read Paul Goodman's *Growing Up Absurd* or Erich Fromm's *Man for Himself* found carefully argued indictments of the superficiality of modern culture as well as support for the need to search for a more "authentic" self, rooted in an individual quest for life's transcendent meaning rather than being satisfied with the conventional trappings of corporate success.

Indeed, the literature of the 1950s was rich in nurturing second thoughts about the value of a life spent serving the "organization," accumulating material goods and being caught in the upward mobility trap. One might play the game, but it was foolhardy to believe in it because despair was the ultimate outcome, according to novelists as diverse as Ralph Ellison (*Invisible Man*), Joseph Heller (*Catch-22*), and Saul Bellow (*Augie March*). Whether the "system" was the oppressive paternalism embodied in Ellison's black college president or the robotlike allocation of military flying assignments in Heller's satire on war, individuals were not in control. All they could do was "play the game without believing it" and hope that somehow they could preserve enough of an inner self to avoid losing all sense of individuality.

The same message, delivered in a different way, came from playwrights and philosophers. In *Death of a Salesman*, Arthur Miller vividly dissected the tragedy of Willie Loman, a salesman caught up in the pressures of an advertising world where selling oneself was literally the price of success—except that all it left was hollow emptiness. Somehow there must be something more. Existentialists like Jean Paul Sartre and Albert Camus provided a philosophical framework within which to understand the human condition. Human beings were always in process, projecting from one moment to the next, never secure or imbedded in a structure of permanent meaning. Rather, they brought to each moment the meaning that they created in it via their choices. The key was that people *had* choices. Thus, in Camus' novel *The Fall*, his hero must choose whether to dive into the Seine River to rescue a man who has just jumped from the Pont Neuf, and in *The Plague*, Dr. Rieux must decide whether to stay and fight the plague in Oran—a metaphor for fascism—or abandon the city to save his own life. As members of the French resistance, both Camus and Sartre made their own choices, and in *The Plague*, Camus argued that standing up for life and staying to fight is the only thing that makes human beings what they are. But the ultimate message was that each person must make that choice—in the American case, whether to conform to the "organization" and its suburban culture or to step back and create a different kind of meaning.

In religion as well, searching questions were being asked, even in the face of the seven-day-a-week all-purpose church or the banal messages conveyed by Norman Vincent Peale's "power of positive thinking"—if only you think good things, they are bound to happen. As young people in increasing numbers flocked to local congregations, youth groups blossomed, and more and more of them began to ask questions about the linkage between the message of the Gospel and the condition of society. Students in the "Faith and Life Community" in Austin, Texas, started to explore what the meaning of Christianity was for the current state of race relations in America. At youth conferences in New England, the same question was asked about the relevance of the Gospel to personal relations between men and women and the larger issue of power and sex. Eventually, individuals involved in such groups questioned the conventional orthodoxy of the comfortable church, turning away from complacency to prophecy and challenging people to use their faith as the cutting edge of change.

Even in politics, signs of agitation appeared just beneath the surface calm of centrist conformity. Although anticommunism reigned supreme, barely questioned by even the most ardent critics of the status quo, more and more political activists dared to challenge political complacency about the current state of the nation. An Edward R. Murrow documentary, *Harvest of Shame*, highlighted the tragic plight of migrant farmworkers, uncovering the scandalous abuse of children and fathers and mothers taking place right under the noses of state and federal farm officials. Americans started to rediscover poverty, from the rural countryside of West Virginia to the Delta cotton fields of Mississippi. New peace groups formed to demand the abolition of nuclear testing; student social action organizations, encouraged by people like former National Student Association president Allard Lowenstein, started to mobilize around issues of social justice.

Thus in virtually every segment of a society supposedly content with the status quo, probing questions existed just beneath the surface, with fault lines ready to burst into open view. Yet it took the oldest and most oppressed minority in American society to explode those contradictions into full consciousness. With increasing urgency, black Americans focused the national spotlight on the contradictions that lay at the heart of the affluent society, in the process creating the most far-reaching social movement America had ever seen.

V. RACE IN THE 1950S: THE CIVIL RIGHTS MOVEMENT IS BORN

J. A. DeLaine was a black preacher and schoolteacher in Clarendon County, South Carolina. In a segregated society, he held a privileged position, economically secure and widely respected. But J. A. DeLaine was not satisfied with being privileged in a racially oppressive society. Once, as a child, he had been whipped for pushing a white boy after the white boy had forced his sister off a sidewalk. At church, he preached the gospel of liberation. And in 1947, after being turned down in his request for a second-hand school bus to transport black pupils to school, he mobilized his parishioners and neighbors to sue the school board for failing to provide "separate but *equal*" facilities for black students. It was one of five cases that eventually became *Brown v. Board of Education* before the Supreme Court in 1953.

Rosa Parks was a seamstress in Montgomery, Alabama. She had lived in Montgomery all her life. Respected, genteel, a devoted churchgoer, she held high standing in the black community. But she was more than that. A charter member of the NAACP, she had become secretary to that body. Together with other people interested in racial equality, she had attended a retreat at the Highlander Folk Center in Tennessee, where Myles Horton and his associates encouraged people to stand up for their rights. When a young black woman in Montgomery was brutally raped and beaten by white police in the 1940s, Rosa Parks was one of those who took on the establishment and vocally supported the woman when she brought charges against the police. In that activity, Parks joined with E. D. Nixon, head of the local chapter of the Brotherhood of Sleeping Car Porters union—an all-black union—who also knew no bounds to his courage. Throughout the early 1950s, Parks helped plan community projects to secure dignity and proper treatment of black folks. Now she acted herself, refusing to give up her seat on a segregated bus to a white person when the bus driver ordered her to do so. Four days later, the Montgomery Bus Boycott began, bringing to the fore a new young preacher named Martin Luther King, Jr.

J. A. DeLaine and Rosa Parks exemplified the grassroots insurgency that haunted the conscience of white America and helped to transform a nation. Each demonstrated how a local action, grounded in daily struggles that took place over a generation, could trigger events soon emblazoned on the front page of every newspaper in the land.

When the Supreme Court in 1954 ruled in *Brown v. Board of Education* that segregation was inherently unconstitutional, reversing its own *Plessy* decision fifty-eight years earlier, it redeemed the dignity of black Americans and honored nearly six decades of tenacious protest. The ruling itself did not come easily. First, Thurgood Marshall and the NAACP Legal Defense Fund had to make the heroic decision to attack the very principle of segregation in the courts, challenging the legal cage in which they had been imprisoned since *Plessy* and taking the huge risk that if they failed, it might take another half century before they could be free. Second, they had to mobilize a decisive majority on the Court. Supreme Court judges, by definition, operate in an environment constrained by past precedent. To overturn a ruling of such immensity, after so long a period of time, meant violating the overwhelming power of stare decisis, the doctrine that past legal precedent is binding. A 5–4 decision would not help. Indeed, any division on the Court would simply rationalize the development of an anti-Court movement that would subvert if not destroy the Court's intent.

In the heat of the legal arguments before the Court, two critical events intervened. First, Felix Frankfurter, a Roosevelt appointee to the court who opposed segregation, recognized that at best his side had a 6–3 majority, and so he proposed hearing new arguments in the case the next year in response to a series of questions he had devised. Then, suddenly, the chief justice of the Court, Fred Vinson—an opponent of any change—died of a heart attack, and President Eisenhower had to name a new chief justice. For multiple political reasons, Ike chose Earl Warren. A former GOP vice-presidential candidate and governor of California, Warren was precisely the kind of popular nominee a president hopes to choose. But Warren was more than that. He had been attorney general of California and helped push for the internment of Japanese American citizens during World War II, an act he deeply regretted; and he had been a progressive governor, famous for his ability to build consensus.

Now Warren set out both to redeem his action against the Japanese Americans and to solidify his reputation as a progressive public servant. Carefully, he marshaled the Court, lunching with individual members, talking about the Court's agenda, piecing together common ground on which they could all stand, even those most opposed to the Court's reversing itself. When the case was re-argued, Warren listened carefully to his colleagues, giving due respect to their opinions. Finally, he volunteered to write the Court's opinion himself. In doing so, he took the simplest path possible, stating clearly but briefly that "equal protection" under the Fourteenth Amendment meant exactly what it said and could not be reconciled with creating totally distinct schools for black children, which were inherently inferior and unequal. By the care and compassion with which he consulted his colleagues, he won unanimous support for his argument. But at a price—in return, he and the court agreed to defer any decision on implementation until a new set of arguments the next year.

It was at that point that Dwight David Eisenhower failed the test of moral leadership, and in addition, committed the worst political error of his administration. The situation cried out for decisiveness. Initial white Southern responses were cautious, recognizing that with the *Brown* decision, a watershed had occurred. No one had more credibility with the American people than the general who won the war. Had Eisenhower boldly endorsed the decision, declared that it was the law of the land and that no evasion would be permitted, little if any room would have existed for resistance to set in. Instead, on repeated occasions, Ike refused to offer his opinion on the decision (he would express neither "approbation nor disapproval"), insisted that this was a state and local matter, and averred that no federal forces should be deployed to enforce the court's action. In reality, Eisenhower's opinion was hostile. He told Warren at a White House dinner before the decision that segregationists were simply concerned "that their sweet little girls are not required to sit in schools alongside some big overgrown Negroes." In private, he called his appointment of Warren "the biggest damn fool mistake" he had ever made and later told an aide that *Brown* had "set back progress in the south at least fifteen years."

By abdicating his leadership role, Eisenhower in effect created a vacuum into which white political extremists could step, free of any threat that they might be chastised by the one person people looked to for moral guidance. As a result, in the years after *Brown* massive resistance set in, schools were closed, state legislatures passed bills that guaranteed private school tuition if whites were forced to go to school with blacks, and a state of war developed between those who advocated abiding by the law of the land and those who spoke with contempt of the Constitution and the Court. In a bizarre reframing of the issues, the Ku Klux Klan and the NAACP both came to be dubbed "extremists"; meanwhile, "moderates" in the South who simply believed in obeying the law were left with nowhere to go. Much of the agony of civil rights protests over the next two decades might have been avoided had

Eisenhower met his responsibilities in *Brown* the same way he had met them at Normandy Beach. But he missed his opportunity to become the Lincoln of the twentieth century.

Instead, blacks continued—virtually alone—to bear the burden of forcing the nation to confront its racial past. Hence the need for Rosa Parks to act in Montgomery in December 1955 because no white authority would take the initiative to desegregate the buses. For 381 days, Montgomery's black population trudged the streets, organized car pools, and raised thousands of dollars to carry on the fight—"my feets is tired," one boycott participant declared, "but my soul is rested." A new civil rights leader came to the fore named Martin Luther King, Jr., preaching the doctrine of nonviolent resistance and redemptive love. "We are not wrong in what we are doing," he told the black people of Montgomery. "If we are wrong—the Supreme Court of this nation is wrong....If we are wrong—God almighty is wrong....If we are wrong—justice is a lie." Wrapped in the armor of serving a higher law, blacks persisted until, more than a year later, the Supreme Court ordered the buses desegregated. From there, King went on to organize the Southern Christian Leadership Conference (SCLC) and to galvanize twenty-five thousand blacks gathered in Washington, D.C., in a "Pilgrimage for Peace" with his rallying cry, "Give us the ballot," and freedom shall be ours.

Appropriately, the transition to a new decade witnessed the most dramatic testimony of all, that black Americans would never again accept second-class citizenship. Four first-year college students in an all-black college in Greensboro, North Carolina, talked in their dorm rooms all fall long about the absence of progress in racial justice. Yes, Eisenhower had sent federal troops to Little Rock in September 1957 to enforce a court order to desegregate the schools there—but only after Governor Orval Faubus, in a rank display of insubordination, went back on his word to the commander-in-chief that he would protect the black students there. For reasons of personal pride and his anger at being disobeyed, Ike had to act. But otherwise he had done nothing. The four students had come of age with the expectation that the *Brown* decision would change everything. It had in fact barely changed anything; and now on the verge of adulthood, these students knew that if they did not act, they would become complicit in perpetuating the reign of white oppression.

Three of the four students had attended all-black Dudley High School in Greensboro. There they were taught by teachers who urged them to believe in themselves and stand up for their rights. One told his students about how he had always refused to ride Jim Crow buses or go to Jim Crow movie houses. Another used the literature in her English classes to inspire her students to be noble and courageous. The students attended an NAACP youth group where each week they talked about Montgomery, and Little Rock, and Dr. King. They went to a black Baptist church whose pastor talked about reaching the promised land. Their parents belonged to the NAACP and conveyed a sense of pride. They had heard the lessons of their elders, and now it was their time to act. Thinking of how they could be true to their convictions most dramatically, they struck on a simple course of action: how better to display the moral and economic absurdity of segregation than to go to the downtown department store, Woolworths, where their patronage and money were welcome at every counter except the one where people sat and had their coffee and lunch.

And so, frightened but determined, the four went downtown on February 1, 1960. They bought school supplies and toiletries, held on to their receipts, then went to the lunch counter, where they took seats and ordered coffee. "We don't serve Negroes here," the black waitress told them. "But you served us at the other counters," they replied. Sitting silently, they opened their books and studied for four hours until the store closed. Word spread of what they had done. The next morning they returned, with 23 of their classmates. The day after that it was 66—then 100. And on day five of the "sit-ins," more than 1,000 students occupied downtown Greensboro.

The sit-in revolution had begun. Within two months, sit-in demonstrations took place in fifty-four cities in nine different states. In April, Ella Baker of SCLC gathered student leaders from throughout the South in all-black Shaw University in Raleigh, North Carolina, to discuss next steps. The students

Black students launched the 1960s with a dramatic new form of demanding equality, the "sit-in." Buying various products at department stores, students would then take their receipts and ask to be served with the same equal treatment at lunch counters, where, under the practices of segregation, they were denied service. They would then remain "sitting in" until they were arrested. This depiction of a 1962 sit-in in Little Rock exemplifies this new tactic.

Credit: © Bettmann/CORBIS

heard James Lawson, a Nashville leader, preach about the gospel of nonviolence and the healing power of Christian love that takes upon itself the sins
of the oppressor. With young leaders like John Lewis, the students determined to form their own independent organization, the Student Non-Violent
Coordinating Committee (SNCC). Within months, operating from a small
one- room office in Atlanta, they spread out into Mississippi and southwest
Georgia, organizing voting-rights campaigns and additional sit-ins. Nearly
everywhere they met violence—cruel, vicious violence that left scores injured
and many dead. But they persisted. The government paid them little heed,
but more than anyone else, they would determine the history of the decade
to follow.

VI. CONCLUSION

Although it is customary to think of the 1960s as the decade in postwar America that most dramatically altered the course of the nation's history, a strong
case can be made that the 1950s set in motion all the most important changes
to come. Certainly the prosperity of the 1950s created the core of a new society. Now more white collar than blue collar, more suburban than urban, with
technology and education driving economic innovation, America took on a
new form and structure. Nearly two-thirds of Americans now owned their
homes as opposed to only 40 percent in 1940; the number of young people attending college multiplied from 15 percent to 45 percent. Consumerism not only fueled an economic boom but also helped define a lifestyle,
with recreation now focused on a shopping mall and its stores, restaurants,
and theaters rather than on reading books or playing a musical instrument.
Communication too assumed mass dimensions. Television created nationalizing experiences—whether quiz show games or comedy hours and dance
parties—that dwarfed the impact of radio. A national highway system, and
the unprecedented number of cars traveling on interstates, helped create a
whole new world of recreation, family contacts, and cultural interactions.
To be sure, millions of people were left out of suburban and consumer revo-
lutions. Millions lived in poverty, whether in inner-city ghettoes and barrios
or rural hamlets, and still others suffered the isolation of being cut off from
TVs and phones. But for most, the pace of change—and progress—seemed
astonishing.

In the midst of such rapid-fire transformations, the nation's political life
represented a bastion of stability. Dwight Eisenhower embodied steadiness
and leadership. Sustaining the Cold War and the politics of anticommunism,
he also proved remarkably adept at preserving peace. Although Ike failed
to quash the excesses of McCarthyism, he succeeded in remaining above
the battle and benefiting from the courageous actions of others who stood
up for common sense. Above all, he displayed a shrewd sense of the dangers of military escalation. Perhaps only a five-star general could have kept
so tight a rein on the impulse of the "military-industrial complex" to surge

forward and seek to dominate everything. Only on civil rights did his sure-handedness fail him.

But in the end, it was civil rights that helped define the most important moments of the 1950s and the decade to follow. Black Americans helped to expose the contradictions just beneath the surface of the affluent society. Through the sacrifices of nonviolent protests and sit-ins, they created an ethical counterpoint to the smug self-satisfaction of suburbia. In their insistence on a higher sense of community, they also provided a focus for those seeking something larger from life than simply "getting along" in the world of the organization man.

In the end, it would be difficult to imagine an era more chock-full of drama and transformation. Except that precisely such an era was about to dawn—the 1960s.

9

From Camelot to Fragmentation:
The 1960s

Never before had a decade begun with such optimism or ended with such despair. A buoyant, charismatic John F. Kennedy launched the era speaking on behalf of a "new generation of Americans" who had come to power ready to "pay any price, bear any burden" to fulfill America's destiny as the last best hope of mankind. With the same sense of idealism, more than a quarter of a million Americans gathered before the Lincoln Memorial in August 1963 to hear Martin Luther King, Jr., share his dream that one day black children and white children would walk together in the sunlight of freedom.

Yet just five years later, such hopes seemed like a distant illusion. John F. Kennedy, his brother Robert, and Martin Luther King, Jr., were all dead, victims of assassins' bullets. The slogan "Black Power" had replaced "Freedom Now" as the rallying cry for millions of blacks. Protests wracked the nation, this time over a war in Vietnam that polarized the American people and seemed to have no relation to John Kennedy's heroic rhetoric of "defending freedom at its maximum hour of danger." While 500,000 American troops fought to preserve an unpopular government in South Vietnam, 600,000 other American citizens protested the war's continuation in demonstrations in Washington, D.C. A nation so recently lifted to heights of shared commitment now found its collective idealism shattered. Warring groups of students, construction workers, police, and political leaders seemed to care more about mutual recrimination than about coming together as one. It was as if some demonic force had turned the best of times into the worst of times—and all within a few short years.

It was more complicated than that, of course. The shared idealism of the early 1960s coexisted with significant tensions over how little the government was actually doing to achieve its rhetorical goals. The retrospective sense that "for one brief shining moment" the Kennedy era had been an age of Camelot shrunk in the face of abundant evidence that Kennedy's failures had been at least as great as his successes. Nor did the sense of divisiveness in the late 1960s do justice to the dramatic progress the Johnson administration had achieved in its domestic agenda or to the number of Americans who still believed in a set of values shared by all their fellow citizens. Still, it was a time unlike any other in the twentieth century. The good and the bad were so tied together, it was hard to understand just what distinguished them and how one led to the other.

I. JOHN F. KENNEDY AND THE NEW FRONTIER

There was little in John F. Kennedy's personal and political history to suggest he would become a tribune of change and idealism. The child of privilege (his father, Joseph Kennedy, was a self-made multimillionaire, his money earned in banking and the film and liquor industries), he early became accustomed to getting his way without extraordinary effort. He was a good but not distinguished student. Yet his father—recently the U.S. ambassador to Great Britain—arranged to have Arthur Krock, a *New York Times* writer, edit Kennedy's senior honors thesis at Harvard on England's reluctant march to war. Subsequently published and widely reviewed, the book was thought to be solely the work of a brilliant young intellectual. When he returned from World War II, Jack's father, Joe, also pushed him into politics, arranging to have Michael Curley, a sitting congressman, retire from his seat and run again for mayor of Boston so that Jack could join a crowd of contenders seeking to be his replacement. Bankrolled by his father, Kennedy won. Then, six years later in 1952, he ran for the U.S. Senate against Henry Cabot Lodge, and in another campaign well financed by his father, succeeded again. But throughout fourteen years in Congress, his political record was mediocre. Although he supported traditional Democratic positions on Social Security and the minimum wage, he failed to work hard; was perceived by many as a lightweight; and on crucial issues of character, such as opposing McCarthyism, absented himself from the debate. Only on the issue of Indochina, where in the mid-1950s he made remarkably astute speeches about the danger of getting into a war between nationalist insurgents and colonial oppressors, did Kennedy distinguish himself. "No amount of American military assistance," he declared, "can conquer an enemy which is everywhere and at the same time nowhere, an 'enemy of the people' which has the sympathy and covert support of the people."

On the other hand, Kennedy had a public aura that set him apart. Handsome, boyish, and articulate, he charmed nearly everyone he met, married Jacqueline Bouvier, a stunning Newport socialite, was featured together with his wife on Edward R. Murrow's *See It Now*, and in 1956 astonished the Democratic national convention when he ran for the vice presidency, arguing that having a Roman Catholic on the ticket would be a boon for the party. Although Kennedy lost out in the end to Tennessee Senator Estes Kefauver, a newspaper columnist at the time cogently observed that Kennedy "rates as the one real winner of the entire convention....His was the one new face....His charisma, his dignity, his intellectuality, and in the end his gracious sportsmanship...are undoubtedly what those delegates [will] remember."

Two other aspects of Kennedy's personal life deserve attention. He grew up in an Irish Catholic family of nine children who every day interacted with a fiercely competitive father and a religiously devout mother. Joe Kennedy brazenly carried on extramarital affairs, even bringing his mistresses into the house. Rose Kennedy acted like a saint, seemingly oblivious to her husband's indiscretions. ("Was [Rose] a fool," asked Hollywood star Gloria Swanson, one of Joe's mistresses, "or a saint? Or just a better actress than I was?") Joe Kennedy insisted that his children master the art of debating history and politics while excelling on the athletic field. Rose Kennedy sought to impart piety, all the while worrying about her social status. "When," she once asked, "are the nice people of Boston going to accept us?"

While the other children accepted one or the other of their parents as role models—Joe Jr. his father, Bobby his mother—Jack found a way to detach himself from the bizarre struggle they waged. From infancy, he was a sickly child, almost dying a number of times. His brother Robert noted that Jack "spent at least half his days" in pain. Yet his illnesses provided a basis for removing himself from the day-to-day struggles of the family. He became more an intellectual, reading history and the classics, moving in and out of the larger hullabaloo of the household, observing from the periphery as well as taking part in the action. It was partly this sense of being the observer that made it difficult for Jack, either in his political views or his personal relationships, to develop significant, sustained emotional commitments—hence his reputation as a philanderer, like his father, and as a shrewd, calculating politician without strong political passions.

The second important feature of Kennedy's personal history was his World War II experience in the Pacific. Although he would never have been able to pass a physical on his own, "Daddy Joe" secured a commission for Jack as a naval officer, initially with navy intelligence in Washington and then as commander of a PT boat in the Solomon Islands. It was there, on a night mission in the Blackett Straits, that Jack's PT 109 boat was scissored in two by a speeding Japanese destroyer. His crew knocked into the ocean, some dead, Jack displayed a heroism remarkable under any circumstances. Saving one crewman's life by taking his life preserver in his mouth and towing him through the water, Kennedy led the survivors of PT 109 to an island, then swam himself to other nearby islands until he was finally able to raise a rescue mission. Kennedy's heroism soon became the focus for a best-selling book that helped propel his political career.

But the World War II experience also pierced Kennedy's detachment, producing a gut reaction that would stay with him the rest of his life. "We got so used to talking about billions of dollars and millions of soldiers," he wrote in a letter, "that thousands of casualties sound like drops in the bucket. But if those thousands want to live as much as [my] ten [crewmembers], the people deciding the whys and wherefores had better make mighty sure all this effort is headed for some definite goal, and that when we reach that goal, we may say it was worth it, for if it isn't the whole thing will turn to ashes." Among other things, Kennedy's experience left him deeply skeptical of military officers who had no sense of the price paid by soldiers in the field. "This thing is so stupid," he wrote about the war, "that while it has a sickening fascination for some of us, myself included, I want to leave it far behind me when I go." Although the immediate impact of Kennedy's wartime experience was simply to make his political possibilities far more attractive, the long-term impact would only become clear when he faced the most critical decisions of his White House years.

In the end, both Kennedy's family wealth and his wartime heroism helped fuel his national political trajectory. By 1960, the handsome, tanned senator from Massachusetts was a front-runner. Women and girls screamed excitedly—Kennedy's campaign progress, one reporter said, "was an epic of the history of the sexual instinct in the American female." Young people in particular viewed Kennedy as almost a rock star. Meanwhile, Kennedy's campaign team—headed by his younger brother Robert—pieced together a winning combination through primary victories in states like Wisconsin and West Virginia, support from big city bosses like Richard Daley of Chicago, and endorsements from powerful governors such as Michael DiSalle of Ohio and David Lawrence of Pennsylvania. With machinelike efficiency, Kennedy swept to victory at the Los Angeles convention. In an example of the rhetoric the country would soon take as second nature, Kennedy exhorted the delegates to prepare for a "new frontier" where Americans would conquer space, solve problems of peace and war, and find answers to abiding problems of ignorance and poverty.

The key challenge Kennedy faced in the general election was his youth and inexperience, especially when compared with the eight years as vice president of his opponent, Richard Nixon. The first televised debate between the two neutralized the experience issue as Kennedy—articulate, the master of facts, poised and in control—actually appeared more in charge than Nixon, who looked dark and jowly because of poor television makeup and a recent illness. Eisenhower did not help when, in a press conference, he responded to a reporter's question about which decisions Nixon had helped shape in the White House by saying, "Give me a week and I'll think about it." Crisply, Kennedy handled the issue of his Catholicism by going to a Protestant minister's convention and declaring his deep commitment to the separation of church and state. Perhaps the most decisive moment of the campaign came when Martin Luther King, Jr., was sentenced to hard labor in prison for his civil rights activities. Fearful that he would never come out alive, family members and civil rights leaders pleaded with both Kennedy and Nixon to intervene. Nixon did nothing. Kennedy placed a phone call to Mrs. King, indicating his concern, while his brother Robert called the presiding judge and secured King's release. Overnight, the black community, which had been split down the middle if not supportive of Nixon, became Kennedy supporters, providing him on election day with 70 percent of the African American vote. In a campaign otherwise punctuated by Kennedy's militant rhetoric about a "missile gap" with the Soviet Union, an economy in the doldrums, and a society that was too self-satisfied—"we can do better," Kennedy said repeatedly—it turned out that a single phone call made the greatest difference, providing the key votes in numerous states to carry John F. Kennedy to the presidency.

Despite all his protestations of representing a new generation, however, what remained most notable about Kennedy was the degree to which the youthful president reflected continuity with the politics of the postwar years rather than change. Having been elected by the narrowest majority imaginable (118,000 votes out of 68 million cast), Kennedy clearly lacked a mandate. Nevertheless, a huge chasm separated Kennedy's extraordinarily bold rhetoric from the minimal legislative agenda he proposed on domestic affairs. Like Truman (and Eisenhower), he succeeded in raising the minimum wage and extending Social Security. He also secured more funds for mental health, funneled public works money into depressed areas, won approval of a Federal Water Pollution Control Act, and provided additional federally funded housing. But his biggest initiative—federal aid to education—floundered, at least in part because of what one historian called Kennedy's "inept guidance."

In fact there was nothing in Kennedy's first two years that came close to reflecting the dramatic initiatives the candidate Kennedy had foretold in his campaign speeches. Although the civil rights movement spread like wildfire in 1961 and 1962, Kennedy submitted no legislation addressing the issue of racial inequality. Instead, his top legislative priority for 1962 was a Reciprocal Trade Act. Shying away from confrontation with the conservative coalition that dominated Congress, Kennedy instead focused most of his domestic energies on fine-tuning the economy. There, he demonstrated significant talent, taking the advice of economists like Walter Heller to encourage productivity increases, limit price and wage increases, and launch the a new era of prosperity. (One of Kennedy's most dramatic moments came when U.S. Steel violated the unwritten rules of the Kennedy years by raising steel prices after unions had accepted a modest wage increase and increased their productivity. In response, Kennedy blasted steel executives, waged a vigorous public relations campaign, and in the end forced steelmakers to rescind their price increase). But notwithstanding the success of Kennedy's economic program, there was little to distinguish Kennedy's record from that of his Republican and Democratic predecessors. "We get awfully sick of this 'moderation,'" the *New Republic* observed. "All during the Eisenhower administration there was moderation...and now instead of Kennedy urgency there is more moderation." The "liberal" consensus of 1948 remained intact.

Kennedy devoted most of his energies to the war against communism, the anchor of the "liberal consensus." "Our responsibility," he told one audience, "is to be the chief defender of freedom at a time when freedom is under attack all over the globe." The enemy, he declared to another audience, "is the Communist system...implacable, insatiable, increasing in its drive for world domination....This is...a struggle for supremacy between two conflicting ideologies: freedom under God versus ruthless, godless tyranny." Neither Harry Truman nor John Foster Dulles could have used the rhetoric of holy war more effectively.

Kennedy's inaugural address dramatically exemplified the priorities that would guide his early presidency. Notwithstanding dramatic civil rights sit-ins taking place across the country and a heightened awareness of poverty

In one of the greatest moments of his presidency, John F. Kennedy journeyed to Berlin to affirm his solidarity with West Berliners defending their freedom in resistance to the totalitarian regime of Community East Germany (including East Berlin). "Ich bin ein Berliner," Kennedy proclaimed, to the roaring approval of his audience.

Credit: Time & Life Pictures/Getty Images

in books and news magazines, Kennedy devoted not a single word to race or income inequality. "Let's drop the domestic stuff altogether," he told his speechwriters. Instead—almost as though talking about potentially divisive domestic issues would detract from galvanizing the nation around foreign policy challenges—Kennedy focused exclusively on the challenge communism posed to the survival of freedom. "Let every nation know," he declared, "that we shall pay *any* price, bear *any* burden, oppose *any* foe, in order to assure the survival and the success of liberty." Kennedy seemed intent on conveying a sense of extraordinary crisis, almost as though he were back in England in 1938 trying to awaken his country to unprecedented challenges awaiting them. Of course, America had been mobilized for the Cold War for more than a decade. But Kennedy framed this moment as different, more dire, a time when America faced its "maximum hour of peril."

Not surprisingly in light of this focus, the struggle against communism dominated Kennedy's first two years in the White House. An air of adventurousness pervaded the new administration. Populated by young aides—Walt Rostow's wife called them "an odd lot. You're not politicians or intellectuals. You're the junior officers of the Second World War come to responsibility"—the Kennedy national security team bristled with ideas for combating communism, such as launching the Green Berets, a newly conceived counterguerilla force to fight against Khrushchev's announced plans to wage wars of "national liberation." Adlai Stevenson, Kennedy's UN ambassador, called them "boy commandos." Unlike the hierarchical, stodgy structure of the Eisenhower White House, Kennedy ran an informal "huddle and run" decision-making apparatus. The Kennedy team, British journalist Henry Fairlie wrote, "lived on the move, calling signals to each other in the thick of the action." It was all part of the electric White House culture, which featured fast-paced impromptu gatherings of security planners by day and concerts by Pablo Casals at black-tie dinners at night.

Before too long, however, the vulnerability of such bravado became apparent. To his surprise, Kennedy had inherited from Eisenhower a scheme to invade Cuba, incite a domestic revolt, and topple Fidel Castro. Kennedy never did subject the plans to a thorough appraisal. Instead, his energetic new team signed off on the bold venture as a perfect opportunity to decisively reverse one of America's most disastrous foreign policy defeats, installation of a Communist regime ninety miles from Miami. Except that the plans were flimsy, unworkable, and dependent on everything going right and nothing going wrong. The opposite happened. When Cuban exiles landed at the Bay of Pigs, they found dug-in Castro soldiers who decimated their ranks, not cheering throngs of anti-Castro insurgents. Their air support faltered, then failed. Hundreds were taken prisoner. The entire operation represented a devastating defeat, not just for the Cuban exile fighters but also for a mode of conducting business, which in General Maxwell Taylor's words "had never cleared proper channels of review and consultation."

Severely weakened, Kennedy went to his first meeting with Nikita Khrushchev in Vienna three months later with few diplomatic cards in his hand. He now knew, and recognized, that the "missile gap" had never existed and that America was dramatically superior to the Soviet Union in military resources. In his mind, Kennedy saw the Vienna meeting as an opportunity to create a new dialogue with the Soviets and initiate far-reaching programs for arms control and peaceful negotiation. But Khrushchev treated Kennedy like a youngster who had failed his first Boy Scout test for courage under fire. By turns scornful and intimidating, the Soviet premiere threatened to sign a separate peace agreement with East Germany and provoke a worldwide crisis over Berlin. Kennedy was shaken, telling Harold Macmillan, Britain's prime minister, and James Reston, the senior columnist for the *New York Times*, that Khrushchev had humiliated him.

Partly in response, Kennedy prepared the nation for war, calling up army reserves, urging Americans to build fallout shelters to protect against nuclear attack, and acting as though world war were around the corner. As one part of his counterattack, Kennedy determined to take a stand against communism in another part of the world. Agreeing to send hundreds, and then thousands, of military advisors to South Vietnam to assist Ngo Diem in his fight against Viet Cong guerillas, Kennedy was, as much as anything, sending a message to Khrushchev that the United States was prepared to pursue its policy of containment anywhere and everywhere that communism threatened. In the end, Khrushchev defused the German crisis by building the

Berlin Wall, thereby halting the devastating loss of East German brainpower and technical skill to the West. He also abandoned his threat to sign a separate peace treaty with East Germany. Still, enormous damage had been done, largely a reflection of how counterproductive Kennedy's initial fascination with adventurous improvisation in national security matters had been.

II. THE CUBAN MISSILE CRISIS

Everything else paled into insignificance, however, when the Cuban Missile Crisis shook the world in October 1962. No other event in the twentieth century brought the universe so close to nuclear annihilation. In the summer and fall, Khrushchev daringly sent scores of ballistic missiles to Cuba with the intention of building hardened sites from which they could be fired. Once armed with nuclear warheads, the missiles would have the capacity to destroy Washington, New York, and Miami. Kennedy had warned against any importation of offensive weapons, and the Soviets responded by claiming they were interested only in defensive arms. Until American U-2 spy planes returned from overflights of Cuba in early October with indisputable evidence that these were *offensive* missiles. Immediately, Kennedy convened an executive committee (ex-com) of his top military and diplomatic advisors to resolve how the United States should react. Virtually everyone on the ex-com united behind a recommendation that the United States should respond militarily, carrying out precision-bombing raids on the missile sites and preparing for a full-scale invasion of Cuba. At that moment, there were two negative voices—Robert F. Kennedy, the attorney general, who compared such an attack to the one Japanese planes carried out against Pearl Harbor ("I now know how [Emperor] Tojo felt," he declared), and most important of all, John F. Kennedy. Based on his reluctance to inaugurate what he feared would become World War III, Kennedy instead announced that he would establish a naval "quarantine" that would prohibit any Soviet ship with a weapons cargo from entering Cuban waters.

As a terrified world came to grips with the nightmare everyone had always feared, John F. Kennedy was going through his own journey of the soul. In some ways, he had learned from the horror of the Bay of Pigs. Realizing how poorly he had been served by his military advisors, he was reminded of his skepticism about generals and admirals at the time of the PT 109 disaster. More often than not from that time forward, he resisted many of the recommendations of the Pentagon—for example, their call that he send up to one hundred thousand troops to Vietnam. Now it had all come down to the ultimate crisis. What to do? When Soviet ships stopped just short of the quarantine line, there seemed room for optimism. But then the situation worsened. Construction continued on the missile bases. Antiaircraft guns in Cuba shot down a U-2 spy plane, killing the pilot. The entire membership of ex-com except for Bobby Kennedy endorsed military retaliation.

Virtually alone, with the fate of the world in his hands, John Kennedy said no. Two days earlier, Nikita Khrushchev had sent a rambling, almost incoherent note, offering to withdraw Soviet missiles if the United States pledged not to invade Cuba in the future. Almost immediately thereafter came a second, far more formal letter, offering to trade the withdrawal of U.S. missiles in Turkey for Soviet removal of its missiles in Cuba. Bobby Kennedy came up with the idea of writing Khrushchev back, accepting his first offer, with America prepared to act on the Turkish missiles in due course. Why risk millions of lives, Kennedy reasoned, "when we could have gotten [the same result] by making a deal on the missiles in Turkey?" Impatiently, Kennedy awaited Khrushchev's reply. Soon it came. They had a deal. Russia would remove its missiles under UN inspection, and in a secret agreement, America agreed to withdraw its Turkish missiles within five months. The nightmare was over.

The world now knows far better that it did then how close it had come to nuclear holocaust. Soviet missiles were, in fact, already armed, prepared to fire on Washington and New York. Moreover, local commanders in Cuba had the authority to launch those weapons without prior approval from Moscow—a terrifying prospect. A U.S. air attack or invasion would have precipitated such a response, followed by all-out retaliation from the United States. The resulting casualties would have made Hiroshima and Nagasaki look like a skirmish. John F. Kennedy did not know then what we know now. But as he paced his White House office and thought about his own children, he understood the burden that rested on his shoulders. Perhaps the letters he sent after PT 109 came back to him, accentuating his awareness of the consequences of his actions for all the children of the world. In any event, he averted a nuclear disaster, and in the process, turned around his presidency.

By dint of circumstance and a changed perception of his own leadership role, Kennedy adopted a much more aggressive stance in the third year of his presidency on both domestic and foreign policy issues. For so much of his time in the White House, Kennedy had been constrained by the absence of a mandate to carry forward the domestic initiatives he had talked about in the campaign. His success in resolving the missile crisis seemed to liberate him, creating a new sense of confidence and freedom to pursue his objectives, regardless of congressional stalemate.

III. A NEW PRESIDENCY

In many respects, the civil rights movement offered him no alternative. Despite his rhetorical support for racial equality, Kennedy had done little to deliver on his campaign promises. He waited for two years to sign an executive order banning segregation from federally financed housing (and even then, it was substantially watered down) and failed to introduce any civil rights legislation lest he offend the Southern chairs of powerful House and Senate committees. Only in Robert Kennedy's appointments of black lawyers in the Justice Department (a 1,000 percent increase, from 10 to 100) and a newly invigorated prosecution of desegregation cases had the administration in any way delivered on its commitments. But the movement never lost the momentum created by the sit-ins. SNCC workers entered the most racist counties of Mississippi and demanded the right to vote. Some were murdered, and the federal government did little or nothing to protect them. But blacks persisted. In Albany, Georgia, thousands demonstrated on behalf of desegregating the bus terminals, securing the vote, and getting decent jobs. Virtually every population center in the South witnessed black insurgency, the voices of local people ringing in the streets and in the churches as they sang "We Shall Overcome" and "Ain't Gonna Let Nobody Turn me Round."

Then in the spring of 1963 came Birmingham. Nicknamed "Bombingham" because of its history of explosions aimed at the homes of black protestors, the city exemplified in its purest form the vicious brutality of white racism. Martin Luther King, Jr., selected the city as the "make or break" site for civil rights demonstrations against segregated public accommodations precisely because it encapsulated all that the movement was protesting against. Daringly, he also chose to send children to lead the demonstrations. Predictably, Bull Connor, the notorious sheriff of Birmingham, responded by unleashing teeth-baring dogs against the demonstrators and using high-pressure fire hoses to splay little children against the walls of the stores they were seeking to integrate. "Let those people come to the corner," Connor instructed his police. "I want 'em to see the dogs work. Look at those niggers run." As *Life* magazine and national TV news featured pictures of women and children being brutalized, the entire country awakened to the horror of racist brutality.

No longer could John F. Kennedy remain silent. Taking the initiative, he ordered his entire cabinet to pressure Birmingham businesspeople to desegregate. In the meantime, Bobby worked with state educational authorities to cooperate in letting two black students enter the University of Alabama. When Alabama Governor George Wallace insisted on "standing in the schoolhouse door" to block them, the Kennedys sent Justice Department officials to confront him and to force the university to comply.

That same night in June, Kennedy decided it was time for him to speak to the American people. Virtually his entire staff opposed his doing so, but he insisted, going on national TV with only a few hours notice and with no speech draft completed. Speaking largely extemporaneously, Kennedy asserted the moral leadership he had so long eschewed, telling the nation that this was "above all a moral issue...as old as the Scriptures and...as clear as the American constitution." "We preach freedom around the world," Kennedy said, "but are we to say to the world, and much more importantly to each other, that this is the land of the free *except* for the Negroes; that we have no second-class citizens *except* Negroes...?" With a passion no president had ever shown before, Kennedy declared his support for a civil rights bill that would desegregate all public accommodations and put the federal

No moment in twentieth-century domestic American history embodies the passion for a just society more than the civil rights movement's March on Washington on August 28, 1963. This picture highlights the throngs marching down the Washington Mall to the Lincoln Memorial, where Dr. Martin Luther King, Jr., proclaimed, "I have a dream."

Credit: Rue des Archives/The Granger Collection, New York.

government firmly on the side of racial equality. "If an American, because his skin is dark, cannot eat lunch in a restaurant open to the public, if he cannot send his children to the best school available, if he cannot vote for the public officials who represent him...who among us would be content to have the color of his skin changed and stand in his place...or be content with the counsel of patience and delay." It had been a long time coming, but the civil rights movement had finally forced John F. Kennedy to take a stand.

The same month, Kennedy demonstrated his new freedom by going to American University and launching a peace initiative that fundamentally reversed the Cold War rhetoric he had embraced throughout his administration. For too long, he told his audience, America had used its weapons of war to rule the world in a Pax Americana and had demonized its opponents. Yet, he said, "our attitude is as essential [as that of the Soviet Union]....No government or social system is so evil that its people must be considered as lacking in virtue." The time had come, he declared, for the United States to shed the shibboleths of the past and recognize the bonds of humanity that tied the peoples of America and Russia together. "We all breathe the same air. We all cherish our children's future. And we are all mortal." It was as if surviving the Cuban Missile Crisis had given Kennedy a new sense of the need to abandon past credos and shape possibilities that might break free of the cage of the Cold War. To advance that cause, Kennedy announced that the United States would suspend nuclear testing in the atmosphere and urged Russia to follow suit. Within two months, the Soviet Union had agreed to a nuclear test ban treaty. "Yesterday," Kennedy said, announcing the accord, "a shaft of light cut into the darkness" of the arms race and the "vicious circle of conflicting ideology and interest that had governed the world." "Let us, if we can," he concluded, "step back from the shadows of war, and seek out the way of peace. And if that journey is a thousand miles, let history record that we, in this land, at this time, took the first step."

Whether or not John F. Kennedy would have continued his trajectory of moral leadership would never be known. Three months later, after a national speaking tour in which he focused on the importance of world peace, Kennedy went to Dallas, Texas, to seek to heal divisions within the Democratic Party. There, in Dealey Plaza, he was shot in the neck and the head by a high-powered rifle. Crying, TV newsman Walter Cronkite announced shortly thereafter that the president was dead. "I have lost my only true friend in the outside world," an African chief of state declared. British journalist Godfrey Hodgson called it the "the death of a democratic prince." The country mourned as it had not since FDR died, especially millions of African Americans on whose walls JFK's portrait hung next to those of Martin Luther King, Jr., and Jesus. In his final year of life, John F. Kennedy had begun to realize the possibility for transforming America that for so long he had held forth as his hope. James Reston of the *New York Times* best summarized the nation's sense of loss. "What was killed [in Dallas]," he wrote, "was not only the president but the promise... the death of youth and the hope of youth, of the beauty and grace and the touch of magic.... He never reached his meridian: we saw him only as a rising sun."

IV. THE GREAT SOCIETY

"All I have," Lyndon Johnson told the American people after John F. Kennedy's funeral, "I would gladly have given not to be standing here today." With passion, conviction, and poise, Johnson assured the nation that "John F. Kennedy lives on.... No words are strong enough to express our determination to continue the forward thrust of America that he began." Emphasizing his commitment to Kennedy's agenda of jobs, education, and most important, "equal rights for all Americans whatever their race or color," Johnson effectively wrapped himself in the mantle of his fallen leader, stressing that "no memorial or oration or eulogy could more eloquently honor President Kennedy's memory than the earliest possible passage of the civil rights bill for which he fought so long." John F. Kennedy had exhorted his inaugural audience in 1961, "Let us begin." Yoking himself to Kennedy's legacy, LBJ now enjoined Congress, "Let us continue."

It was a moment that in many ways Lyndon Johnson had spent his life preparing for. The son of parents with diametrically opposite personalities, he had been torn as a child. His mother dressed him in Little Lord Fauntle-roy outfits, let his curly hair grow long, gave him violin lessons, and tried to make him into a refined aesthete. His father, a bawdy, hale-fellow-well-met politician who loved to mix with cowboys and campaign at the county fair, wanted his son to be his spitting image—garrulous, down to earth, a man among men. The conflict proved so great that Johnson felt driven to do any-thing he possibly could to escape it. Every day of his life, he set for himself an impossible task: to bring consensus out of division wherever he was and to be the *single person in the world* who could find the right answers.

Johnson's method was to work people, massage their egos, defer to their sensitivities, all in the service of persuading them to follow him. In college at San Marcos State, he became the indispensable aide of a strong president, got himself elected student body leader, and brought unity to the campus. When he went to the House of Representatives, he did the same with Speaker Sam Rayburn of Texas, whom he saw each day for an after-hours drink—LBJ used to come in and kiss Rayburn's bald pate, saying "how are you today my beloved"—and whose approval he used to rise quickly in the House ranks. The same ritual followed in the Senate, Johnson cultivating another bachelor, the senior senator from Georgia Richard Russell, who was the spine of South-ern leadership. Each man he brought home for dinners with his wife, Lady Bird. Both provided the legitimacy and power that enabled Johnson to rise to a position of national leadership.

By 1954 he had been chosen Senate majority leader—perhaps the most powerful person ever to occupy the office—and overnight became legend-ary for his ability to mobilize consensus behind his legislative priorities. The Johnson "treatment"—compared by one senator to "a great overpowering thunderstorm that consumed you as it closed around you"—consisted of cornering individual senators, finding out what they wanted and needed, striking secret deals with each without telling others what he had done, and in the end putting together overwhelming votes for those bills he deemed most important. Southerners promised to vote for public dams in Western states in return for Western votes to dilute legislation threatening to the South. Nowhere was this more evident than in the compromise he struck on a 1957 Civil Rights bill. But through it all, Johnson succeeded in being known as the master unifier who held the keys to both power and conciliation.

Now, he brought to bear all the skills he had cultivated so caringly through those years as a consensus builder. "I knew what had to be done," he told one biographer, Doris Kearns, about the period of chaos following Kennedy's assassination. "There is but one way to get the cattle out of the swamps. And that is for the man on the horse to take the lead, to assume command, to pro-vide direction. In the period of confusion after the assassination, I was that man." Carrying the Kennedy legacy like a flag into battle, Johnson rallied the country behind an expansive set of liberal programs that made Kennedy's own legislative agenda seem pale by comparison. "Everything I had ever learned in the history books," he declared, "taught me that martyrs have to die for causes. John Kennedy had died....I had to take the dead man's program and turn it into a martyr's cause." Johnson secured enactment of Kennedy's tax cut, refined and strengthened Kennedy's initiative for a War on Poverty (naming Kennedy's brother-in-law Sargent Shriver to head the effort), then moved on to his highest priority, passage of Kennedy's civil rights bill. Strengthening the original measure, marshaling a biracial coalition, Johnson drove the bill through the House, then set out to overcome a filibuster in the Senate. Each week, he hosted Republican leader Everett Dirksen for drinks, swapping politicians' tales into the night, playing up how history would judge the role Dirksen was to play, until finally, the Republican leader embraced civil rights as "an idea whose time has come" and enabled supporters of civil rights to break the filibuster and enact the most sweeping civil rights legislation since Reconstruction. With enactment of the Civil Rights Act of 1964, Congress in one legislative act virtually extinguished the entire Jim Crow system, from separate drinking fountains to segregated hotels and dining rooms to routine discrimination in hiring practices based on race and gender.

At every step, Johnson cultivated Congress like a suitor wooing his lover. "The relationship between the President and Congress has got to be almost incestuous," he said. "Timing is essential. Momentum is *not* a mysterious mistress. It is a controllable fact of political life that depends on nothing more exotic than preparation." For years, Johnson had learned and practiced the art of legislative persuasion. Stated crudely, Johnson declared, "You got to learn to mount this Congress like you mount a woman." Once every detail was pinned down, you "know, know, *know*" you are in control, he said, because (changing the metaphor slightly) "you've got his pecker right here [in your pocket]." Not coincidentally, Johnson's pervasive sexual imagery conveyed a clear sense of how he conceptualized the relationship of leader to followers—intimate exchanges, calculated manipulation, but always with the same result, total mastery and control by the man at the top.

But Johnson had just begun. His true aim was not only to enact Kennedy's legislative program but also to so far exceed it that the Johnson record would compare favorably with, or perhaps even surpass that of LBJ's political "father," Franklin Delano Roosevelt. Johnson found a brand for his vision in a series of speeches he gave in the spring of 1964, culminating in a commencement address at the University of Michigan where he called on Americans to create more than a New Deal or a Fair Deal or even a New Frontier but to go beyond material prosperity to fashion a "Great Society." America, he declared, must decide "whether we have the wisdom to use [our] wealth to enrich and elevate our national life, and to advance the quality of American civilization." The Great Society, he said, "demands an end to poverty and racial injustice, to which we are totally committed in our time." But it focused as much on the "quality of [our] goals" as on their quantity and envisioned a world where "the city of man serves not only the needs of the body and the demands of commerce but the desire for beauty and hunger of community." In effect, Johnson dreamed of a day when America moved beyond equality of opportunity for all citizens to a shared richness of culture and civilization.

Nothing better served Johnson's aspirations than his opponent in the 1964 presidential election. Barry Goldwater, the Republican senator from Arizona, rejected the consensus that had evolved in American politics. He wished to cut taxes, modify Social Security, end the New Deal welfare state, and radically curtail the role of government in American life. "A choice, not an echo" screamed one of his campaign slogans. "In your heart you know he is right," declared another. To which Democrats responded, "Yes, far right!" Aiding Johnson even further was Goldwater's proposal that military commanders in the field in Vietnam be given independent authority to launch nuclear weapons—an idea that terrified citizens who had just survived the Cuban Missile Crisis. Although Governor George Wallace was also leading a conservative crusade against federal intervention, especially around issues of race, most Americans were sufficiently appalled by racial atrocities in Birmingham and Mississippi that they were not ready to accept Wallace's critique. By contrast, Johnson was a voice of reason. Rather than dismantle three decades of reform, he promised to extend and enrich America's commitment to a better life for all its people. In response to Goldwater's military adventurism, Johnson declared, "We're not about to send American boys nine or ten thousand miles from home [to Vietnam] to do what Asian boys ought to be doing for themselves." The election results amounted to as popular a victory as any recent president had achieved. Winning 61 percent of the popular vote, Johnson could now claim to have resounding support from the entire country—as close to a mandate as anyone could achieve.

Immediately, LBJ seized the initiative. "Every day...I'm in office, I'm going to alienate somebody," he told his staff. "We've got to get this legislation fast. We've got to get it during my honeymoon....You've got just one year when they treat you right." The results were astonishing. First came federal aid to elementary and secondary education, then Medicare—providing government-sponsored health care to all citizens over sixty-five. Higher education, Operation Head Start, a teacher corps, demonstration cities, a housing program (including rent subsidies), mass transit, mental health, and the environment soon followed. Culminating it all was the Voting Rights Act of 1965, which placed federal registrars in counties throughout the South with histories of racist disenfranchisement. Prompted by mass demonstrations in Selma, Alabama, and vicious police brutality by Sheriff Jim Clark against the protestors, Johnson went before a joint session of Congress in the spring of 1965 demanding that America deliver on her promissory note of equal citizenship for black as well as white citizens. "We shall overcome," Johnson concluded, personally embracing the most powerful movement in America's history by using the slogan of the civil rights movement's anthem.

Nothing matched the legislative legerdemain that Johnson displayed day after day. Reading Congress like a road map, he vaulted from one success to another, transforming the nation's domestic landscape in a manner that surpassed even the legendary accomplishments of FDR. "Johnson asketh and the Congress giveth," one reporter joked. Not all the achievements of the Great Society were as clear cut as others. Solving poverty, for example, entailed more than simply giving poor people a voice in devising their own strategies for change: "Maximum feasible participation" by the poor in Community Action Programs (CAPs) did not perforce slash welfare rolls or redistribute income from rich to poor. On the other hand, entitlements like Medicare (and its state subsidiary Medicaid) made stunning inroads into poverty among people over sixty-five while carrying the country at least partway toward national health insurance. Operation Head Start brought education to youngsters in inner-city ghettoes during the preschool years when psychologists said most learning took place. And nothing could gainsay the revolutionary impact of the Voting Rights Act, which overnight led to an increase in voting among African Americans in the South from 10 to 65 percent of the population—approximately the same proportion as among white people. The Immigration Act of 1965 radically altered the exclusionary policies inherited from the 1920s, facilitating a dramatic if unintended influx to America, especially of Asians and Latinos. If this kind of change were the product of a "liberal consensus," it meant a measure of progress significantly greater than had been anticipated at any other time in the postwar era. Never had the ability of the state to act on behalf of the general good of the whole been more visibly triumphant.

V. VIETNAM

Yet even as Johnson soared to the greatest heights of his success, he was already in the process of undermining the faith in government that had made it all possible. From 1947 forward, the anchor of the "liberal consensus" had been ardent anticommunism. First enunciated in George Kennan's "containment" policy, then carried forward in the rhetoric of a holy war that infused the statements of Harry Truman, John Foster Dulles, and John F. Kennedy's inaugural, the struggle to fight the Communist menace whenever and wherever it appeared served as the undisputed (and unexamined) premise of all American foreign policy. Any nation hostile to the Soviet Union, however undemocratic—Portugal or Paraguay—was America's friend; any nation friendly to Russia, however freedom-loving—India—was on the other side. The United States had survived one unpopular war based on such a policy. Costly in casualties, Korea represented a deep scar on the otherwise unbroken surface of anti-Communist successes. But now, under Lyndon Johnson, came a conflict that threatened to tear apart the unwritten rule that Americans would pay *any* price and bear *any* burden to defeat worldwide communism.

Vietnam had not always been an enemy of the United States. During World War II, American intelligence officers worked in close collaboration with Ho Chi Minh in a common effort to defeat the Japanese. When North Vietnam announced its independence from France in September 1945, American air force planes flew overhead in tribute to the new nation, and Ho pointedly quoted Thomas Jefferson's words—"We hold these truths to be self-evident, that all men are created equal"—while aides to Ho warmly embraced the "particularly intimate relations" the Vietnamese had with the United States, "which it is a pleasant duty to dwell upon." Given the anticolonial policies FDR had endorsed at Teheran and Yalta, there seemed good reason to be optimistic about future relations.

Yet the Cold War changed all that. As we have seen, America's first priority in the late 1940s was to unify Western Europe in an alliance against Communist aggression. France represented a key player in that policy, sufficiently important for the United States to waive its general anticolonialist position to support French domination of Indochina as a fair price to pay for securing French support for NATO and the Western alliance. That support persisted through the 1950s, in many ways reinforced by American determination to extend its containment policy throughout Asia.

Ngo Diem, the ruler of South Vietnam after the 1954 Geneva Accords, was in large part an American creation. Schooled at Maryknoll Seminary, friend of American Catholics like Cardinal Spellman and John F. Kennedy, he brought to his duties as president of South Vietnam an imperious arrogance, untempered by deep familiarity with either the Buddhist culture of his country or its agrarian peasantry. From the beginning, many Americans questioned Diem's ability to bring peace and reform to Vietnam; yet there were few alternatives, and when John F. Kennedy decided that he needed to signal Nikita Khrushchev that he was determined to fight communism, Vietnam became his test case. Although Kennedy resolutely opposed sending tens of thousands of troops to Vietnam—"the troops will march in," Kennedy said prophetically, "the bands will play; the crowds will cheer; and in four days everyone will have forgotten. Then we will all be told we have to send more troops. It's like taking a drink. The effect wears off, and you have to take another"—he nevertheless agreed to increase the number of American military advisors there from 800 to 17,000. Moreover, Kennedy implicitly agreed to a plan conceived by U.S. Ambassador Henry Cabot Lodge to sponsor a coup d'etat against Diem. When Kennedy heard that Diem and his family had been brutally murdered as a result, he rushed from the room in dismay, haunted by what the United States done and what it suggested about ever deeper American involvement in Southeast Asia. Less than two months later, Kennedy himself would be assassinated.

As with domestic affairs, Lyndon Johnson did not miss a beat in affirming his intention to continue Kennedy's policies. "I am not going to lose Vietnam," he told Henry Cabot Lodge right after Kennedy's death. "I am not going to be the president who saw Southeast Asia go the way China went." Based on his long experience with Congress during the McCarthy era and his own participation in Communist witch hunts, Johnson was terrified of what might happen to his domestic aspirations were he to show any softness toward aggressively advancing the cause of anticommunism in Vietnam. Although many American historians believe that Kennedy, bolstered by his new sense of self-confidence and mastery in the diplomatic arena after the Cuban Missile Crisis, would never have escalated the war in Vietnam, Johnson had neither the experience nor the confidence of Kennedy. Genuinely, he seems to have believed in the domino theory articulated by Dwight Eisenhower in his 1954 comments on Vietnam. "You knock over the first one, and what will happen to the last one is a certainty.... The loss of South Vietnam would have grave consequences for us and for freedom." Translated into Johnsonian vernacular, that meant "if you let a bully come into your front yard one day, the next day he will be up on your porch and the day after that he will rape your wife in your own bed." Hell, Johnson said, "Vietnam is just like the Alamo."

Thus, Johnson never questioned the necessity of America fighting to the end to prevent Communist victory in Vietnam. Indeed, in his view, carrying forward the war in Vietnam was inextricably tied to achieving success for the Great Society. If he "left that war and let the Communists take over," Johnson said, "I would lose everything at home. All my programs. All my hopes to feed the hungry and shelter the homeless." To some, the reasoning might be convoluted, but to Johnson it was compelling. And among other things, it helped explain the hows and whys of Johnson's conduct of the war. The president felt trapped by a vicious cycle. If he were open with the American public about his intention to ratchet up the war in Asia, it might endanger support for the Great Society on the grounds that it was impossible to pay for both "guns and butter." On the other hand, were he to abandon Vietnam, he would generate a McCarthyite political backlash that would also doom

Slowly but inexorably, America became bogged down in a brutal war in Vietnam during the 1960s. American troop deployments increased from 15,000 in 1963 to 540,000 in 1968. The war divided America into bitter factions and dramatically undermined America's popularity in the world.

Credit: Associated Press

his program. Hence Johnson's peculiar choice of tactics: he would save his domestic agenda by accelerating American involvement in Vietnam *but would hide his policies of escalation through a politics of deception* that would obscure the full measure of America's growing commitment to Vietnam and allow continuation of the Great Society, "the woman I really love." It was a desperate bid to preserve consensus, both about domestic reform and the need to fight communism, but based as it was on duplicity, Johnson's choice of how to proceed ultimately shattered consensus in America and brought the nation to the greatest internal division it had experienced since the Civil War.

Notwithstanding his comments to Henry Cabot Lodge in November 1963, Johnson gave no public indication of his intention to increase American involvement in Vietnam. On the contrary, he scored huge points with American voters when, in the 1964 campaign against Barry Goldwater, he pledged not to send American boys to fight a war nine thousand miles from home. Yet even as he was upholding a policy of restraint, Johnson carried around in his pocket a congressional resolution that he planned to introduce whenever a North Vietnamese assault provided him with the occasion to do so. Its purpose: to give the president unrestricted authority to pursue the enemy. Such was the context when North Vietnamese torpedo boats allegedly attacked American destroyers in international waters in the Gulf of Tonkin. Although we now know that the evidence for such "attacks" was flimsy if not nonexistent, Johnson galvanized patriotic sentiment to secure immediate passage of his resolution, with only two United States senators dissenting.

Soon it became necessary to escalate further and practice even greater deception. In the midst of Johnson's giant push for Great Society legislation in the winter and spring of 1965, conditions in Vietnam steadily deteriorated. The government of Vietnam changed regularly—six times in one year. Intelligence experts estimated that the South Vietnamese regime had at best a fifty-fifty chance of surviving unless America became more directly involved. Earlier, the argument had been that once a strong government was in place, America could increase its support for that regime. Now the argument became that unless America intervened, no government could survive. Once more, as with the Gulf of Tonkin, the alleged rationale was a Viet Cong attack on an American air base at Pleiku. In response, the United States determined that it not only needed to launch a massive bombing attack on North Vietnam— Operation Rolling Thunder—but also send thousands of additional troops to Vietnam to protect the air bases from which the planes would carry out their missions. It was all "Catch-22"—to stabilize the South Vietnamese government, America needed to increase its attacks on North Vietnam, thereby demonstrating its commitment to the South Vietnamese government, and then in order to protect the planes, it needed to commit more troops on the ground. But Pleiku was just an excuse. As presidential aide McGeorge Bundy said, "Pleikus are like streetcars. There's always another one coming along." And so the process of escalation continued.

Significantly, the escalation did not occur without a rising tide of dissent within the administration. On two occasions in the spring of 1965—the

February launch of Rolling Thunder and a June decision to raise American troop levels to one hundred thousand—the critics, led by Undersecretary of State George Ball, raised the kind of fundamental questions about American policy that should have framed discussion of America's commitment all along. Painfully cognizant about the parallels between America's growing role in Vietnam and the French experience in Indochina, Ball worried that the escalation might never end, and America would become a colonial oppressor. "Once on the tiger's back," he noted, "we can not be sure of picking the place to dismount." State Department advisor James Thompson echoed Ball. "It seems to me," he wrote, "[that] we have slipped into a gross overcommitment of national prestige and resources on political, military and geographic terrain which should long ago have persuaded us to avoid commitment. Our national interest now demands that we find ourselves a face-saving avenue of retreat." What the United States was asking, Ball suggested, was for North Vietnam to engage in an unconditional surrender—clearly something Ho Chi Minh would never consider. A negotiated settlement provided the only sensible option from Ball's point of view.

The debate reached new intensity when General Westmoreland requested a commitment of 150,000 troops in June. Presciently, Ball retorted that this would make the war irretrievably an *American* battle, predicting that even with 500,000 troops, the United States could not achieve its goal. (McNamara accused Ball of using scare tactics with his 500,000 figure, although three years later that was exactly the total of American troops that were fighting in Vietnam). "When we have put enough Americans on the ground in South Vietnam to give the appearance of a white man's war," Ball pointed out, "the distinction [between us and the French] will have less and less practical effect." Johnson must take advantage of this last opportunity, Ball concluded, to "extricate ourselves without unacceptable costs....*In my view, a deep commitment of United States forces in a land war in South Vietnam would be a catastrophic error. If ever there was an occasion for a tactical withdrawal, this would be it.*"

Although Johnson gave the appearance of encouraging debate, he in fact conceptualized the options in a way that created the impression of following a moderate course while in reality pursuing escalation. There were three possible courses of action, he declared: (a) cut and run, abandoning Vietnam; (b) commit additional forces in a reasonable fashion to stabilize the political situation and punish the aggressors; and (c) engage in all-out combat against the North. Neither the extremes of a or c were acceptable. Hence, Johnson would pursue a consensus and choose b.

In the meantime, Johnson continued to deceive the American public about the decisions he made. Just before committing American ground troops to offensive action in Vietnam, he told reporters that "I know of no far-reaching strategy change that is being suggested or promulgated" and ordered Pentagon officials to "minimize any appearance of sudden changes in policy." When the president agreed in midsummer to increase America's troop levels to 125,000, with more to come later, he once again denied there was any significant shift in United States policy. Significantly, Secretary of

Defense McNamara and most of his other advisors agreed that if he were to pursue this escalation, Johnson should call up 100,000 reservists to assume responsibility for other American military commitments and that he should raise taxes to pay for the war. Johnson refused to do either one, explicitly stating to the American public that no reserves would be called up and no taxes raised. Instead, he advised his staff to implement the new policy in "a low-key manner in order...to avoid undue concern and excitement in Congress and in domestic public opinion." Or, he might have added, to in any way undermine his current legislative initiatives for the Great Society. It was a perilous course, destined eventually to explode the consensus Johnson so deeply cherished.

All of George Ball's worst fears proved prophetic. Each escalation of military involvement failed to achieve its stated objectives. The more American planes bombed Vietnam—and the total tonnage of bombs far exceeded all the bombs dropped by the Allies during World War II—the more resilient the North Vietnamese became. Intelligence studies found that North Vietnam's morale actually improved as the bombing intensified. In the ground war, meanwhile, the difficulty of identifying an enemy that blended into the population proved an insurmountable barrier to U.S. troops. On the one hand, a group of innocent-looking South Vietnamese peasants could turn in a second into a grenade-throwing Viet Cong battalion. On the other hand, viewing all Vietnamese peasants as potential enemies could lead to massive atrocities like the My Lai massacre, when American troops, frustrated by losses among their comrades, vented their rage against a Vietnamese village by burning down every village hut and slaughtering the men, women, and children who tried to escape. Despite America's military might, one journalist noted, every blow against the enemy "was like a sledgehammer [hitting] a floating cork....Somehow, the cork refused to stay down." In the meantime, the presence of American troops, money, and consumer goods turned Vietnam's cities into American-style enclaves. As one reporter wrote, "There evolves here a colonial ambience that can sometimes be worse than colonialism itself."

In the end, Johnson's Vietnam policy turned into a long national nightmare, the horror of which was summarized in a comment made by one American major about the "victory" he had just won: "We had to destroy the village," he declared, "in order to save it." All Vietnamese in some ways became the enemy—"gooks," the "other." America had set forth to "save" those unable to save themselves, to Americanize the Mekong Delta and make it into a replica of the Tennessee Valley Authority, to bring "progress" to a backward civilization through uprooting ancient villages and creating new "strategic hamlets." Yet almost inexorably, it seemed, that mission entailed destruction rather than construction. Even government officials ultimately recognized the price. "We seem to be proceeding on the assumption," a Defense Department official said, "that the way to eradicate the Viet Cong is to destroy all the village structure, defoliate all the jungles, then cover the entire surface of South Vietnam with asphalt." The ritual optimism of

Pentagon and White House pronouncements became a ready foil for comedians and social satirists. After the umpteenth time that a government official said that the country was "turning the corner," one columnist described a mock street corner, stored in the Pentagon's theatrical effects section, that government officials brought out and "turned" every few months to create the impression that the situation was improving. Only humor could attempt to redeem tragedy.

Inevitably, opposition mounted to what now seemed self-evidently a failed policy. Initially, Americans were supportive of Johnson, believing their president when he said there had been no major change in policy. Senators and congressmen followed a long tradition of bipartisanship, giving the president the benefit of the doubt on virtually every foreign policy issue. But eventually, the casualty reports and news analyses took root. David Halberstam of the *New York Times* and Peter Arnett of the Associated Press wrote about the "quagmire" in which America was sinking. When two or three combat deaths a week became thirty or forty, hometown America started to ask questions, especially when there was a new South Vietnamese government every few months, and the Vietnamese themselves seemed notoriously reluctant to fight for their own freedom. By 1966–1967, more and more senators started asking hard questions. J. William Fulbright conducted Senate hearings on the war that were televised nationally, bringing into every American home a new debate on the very premises of America's foreign policy and the viability, in particular, of what the country was doing in Vietnam.

But it was on the nation's campuses that the antiwar movement primarily took root. A generation of young people had been politicized by the moral thrust of the civil rights movement. Acutely sensitive to hypocrisy in their elders, and the call for social and economic justice prompted by black Americans, college students demanded accountability from their elected officials. Students for a Democratic Society, a left-of-center group, formed in 1962 to express their concern about "the permeating and victimizing fact of human degradation." "We are the people of this generation," their founding statement declared, "bred in at least modest comfort, housed now in universities, looking uncomfortably to the world we inherit." Well before the Vietnam war became an issue, SDS passionately embraced the cause of making America more humanistic, compassionate, and committed to "an environment [where people can] live...with dignity and creativeness." At the University of California, Berkeley, they took aim at the dehumanizing bureaucracy of the megauniversity where people became machines of capitalism and were denied their ability to shape their own futures. The Free Speech Movement in 1964 became the first manifestation of radicalization among veterans of the civil rights era as young people mounted their own campaign for autonomy and freedom.

Now, the war heightened the sensitivity of college students to injustice in the world and hypocrisy among their leaders. Although attending a university automatically exempted a person from the military draft, students quickly seized on the war as an illustration of evil in the world, which they would not tolerate. With a moral self-righteousness fully equal to the strident rhetoric of the country's national leaders, they condemned the complicity of their universities with the Pentagon war machine, attacked the inhumanity of destroying Vietnam villages, and called into question the values of the entire capitalist system. Initially, students sought to focus attention on the shortcomings of the war by holding "teach-ins" and inviting defenders of the war, as well as critics, to debate the war's merits. But soon it became evident that although government spokesmen might agree to participate in such exercises, they would not suddenly discover the error of their ways and change policies. At that point, students adopted a more aggressive approach, sponsoring street demonstrations in protest, picketing draft boards, and harassing government representatives when they came to speak on campus. Eventually, these demonstrations turned into an antidraft movement, the burning of selective service cards, the ransacking of government records, and more and more overt confrontations with authorities. Dissent ceased being civil and became raucous. "Hey, hey, LBJ, how many kids did you kill today?" was the new slogan. The police became "pigs," government officials "murderers," university presidents a tool of ruthless capitalists. The country was on its way to civil war.

As the Vietnam War became ever more divisive, protestors took to the streets to demand peace, with hundreds of thousands demonstrating all over the country. Here "May Day" protestors are blocking the main entrance to the House of Representatives in Washington, D.C.

Credit: © Wally McNamee/CORBIS

VI. FRAGMENTATION

Although it was the antiwar movement that brought the nation to the precipice of breaking apart, the process of fragmentation had begun in 1964 at the height of Lyndon Johnson's success. The civil rights bill had been enacted, the War on Poverty begun, and Kennedy's tax cut passed. But just as it seemed that the liberal consensus was at its peak of effectiveness, the principle tenets undergirding it began to erode. For more than a decade and a half, various constituencies—labor, blacks, intellectuals, urban bosses, moderates from suburbia—had carried around in their heads a common picture of their society. They believed in equal opportunity, in making appropriate incremental reforms to help those most aggrieved, and in working together toward common goals at home even as they united behind a posture of anticommunism abroad. Now, multiple constituencies began to feel that those ground rules had been betrayed and that their own interests were being trampled for the benefit of others. Not surprisingly, the fragmentation began over the issue of race.

The fracture began in Mississippi and spread to Atlantic City, where the Democratic national convention was meeting to nominate Lyndon Johnson for president in his own right, not just as the successor to John F. Kennedy. In no place in America were black people more brutalized and exploited than Mississippi. After years of struggling to secure the right to vote, only to be beaten, killed, and fired from their jobs (and never given the protection promised them by the Justice Department), black Mississippians, under the leadership of Bob Moses, concluded that having white people put their lives on the line, together with blacks, offered the only hope for securing justice. In the fall of 1963, a white civil rights advocate, Allard Lowenstein, collaborated with black leaders to bring white students into the state and sponsor a "Freedom Vote" where blacks would show their commitment to the political process by casting ballots in a mock election. More than eighty thousand did so. Now Moses decided that bringing one thousand white volunteers into the state in the summer of 1964 from campuses like Yale, Stanford, Swarthmore, and Antioch would provide the occasion to replicate the success of the freedom vote, start a series of "freedom schools" for young African Americans, and organize a new party—the Mississippi Freedom Democratic Party—which could go to the national Democratic convention in Atlantic City and secure the recognition that blacks deserved.

The summer started with tragedy when James Chaney, Michael Schwerner, and Andrew Goodman—two of the three were white summer volunteers from New York City—were arrested by the Neshoba County sheriff, then brutally beaten and lynched, their bodies sunk in a damn near Philadelphia, Mississippi. But the movement did not stop. Freedom schools taught young black students African American history, writing, and civics. White volunteers joined blacks in seeking to register black voters, then collected mountains of affidavits testifying to the manner in which they had been denied basic citizenship rights. The MFDP elected a biracial slate of delegates to go to Atlantic City, where, with legendary labor lawyer Joseph Rauh as their legal counsel, they petitioned the Credentials Committee to seat them in place of the all-white "regular" Democratic Party delegates, all of whom were pledged to support Barry Goldwater, the Republican nominee for president. "Are you going to throw out of here the people who want to work for Lyndon Johnson," Rauh asked the Credentials Committee, "who are willing to be beaten and shot and thrown in jail to work for Lyndon Johnson? Are we for the oppressor or the oppressed?" When Mrs. Fannie Lou Hamer, a legendary heroine of the movement, testified on national television about how she had been beaten and sexually abused by white sheriffs when she tried to register, then fired by her employer, it seemed the case had been clinched. More than enough delegates believed in the MFDP for the fight to be taken to the floor for a vote, and everyone knew that in that instance, the MFDP would win. The MFDP had played by the rules of the game, and it had faith that within the democratic process, it would win.

But that expectation did not take into account Lyndon Johnson's ego. He did not wish anyone, white or black, to take the spotlight away from him or to undermine his total domination of the convention. In response, Johnson mobilized his own forces, telling Hubert Humphrey that if he wished to be LBJ's vice president, he had to quell the MFDP dissent. He also mobilized his traditional allies in the civil rights movement, from Bayard Rustin to Walter Reuther of the United Automobile Workers, to Martin Luther King, Jr., to support a compromise—that the MFDP would get only two seats out of forty, both to be chosen by the credentials committee, not the MFDP. From the point of view of the freedom movement in Mississippi, Johnson's proposal represented an insult. They had played the game, done what they were told to do, produced the evidence, and for what? As one black woman from Mississippi said, "The compromise would let Jim Crow be.... Ain't no Democratic Party worth that. We've been treated like beasts in Mississippi. They shot us down like animals. We risked our lives coming here.... Politics must be corrupt if it don't care none about people down there." The MFDP had believed in the "system." Now the system had failed them, severing the ties that had sustained hope among blacks in Mississippi in the liberal tradition. So the MFDP said no to the compromise and went back home—but now with a different spirit, one of anger and alienation as opposed to hope and faith.

The MFDP blowup at the convention represented a pivotal fissure in the liberal coalition. To be sure, Johnson went on to a resounding victory over Goldwater, with massive black support. Still, activists—especially among the young and more militant members of SNCC—started to question whether they could ever again trust white liberals. Their doubts were reinforced, innocently enough, by the presumptive authority that many white volunteers brought with them to Mississippi. Members of the "best and brightest" generation, these white students had grown up self-confident and authoritative. They "knew" what was best. With all the good intentions in the world, they conveyed this sense of the best way to proceed to the blacks they encountered both inside the movement and in their work with rural African

Americans, whom they were trying to convince to go to register. The difference was highlighted in Alice Walker's novel *Meridian*, a fictional recounting of how differently a black and white volunteer handled a reluctant sharecropper whom they were trying to recruit. The black was patient, hearing out the sharecropper's fears and anxieties, not pushing too hard or fast. The white was overbearing, lecturing the sharecropper on her responsibilities, displaying anger when the sharecropper declined to sign up immediately to go to the courthouse. In the end, many blacks came to resent the implicit but imperious message that whites conveyed, however unintentionally—*they* were the ones with the answers.

At the same time, sexual tensions exploded within the movement, especially during Freedom Summer. Whites and blacks lived together in intimate circumstances. Inevitably, sexual liaisons developed, usually between black men and white women. But these were relationships that struck at the volatile nexus between race and sex. Black men having intercourse with white women was taboo, highlighting the apprehension among whites that blacks might finally seek retribution for the centuries of oppression where white men exploited black women sexually. For native Southern whites and for many older blacks, such sexual relations inside the movement were scandalous. For black civil rights workers, on the other hand, engaging in such activities with white women provided final confirmation that they were "free." Because many white women felt that saying no to black men was racist, they responded positively. Many black women, however, saw such behavior as demeaning, threatening, and destructive. As sexual tensions proliferated, so too did the divisions between black and white women and more generally between blacks from the South and Northern white volunteers.

By the fall and winter of 1964–1965, these stress lines came to the fore. SNCC debated whether or not whites should be permitted to remain on the staff of the nation's most cutting-edge civil rights organization. At the same time, white women, led by SNCC old-timers like Casey Hayden and Mary King, introduced the issue of how women were treated in the movement. Too often, King and Hayden argued in "Sex and Caste: A Kind of Oppression," women were expected only to clean up, make coffee, and serve men while being denied an equal voice in decision making. In so many instances, they suggested, women in SNCC were treated by men just like blacks in America were treated by whites. With an attempt at ironic humor, Stokely Carmichael infamously commented, "The position of women in the movement should be prone"; but the conflicts suggested in the King-Hayden memo eventually resulted in white women leaving the movement and becoming the leaders of a new women's liberation struggle.

By 1966, the idealism of whites and blacks working together as a "beloved community" had fallen victim to fratricide, with "Black Power" now the slogan of choice rather than "black and white together." SNCC berated Dr. King, snidely called him "de Lawd," mocked his elitism, and ridiculed his philosophy of nonviolence. The growing chasm exploded into public view when Dr. King and SNCC chair Stokely Carmichael led a march to

Jackson, Mississippi, that had been started by James Meredith before he was wounded by a roadside sniper. At each town the marchers entered, blacks rallied to hear their leaders. "Freedom Now," King repeated, with little response. "Black Power," Carmichael chanted, and the crowd erupted. White America had betrayed black dreams, Carmichael declared. "The only way we are going to stop them from whuppin' us is to take over.... Black Power. It's time to stand up and take over; move on over [Whitey] or we'll move on over you."

A fearsome new phrase had entered national political discourse. Although the substance of black power and black nationalism had a long history in the black community, it had always been in the context of a larger commitment to work for progress within a white-ruled America. Now, the old ground rules were gone. Black Power represented the equivalent of a racial nuclear bomb, suggesting new ground rules where blacks alone would determine what was best for them and where racial antagonism became a cause for celebration, not regret. Moreover, the new militancy went hand in hand with growing white apprehension over blacks taking to the streets, viscerally attacking white America. First there was Watts in Los Angeles, with thirty-five million dollars in property damages; then riots in Cleveland, Chicago, and Milwaukee. "Burn, baby, burn," the rioters chanted. The old biracial coalition of blacks and white liberals seemed like a romantic dream.

If many blacks no longer felt invested in the ground rules of the "liberal consensus," the same was true of millions of white Americans. There had always been a strong conservative movement in the country. Barry Goldwater and *National Review* founder Bill Buckley preached the doctrine that the best government was no government, embraced laissez-faire capitalism, accused Democrats of being "soft on communism," and opposed tinkering with the American social system. But millions of average Americans rallied in support of civil rights when they heard Dr. King speak at the March on Washington and saw Bull Connor's police dogs snarl at black women and children. Now, however, these "middle-Americans," as news magazines dubbed them, became angry at black militants, resentful of the peremptory tone of their demands and the threatening implications of their call for "Black Power." Many of them were white ethnics. They had worked hard to make it into the middle class, buy a home, and give their kids a better life. "[They] don't want to penalize the Negro," one political scientist noted, but "they feel strongly that the rules they came up by should apply." That meant no special treatment, no loud protests, no rioting in the streets. Their changing views were reflected in one simple statistic. In 1964, only 34 percent of white Americans believed that blacks wanted too much too fast. Two years later, that figure had soared to 85 percent. It was all too much. Women were denouncing traditional marriage, forming women's liberation groups, and trashing monogamy; young people were defaming the flag and calling police officers "pigs"; and black militants were talking about walking all over "Whitey" and taking over. Everything was coming apart.

VII. 1968: THE YEAR OF DISINTEGRATION

If there were a day when America's public optimism about Vietnam started to shatter, it was January 30, 1968, the beginning of the Tet holiday celebrating the lunar new year. In one 24-hour period, Viet Cong forces attacked 36 provincial capitals, 64 district capitals, and 5 major cities. In Saigon, they seized control of the grounds of the United States Embassy. Just a few weeks before, General William Westmoreland had one more time announced that he could see a "light at the end of the tunnel" in Vietnam. Now, despite huge Viet Cong losses in the ensuing battles, it appeared that the tunnel was endless, with no end in sight. "What the hell is going on," CBS anchorman Walter Cronkite asked, reflecting the incredulity of his audience. "I thought we were winning the war!" To act as though this was just one more defeat for the enemy, humorist Art Buchwald wrote in his column, was like Custer at Little Big Horn announcing that "we have the Sioux on the run....Of course we still have some cleaning up to do, but the Redskins are hurting badly and it will only be a matter of time before they give in." What had once been a credibility gap for the White House now became a chasm, with Johnson's approval rating plummeting from 40 percent in November 1967 to 26 percent in the aftermath of Tet.

Newly galvanized by the shock of the Tet offensive, antiwar forces in the United States took on new energy. Allard Lowenstein, the civil rights activist and political gadfly, had spent a full year seeking a candidate to "dump Johnson" in the Democratic primaries of 1968. Deeply torn, Robert Kennedy ultimately turned him down, believing that everyone would attribute a Kennedy candidacy to his history of bad personal relations with Johnson rather than policy conviction. But Minnesota Senator Eugene McCarthy said yes, agreeing to bring his satirical tongue and biting eloquence to bear on the most pivotal issue of his lifetime. "There comes a time," he declared, "when an honorable man simply has to raise a flag." Although initially McCarthy failed to marshal any support in the New Hampshire primary(6 percent in December), Tet changed all that. Backed by thousands of college antiwar demonstrators who flooded New Hampshire's rural hamlets ("be clean for Gene," they said, as they cut their long hair and donned sport coats, ties, and dresses), McCarthy suddenly became a contender and on the night of the New Hampshire primary ended up winning twenty of twenty-four delegates and coming within 4 percentage points of outpolling Johnson in the overall vote count. Although a significant portion of McCarthy's support came from prowar citizens angry at Johnson, the fact remained that most Americans saw his "victory" in New Hampshire as a dramatic repudiation of the sitting president.

Suddenly, what had looked to be a surefire renomination of Lyndon Johnson became a front-and-center political question. Robert F. Kennedy reconsidered his earlier rejection of a presidential candidacy, rationalizing that McCarthy's showing now made the war the major issue, not Kennedy's personal relationship with Johnson. Leaping into the fray, Kennedy engaged in searing attacks on America's Vietnam policy, and in addition, galvanized substantial support among black Americans, Latinos, and the poor as well as big-city bosses. Just as he had identified with the most malnourished sharecroppers of Mississippi, Kennedy became the champion of Chicano grape-pickers in California.

As if that were not enough, just as Kennedy's candidacy was taking off, Johnson foiled everyone's expectations. In a nationally televised speech on March 31, the president announced a halt in America's bombing raids of North Vietnam, signaling a readiness to de-escalate the war and initiate peace negotiations; then, to the astonishment of virtually everyone, he announced that under no circumstances would he be a candidate for reelection. Overnight, the entire political stage was transformed, its central character having withdrawn.

The Johnson shock waves had barely subsided when four days later, a white racist gunned down Martin Luther King, Jr., on a Memphis hotel balcony, killing him instantly. The night before, King had preached a sermon he had given oftentimes before, seeking to rally Memphis blacks in support of the Poor People's Campaign he was organizing as well as on behalf of the sanitation workers strike in Memphis. But this time, his closest aides noted something different in his voice, almost as if he were prophesying what was about to happen. "I've been to the mountaintop," he told the congregation, and "I've seen the glory" of a better day. "I may not get there with you," he said, "but I want you to know that we as a people will get to the promised land." As the nation mourned, riots broke out in more than one hundred cities, army machine guns were installed on Capitol Hill, and millions who had looked to King for moral guidance felt as though they had lost their only hope for lasting peace.

Even then, the staccato-like blows at America's sense of order and stability did not cease. "It was as if the future waited on the first of each month," journalist Theodore White wrote, "to deliver events completely unforeseen the month before." In one of the periodic eruptions spotlighting the growing alienation between antiwar student radicals and ordinary "middle-Americans," a group of SDS students at Columbia University seized the main administration offices of the president and occupied numerous academic buildings. "Up against the wall, motherfucker," SDS's Mark Rudd told Columbia president Grayson Kirk, "this is a stickup." The students were protesting both Columbia's collaboration with secret national security agencies on military matters and the university's decision to build a new gymnasium bordering Harlem *with no access available to Harlem residents*. The administration refused to negotiate, and after six days, thousands of New York City police were sent in to empty the buildings. In the course of the raid, faculty members seeking to provide a buffer zone were beaten in addition to students. The next day, even moderate students joined a university-wide strike against the administration's action while countless parents of college-age students wondered just what the world was coming to when student protestors used such language against college presidents and stole or destroyed the files of professors whose offices they were occupying.

The final blow against those who hoped against hope for some political solution to the nation's malaise came when Robert F. Kennedy, brother of the slain president, was murdered in a hotel kitchen shortly after he had delivered his victory speech the night of the California primary. In some people's opinion, Kennedy had experienced a virtual transformation as a political personality in the aftermath of his brother's death. Depressed, brooding, worried that he himself might have been responsible for JFK's death because of his pursuit of the Mafia, Kennedy became less sharp-edged, more introspective. He reflected on the mysteries of life and death; contemplated the wisdom of the Greek philosophers; and focused on the preaching of modern-day moralists like existentialist Albert Camus, who argued that human beings were responsible for making the world better or worse and that the least one could do was to leave children better off than they were. When Kennedy was elected U.S. senator from New York, he made issues of poverty, race, and injustice his priorities. Visiting the dirt-floored shacks of black sharecroppers in Mississippi, he held little children in his arms whose bodies were covered with sores and who suffered from malnourishment. He embraced the cause of Latino farmworkers of California, went to South Africa to encourage valiant black Africans fighting against apartheid, and in the coal mines of Peru stood side by side with workers seeking a better life. It was as though in seeking to redeem his brother's death he had become a tribune for the underclass.

Now, in the spring of 1968, Kennedy carried those same messages—plus an almost prophetic denunciation of the war in Vietnam—to dissatisfied Americans. When Martin Luther King, Jr., was killed, Kennedy told blacks in Indianapolis that he understood their pain because he too had a brother killed by a white man. Across the country, black Americans rallied to Kennedy as their last best hope. But so too did millions of working-class whites, otherwise alienated from blacks, who saw in Kennedy the hope and inspiration of his brother. Perhaps, they believed, just perhaps, there could be a new coming together led by this man whose shy smile, affection for young children, and passionate concern for justice signaled the promise of a better day. But it was not to be, and now the second social crusader in two months had been shot down, casting millions of Americans into despair, shattering what at least some saw as the last chance the country had to recover its soul and feel as one again.

Instead, the disintegration continued. At the Democratic convention in Chicago, police and national guardsman brutally beat student demonstrators who had come to protest the war and seek a nominee who shared their views. It was a "police riot," a review commission subsequently declared. Richard Daley, Chicago's mayor, had ordered his police to "get tough," but perhaps no one could have anticipated just how tough they would be. Inside the convention hall, Abraham Ribicoff, a Connecticut senator sympathetic to the protestors, bemoaned their treatment while the national TV audience could read Daley's lips as he shouted back, calling Ribicoff a "motherfucker." The country could not believe what it was seeing, as on the streets the dramatic confrontation between student radicals and angry "middle-Americans" was acted out while in the convention hall, the national party seemed to fall apart, reflecting the larger disintegration occurring in the country as a whole. In the end, Vice President Hubert Humphrey was nominated, but his acceptance speech celebrating the "politics of joy" in America seemed almost a theater-of-the-absurd confirmation of just how distant America truly was from the politics of consensus that had driven the past two decades.

When Richard Nixon was chosen the Republican nominee, he understood exactly how to pull together all the issues that were dividing the American people. Nixon claimed to have a "secret plan" for ending the war in Vietnam and would bring American troops home. Speaking for those Americans— later dubbed "the silent majority"—who were patriotic, religious, and devoted to law and order, Nixon pledged to "bring us together" as a nation, once more restoring respect for the nation's institutions, especially the family. For those upset with racial protest, Nixon pledged a country that would enforce "law and order," all the while pursuing a Southern strategy to win over historically Democratic white Southerners by deemphasizing school desegregation and opposing aggressive federal intervention on racial issues. In short, Richard Nixon understood profoundly the degree to which disintegration had supplanted consensus and used the depth of popular alienation to build a winning coalition. If there was a surprise in his ultimate electoral victory in the 1968 presidential election, it was only the slim margin by which he eventually was elected. Now there would be a new regime in power, one that would seek to create a very different kind of consensus for American politics than had existed for more than two decades.

VIII. CONCLUSION

In just four years—1964 to 1968—a country that had been united as never before fell apart, fragmented into polarized factions. Whatever the ineffectiveness of his early months in office, John F. Kennedy had rallied the nation to a romantic sense of possibility. His call to national service inspired young people everywhere, rousting them from their complacency, giving them through the Peace Corps and participation in the civil rights movement the sense that they could make history and create a better America. Especially in the aftermath of the Cuban Missile Crisis, Kennedy started to put markers on the wall—toward peace, toward racial equality, toward a campaign to end poverty. Then when he died a martyr's death, Lyndon Johnson took Kennedy's dream and soared with it to the greatest heights of domestic achievement seen since FDR and the New Deal. Almost nothing seemed unimaginable as Congress and the president strode in vigorous partnership to provide health care for the aged, education for the young, rent supplements for the poor, job training for the unemployed. The liberal consensus, with its faith in capitalism, democracy, incremental reform, and anticommunism, had reached heights never dreamed of before and seemed undefeatable.

What caused it all to come apart? First, and perhaps most important, the disintegration came from ingredients in the liberal consensus itself. The progress that had been made on America's central domestic issue—that of race—was premised on a good-faith relationship between black Americans and liberal whites. As with every social movement, aspirations rose as victories were won. Blacks became more vocal in their anger at white betrayal of promises made. Some began to question whether it made sense to be integrated into a world where they would continue to be controlled, even if this time by white liberals. The MFDP became one test of that relationship, the dispute over who would determine the course of the civil rights movement another. In both instances, enough blacks felt betrayed by white liberals that they began to turn away from the biracial coalition that had triumphed in 1964 and 1965 and toward a critique of American society as a whole. A significant minority of white activist students did the same, arguing that there was a corruption within the capitalist system itself that militated against social and racial equality. That perspective, in turn, generated backlash from many ordinary white Americans who might be willing to go along with incremental reforms over long-standing grievances like voting rights and access to public accommodations but who rebelled when confronted with militant demands from Black Power advocates and student radicals. Thus in many ways the domestic successes of the liberal consensus planted the seeds of its own self-destruction.

But the fundamental flaw turned out to be the determination by Lyndon Johnson to combine domestic reform with a huge national war against Communism in Vietnam. As Johnson envisioned it, an inextricable relationship existed between the two. If one did not stand up to Communists in Asia, it would never be possible to fight poverty in America. Yet he could not be candid about the costs of the war if he wished the country to support his domestic initiatives. Hence the Catch-22 of LBJ's policies. In order to maintain consensus, he had to dissemble about the choices he was making, never realizing that he was pursuing a course guaranteed both to undermine his policy in Vietnam and erode the political support he needed to achieve a Great Society at home. In the end, the "inextricable" relationship between anticommunism abroad and reform at home was not sustainable. The one undermined the other. Unlike the war against Soviet Communists in Eastern Europe, in Vietnam there was no clear enemy. Defeating a foe indistinguishable from one's "friends" overwhelmed military strategists and set in motion a series of escalations that ultimately turned much of the country against its leaders. As antiwar sentiment increased, so too did polarization among the American people.

Ultimately, then, disintegration grew directly out of the "liberal consensus." It became impossible to perpetuate a healthy tension between social change at home and aggressive containment of communism abroad when each led to results that undermined political comity. In the end, the liberal consensus imploded, the victim of its own centrifugal impulses. The irony was that it reached its apex in the summer of 1965 with the passage of the Voting Rights Act, Medicare, and Federal Aid to Education—the same months when America committed over one hundred thousand troops to Vietnam and the president claimed that there was "no change in policy." Nothing better encapsulated the intrinsic connection between triumph and tragedy in the 1960s.

10

Polarization, Paranoia, and a New Conservatism: America in the 1970s

I f the 1960s witnessed both the apex and the nadir of America's post-war "liberal" consensus, the 1970s saw the emergence—gradually but inexorably—of a different politics, significantly more conservative. In reaction to the divisiveness of the late 1960s, politicians had used the polarization between "middle-Americans" and blacks, those devoted to traditional social values and those seeking to dismantle the "old rules," to create a new majority based on conservative cultural norms. The axis of politics shifted from horizontal concerns—social class, income level, education—to more vertical issues such as religious faith, law and order, and family values. Not coincidentally, the shift came at precisely the time when the economy slowed, America lost its position of unchallenged preeminence in the world, and a sense of anomie spread across the land. No one knew where the country was going. A president was forced to resign for moral turpitude, Americans fled in humiliation from the rooftop of the American embassy in Vietnam, oil-producing nations in the Middle East declared an embargo that made American drivers wait in line for hours to get gas, both inflation and unemployment hit double digits at the same time, and an Islamic fundamentalist regime in Iran held more than fifty American diplomats hostage for more than a year.

Out of all of this evolved a new set of shared understandings. There were limits to what government could do, especially domestically. A powerful religious community was intent on passionately defending the traditional rules of family and morality against change. America's unchallenged supremacy in the world was no longer a given, and if the nation needed to choose among competing priorities, national defense and the defeat of communism trumped social reform. In many respects, the emerging political consensus was not that different from the old; it still believed in capitalism and democracy and that communism and dictatorship must be defeated—except that now it no longer envisioned exuberant government support for social equality and justice. Instead, the locus of power had shifted to those committed to maintaining traditional cultural values and strengthening the domestic status quo.

I. THE MYSTERY OF RICHARD NIXON

No one better embodied the political dynamics at work in shaping the new era than Richard Nixon. Raised in a middle-class Quaker family in Whittier,

California, Nixon from the beginning demonstrated two qualities that would persist through his life: he was a loner who took every opportunity to go off by himself, whether working in the family store or plotting his lifetime career; and while alone, he envisioned himself doing great things, often against the tide of public opinion. Pervading both qualities was a sense of insecurity and alienation. Always fearful of not being liked, he resented those to whom power and success came as second nature, and he sought to strike out at and to destroy—vindictively—those who got in the way of his own ambitions. He wished to transform the world but to do so alone. He often displayed contempt for those around him. "He seemed lonely and so solemn," his first girlfriend commented. "He was smart and sort of set apart. I think he was unsure of himself deep down."

These character traits help explain the dualism of Nixon's political personality. On the one side, he talked of noble aspirations to improve the world and live a life of virtue, consistent with his mother's Quaker philosophy; on the other, he engaged in crude, petty, and vicious tactics to defeat his foes and ensure his invulnerability against those who might threaten his position. While at Duke Law School, the otherwise sanctimonious Nixon broke into the dean's office to determine his grades, so fearful was he that he might have fallen below the class standing necessary to retain his scholarship. When he came back from World War II, where he served as a naval officer, he decided to run for political office on a platform that celebrated the heroic virtues of America's fight for democracy and justice in the world, but he employed tactics that were abusive and demeaning. His opponent, Nixon declared in the congressional campaign of 1946, was a "lip-service American" who "fronted for un-American elements" and whose "voting record in Congress is more Socialistic and Communistic than Democratic." When a friend asked why he was using such dirty techniques, Nixon responded, "Because sometimes you have to do this to be a candidate. I'm gonna win."

Having learned well the lessons of his first victory, Nixon rode the politics of anticommunism to the vice presidency. As a freshman member of the House Un-American Activities Committee, Nixon single-mindedly pursued Alger Hiss, purported to be a Communist spy during the Roosevelt administration and one who had accompanied the president to Yalta. While other HUAC members shied away from confronting someone so supported by the "establishment," Nixon studied the issue in isolation, determined that Hiss was guilty, and assumed responsibility for leading the successful attack to expose him. Eventually, Hiss—subsequently shown to be a Russian spy—was convicted of perjury, and Nixon's career took off. Running for the U.S. Senate in 1950, he accused his liberal Democratic opponent, former Hollywood actress Helen Gahagan Douglas, of being a "pink lady" who in Congress voted "time after time against measures that are for the security of this country." Douglas, Nixon declared, was "pink right down to her underwear."

Victorious in his Senate race, Nixon then conspired to deliver California's Republican delegation to Dwight Eisenhower in 1952, all the while professing to support California Governor Earl Warren for the nomination. When

Eisenhower triumphed, he turned to Nixon, the youthful embodiment of Republican conservatism, to serve as his vice-presidential nominee. In the ensuing campaign, Nixon continued to fulfill his self-assigned mission, denouncing Democratic nominee Adlai Stevenson as "a graduate of Dean Acheson's spineless school of diplomacy which cost the free world six hundred million allies in the past seven years of Trumanism." In six years, Nixon had risen from being a neophyte congressional candidate to become vice president of the United States, displaying at every stage of the journey how to marry noble appeals to patriotism with the vicious smears of red-baiting.

During the next decade and a half, Nixon continued to exemplify a politics of aggressive anticommunism combined with deep personal insecurity. As vice president, he was Eisenhower's "hatchet man," denouncing the Democrats as "soft on communism" and graduates of "Dean Acheson's Cowardly College of Communist Containment." Traveling abroad, he delivered America's message of combating Communists in multiple capitals, celebrating the superiority of American commercial products like dishwashers at his famous "kitchen debate" with Nikita Khrushchev in Moscow. Yet on a personal level, Nixon never got over the snub of Eisenhower failing to invite him to the family quarters of the White House or a tentative effort to "dump" him from the ticket in 1956. Ike, for his part, noted how few friends Nixon had and his secretary observed that "the Vice-President sometimes seems like a man who is acting like a nice man rather than being one." Ike's failure in a 1960 press conference to be able to name a single policy area where Nixon had made a major difference helped undermine the vice president's claim that experience was the major reason for electing him. By all odds, Nixon should have been elected, but in contrast to the grace, humor, and self-confidence of a Jack Kennedy, he came up short. In a maudlin confirmation of this least attractive side of his personality, Nixon responded to his subsequent defeat for the governorship of California in 1962 by playing the victim and telling reporters, "Well, you won't have Nixon to kick around anymore."

Yet such was the complexity of the Nixon persona that within two years he was back, moving full speed ahead to redeem his political career and claim the prize he had always dreamed of. With tenacity and shrewd calculation, Nixon buttressed his reputation as a man of the world by visiting international leaders in every capital. At home, meanwhile, he moved to New York City, established a richly remunerative law practice, and collected hundreds of political credits by campaigning for state, local, and national Republican candidates across the country. Redeeming those chits in 1968, he crushed the political opposition and seized the Republican Party nomination for president. Although he won the White House with a far smaller margin of victory than might have been anticipated, the fact remained that four years after the Democrats had triumphed with more than an eleven-million-vote plurality—the largest in history—the Republicans were now back.

True to form, President Richard Nixon had secured victory by pursuing two strategies simultaneously: he promised to "bring us together" as one nation, reconciling the deep divisions that were tearing the country apart, and he practiced the politics of polarization, using a "southern strategy" to rally white voters alienated by black civil rights gains and trumpeting the cry for "law and order" to turn middle-Americans against hippies and antiwar protestors.

II. THE NIXON PRESIDENCY

Not surprisingly, these two contradictory patterns characterized Nixon's approach to domestic affairs during his first term. One side of Nixon cleaved to the idea advanced by his domestic aide, Daniel Patrick Moynihan, of becoming a Tory reformer, acting from above to implement national programs that would correct social injustices and permit him to go down in history as a patrician progressive, like the nineteenth-century British Prime Minister Benjamin Disraeli. Hence, Nixon signed Title IX legislation that banned discrimination against women in higher education and supported the National Environment Policy Act that created the Environmental Protection Agency, a new water pollution control act, and an endangered species act. Most impressively, he backed Moynihan's bold initiative to create a Family Assistance Program that would guarantee every American family an income of one thousand dollars per year. (The law never came close to passage, partly due to opposition from welfare rights groups, partly because Nixon cooled in his support). Nixon even endorsed a plan of his secretary of labor, George Shultz, to set aside a certain quota of jobs for minorities under all federally funded construction projects. On one level, therefore, it appeared that Nixon was seeking to personify the "conservative as progressive."

Yet the image was illusory. For at bottom, Nixon cared most about promoting the politics of polarization. Ever since he met with Strom Thurmond, the former archsegregationist from South Carolina, before the Republican convention to secure his support, Nixon had been committed to wooing white Southerners to the Republican Party. Kevin Phillips, an assistant to campaign manager and future Attorney General John Mitchell, outlined the Nixon strategy in his subsequent book, *The Emerging Republican Majority*: if Republicans played up the "social issues" of law and order, opposed aggressive intervention on behalf of desegregation, and defended Americanism, they could surge to the forefront in Southern and Western states. The key to American political success, Phillips said, was knowing "who hates who."

Now Nixon proceeded to implement the "southern strategy." He opposed renewal of the Voting Rights Act, defended Mississippi whites who fought court-ordered desegregation, worked to prevent the termination of federal funding for schools that continued to segregate, and—after the Supreme Court mandated school busing to achieve racial balance in *Swann v. Mecklenburg*—called for a moratorium on busing. Most dramatically, he sought to appoint to the Supreme Court two judges, Clement Haynesworth of South Carolina and G. Harold Carswell from Florida, whose judicial records reflected sympathy with segregationists. Carswell had even attempted, in conjunction with a private country club, to purchase a public golf course in Tallahassee to prevent its being integrated. In the end, both nominees were turned down by the Senate, with numerous Northern Republicans joining Democrats in opposition. But even in losing, Nixon had won—white Southerners now would know that deep in his heart, Nixon was one of *them*.

Building on his Southern strategy, Nixon used Vice President Spiro Agnew to spearhead the politics of divisiveness. Agnew had "earned" his nomination as vice president by taking a tough stance against black protestors when he was governor of Maryland. Now, using a high-powered speechwriting team who specialized in alliteration, Agnew lacerated the "sniveling, hand-wringing power structure [that] deserves the violent rebellion it encourages [on the nation's campuses and urban streets]." He denounced the "nattering nabobs of negativism" in the media who encouraged dissent, linking them with "small cadres of professional protestors [who with] avowed anarchists and commu- nists...detest everything about this country." The time had come, Agnew said, "to question the credentials of [protest] leaders. And, if in...challenging, we polarize the American people, I say it is time for a positive polarization....It is time to rip away the rhetoric and to divide on authentic lines."

Nixon himself joined the battle when he told a reelection crowd in 1972 that it was time to confront the rock-throwing protestors who "hate this country." "The time has come," he roared, "to draw the line...for the Great Silent Majority...to stand up and be counted against the appeasement of the...obscenity shouters of America." It was a long way from Nixon's pledge in 1968 to "bring the Ameri- can people together...to be open to men and women of both parties, open to the critics as well as those who support us...to bridge the gap between the races." When push came to shove, Nixon's real politics were those of forging a majority coalition based not on love and conciliation but on "who hates who."

In the end, however, it became clear that Nixon did not really care about domestic politics. Whatever he achieved or did not achieve at home simply served as a departure point for his real ambition—to be a transformative world leader who would dramatically revise international geopolitics. This was his forte, the focal point for his visions of heroic greatness. It was here that Nixon brought his innermost desires to bear, sketching out in solitary reflection his plans to remake the world.

Nixon's modus operandi as president highlighted the complexities of his personality and politics. Most presidents spend their days in nonstop meet- ings, usually half an hour or less in length, often with cabinet officials, aides, foreign dignitaries, members of Congress. They have multiple staff members, each feeding ideas and information to their chief, often through meetings where major decisions are argued, then decided. Not so Richard Nixon. "The idea," historian Richard Reeves noted, "was to make the President's world secure from outsiders." Nixon's favored schedule was to sit alone in his pri- vate study, doodling on a yellow legal pad, reflecting on long-range strategies, plotting how he would reach his grand objectives. "The problem is time to pre- pare," he wrote. "I must take the time to prepare and leave technical matters to others." Particularly when big decisions loomed, Nixon insisted on clearing his calendar and being alone. Almost obsessed with protecting his isolation, he repeatedly jotted notes to himself about the importance of being "a spiritual leader," a "moral leader." "Each day," he wrote on his legal pad, "[I have] a chance to do something memorable for someone....Goals: set example, instill pride....I have decided my major role is moral leadership. I cannot exercise this adequately unless I speak out more often and more eloquently."

In his fixation on self-isolation, Nixon intentionally limited the number of people with whom he had daily contact. He detested Agnew, his vice president, notwithstanding his callous exploitation of Agnew's role as a spear-carrier for polarization. Other cabinet members received short shrift. "Time," Nixon wrote, "is a person's most important possession. How he makes use of it will determine whether he will fail or succeed in whatever he is under-taking." Nixon chose to spend most of his time with only three people—H. R. Haldeman, White House chief of staff, John Ehrlichman, his domestic counselor, and Henry Kissinger, his national security advisor. Each partici-pated actively in weaving a web of secrecy around their boss, recognizing that only by reinforcing his paranoia about contact with others could they protect their own influence. Nixon would read lengthy briefing papers each morning, then dispatch memoranda to Ehrlichman and Haldeman—satirically dubbed "Prussian" acolytes by the press—about how to handle the business of the day. Their job was to please the president, and if doing so meant deceiving cabinet officers or misleading the public, so be it. In nearly total secrecy, four men, walled off from the world, controlled the power of America.

The Kissinger-Nixon relationship highlighted both the genius and the pathology of Nixon's presidential style. Both men were consumed by a pas-sion for secrecy and intrigue. "Loners and outsiders," diplomatic historian George Herring has written, the two men shared "a penchant...for the unex-pected move" and for keeping others in the dark about their plans. Kissinger earned his spurs with Nixon when he violated the confidentiality of his role as White House advisor to Lyndon Johnson on Vietnam by alerting Nixon to the possibility of an impending breakthrough in negotiations with Vietnam, thereby giving candidate Nixon an opportunity to undermine a potential set-tlement. "Kissinger had proven his mettle by tipping us," said one Nixon cam-paign advisor. "It took some balls to give us those tips...[and after that] it was inevitable that Kissinger would have to be part of our administration." The two men reinforced each other's dedication to duplicity, intent on using their secrecy to shape policies totally independent of the rest of the government.

Nowhere was the Nixon penchant for secrecy and isolation more evident than in his treatment of his two most important cabinet officials, Secretary of State William Rogers and Secretary of Defense Melvin Laird. Rogers was never told that Kissinger conducted secret "back-channel" meetings every week at the White House with Soviet Ambassador Anatoly Dobrynin; nor did he know until the very end that Kissinger flew many weekends to Paris to hold secret meetings with North Vietnamese negotiators. Each major ini-tiative undertaken by Nixon with regard to Vietnam, Cambodia, and Laos occurred without any consultation with Melvin Laird at the Pentagon. Flight logs were altered to hide incursions into Cambodian airspace from generals.

Henry Kissinger, an American of German extraction, became the most powerful diplomat of the late 1960s and early 1970s, serving as national security advisor and then
secreatry of state to Presidents Nixon and Ford. Brilliant, clever, and tenacious, Kissinger witnessed both the end of the Vietnam War and the beginning of a new era of
diplomacy with China and Russia.

Credit: Time & Life Pictures/Getty Images

It was almost as if there were two governments—one a public shell that the
outside world believed was the deliberative policymaking body in America,
the other a private junta of four men who wielded the real power and shared
with no one their plans for shaping the country's path.

III. VIETNAM

Vietnam provided one example of this secret decision-making process.
Although Nixon proclaimed that he had a "secret" plan to end the war, there

was in fact no blueprint, only a determination to steadily diminish American forces in Vietnam on the one hand—what he called "Vietnamization"—while boldly and unpredictably escalating military activity on the other, particularly through the use of airpower. Nixon believed that Ike had ended the Korean War by letting it be known that the United States might use nuclear weapons. Similarly, Nixon adopted his own "madman theory." "I want the North Vietnamese to believe," he told Haldeman, "[that] I might do *anything* to stop the war. We'll just slip the word to them that, 'for God sakes, you know that Nixon is obsessed about Communists. We can't restrain him when he's angry—and he has his hand on the nuclear button'—and Ho Chi Minh himself will be in Paris in two days begging for peace."

The "madman theory," in fact, proved to be the consistent theme of Nixon's policy from beginning to end, always leaving open the question of if, or whether, the president might push the nuclear button. Hence, his bombing raids of Vietnamese supply bases in Cambodia, dropping more than 110,000 tons of bombs—*all done in total secrecy out of Kissinger's office* and never revealed even to the Pentagon. Or his placing the Strategic Air Command on full alert for twenty-nine days, nuclear armed B-52s constantly in the air, creating the apprehension that at any moment, the order might come to release the bombs. Or Nixon's implementation in the fall of 1972 of Operation Duck Hook, involving the mining of Haiphong Harbor, and nonstop American air raids—dropping 110,000 tons of bombs on the north; and finally the Christmas 1972 attacks directly on Hanoi and Haiphong, seeking to obliterate all infrastructure—hospitals, factories, airports, train stations. All to demonstrate that Nixon might do *anything* to win. Presciently, one critic observed that Nixon was acting like a "madman," waging war "by tantrum."

Typical of Nixon's approach was his decision to invade Cambodia in the spring of 1970 in a bold "make or break" move that would verify that Nixon had no sense of limits. Cambodia was a neutral country. Both Secretary of State Rogers and Secretary of Defense Laird opposed sending America troops into a country they had never entered before. (On other occasions, Laird simply did not implement Nixon's orders, as when he told Nixon that "bad weather" had made it impossible to launch air strikes that Nixon had ordered in the Mideast after a hijacking crisis). But the Cambodian invasion was part of Nixon's "big play philosophy" that he hoped would paralyze the enemy and mortally wound his critics at home. "Those senators," he said, "think they can push Nixon around on Haynesworth and Carswell [but] we'll show them who's tough."

In fact, the Cambodia invasion accomplished little except to confirm Nixon's bravado. "If when the chips are down the U.S. acts like a pitiful helpless giant," he told the nation, "the forces of totalitarianism will threaten free nations...throughout the world. It is *not our power but our will* that is being tested." That definition of the issues described perfectly Nixon's persona: his will and determination were what was at stake. Rogers and Laird might be outraged, National Security Council members might resign in protest (they did), and students might protest—hundreds of thousands took to the streets, four of them shot down by National Guardsmen at Kent State on their way to class. But

Nixon had made his point. He was in charge, simultaneously reducing the number of American troops on the ground while accelerating the aggressiveness of American attacks. A similar invasion of Laos took place in early 1971, again with the twin purpose of buying time to reduce American troop levels and testing the combat-readiness of the South Vietnamese. Although both Cambodia and Laos turned out to be failures—and only intensified the furor of the antiwar campaign in America—Nixon continued to keep the enemy guessing about his next move, until with Operation Duck Hook and the Christmas bombing in 1972, he finally had created the circumstances for a negotiated settlement at the beginning of 1973. Throughout, secrecy and intrigue were his bywords.

In reality, the peace treaty with Vietnam was similar substantively to the one that could have been secured four years earlier or anytime in between. The North Vietnamese would stay in South Vietnam, the Viet Cong were to participate in a National Council of Reconciliation, and—for the moment at least—President Thieu would continue in power in Saigon. POWs on both sides would be freed. Nixon's "secret" plan had finally worked. Most important, from his perspective, he had done it *his* way. But in the meantime, 21,000 additional Americans had died in battle as well as half a million North Vietnamese and more than 120,000 South Vietnamese.

IV. THE NIXON GRAND SCHEME

All of this permitted Nixon to deliver the pièce de résistance of his schemes for world transformation, rapprochement with Communist China. Nothing better illustrated the Nixon "MO"—total secrecy; the use of "back-channel" contacts with diplomats in Romania, Pakistan, and Beijing; the intrigue with Kissinger; the total exclusion of Laird and Rogers from the entire process. It was an act of genius as well as pathology. But it ended up securing precisely the kind of tectonic shift in the geopolitical plates undergirding the world that Nixon had always dreamed of.

Such was the vision Nixon toyed with as he sat alone in his study with his yellow legal pad. He had told presidential journalist Theodore White in 1968 that his dream was to open relations with Beijing. In 1971 he repeated his wish: "If there is one thing I want to do before I die," he told *Time*, "it is to go to China." The run-up to the breakthrough reflected all the delicacy of a fine piano concerto. Nixon representatives met with Chinese diplomats in Warsaw to craft the movements for the next stage. Nixon for the first time used the words "People's Republic of China," not "Red China," in a toast to the Romanian president; China asked an American Ping-Pong team to visit Beijing; and Nixon announced trade concessions. Then, on a previously scheduled trip to Pakistan, Henry Kissinger pleaded illness and flew off to Beijing, where he met Premier Chou-en-Lai and orchestrated the final stages of the breakthrough (his notes to Nixon on that conversation took up five hundred pages). No one at the State Department, including Secretary of State William Rogers, knew anything of this until after Kissinger had arrived. The result: an agreement that American troops would leave Taiwan and a pledge from China to support negotiations with the North Vietnamese that would keep Thieu in office.

Four months later, Richard Nixon achieved his dream. In a visit televised around the world, the president entered the Forbidden City, walked the Great Wall, and conducted hours of intense discussions with Chou En-lai and Chairman Mao Tse-tung. As with all such pivotal moments in his past, Nixon prepared for these encounters in isolation, absorbing all of Kissinger's notes, creating his own grand design of what a new tripolar world might look like. Without a piece of paper in front of him, for ninety minutes he held Mao spellbound with his tour de force survey of world politics. At the end, the two men came to an agreement. Richard Nixon, the inveterate anti-Communist, whose political career had been propelled by his tenacious pursuit of anyone "soft" on communism, had done what only Richard Nixon could have done—reached out to make peace with his archenemy. It was a maneuver worthy of the boldest Hollywood director.

Not willing to stop there, Nixon then went on to pursue a similar détente with Russia. Having visited China, Nixon subsequently went to Russia for a summit meeting, where he could leverage the new triangular relationship

In his greatest foreign policy triumph as president, Richard Nixon reversed over two decades of America refusing to deal with Communist China by boldly journeying to Beijing to recognize the People's Republic of China. Here he is shown at the Great Wall, accompanied by the Chinese deputy premier and Secretary of State William Rogers, who was never even told of Nixon's initiative until it became a fait accompli.

Credit: © CORBIS

in the world to create new flexibility in the previously bipolar universe. Here too, the "back-channel" relationships that Kissinger had cultivated with Ambassador Dobrynin came into play, making possible a new Strategic Arms Limitation Treaty (SALT); a rapid expansion of trade; and perhaps most important, Soviet willingness to facilitate rather than obstruct achievement of a peace settlement in Vietnam. The price for Nixon's isolation, secrecy, and intrigue was enormous—not least the arrogant disregard of normal processes of government and the contempt Nixon showed for his most important cabinet aides. Yet in the case of China and the Soviet Union, at least, all the plotting and circumvention of normal channels had a positive payoff.

V. WATERGATE

Ultimately, however, the negative consequences of Nixon's "MO" were more powerful and destructive. Central to Nixon's personality was his insecurity, vengefulness, and sadism. No internal "Stop" sign constrained his impulse to exercise total control. When the *New York Times* reported that the United States was secretly bombing Cambodia, Nixon ordered wiretaps on White House aides to see who might have tattled. Then, when former Defense Department consultant Daniel Ellsberg published the Pentagon Papers, a secret history of the war in Vietnam, Nixon signed off on a plan to break into Ellsberg's psychiatrist's office to unearth private information that could be used to destroy him. As early as 1971, White House aide Thomas Houston had proposed a massive program of surveillance, wiretaps, and infiltration by which Nixon could garner information on his political foes to prevent their ever being able to mount an effective opposition to the White House. Ironically, only a "veto" by J. Edgar Hoover—who did not want anyone else intruding on "his" territory—deferred implementation of the plan. But ultimately, the White House did create its own PLUMBER unit, ostensibly to plug the "leaks" that occurred from government offices but in reality to undermine any and all political enemies of the White House. Staffed by White House operatives such as E. Howard Hunt and Charles Colson and employing former CIA agents like G. Gordon Liddy, the PLUMBERS would soon be blazoning national news headlines and setting in motion the final implosion of the Nixon presidency.

It all started when money raised by the Committee to Re-Elect the President at Republic national headquarters was diverted to finance a series of undercover operations by the PLUMBERS to disrupt the Democratic campaign of 1972. Some of these were "dirty tricks" enterprises, where Republican "plants" were hired in Democratic campaigns to spy on them, Republicans wrote anonymous letters accusing Democrats of sexual infidelity, and plans were made to spend as much as one million dollars bugging Democratic organizations. One idea that came to fruition was to break into National Democratic Party headquarters at the Watergate hotel to steal campaign documents and wiretap the phone of Lawrence O'Brien, head of the DNC. When the burglars went in a second time in June 1972 to fix a phone bug, they were captured by an alert security officer. Bob Woodward and Carl Bernstein, young reporters for the *Washington Post* were assigned the police beat. Soon they discovered that James McCord, one of the five burglars, claimed a past with the CIA, and another had a phone book with the name of E. Howard Hunt, whose address was listed as the White House. Within a short time, people knew that David McCord was security chief for CREEP and that someone in the White House—probably campaign manager and former attorney general John Mitchell—knew all about the planned break-ins and wiretaps.

Initially, White House denials of any connection to the Watergate escapade were successful. Nixon coasted to an overwhelming 61 percent victory over Senator George McGovern, the Democratic nominee who seemed almost handpicked to give Nixon maximum support from voters because of his support for the legalization of marijuana and his identification with antiwar dissidents. But Woodward and Bernstein continued their investigation. A senior official dubbed "Deep Throat" by Woodward and Bernstein—subsequently identified as FBI Deputy Director Mark Feldt—provided the reporters secret leads. Then the floodgates burst when the five burglars were tried and convicted the following spring. McCord, refusing to be the "fall guy" for the White House, handed Judge John Sirica a letter saying that senior officials in Washington were implicated in the burglary, that perjury had been committed, and that payoffs from powerful politicians had prevented testimony that would have led to indictments of other highly placed individuals.

From that point forward, one stunning revelation after another poured forth. John Dean, White House counsel, saw the handwriting on the wall and went before the grand jury to testify. The acting director of the FBI revealed to Congress that he had "deep-sixed" critical documents in the case on White House orders. A Senate Select Committee chaired by Senator Sam Ervin initiated televised hearings grilling senior White House officials about "what the president knew and when did he know it." Then the dramatic bombshell—White House aide Alexander Butterfield disclosed that Nixon had taped *every* conversation in the White House, so there was an incontrovertible record of exactly what Nixon knew and when he knew it. When the special prosecutor appointed to oversee the Watergate prosecution insisted on hearing the tapes, Nixon ordered Attorney General Elliot Richardson to fire him. When Richardson refused, he and his aide were dismissed in what became known as the "Saturday night massacre." Soon, there was no room left. A House committee started impeachment proceedings; a grand jury indicted seven top Nixon aides, including Haldeman, Ehrlichman, and Mitchell; and Congress went to the Supreme Court to demand access to the original tapes. When the Court ruled, unanimously, that the tapes must be turned over in their entirety, the game was up. By then, everyone knew that the most critical evidence involved a meeting Nixon convened on June 23, 1972. There, the president of the United States had ordered the CIA to call off the FBI in its investigation of the Watergate break-in. He thereby both initiated the cover-up and participated in a criminal conspiracy to obstruct justice. Within days, Nixon had resigned.

The other side of Nixon's grand vision for world diplomacy was his indulgence in petty, vengeful political sabotage at home. This was typified by the break-in into Democratic Party headquarters in 1972. When links were finally made between the break-in and the White House, the Senate created a Select Committee to investigate, which eventually led to Nixon's resignation.

Credit: © Wally McNamee/Corbis

The White House tapes highlighted the petty and venal side of Nixon's dual personality. Filled with "expletives deleted" language denouncing his political enemies, the tapes also highlighted Nixon's xenophobia, with his denunciations of blacks and Jews. "Most Jews are disloyal," Nixon spat at Haldeman in a typical outburst. "You can't trust the bastards. They turn on you." Blacks, Nixon said, were genetically inferior. Not only did the tapes reveal that Nixon had ordered the Ellsberg break-ins, initiated the obstruction of justice, and sanctioned payoffs to members of the PLUMBERS who might turn states evidence but more tellingly, they revealed a personality consumed with hatred for his political enemies. "One day we will get them," he told Haldeman and Ehrlichman. "We'll get them on the ground where we want them. And we'll stick our heels in, step on them hard, and twist—right—get them on the floor and step on them, crush them, show them no mercy."

It was all of a piece—the isolation, the secrecy, the intrigue, the insecurity, the need to seek vengeance, to exercise total control. If at its best the Nixon persona could create the circumstances for a world-shattering breakthrough in relations with China, at its worst, it came close to destroying the Constitution, America's system of checks and balances, and the accountability of elected officials to laws and due process. At the end, Richard Nixon destroyed himself. As Gerald Ford observed when he assumed the presidency after Nixon's resignation, "Our long national nightmare is over."

VI. A COUNTRY IN TROUBLE

Ironically—though that was not his intention—through his excesses Richard Nixon had achieved his goal to "bring us together." Republicans as well as Democrats rejected Nixon's abandonment of the Constitution's safeguards and breathed a sigh of relief when he resigned. But the more disturbing reality was the degree to which, notwithstanding people's gratitude that they had survived such an abuse of presidential power, deep fissures continued to divide America. The economy plummeted; disagreements over cultural values, family norms, and sexual behavior surfaced with growing intensity; and the nation entered an era where humiliation rather than proud dominance became the norm of foreign relations. Out of all this, a new conservative consensus emerged, in Democratic as well as Republican administrations, as the prevailing political mentality of the age.

The underlying symptom of national malaise was an economy teetering on the edge of breakdown. After nearly a quarter of a century of unbridled growth—which had done so much to fuel the commitment of the "liberal consensus" to economic progress for *all* people—economic stagnation set in. Both Johnson and Nixon had sought to wage war without raising taxes—an invitation to disaster. As deficits increased, so too did inflation. Nixon responded initially by raising interest rates and slowing down the economy, then in an election year maneuver, imposed price controls in 1971. The problem was that once controls were removed, everything fell apart. Inflation doubled to 8 percent, and the deficit soared to a then unheard of forty billion dollars. In the meantime, America lost its industrial dominance to Japan and Germany. More and more a service-based economy instead of a manufacturing one, for the first time America started to run a balance of payments deficit as foreign cars, electronics, and textiles made deep inroads into the American market.

The Arab oil embargo of 1973, precipitated by the Yom Kippur war between Israel and Egypt, confirmed that America no longer controlled her own economic destiny. In one winter, gas prices shot up 33 percent. Moreover, America's dependency on foreign oil increased dramatically over the decade from an annual expenditure of $4 billion in 1970 to $90 billion a decade later. Inflation skyrocketed as a result, hitting double digits in 1974 and continuing to rise throughout the decade. Meanwhile productivity fell, unemployment rose—soon to reach double digits as well—and worker alienation soared as manufacturing jobs left the country and the expectation of steady annual increases in real income evaporated. Whereas in 1969, 79 percent of noncollege young people believed that "hard work always pays off," by the mid-1970s, that figure had fallen to 56 percent, and by the end of the decade, more than half of all Americans believed that "next year will be worse than this year." "Stagflation" had become the word of the day, with nine out of ten Americans anticipating that inflation was a permanent presence and two-thirds agreeing that the country was entering a period of lasting shortages, with a continued decline in the standard of living. According to one public opinion poll, nearly three out of four Americans by the end of the decade agreed with the statements "We are fast coming to a turning point in our history. The land of plenty is becoming the land of want." It would be hard to imagine a more dramatic turnaround.

But the sense of malaise was not limited to jobs and economic expectations. Although the activism of the New Left had largely dissipated by the time Nixon resigned—partly through self-inflicted wounds such as when members of the Weathermen, an offshoot of SDS, blew themselves up in an abortive bomb-making enterprise—large numbers of well-off students and former students embraced the counterculture instead, a set of ideas and living practices designed to create norms for group living that rebelled defiantly against middle-class conventionality. If creating a new politics would not work, perhaps finding a new way of relating to each other, sharing, and getting high on drugs might undermine the perceived shallowness of bourgeois existence. Smoking marijuana and hashish or taking LSD became the ritual symbols of the counterculture, celebrated by people living in communes; engaging in free love with multiple partners; and seeking what one apologist, Theodore Roszak, called "a new culture in which the non-intellective capacities of personality" became dominant. It was almost a religious transformation, social critic Paul Goodman said, creating new ideas of what constituted human community, family, and morality.

Even if only a minority of young people embraced such values, the behavior of those pursuing the counterculture seemed to mirror a more

If antiwar demonstrations represented one side of radicalism among young people in the 1960s and 1970s, a movement to create a "counterculture" of free love, communes, and potsmoking represented the other side. Here two people share a "joint" as they watch a Bay Area concert.

Credit: © Steven Clevenger/Corbis/Corbis

far-reaching change taking place in sexual norms and gender roles. By the early 1970s, feminism and the women's liberation movement—not necessarily the same thing—had sunk deep roots in the psyches of American women, particularly the young. More than 50 percent of women now worked, even if at unequal wages and with limited opportunities for promotion. Of equal importance, two out of three now declared their unhappiness with women's "place" in America—a direct reversal of ten years earlier—and the young in particular no longer saw marriage and motherhood as their primary source of fulfillment. The numbers of women college graduates aspiring to graduate degrees in business, medicine, and law skyrocketed while those envisioning having more than two children plummeted. Even mainstream feminist groups like Betty Friedan's National Organization for Women (NOW) had come to embrace lesbianism as a cause of all women, while radical women's liberation groups discussed ending the nuclear family as an oppressive institution and creating a new culture based on women's distinctive values.

A revolution appeared to be happening in women's lives as well as in feminist literature. As one conservative columnist wrote, "The 1970s blew to smithereens an entire structure of sexual morality." By 1978, more than half of Americans saw nothing wrong with extramarital sex—double the figure of a decade earlier. Some saw a direct correlation between that figure and the fact that the nation's divorce rate doubled between 1965 and 1975; soon more than 40 percent of all marriages would end in divorce. Even in the 1970s, 40 percent of all children could expect to spend at least part of their time growing up in a single-parent home. During the same decade, the percentage of children born to unmarried mothers went from 11 to 18 while among black and Hispanic populations, it soared to 50 percent. A sea change was happening. Sex became more and more a feature of adolescence, not adulthood, for women as well as men. The number of nineteen-year-old unmarried white women engaging in sexual intercourse climbed from 25 percent in the mid-1950s to 75 percent by 1990, with the major change occurring in the 1970s. Nothing of a comparable nature had occurred at any previous time in American history.

To those given to conspiracy theories, all of this seemed connected to actions at the governmental level that appeared to sanction liberation from traditional social mores. In 1973, the Supreme Court by a vote of 7–2 broke new constitutional ground in *Roe v. Wade* by declaring that women might choose abortion, if pregnant, rather than carry a fetus to full term. Based on a previous ruling on privacy rights (*Griswold v. Connecticut*), which denied the state the right to regulate birth control, this new decision made legal what for decades had been a crime. Feminists had long petitioned for women's right to choose. Now the Supreme Court had said yes, at least through the first two trimesters of a pregnancy. In the aftermath of the decision, abortions averaged 1.5 million per year, or 4 terminated pregnancies for every 10 babies born. To conservatives, and especially many Roman Catholics who had been taught that abortion was murder, these figures suggested that the entire moral structure of the nation had been turned upside down, with no one defending society's interest in stable family life or strict sexual standards.

In the context of these developments, it was no surprise when fundamentalist Christians felt compelled to engage in political action. Throughout the 1960s, conservative evangelists forswore the idea of mixing religion and politics. Church and state were separate, they had argued, and the world of Caesar should not mix with that of Paul. But that was before the gay rights movement came into full bloom, the Equal Rights Amendment was sent to the states for ratification, busing for purposes of racial balance was ordered by the Supreme Court, abortion on demand became legal, the divorce rate doubled, and prayer in public school classrooms was deemed unconstitutional. Each of these changes seemed to threaten the very foundation of society. Liberals might claim that these developments simply reflected the expansion of civil rights—a new level of support for individual freedom. But from the point of view of God-fearing conservatives, they amounted to an assault on sacred values. The traditional church deemed homosexuality a sin; believed that wives should be subordinate to their husbands; that women occupied a separate sphere from men; that life, from conception, was sacred; and that worship of God should be as much a part of civil activities as the Pledge of Allegiance to the flag.

The "New Right," as it came to be called, erupted in outrage at these changes. Tens of thousands joined antifeminist activist Phyllis Schlafly in opposing the ERA—a constitutional amendment that in effect stated that women should be treated under the law exactly as men were treated— claiming that it would lead to homosexual marriages, unisex toilets, and drafting women into the army. Jerry Falwell, an evangelical preacher who had renounced politics in the 1960s, now organized the Moral Majority to fight pornography, sex education, and homosexuality, becoming in the process a pivotal figure in national politics. Pat Robertson, host of the nationally syndicated *Praise the Lord* television show, enjoined his audiences to fight the "humanistic/atheistic/hedonistic" influences that were taking over the government. Robertson and Falwell declared they would not let this happen. "We have enough votes to run the country," Robertson said, "and when the people say 'we've had enough,' we're going to take over." Falwell specifically targeted "those people in government who are against what we consider to be the Bible, moralist position." Lest anyone doubt the importance of this new political force, TV evangelists pointed out that more than fifty million Americans called themselves evangelical Christians. In many respects this was a social movement almost as pivotal to the politics of the 1970s as the civil rights movement had been to the politics of the 1960s.

Nothing that was happening in Washington diminished the spreading sense of alarm. Although Gerald Ford began his time in the White House with enormous support from the American people, that support quickly evaporated. One month after becoming president, Ford—without warning—issued a blanket pardon for any crime for which Richard Nixon might be charged. In many respects, Ford's action made eminent sense. It eliminated the possibility of endless controversy over Watergate and any further demeaning of the office of the president. But to most Americans, it seemed one more violation of due process, an unconscionable intervention that prevented the justice system from taking its own course. The voters responded by turning out forty-eight Republican congressmen in the midterm elections of 1974—the second largest turnover ever. The nation's sense of vulnerability only deepened when North Vietnamese forces seized Saigon, removed President Thieu from office, and in an ignominious blow to American pride forced hundreds of American officials to flee from the rooftop of the U.S. embassy on helicopters dispatched from naval vessels standing offshore. Worldwide television showed the United States experiencing abject humiliation. The country that once told everyone else what to do now appeared to be a diminutive weakling.

Ford never became an assertive chief executive. He had no clear-cut positive agenda. For the most part, his leadership style was negative. He vetoed sixty-eight bills in two years, setting a record for saying no to Congress. His approach to inflation was to jawbone consumer industries, tighten the money supply, and raise interest rates—but no relief was in sight. Nor did Ford have any original ideas for dealing with America's new trade deficit or the increased domination of the American economy by foreign industry. Stalwart, dignified, and hardworking, he nevertheless achieved few victories either in foreign or domestic policy that would help revive America's flagging spirits. The politics of the nation remained a quagmire, with citizens of all partisan persuasions simply seeking some way to pull themselves together and return to a path of optimism and progress.

VII. CARTER, THE CONSERVATIVE

The presidential election of 1976 took place amidst this miasma of depression, angst, and confusion. Not since the Great Depression had the nation seemed less sure of its destiny or more apprehensive about finding its feet and moving forward. Evangelical Christians believed the country's morals were collapsing; average workers saw their paychecks diminish, their jobs disappear, and inflation destroying their pensions. Washington had come to symbolize misdeeds and corruption rather than bold statesmanship. Even the military appeared weak and helpless. In such a swamp of negativism, where would the country find a bedrock of sanity and stability around which to rally its wounded pride and begin the process of recovery?

During the months preceding the election, Jimmy Carter appeared to offer an answer. Son of a Georgia peanut farmer, graduate of the naval academy, respected former governor of Georgia, Carter represented the antithesis of smooth, polished Beltway politicians. Over and over again, he told the American people—from the quiet small towns of Iowa to the mountain villages of New Hampshire—that they deserved a government as moral, as competent, and "as filled with love" as were average American citizens. The people of America were good, Carter affirmed. It was the government that had failed them. But Jimmy Carter was not of that government. He was an outsider, from the heartland, dedicated to sweeping clean the corruption and sophisticated double-talk of Washington and substituting for it the simplicity, virtue, and morality of small-town America. Government had betrayed the people, and Carter was now ready to offer redemption.

Carter's message resonated with those who were distraught at the degree to which America seemed to have lost her moral compass. An avowed "born-again" Christian, Carter offered a message of faith and dedication to old-fashioned morality that could only reassure the millions who shared his religious convictions and wished a reaffirmation of America's core values. At the same time, his campaign against Washington duplicity and sophistication rang a bell with average citizens—workers, farmers, secretaries—who valued straight talk and craved the simplicity of forthright values and a sense of direction. When he swept to victory at the Democratic convention, Carter seemed to validate the hopes of all those who saw him as the answer to their anxiety. Denouncing corporate corruption and declaring his solidarity with "the little man," Carter pledged to cleanse the American political system, end favoritism, and create once more a government as good as its citizens.

Under the circumstances, there should have been no contest. As one Democratic wag observed, "We could run an aardvark this year and win." But even with a thirty-three-point advantage in the polls going into the campaign, it was not easy for Carter. After turning back a nomination bid from California Governor Ronald Reagan based on his opposition to détente and a proposed Panama Canal Treaty—"we bought it, we paid for it, it's ours and we're going to keep it," Reagan said—Ford gained momentum even as Carter floundered. In an embarrassing interview with *Playboy*, Carter disclosed both the sincerity of his faith and his naivete as a political communicator, declaring that he had "looked upon a lot of women with lust. I have committed adultery in my heart many times." Meanwhile, Ford rallied his party, moving beyond the hilarious spoof of him on *Saturday Night Live* as someone who could not walk and chew gum at the same time. "What town is named for the president?" one punster asked. "Marblehead," was the answer. Neither candidate, in fact, was perceived by the voters as "presidential." But even as he cut Carter's lead to a few points, Ford faltered, telling a presidential debate audience, "There is no Soviet domination of Eastern Europe." On election day, Carter squeaked to victory with 51 percent of the vote while Democrats won two-thirds of all seats in Congress. Seven out of ten voters identified the economy as a basic concern, with Carter winning three out of every four votes cast by those who were worried about their jobs.

Unfortunately, all the positives that enabled Carter to win represented only one side of a two-sided coin. The other side—the direct opposites of Carter's virtues—helped undermine his presidency from its inception. Carter celebrated being an outsider to Washington, with none of the inbred characteristics of its smooth political operators; but that same trait denied him the familiarity with the capital's inner workings that would have facilitated effective relations with Congress and the Washington "establishment." Stated bluntly, Carter betrayed both ignorance and contempt for how Washington worked. His chief aide, Hamilton Jordan, boasted of not returning phone calls from Capitol Hill. Carter himself told Speaker of the House Tip O'Neill that he did not need any advice on how to work with Congress—if need be, he would go over the heads of Congress to the American people. Summarizing the problem, Vice President Walter Mondale observed, "Carter thought politics was sinful. The worst thing you could say to Carter...was that it was politically the best thing to do."

A direct corollary to Carter's disregard for how Washington worked was his belief that a president should be the "steward" of the country's well-being, not a power broker. In that role, he would be a wise man charged with acting in the best interests of those he represented. He would study a problem, arrive at a solution, and then present his answer from on high. In that sense, he was like a "trustee," responsible for the well-being of his clients but not accountable for negotiating with his subordinates, whether they be Congress or interest groups. Such a top-down approach might work in a charitable foundation, but it violated all the ground rules of Washington. By adopting the role of steward, Carter cut off the possibility of communicating with, and learning from, those responsible for enacting his proposals. Consequently, his preconceptions about leadership in theory almost guaranteed the failure of his presidency in practice.

Finally, Carter's moralism led to disaffection among those charged with implementing his ideas even as it gratified millions of "middle-Americans" longing for a voice of ethical clarity in the White House. When issues of policy were framed largely in a moral framework, there was no room for compromise. It was all or nothing, right or wrong—no middle ground. The opposition, as one historian has noted, by definition came to represent "some selfish or immoral interest." Yet politics had always operated on a middle ground, and if one were not willing to play on it, there could, in effect, be no game.

All of these "negatives" came together to undermine what might have been a successful presidency. Two-thirds of Congress came from the president's party, an almost guaranteed majority for initiatives that emanated from party leaders in both branches of government. Not since FDR in 1935 and LBJ in 1965 had such an opportunity for effective legislative change existed. The energy crisis cried out for action and was directly tied to stagflation and the economic downturn. To his credit, Carter recognized the problem, pointing out that Americans consumed 40 percent more oil than they produced. But instead of going to Congress, enlisting the expertise and ideas of relevant committee chairs, and drafting bills that reflected their views, Carter created an energy task force made up of *his* experts. Then he developed a bill that had 113 separate provisions. Finally, he demanded that Congress pass the legislation in its entirety because after all, it reflected the insights of wise men whom he, as steward for the country, had mobilized. Not surprisingly, Congress resisted. On the central domestic policy issue of his time, Carter had failed. Tellingly, the president's response was to go off to Camp David, the president's retreat in the Maryland mountains, to ponder his future course. When he returned to address the American people, he blamed the crisis not on energy but on a paralysis of will "at the very heart and soul" of the American people. Americans had lost their spiritual compass. Only by restoring their "faith and confidence" in traditional American values could they recover. Yet an Old Testament jeremiad did not necessarily translate into good social policy.

To Carter's credit, he scored some remarkable victories in foreign policy using the same moral leadership style that had crippled him in domestic politics. For the first time since John F. Kennedy, an American president seemed to appreciate the struggles for independence and freedom taking place in developing countries of the third world. Carter refused to condone right-wing dictatorships in Africa and Latin America, even if they were anti-Communist, and he loudly proclaimed America's commitment to human rights. With courage and strength, he pushed through a Panama Canal Treaty that restored to that country, as of 1999, sovereignty over a waterway that had been owned by the United States since 1903. Most important, Carter showed moral vision by bringing together at Camp David Israeli Premier Menachem Begin and Egyptian President Anwar Sadat and refusing to let them leave until—with his direction and aid—they agreed to make peace in the Middle East.

Nevertheless, it was also foreign policy that, in the end, destroyed the Carter presidency and brought American prestige to an all-time low. In the fall of 1979, Islamic militants, encouraged by their leader Ayatollah Komenei, invaded the American embassy in Teheran, Iran, and took captive more than fifty U.S. diplomats and soldiers. In 1953 the CIA had helped topple a nationalist regime and impose a pro-Western monarch, Shah Pelavi. No leader had been more loyal or subservient to American interests, even as he proceeded to westernize Iran. A year earlier, ill with cancer and out of touch with a growing Iranian insurgency, the shah had been deposed by Komenei in what amounted to an Islamic fundamentalist revolution. Now the United States permitted the shah to come to the United States for medical treatment, and militant Iranian students showed their contempt by their brazen assault on American property. After Vietnam and the OPEC oil embargo, this was the ultimate humiliation. Carter appeared helpless. Furthermore, he magnified his powerlessness by refusing to leave the White House to campaign or conduct ordinary presidential business lest he appear to be taking lightly the insult done to America. His "Rose Garden" strategy simply highlighted America's isolation. Desperately, Carter signed off on a rescue operation that envisioned eight helicopters full of soldiers landing in a remote desert in Iran; being refueled by cargo planes; then proceeding to another landing strip one hundred miles from Teheran; riding trucks into the city (all this time unnoticed); rescuing the hostages from the embassy; then going back to a deserted airfield, where other cargo planes would take them home. In retrospect as foolhardy as the Bay of Pigs, the plan collapsed at stage one when a helicopter crashed into a cargo plane and exploded. With eight soldiers dead and the rescue mission aborted, the United States became the laughingstock of the Islamic world, pitiful in its seeming incompetence. As nightly news commentators signed off the air—"And that's the way it is, June 15th, the 300th day of captivity for the American hostages in Iran"—Americans had barely a moment to gather up their spirits and imagine a world where they were once more in charge. No one cared more passionately about redeeming the name of America than Jimmy Carter. No one tried harder to find a solution to the crisis. But it would not be until the last day of his presidency—and one hour after he had given up the office—that in a final insult, the Iranians finally sent the hostages home. By then, Carter had spent all his resources and lost the political power he had struggled so mightily to achieve four years earlier as the farmer from Georgia who wished only to give the American people a government as moral as they were. Now that task fell to someone else, cut from the same moral conservative cloth as Jimmy Carter but with a political approach that was worlds apart.

VIII. CONCLUSION

There was a certain logic to developments in America during the 1970s. Toward the end of the 1960s, the country had engaged in repeated displays of excess—in political protests, racial divisions, cultural holy wars, and above all military adventurism. Despite having been elected on a platform of ending the war and "bringing us together," Richard Nixon simply carried the politics of excess to a new level. From his "madman theory" of frightening the North Vietnamese into surrender to his brazen practice of the politics of polarization, Nixon exhibited a hubris rarely if ever manifested in American politics before. No law was too sacred to circumvent, no political innuendo too bizarre to hurl. Sitting alone in his presidential study, alternating back and forth between dreams of world transformation and plots to stomp on his political enemies, Nixon gave new definition to the politics of arrogance. Eventually, his administration seemed destined to implode. No one could stretch a political and social system to such extremes without its breaking.

When it did, the whole bubble of American postwar confidence seemed to burst as well. Grievances of long standing within the society exploded into public view. Racial tensions persisted, the newly energized war between the sexes took on sharpness, and a significant minority among the young challenged traditional codes of social behavior, whether these involved sex, drugs, marriage, or patriotism. Economic progress not only stopped but also started heading backward, jobs leaving the industrial sector, Japanese and German products taking over. Suddenly, as well, individual freedoms appeared to become more important than social cohesion, from the Supreme Court ruling that every person arrested for a crime had the right to counsel to the determination that every woman could abort a fetus during the first six months of pregnancy if she chose, without either consulting her husband or—if a minor—her parents. Gay Americans, meanwhile, demanded the same civil rights as other minorities had achieved during the 1960s, including the freedom to champion publicly their distinctive sexual preferences. Everything now seemed up in the air.

It was in response to all this that the conservative insurgency of the New Right rose to prominence in the mid 1970s. Sick and tired of having people question their flag, the sanctity of the family, the right to pray in school, or the value system embodied in practices of sexual fidelity and monogamy, millions of Americans—many of them evangelical Christians but some more traditional Roman Catholics—rallied to the "old-fashioned" way of doing things. They were sick and tired of rampant secularism and dedicated to revitalizing old religious covenants of virtue and moral behavior. Tired of seeing their country made an object of scorn, they yearned for strong moral leadership both at home and abroad.

It seemed that Jimmy Carter was the answer. Decent, pious, "born again" and proud of it, he embodied traditional values and praised the American people for their competence and morality. Despite being a Democrat, Carter was conservative—in his ethics, his political philosophy, his sense of what was possible. "Government cannot solve our problems," he told Congress in his second State of the Union address. "It cannot eliminate poverty, or provide a bountiful economy, or reduce inflation, or save our cities, or cure illiteracy, or provide energy"—a statement that would have confounded Franklin Roosevelt and Lyndon Johnson. So from the perspective of both conservatives who wished to restore traditional values and those who wished to limit the role of government, Carter seemed an ideal leader. Yet his assets became his liabilities, his strengths his weaknesses, and instead of recovering the exuberance, direction, and purposefulness of America during the postwar era, Americans plunged deeper and deeper into the morass of uncertainty and despair.

It had been a humbling decade, more full of disillusionment and anxiety than any since the 1930s. But it also highlighted important fault lines in American society—in the "culture wars" that would persist through the 1980s and 1990s, in an economy that seemed directionless and immobile, in an international posture that lacked firmness and confidence, and above all in the sense of despair that permeated people of all political and social backgrounds. Americans wanted to feel good about themselves again and were looking for a leader who would accomplish that goal. The stage was thus set for the election of 1980.

11

Morning in America: Ronald Reagan

The difference was as day to night. Ronald Reagan was breezy, ebullient, funny, and inspiring, Jimmy Carter pensive, ponderous, and dour. The one brightened a room with his laughter and self-confidence; the other engendered concern and spurred reflection as to whether the country was going in the right direction. At some deep level, both reflected conservative values—that government should be lean, individuals should be responsible for their own well-being, families should be strong, and religion was important. But whereas Reagan trumpeted these with a cheery patriotism that promised a better day for an America just coming into its prime, Carter worried aloud that the nation might be seeing its glorious past enter a period of decline. Coming from so many shared presumptions, the two could not have been more diametrically opposite in their approach to governing. In this instance at least, temperament and personality made a difference. What had only yesterday seemed to be the twilight of American power suddenly became morning time in America, launching an era that would see the Cold War end and the country recover its sense of pride and power, even in the midst of White House shenanigans reminiscent of Watergate and economic policies seemingly aimed at creating out-of-sight deficits.

I. REAGAN BEFORE THE PRESIDENCY

The key to Reagan's lifelong optimism was his ability to overcome the childhood traumas of family disarray and craft for himself a role as rescuer and spokesperson for transcendent national values. Born in a small midwestern town, Ronald Reagan grew up amidst economic uncertainty. His father was frequently unemployed and during the Great Depression depended for his living on a government job, which made Franklin Roosevelt a Reagan family hero. More important, he was an alcoholic whose wife chastised him for drinking. One day, young Ronald came home to find his father passed out on the porch, unable to move. In the face of such conflict, Reagan developed a keen sensitivity to the people around him, learning early to find ways of overcoming disharmony and bring people together by the force of his personality. He ingratiated himself with peers and authority figures, took a job as a lifeguard for six summers during which he rescued seventy-six people, and became enamored of playing roles full of romance and heroism. Always ready with a self-deprecating quip—"We didn't live on the wrong side of the

239

tracks," he said of his less-than-secure childhood, "but we lived so close we could hear the whistle real loud"—he quickly ingratiated himself with his friends at the small church-related college he attended and prepared to hone his "people" skills by pursuing a career in acting.

Moving to Hollywood from the rural Midwest, Reagan—handsome and debonair—soon became a "character" actor specializing in all-American, romantic, "good guy" roles. He married Jane Wyman in 1940, starred in a series of patriotic films during World War II, in many of which he played "down home" soldiers, and later became sufficiently popular that he was elected president of the Screen Actors Guild, the union that negotiated on behalf of actors with movie studios. Reagan was never a superstar—rather, he was what he called "Errol Flynn of the Bs," those who became known for their reliable efficiency at playing a certain kind of role. But he loved movies and identified with the parts that he and others enacted. Throughout the rest of his life, Reagan responded to crises or political dilemmas by telling an anecdote from his Hollywood days. For him these stories were real, not fictional. Over and over in patriotic moments, he recalled—tears in his eyes—the bomber pilot whose plane was hit by enemy fire and who decided to stay with a wounded crew member as the plane went down and subsequently received a Congressional Medal of Honor. Or his own experience seeing concentration camps in Germany and being profoundly moved. Except that neither event ever happened. The first was from a war film he loved, the second from a role he played in another movie. (Reagan never went abroad during the war.) Yet these acting parts meant so much to him that they became, in their own way, his personal reality, and in retelling the stories, he was transported back into those roles, not distinguishing them from what actually occurred.

Reagan was a liberal Democrat during the 1940s and 1950s. He venerated Roosevelt (and always would), joined the Americans for Democratic Action, and voted for Helen Gahagan Douglas in her Senate race with Richard Nixon. But he also became deeply suspicious of Communist infiltration in Hollywood and voluntarily shared with congressional investigators the names of Hollywood personalities he suspected of being "soft" on communism. After Jane Wyman divorced him—the relationship, she claimed, was too superficial—he married Nancy Davis, another actress, but someone far more conservative. Gradually, his politics shifted toward hers, his concerns with communism, big government, and individual liberty occupying an increasingly important influence in his life. By the 1950s his career as an actor declined, and soon he became the chief spokesman for the General Electric Company, a conservative corporation.

Using the same talents he had excelled with as an actor, Reagan now became a supersalesman for GE, whose slogan "Progress is our most important product," resonated completely with Reagan's upbeat outlook. Spending hundreds of days on the road over the course of his GE career, Reagan "pitched" his message to more than 250,000 GE employees in what became famously known as "The Speech." Always delivered with the appearance of spontaneity, "The Speech" embodied Reagan's basic political credo, conveyed with fervent patriotism. America was a great nation, he exhorted, blessed with a passion for liberty that made her a "city upon a hill" for the rest of the world to emulate. But America's greatness faced profound challenges. Communism represented an evil ideology that must be fought at every step and eventually conquered. Dangerous as well was big government with its intrusion on people's individual freedom through excessive taxes and cumbersome bureaucracies. America must resist its twin enemies with a twofold commitment: reduce taxes and get the "monkey" of big government off the people's backs so that they could grow their riches and insist on a strong military that would confront the Soviet Union wherever it sought to intervene in America's business, and in the end, triumph over totalitarianism. "The Speech" was inspiring and always fresh, however many times it was given, because Reagan believed in what he was saying, just as he believed the story of the bomber pilot who went down with his plane in order to stand by a wounded comrade.

Reagan's ascendancy as a national conservative hero began when he delivered "The Speech" in a campaign appearance for Barry Goldwater in 1964. During an election ordeal that every day brought more bad news for Goldwater, "Mr. Conservative," Reagan's speech was like a transfusion to a patient dying from blood loss. Conservatives came alive, proud to finally have an advocate who brimmed with enthusiasm—and optimism—for the cause of recovering America's greatness and rolling back the creeping encroachment of big government. Soon Reagan was being touted for political office himself and in 1968 rode his fame—and his biting rhetoric against student protestors at Berkeley—to a resounding victory as governor of California.

In many respects, Reagan typified the state he ruled. California was known for its mixture of political views. The largest, fastest-growing state in the union, it had always boasted of its independent, individualistic views. Orange County has been seen by some historians as the birthplace of conservatism. Yet California was also in many ways a microcosm of the nation. It might trumpet its independence from Washington, but to an extraordinary degree its existence required extensive national government involvement, from issues of water supply, irrigation, and dams to preservation of its environment to policies dealing with immigration. The state thus boasted conservative attitudes at the same time it sanctioned, and often championed, government involvement. Ronald Reagan personified the same paradox— simultaneously articulating a rhetoric of conservatism while practicing a politics of moderation.

For eight years Reagan reigned as a popular chief executive of this, the nation's largest state, forging a remarkable bipartisan coalition on most issues and for the most part staying above the battle. But perhaps most important, he remained the iconic hero of conservative Republicans, and as splits within the party intensified, Reagan proudly carried the banner of the right, pleasing evangelical television preachers like Pat Robertson and Jerry Falwell as well as Goldwaterites still furious at their candidate's defeat by Lyndon Johnson.

Although on policy matters—including abortion—he partnered with his Democratic colleagues, for most of the body politic he was "Mr. Conservative." At age sixty-five—in 1976—Reagan almost took the nomination away from Gerald Ford, and in 1980, he finally achieved the prize conservatives had been waiting for since 1964 when he outlasted George Herbert Walker Bush to win the Republican nomination for president.

In retrospect, Jimmy Carter never had a chance. Notwithstanding their shared conservative values, Carter had come to symbolize the weakness of a country beset by Islamic revolutionaries and double-digit inflation, whereas Reagan personified a tall Westerner riding into Dodge with his six-shooters blazing to rescue the innocent and destroy their oppressor. The clear beneficiary of white, "middle-American" anxiety about America's lost prestige and values, Reagan trumpeted his commitment to a strong military, a more aggressive policy toward communism, and a determination to recapture the spirit of fearless competition in the American economy. "Are you better off than you were four years ago?" Reagan asked. Clearly, the answer was no. And for that dilemma, Reagan had a solution. "A recession," he declared, "is when your neighbor loses his job, and a depression is when you lose yours...and recovery is when Jimmy Carter loses his." When Carter tried to raise doubts about Reagan's trustworthiness as a commander in chief, a self-assured Reagan—now

Ronald Reagan personified optimism, confidence, and strength to the American people. In a time of despair and disillusionment, he offered the positive leadership people had been looking for. Here he is shown at his desk, surrounded by key staff members.

Credit: Time & Life Pictures/Getty Images

sixty-nine years old—chastised his younger rival, "There you go again!" Even on traditional economic issues, Carter lost, with Reagan winning 67 percent of the vote from those for whom inflation was a major concern. Ironically, Reagan was the "cultural democrat" who seemed comfortable with citizens of all backgrounds, Carter the aloof, Hoover-like leader preaching austerity. At bottom, Reagan triumphed because he reignited in Americans the sense of hope that for so long had been smothered by news of recession, national weakness, and malaise. It was time, he declared in his inaugural address, for Americans "to believe in ourselves and to believe in our capacity to perform great deeds, to believe…we can and will resolve our problems.…[And] why shouldn't we believe that? [After all] we are Americans."

II. THE REAGAN WHITE HOUSE—DOMESTIC POLICY

In the event any Americans believed that Reagan was simply Carter with an optimistic smile, the new president's first year in office proved them totally wrong. Reagan actually believed all the certitudes he preached in "The Speech" and set forth immediately to put them into action. Restarting the B-1 bomber project that Carter had killed, he also launched the B-2 initiative and increased defense expenditures by nearly 40 percent in his first three years in office. Closer to home, he proposed slashing taxes by $750 billion while curtailing food stamp benefits, cutting 300,000 federally funded jobs for the unemployed, and reducing the welfare rolls by 10 percent. When air traffic controllers went on strike, Reagan ordered them back on the job, then destroyed the union when they refused. It was a flurry of activity matched in the twentieth century only by the first one hundred days of FDR and the first six months after LBJ's inauguration in 1965.

The tax cut and explosion of military expenditures succinctly encapsulated Reagan's legislative agenda. From his days as a Hollywood actor, when he paid 90 percent of his income to the federal government, Reagan had been determined to "free" the American taxpayer from the burdens of an oppressive central government. Under his new plan, the top tax rate would fall from 70 to 50 percent (eventually falling to 34 percent under subsequent Republican administrations). Overall, a 23 percent reduction would occur in federal taxes over a three-year period. Astonishingly, Reagan predicted that the tax cut would help eventually to achieve a balanced budget. Based on the "Laffer curve"—named for an economist—once taxes reached a certain level, investor confidence would rise, more business enterprises would begin, resources would "trickle down" to consumers, and as the economy thrived, more tax dollars would pour into federal coffers, balancing the budget. Scream as they might about the logic and consequences of the Reagan proposals, Democrats soon learned they were up against a political pro. Reagan lobbied congressmen by telephone and in personal meetings, seeing more than 400 members of the House and Senate during his first 100 days in 69 different encounters. "I'm getting the shit whaled out of me," Democratic

Speaker of the House Tip O'Neill complained, while his Majority Leader Jim Wright declared that in terms of political skill, "I am not sure that I have seen [his] equal."

With little acknowledgment that there might be a conflict between a tax cut and a huge increase in defense expenditures, Reagan proceeded to increase the military budget by $1.2 trillion over five years. In addition to resuming production of the B-1 and starting the B-2, Reagan proposed to build seventeen thousand additional nuclear weapons and to modernize substantially the navy. It was as if the government's right hand had no idea of what the government's left hand was doing. While hundreds of billions of dollars in revenue were being *cut* by the tax plan, hundreds of billions of expenditures were being *added* by the military buildup. Even David Stockman, the youthful (and ideological) guru of Reaganomics who managed the Office of Management and Budget, finally recognized the unworkability of the plan and sought to rally support for new taxes and lower defense expenditures. But Reagan would not abide such doubts, convinced in his heart of hearts that slashing taxes would inevitably liberate the economy and result in a balanced budget. Here, as in so many instances, Reagan revealed how totally oblivious he could be to facts. As *Washington Post* columnist David Broder noted, "When someone approaches Reagan bearing information, he flees as if from a leper's touch." With breezy equanimity, he told people that ballistic missiles could be called back after they were launched and that submarines did not carry nuclear missiles. Clearly, all that mattered were the simple propositions on which Reagan based his political life and identity: taxes were bad, communism was abhorrent, a strong military was good, and America would triumph as soon as it released the stranglehold of government on the economy and determined to destroy its archenemy.

III. THE REAGAN WHITE HOUSE—FOREIGN POLICY

Not surprisingly, Reagan brought the same faith in simple ideas to his conduct of foreign policy. Quickly, he enunciated what became known as the "Reagan Doctrine"—a commitment that America would provide military and economic aid to forces resisting communism anywhere and everywhere in the world but especially in developing countries like Angola, Ethiopia, and Afghanistan. Latin America was especially pivotal to Reagan. He committed millions of dollars to a reactionary dictatorship in El Salvador that killed thousands of its domestic political opponents, including Roman Catholic priests and nuns, and he made the overthrow of the Marxist Sandanista regime in Nicaragua one of his primary objectives.

Central to Reagan's entire foreign policy enterprise was the simple credo that communism was satanic. He accused the Soviets of possessing a national trait of lying and cheating, as if they were genetically preordained to be untrustworthy. Consistent with that view, he declared the arms race to be a struggle of "good versus evil, right against wrong," matching in rhetorical flourish the most ardent Cold War rhetoric of Harry Truman and John F. Kennedy. But he exceeded even them when in the spring of 1983 he called Russia an "evil empire" with no redeeming virtues. Six months later, after Soviet planes shot down a Korean Airlines jet over Soviet territory (unaware it was a passenger plane), he accused the Soviets of being "inhumane," "barbarous," and "uncivilized," having perpetrated a "massacre" by their military action. The standoff between America and the Soviets had rarely been more strident or threatening. By his arms buildup, Reagan clearly signaled his intention to defeat any Soviet military initiative. Even more frightening from a Soviet perspective was the new president's commitment to "SDI," the Strategic Defense Initiative, which he believed would produce an antiballistic missile laser weapon that would make America invulnerable to Soviet attack. Inspired by a movie he had seen, the idea of SDI, or "star wars" as it came to be dubbed, might have lacked significant scientific backing as a viable weapons system, but to Reagan it took on the aura of a magic bullet that would forever protect the land of freedom from the "evil empire." Needless to say, Soviet leaders were terrified of the concept, being ill-equipped to afford a parallel effort on their side of the arms race.

Throughout his first term of office, Reagan exhibited a remarkable ability to escape even the negative consequences of his policies. He was a "political phenomenon," *New Yorker* commentator Elizabeth Drew wrote, "a man who by force of personality and marvelous stage-management super-imposes himself over his own mistakes." Congresswoman Patricia Schroeder called him the "Teflon president" because even bad things that happened refused to stick to him. Despite the tax cuts he passed, the country went into the worst recession of the postwar years in 1981–1982, with unemployment soaring to 11 percent and savings and investment in decline. Democrats won twenty-five additional congressional seats in 1982 as a result. Yet by the next year, prosperity had returned, and Reagan took the credit, celebrating the degree to which his tax cut had kicked in.

Foreign policy was the same. Reagan had committed American troops to Lebanon as part of an effort to stabilize a part of the world that would remain volatile for decades thereafter. Then, as one of the first signals of what soon would become a threat worse than communism, Islamic jihadists drove a truck jammed with explosives into the U.S. Marine compound in Beirut, killing 274 American soldiers. (A subsequent blue-ribbon panel blamed politicians in Washington for rejecting military requests that the compound be fortified.) Then just two days later, Reagan sent 5,000 marines into the Caribbean island of Grenada to quell what the administration saw as a threat by Cuban Communists to take over that island and hold Americans hostage. They swept to victory. One night later, Reagan went on national television and fused the events of Beirut and Grenada into a celebration of American patriotism and sacrifice, ending his speech with a tear-filled tribute to an American marine in Lebanon, unable to speak, who scratched the marine motto "Semper Fi" on a piece of paper and gave it to a visiting general. The next day Reagan's popularity rating went up fifteen points.

IV. THE 1984 ELECTION AND REAGAN'S SECOND TERM

By 1984, Ronald Reagan had succeeded in becoming "Mr. America." No one could come close to him. "We kept apple pie and the flag going the whole time," Reagan's aide Michael Deaver said. The Democrats nominated Walter Mondale, one of the most talented men in the country, to contest Reagan in the 1984 presidential election. The vice president under Jimmy Carter and a highly respected former Democratic senator from Minnesota, Mondale sought to pull together the old New Deal coalition—labor, minorities, women—and to focus on the economic issues of fairness that Reagan's tax cut highlighted. But Mondale never had a chance. Reagan tarred him with the brush of being a candidate of the "special interests"—labor, women, and minorities had now taken on that label—while portraying himself as the candidate of "equal opportunity." Sustaining his popularity among New Right voters like "middle-Americans," born-again Christians, and those dyspeptic over the idea of abortion on demand and homosexuality, Reagan flew the flag, identified with the triumphs of the U.S. Olympic team in Los Angeles—"let's go for the gold!"—and celebrated the grand comeback of America after years of humiliation.

"Just about every place you look," one Reagan TV ad said, "things are looking up. Life is better—America is back—and people have a sense of pride they never thought they'd feel again." In the face of all that, Mondale could only feebly attempt to prick the Reagan bubble. Although the president might say that "it's all picket fences and puppy dogs [and] no one's hurting," Mondale declared, there were millions of people out there who were hungry, unemployed, and suffering. But his message never got through and on election day Ronald Reagan soared to one of the great triumphs of modern political history, winning 59 percent of the popular vote and 49 out of 50 states. He even won majorities among the core Democratic constituencies—57 percent of the women, 61 percent of the elderly, a majority of Catholics, even half of the union vote. Reagan had achieved his lifelong dream. He had become, in commentator Elizabeth Drew's words, "the personification of America."

Yet even as Reagan reached the zenith of his political trajectory, his fortunes started to plummet. Like Franklin Roosevelt at the height of his success in 1937, or LBJ at the flood tide of the Great Society in 1965–1966, Reagan overreached, engaging in failed policies that set off a backlash of criticism and put at risk his entire administration. For FDR it had been an ill-conceived plan to pack the Supreme Court, for LBJ the rapid-fire escalation of the Vietnam War. In the case of Reagan, it was the Iran-Contra imbroglio, where—in a desperate attempt to free American citizens held hostage by Iran and simultaneously fulfill the Reagan Doctrine by helping the contras overthrow the Sandanista regime in Nicaragua—the president and his aides directly violated laws enacted by Congress, betrayed their own pledge never to pay ransom for hostages, and even contemplated setting up a secret arm of government intelligence to engage in rogue military action beyond the oversight of any congressional committee.

It all began with Reagan's passion to be a "rescuer" and to save American hostages kidnapped by Hezbollah and other groups beholden to Iran. Nothing galvanized Reagan's patriotic impulses more than his wish to save American citizens held captive, and so, despite his repeated promises never to negotiate with terrorists, he said yes when members of his National Security staff learned that Israel could transfer American arms to Iran in return for which a hostage would be freed. After all, it was Israel conveying the arms—even if secured from America—not the United States. The plot thickened when Robert McFarlane, Admiral John Poindexter, and Colonel Oliver North of the National Security team saw a way of using the arms deal to raise monies to support the contra guerillas in Nicaragua. They could overcharge the Iranians for the weapons, then transfer the proceeds and supply anti-Communist forces with arms and supplies. Except that in 1982 Congress had specifically refused to permit American aid to go to the contras and then two years later unanimously reaffirmed the ban, this time extending it to any and all forms of government support. Clearly, the Reagan administration was both breaking its own promise never to ransom hostages and violating a precise congressional instruction.

It was only a matter of time before news spread of the Iranian arms deal and the aid being sent to the contras. The administration tried one cover story after another, but they all imploded, with Reagan finally having to admit that his administration had broken all its own injunctions, not to mention an act of Congress. A special blue-ribbon commission, two-thirds Republican, concluded that the administration had wantonly abrogated the law and its own pronounced policies. More disturbing, subsequent testimony by North and Poindexter pointed to a long-range plot to take the monies raised from the Iran arms deals to fund "an overseas entity capable of conducting activities similar to the ones we had conducted here [with the contras]"—in short a parallel arm of government answerable to no one. North proudly admitted to having lied on repeated occasions to Congress and to having shredded incriminating documents fifteen feet away from where Attorney General Edward Meese was standing. "What we have here," one commentator said, "is a combination of right wing fervor, militaristic nationalism, and religiosity...reminiscent of the stirrings of authoritarianism in Europe." Less than two years after his triumphant reelection, the Reagan presidency seemed doomed to failure, reminiscent of the self-destructive path that had beset the Nixon administration just a decade earlier. How could such a turn of events have occurred?

V. THE REAGAN STAFF AND PERSONALITY

Fundamentally, the answer rested with two factors that explained both Reagan's greatest successes and his most abysmal failures. The first involved the staff who shaped his presidency—when they were good, he vaulted to triumph, when bad, he was helpless and incompetent. The second revolved around the Reagan personality—his simple credo, wonderful sense of humor, and inspired capacity to relate to and speak on behalf of the American people made it possible for him to pursue a few "big" ideas with passion and success. On the other hand, Reagan's hands-off style, indifference to detail, ignorance of policy implementation, and detachment from the daily routine of government management set up executive practices that at best invited abuse and at worst created disaster.

Reagan cared not a whit about the qualifications of many of the people he appointed to high positions. The only conversation he had with Alexander Haig, his first secretary of state, focused primarily on Reagan anecdotes about his old friend, the ventriloquist Edgar Bergen, and never touched on the views of either Reagan or Haig about how to conduct foreign policy. Donald Regan, the new secretary of the treasury, came into office having held only one brief phone conversation with the president. "I was flying by the seat of my pants," he recalled. "The President never told me...what he wanted to accomplish in the field of economics." With regularity, Reagan forgot the names of members of his senior staff and even failed to recognize some of his own cabinet members, at one point referring to Samuel Pierce, secretary of housing and urban affairs and the only black cabinet member, as "Mr. Mayor." Six different individuals served as Reagan's National Security advisor over eight years, with only the last two—Frank Carlucci and Colin Powell—performing with distinction.

The stunning success of Reagan's first term depended almost totally on the skill of his personal staff. Here, Reagan relied on solid political instinct and long-standing friendships with aides who had proven their loyalty and talent. Shrewdly, Reagan chose James Baker, formerly the campaign manager of his archrival and now vice president, George H. W. Bush, to be his chief of staff. A powerful lawyer and business figure, Baker understood how to make government work and possessed the single quality most indispensable to someone in his role—total devotion to making his boss look good, with minimal concern for his own status and well-being. Assisting Baker were Edwin H. Meese, the chief domestic counselor who had worked with Reagan throughout his gubernatorial years, and Michael Deaver, a brilliant public relations expert who recognized the importance of scripting every Reagan public statement and appearance to highlight his telegenic personality and ensure that the public saw him as the master of his, and the country's, fate. With these three individuals at the helm—Meese literally "ran" every cabinet meeting, moderating the discussion and setting the agenda while Deaver orchestrated each day's "sound bite" to maximize Reagan's public impact—the White House seemed to run like a smooth ocean liner. Reagan worked a less than nine-to-five day, taking an hour each morning to feed the pigeons outside the Oval Office and write personal correspondence while reserving more than an hour of each afternoon for "personal" time (a nap). Yet it all seemed to be a "splendid routine," as one observer noted, even if "often [Reagan] held the reins of power so lightly that he did not appear to hold them at all." The skill of his staff ensured that only the most positive sides of

Reagan's staff proved all important to both his success and his failure. During his second term, staff turnovers brought people like Colonel Oliver North to Reagan's National Security team. North, together with others, engaged in a deal to sell arms to Iran in order to get American hostages released and then use the profits from those sales to arm Nicaraguan rebels. Such aid was a direct violation of a congressional act and led to the "Iran-Contra" scandal.

Credit: Associated Press

the Reagan persona received attention while the way his words and public appearances were shaped guaranteed that the President's skill as an actor would register with maximum impact, from his State of the Union addresses to his nationally televised speeches such as the one on Beirut and Grenada that left his audience in tears.

Yet what would happen if Baker, Deaver, and Meese disappeared? To Reagan's detriment, that is precisely what occurred after he won reelection. All three of the most critical staffers were tired. One had an alcohol problem. None felt appreciated by the president, who seemed to take them for granted. Now, in the most critical shift of all, James Baker decided to switch jobs with Donald Regan at Treasury—except that Regan had none of Baker's skills. Instead of being a consensus-builder who worked smoothly with those around him, he was a loner and sufficiently egotistical to always want his own way. Whereas Baker put his own interests second, Regan put his first. The entire National Security team turned over, working less closely and harmoniously with the rest of the staff. Particularly worrisome was Regan's personality conflict with the First Lady. Nancy Reagan had always been the power behind the throne, with her own maverick qualities. She regularly consulted an astrologer about her husband's schedule, frequently demanding changes if the stars were not in alignment. Baker handled the conflicts diplomatically; Regan muffed the relationship completely. As a result, a smooth operation suddenly became erratic, with Reagan's bad side now more regularly displayed. As Reagan biographer Lou Cannon noted, the president suddenly became "a remote and disengaged monarch." In truth, the president himself had not changed, but now there was no team to worry over every detail and make sure that every word and picture fit a predetermined positive outcome.

The consequences of the shift first became apparent when Regan scheduled a wreath-laying ceremony for the president on a visit to Germany at a military cemetery in Bitburg. When it was revealed that members of Hitler's SS who had participated in the slaughter of Jews were buried there, Regan refused to cancel or change the event, exposing the president to international embarrassment. In 1984 Reagan had achieved one of his greatest triumphs when at Normandy he celebrated the heroism of those who had taken part in the D day invasion. There, he became the symbol of all that was good about the World War II experience. Now, in Bitburg, that symbolism was tarnished. So too was Reagan's luster.

Iran-Contra constituted the worst example of staff incompetence, however. Although Reagan himself bore much of the responsibility for setting the stage through his insistence on freeing hostages, the reckless actions of his National Security staff created the constitutional crisis of brazenly violating a congressional mandate and contradicting a national pledge. In the Baker-run White House, it would be inconceivable that maverick military officers could set national policy without oversight to assure that the president was not embarrassing himself. But now Poindexter and North were given free rein, no one taking responsibility to protect the president from being manipulated and used by his National Security aides. When the blue-ribbon commission headed by former Republican Senator John Tower investigated what had occurred, they could not believe the disarray they discovered. It was Donald Regan, the commission concluded, who "must bear primary responsibility for the chaos that descended upon the White House" after the Iran-Contra disclosures occurred. No one was overseeing the decision-making process or protecting the president from embarrassment. Instead, the commission declared, North, Poindexter, and McFarland had operated "largely outside the orbit of the U.S. government." In perhaps the most delicate understatement ever uttered, one commission member observed that "the system [of decision making at the White House] did not compensate adequately for the management style of the president."

And that, of course, was the ultimate problem—Reagan simply did not care about, or get involved with, the day-to-day details of running his own administration. He did what he was told, and as long as the people directing him understood their task and were dedicated to protecting his image, the results were acceptable. Congenial, self-deprecating, always ready with an anecdote, Reagan could charm people once given the opportunity. But others set the scene and gave him his cue cards. Never did Reagan meet a senator, congressman, or foreign statesman without a set of 4 × 6 cards in large type that told him what to say. James Baker tried desperately to prepare Reagan for a world economic summit, boiling down a complicated set of briefing documents to a few pages, only to be told by Reagan the next morning that he had not even read those because "well, Jim, the *Sound of Music* was on last night." Lou Cannon had observed the problem from the state capital of Sacramento all the way to Washington. Reagan's "biggest problem," he wrote, "was that he didn't know enough about public policy to participate fully in his presidency—and often didn't realize how much he didn't know." As long as Deaver and Baker were in charge, things were under control. "[Deaver] tried to see to it," Cannon noted, "that the script, staging, and lighting of each scene provided Reagan an opportunity to give a smashing performance." Which for most of the first term he did.

On the other hand, once the wrong people were in charge, the directions faltered, the performance disintegrated, and the nation—as well as the presidency—floundered and started to sink. So unengaged was Reagan in the actual details of Iran-Contra, one witness told the Tower commission, that "he can't remember anything about it, my God!" Not only did his staff manipulate him but they also actually believed that they had the right to pursue such policies because, they claimed, *they* knew what Reagan wanted. A clear pattern was evident. Reagan was a man of simple and grandiloquent ideas. He had a vision that he cared about deeply. Others would handle the details. In the meantime, like the good actor he was, he would await their direction on how he should behave, trusting that they would be true to his goals and protect his image. To get more involved, or immerse himself in policy details a la Jimmy Carter, was not part of his role. But that left the burden of his own performance totally on the shoulders of others.

The same detachment characterized Reagan's personal life. Although gracious in every social setting, he devoted little if any attention to his friends, his staff, or even his own family members, with the exception of Nancy. "He's a genuinely nice man," his longtime associate Lynn Nofziger said, "but there's a kind of barrier between him and the rest of the world, a film you can't get through. You can't get inside of him." Those who had dedicated their lives to his service felt hurt by Reagan's distance. "He didn't make you feel needed," his aide David Gergen wrote later. "People left, and didn't hear from him, and there was no real sense of connection." His children, especially, experienced the sense of detachment. Ronald, his son, reported that his father "got antsy [if I tried to] get too close and too personal" to him, and his daughter said, "I could never get through to him....I never knew who he was." Even Nancy acknowledged that "he often seems remote and doesn't let anybody get too close. There's a wall around him."

Thus in personal relationships, as in policy matters, Reagan remained above it all, playing to perfection the part he was assigned but unwilling to engage intimately the people and policies that constituted the heart of his presidency. The results were dismaying: his inability to recognize the contradiction between cutting taxes, ballooning the military budget, and still believing he was fighting for a balanced budget; and his inability to understand that sending money and arms to the contras was prohibited by law. All that mattered, in his eyes, was that he was being true to the vision distilled in "The Speech." If he was successful in slashing taxes, fighting Communists, and growing the military, everything was on course. The tragedy of all this was that when the wrong people were on board as one's crew, everything could go dreadfully wrong while the president—by virtue of his detachment—had no independent source of information to realize the problems besetting the society and his own administration.

VI. THE SOCIAL REALITIES OF 1980S AMERICA

And problems there were. The most notable involved the economy and were direct consequences of policies Reagan had introduced. By virtue of a $750 billion tax cut and a $1.2 trillion defense budget increase, the federal deficit skyrocketed, soaring from $90 billion in 1982 to $283 billion in 1986—almost ten times larger than the highest previous deficit. During the entire Reagan presidency, the nation's indebtedness increased 300 percent. To finance that debt, the United States raised interest rates and came increasingly to depend on foreign investment. As a result, the value of the dollar artificially increased, which in turn made imports cheaper and sent more American jobs flying out of the country. American exports went down for the same reason—given the value of the dollar, foreign markets could not afford them. The bottom line: America lost thousands of high-paying, skilled jobs in the manufacturing sector to foreign companies; the trade imbalance grew deeper year by year; and instead of being the world's largest *creditor* nation, which had been true when Reagan took office, it now became the world's largest *debtor* nation.

Another consequence of the shift was that as more skilled jobs left the country, employment growth occurred primarily in the service sector—hotels, restaurants, laundries. Yet most of these jobs paid low wages, offered little chance for promotion, and in almost all cases, provided no benefits such as health care. Unionization fell as skilled jobs evaporated, with membership in the AFL-CIO falling from 25 percent of all employees in 1980 to 16 percent in 1990. In fact, more than half of all the new jobs created in the 1980s paid wages that left a family of four below the poverty level. As a result, the social structure of the nation's workforce became increasingly bifurcated. Minorities—particularly blacks and Hispanics—lived in inner-city ghettoes and barrios, dropped out of high school, and were limited to subsistence wage jobs; middle-class workers, meanwhile (including blacks and Hispanics with sufficient education to take advantage of desegregation), increasingly moved out of the city, sharing in the larger phenomenon of "white flight" that exacerbated ethnic tensions.

The two-tier society that emerged was full of ironies for women and minorities. Despite the existence of a "glass ceiling" for most women executives and lawyers, more and more women graduates of business, law, and medical schools succeeded in securing decent jobs and significant remuneration. The number of blacks attending college multiplied five times between the 1960s and the 1980s. As a result, as many as one-third of African American families were able to join the middle class, move to the suburbs, and enjoy the "good life" promised by the consumer culture. By the end of the decade, a black husband and wife who both worked and had both graduated from college earned as much as their white peers in a similar situation.

Yet at the same time, women and minorities suffered most under the new economic regime. As high school dropout rates in the inner city reached the 50 percent level, more and more young women had pregnancies out of wedlock and entered the world of welfare. Nearly two-thirds of black children were born in female-headed households as well as 50 percent of Hispanic children. Poverty was the almost inevitable outcome. Whereas a child born into a home with two parents had only a 5 percent chance of being poor, the figure for black children born into a female-headed household where the mother was under twenty-five was 90 percent. The paradox of success for some and misery for others stood out as one of the outstanding consequences of economic developments in the 1980s.

Nor did the economy stand alone as a source of concern. More and more Americans viewed with alarm threats to the environment. The 1979 Three Mile Island accident at a Pennsylvania nuclear plant nearly resulted in dispersal of massive radiation through the atmosphere—a close call made all the more relevant by the disaster at Chernobyl in the Soviet Union in 1986 that left millions affected by nuclear poisoning after the power plant there melted down. Global warming also became a source of increasing concern as ozone-depleting fluorocarbons created the danger that carbon monoxide would overheat the world's atmosphere, melt the planet's ice caps, and create a disaster of international proportions. In the face of such fears, the Reagan administration's posture was hardly reassuring. The president's first secretary of the interior, James Watt, did all he could to eliminate environmental regulations, proclaiming that the environment was of little importance compared with the imminent Second Coming of Christ. His EPA administrator, Anne Burford, resisted imposing penalties on chemical companies that had been found responsible for creating toxic waste dumps. Indifference to environmental crisis seemed the byword of the Reagan years, terrifying those who perceived, correctly, that unless action were taken quickly, the world might well become uninhabitable for hundreds of millions of people.

The same indifference greeted the emergence of AIDS, a new worldwide health epidemic. Word began to spread about AIDS (Acquired Immune Deficiency Syndrome) as the decade dawned. The disease, at least initially, was largely confined to homosexual men. Throughout the postwar years there had been a quiet, "respectable" gay rights movement among business and professional people called the Mattachine Society that had fought police harassment and tried to educate the larger population about homosexuality. Then in 1969, when police violently disrupted a gay bar in Greenwich Village New York called the Stonewall, large groups of gay activists for the first time responded by fighting back, hurling bottles at the police and overturning patrol cars. From that point forward, a different, more militant, more "in your face" gay movement spread through the country, holding "coming out parties" and gay rights marches in most large cities and seeking political recognition. Now the gay world buzzed with terrifying news of the new virus that destroyed the immune system and brought quick death from virtually any disease that took over the body after the immune system

Although not recognized as a crisis by the government until the end of the Reagan administration, the HIV/AIDS epidemic spread throughout America and the world in the 1980s. Here supporters of those victimized by AIDS demonstrate their solidarity with those afflicted with the disease.

Credit: © Roger Ressmeyer/CORBIS

was dead. The medical community quickly recognized the immensity of the problem and spread the word to government officials. Neither the president nor any of his health aides responded. By 1985, fifty-six hundred people had died from AIDS. Only in February 1986—after his friend, actor Rock Hudson, died from AIDS—did Reagan ask Surgeon General Everett Koop for a report. Even then, the administration budget called for a reduction in AIDS research.

By the end of the decade, nearly 50,000 people had died of AIDS in America alone and it no longer was possible to sweep the issue under a rug. AIDS activists came together in a group called ACT-UP (Aids Coalition to Unleash Power) and held demonstrations throughout the country. On Columbus Day 1987 more than 500,000 gay activists and their allies marched through New York City demanding action. "AIDS is our holocaust," ACT-UP leader Larry Kramer declared, "and Reagan is our Hitler." With the disease sweeping the world and affecting women and children as well as gay men, even Reagan recognized the need for decisive action. Eventually—well after he left office—Reagan apologized for his failure to speak out forcefully when he was president. But AIDS was only the latest in a long line of crises in American society that never appeared on Reagan's radar screen for the simple reason that as president he paid so little heed to glaring realities that otherwise should have galvanized his attention. Although he was speaking of Iran-Contra, Republican Senator William Cohen might well have been describing virtually any issue when he said in 1987, "With Ronald Reagan, no one is there. The sad fact is that we don't have a president." It looked as if Reagan would go down in history, like Richard Nixon before him, as a failed leader. "No sadder tale could be spun in this holiday season," columnist David Broder wrote at Christmastime, "than the unraveling of yet another presidency." Elizabeth Drew agreed. "It is hard to see how [things] could change sufficiently," she wrote, "to give us a presidency that is not—and does not put the country—in danger."

VII. THE MIRACULOUS RECOVERY

Such forebodings of doom failed to take into account the core of Ronald Reagan's character—boundless faith in his vision and an optimistic determination that if he willed it hard enough, he could bring that vision to fruition. On the surface it seemed there could be no president less likely to reach out to the Soviet Union for détente than Ronald Reagan. Here was a man who called his country's archenemy an "evil empire," who pledged in the Reagan Doctrine to fight communism wherever in the world it reared its ugly head, and who—literally—suggested there was something genetic in the Russian character to make the nation untrustworthy. But John F. Kennedy had used some of the same rhetoric, and it was John F. Kennedy, who in his 1963 American University speech, reversed virtually every axiom he had articulated to reach out for peace.

For different reasons, but in parallel fashion, Ronald Reagan pursued the same course. As someone who believed passionately in simple absolutes—and who exhibited little difficulty in embracing contradictions, for example, a belief in a balanced budget, tax cuts, and soaring defense expenditures—Reagan saw no contradiction between committing to destroy world communism by deploying the most expensive weapons system ever developed by the American military and also believing in total world disarmament. Ironically, the two were inextricably connected. SDI, or "star wars" as the media dubbed it, would in his view create an antiballistic missile system that could then be shared by all nuclear powers. As a consequence, all systems capable of delivering nuclear weapons would lose their raison d'etre and could be destroyed because with SDI, they could never be used effectively. Thus in an almost bizarre fashion, Ronald Reagan believed that he could use his greatest weapons system, to be constructed as a means of defeating the Soviet Union, to also bring about a world peace never before imagined possible. In all of this, a characteristic aloofness separated Reagan, the "believer," from any of the realities of SDI. But as in every other aspect of his administration, from tax cuts to Iran-Contra, what mattered were a few simple beliefs, not murky details.

Reagan seized his chance to leap from irrevocable condemnation of Russia to passionate wooing when the Kremlin leadership turned over in 1985. Prior to that time, tedious "apparatchiks" like Leonid Brezhnev and Konstantin Chernenko were in power. They exhibited little imagination (or life) and simply dug in deeper to defeat capitalism. But now a new, dynamic young leader took over. Mikhail Gorbachev may have had a traditional party past, but he dressed like a Westerner, had a sparkling wife with a fashion taste of her own, and immediately started talking a new line. "This is a man we can do business with," the conservative British prime minister, Margaret Thatcher, declared. Gorbachev talked about encouraging entrepreneurship, licensing private restaurants, decentralizing the economy, and embracing glasnost, the free exchange of ideas. Artists started to display their works (some of them political) in Gorky Park, poets started to publish more widely their works criticizing the Soviet regime. Most important, Gorbachev recognized that were he to try to match, weapon for weapon, Reagan's defense buildup, he would bring his country to bankruptcy. There was only one way to go, he determined, and that was to follow the winds of change that were already blowing through Eastern Europe, particularly with the Solidarity labor movement in Poland, and to open the USSR to changes that might thaw the most frozen structures of state power.

Now, with Nancy Reagan's ardent encouragement, Ronald Reagan stepped up to seize the moment of opportunity that Gorbachev had presented. Even as the disaster of Iran-Contra seemed to consign his presidency to the rubble heap, Reagan imagined a moment when he and his Soviet counterpart could break the chains of "mutual assured destruction" (MAD) and walk together into a Shangri-la of peace. So intent was Reagan on bringing his vision to pass that he threw away all his briefing papers at their first summit

Although Ronald Reagan had denounced the Soviet Union as an "evil empire" during his first administration, he ended his presidency by proposing an arms reduction treaty with the Soviets and achieving a major breakthrough toward world peace in partnership with Soviet Premier Mikhail Gorbachev. Here they are shown in Red Square.

Credit: Associated Press

in Reykjavik, Iceland, and in a move that stunned (and appalled) all of his advisors, proposed to Gorbachev that they destroy all nuclear weapons in the world. Of course, the price of doing this would be Soviet acceptance of SDI or "star wars"—something Gorbachev could never agree to because it would give the United States ultimate power. Yet the very idea of abolishing nuclear weapons was one that perhaps no other American president in the postnuclear age could ever entertain—unless that president too was an actor who had seen a movie where "star wars" had precisely that effect.

Even if Gorbachev could not agree to Reagan's vision, a start had nevertheless been made. In three additional summits over the next two years, the two men found more common ground than at any time since Kennedy's American University speech and prepared the way for Reagan to exit his presidency, not shamed by the betrayals, incompetence, and willful power grabs of his National Security staff in Iran-Contra but instead wrapped in the glory of having negotiated a major reduction of intermediate nuclear weapons (the INF treaty). Together the Reagans and Gorbachevs celebrated by attending the Bolshoi Ballet. Nancy and Ron walked hand in hand at midnight through Red Square, and the world marveled at the miracle that détente had produced—the "evil empire" had turned into a newfound friend, and Ronald Reagan, once the most intrepid firebrand that anticommunism had to offer, had now become what one American expert on Russia described as "a romantic, a radical, a nuclear abolitionist."

As President and Mrs. Reagan winged their way over the Atlantic back to Washington from Moscow, the resident crystallized the significance of what had been achieved in a discussion with reporters. The trip, he said, had been like a "Cecil B. DeMille [Hollywood] production," and he had been fortunate enough to "drop into a grand historical moment." And what about the evil empire, the press asked. "That was a different time and place," Reagan responded.

It was all like a fairy tale but one where, if you believed passionately enough in the possibilities of magic, disaster could become triumph, and defeat could turn into victory.

VIII. CONCLUSION

In the end, there was an intrinsic relationship between the best and worst sides of Ronald Reagan. His visionary goals for America—back to #1, an economy liberated by tax cuts, unchallenged military supremacy, pride in the "can do" qualities of the national character, a Pax Americana—all grew directly from his ability to identify, deeply and totally, with the transcendent and heroic roles in the patriotic movies he loved the most. He had become "Mr. America," embodying the inspiring ideals he had learned growing up and had communicated to his fellow countrymen from "The Speech" he gave for General Electric to his years in the White House. But the other side of that visionary inspiration was a peculiar indifference to facts, to complexity, to the nitty-gritty details of how you put together a plan to translate idealism into policy. There Reagan was a cipher, alternately oblivious or contemptuous to those who would seek to ground him in reality. As long as someone gave him his lines, told him where to stand and how to behave, he was untouchable. But without superb direction and attentive care, he was like a nomad in the desert lacking a compass to tell him where to go. Hence the absurdity of believing simultaneously in cutting taxes, exploding the military budget, and balancing the budget. Or of trading arms for hostages and violating the Boland Amendment, all the while insisting he would never negotiate with kidnappers or break the law. It was like a computer with a huge blank spot on the drive that distinguished desired outcomes from programmed realities. As one of Reagan's biographers said, "There was no *there* there."

Hence, a president who could transform the national agenda and global geopolitics but who also lacked an emotional connection to his children and professed total ignorance of the whys and wherefores of his most important policy initiatives.

All of this accentuated the critical importance of those who took it upon themselves to fill the blank spots and make sure Reagan had his lines right—his staff, his wife, Nancy, his closest associates. They were really the ones in charge. Reagan might have the ideals and the vision, but only those who scripted him and directed his lines knew how to get from here to there. In that context, one commentator presciently noted that there were in fact three Reagan presidencies—the first under Chief of Staff James Baker, where Reagan was the "Teflon president," who could do only good; the second under Donald Regan, where oversight was totally lacking and disasters like Iran-Contra dominated the news; and the third under retired former senator Howard Baker, who was persuaded to "rescue" the Reagan White House and under whom the great triumphs of détente with the Soviets occurred.

At his best, Reagan gave to America what it had been thirsting for during years of divisiveness and turmoil—a sense of direction and purpose. Nixon had threatened to undermine the very sanctity of the constitution while carrying on a war against his personal "enemies" list that poisoned the political process and called into question the moral rationale for public service. In the meantime the country became polarized by cultural conflicts over religion, family values, and personal freedoms such as the right to an abortion and one's own sexual preference or collective rights such as affirmative action for black Americans who had been victims of centuries of discrimination. Demoralized by a loss of economic control due to the oil crisis and humiliated by foreign policy defeats, Americans became more conservative and sought reassurance. Jimmy Carter had tried to restore the moral center and sense of well-being of his fellow citizens but ultimately failed. Into that morass Ronald Reagan rode on horseback with a message of hope, inspiration, and moral revitalization. As he told a group of Russian artists on his trip to Moscow, acting had helped him greatly "in the work I do now.... The most important thing is to have the vision. The next is to grasp and hold it...to fix it in your senses.... [T]hat is the very essence, I believe, of successful leadership." By those criteria, Reagan had "rescued" his country, just as he had saved countless swimmers who had gotten in trouble when he served as a teenage lifeguard. He knew how to perform that role.

What he did not know was how to address the ongoing fissures that plagued the country and which required intimate knowledge of complex economic and social data as well as a willingness to plunge into the process of finding creative solutions. How to cope with a skyrocketing trade deficit and make the connection between cheap imports, the outsourcing of skilled American jobs to foreign countries, a soaring national debt, and the growing ownership of American bonds by Asian and European banks. What was the answer to a rapidly growing chasm between the rich and the poor when tax breaks benefited primarily the wealthy and new jobs concentrated in service industries that paid minimum wages which often increased, rather than diminished, the number of those who were poor? What to do about the continuing—indeed intensifying—split between those who believed abortion and homosexuality were mortal sins and others who prized the individual freedoms they believed the Constitution guaranteed them. On issues of race, family values, affirmative action, sexuality, AIDS, health care, and economic despair among the poor, Reagan and his colleagues in the administration had little to offer. The president excelled in rhetoric but more often than not spoke words that failed to engage the most intractable problems of a society continuing to seek realistic answers to its ongoing domestic dilemmas.

Ronald Reagan had succeeded in his dream of bringing "morning [back] to America." The Cold War was on its way to an end, the national spirit had revived, and people felt "good" once again to be citizens of the United States. But in a deeper sense, the problems that emerged out of the challenges and confusions of the 1970s remained intact, waiting for answers that would reflect the realities of a society still torn by clashes over race and gender, divides over cultural values, and a disparity of economic resources that threatened the viability of still speaking in terms of "one America." Would the nation be able to rise to the challenge?

12

The End of One War, the Start of Another: Politics, Culture, and the Specter of Terrorism in the 1990s

The successful conclusion of the Reagan presidency served as a harbinger for an era of triumph, at least on the surface. The Cold War, which had anchored American history for more than four decades, was about to end in glorious victory for the cause of freedom. An era of unprecedented prosperity soon swept the land, marked by the power of information technology to create unheard-of fortunes in a dot.com world. Like a giant bestriding the universe, America seemed to reign supreme in the world, unchallenged in its economic energy, its military strength, and its cultural hegemony.

Yet at the same time, the nation remained torn by divisions over political and social values as severe as at any time since the 1920s split between urban and rural America. Back then, the flappers and immigrants from the cities, with their independence and worldly lifestyles, fought the Ku Klux Klan and fundamentalists who detested Jews and Catholics and fought the teaching of evolution in the schools. Now the cultural wars involved not only the "moral majority" against feminist libertarians *within* the United States but also what political scientist Samuel Huntington called a "clash of civilizations" in the world at large, between Islamic fundamentalists from the Arab and Asian world, on the one hand, and Judeo-Christian believers from Europe and America on the other.

Playing the central role during all this was a man named Bill Clinton. A child of the 1960s, Clinton became president displaying a political flair, a policy panache, and a penchant for self-destructive behavior that made his administration as fascinating—and bizarre in its contradictions—as even those of Richard Nixon and Lyndon B. Johnson. No one better encapsulated the tensions of the decade or its roller-coaster journey through triumph and disaster. And no one came more to symbolize, personally, the cultural passions that tore apart political consensus in the country. Clinton and his wife, Hillary, polarized the nation, attracting on the one hand unconstrained vituperation for being slick, expedient messengers for the devil while on the other sustaining a level of public approval—up to 70 percent in the late 1990s—that exceeded that of any other modern administration. Although Monica Lewinsky highlighted Bill Clinton's capacity to succumb to his worst instincts, public support of Clinton, even in the midst of impeachment proceedings, suggested his abiding appeal to a majority of the American people.

It was a decade, and an administration, somehow appropriate to the passing of one age and the dawning of another.

I. THE BUSH YEARS

Launching the time of triumph was a New England Brahmin turned Texas oil-man who personified the American political establishment. George Herbert Walker Bush was a graduate of Phillips Andover Academy; the son of a Republican senator from Connecticut who was a former Wall Street tycoon; a Phi Beta Kappa from Yale; and on top of all that, a war hero. Turning to Texas to try to make his political fortune, Bush embarked on a career trajectory that seemed like a prescripted resume for national prominence. Although chosen for elective office only once—as a congressman from Houston—Bush became head of the national Republic Party, director of the Central Intelligence Agency, and U.S. ambassador to China. Having closely contested Ronald Reagan for the Republic nomination in 1980 (he coined the phrase "voodoo economics" to describe Reagan's budget plans to simultaneously cut taxes and increase military spending), he gracefully accepted the nod to become vice president under Reagan for eight years. Although he often tried to avoid responsibility for Reagan disasters (he was "out of the loop," he claimed, during Iran-Contra, even though subsequent evidence showed him very much involved), Bush banked on the momentum of Reagan's successes to fuel his own bid for the presidency in 1988.

Too "moderate" and "establishment" for many on the New Right, Bush nevertheless held his own and won the Republican nomination. His foe, Massachusetts Governor Michael Dukakis, meanwhile, blew a seventeen-point lead in the polls after being nominated. Disowning the label of being a "liberal" (it had become a dirty word for many), Dukakis boasted that the key issue was "competency." Dry and pedestrian, Dukakis provided little inspiration to the Democratic base while quickly showing vulnerability to Bush's all-out attack on his "liberal" character. Dukakis had vetoed a Massachusetts bill requiring the Pledge of Allegiance in the schools (it was unconstitutional, his attorney general told him), opposed the death penalty, and according to Bush was a "card-carrying member of the American Civil Liberties Union"—horror of horrors! Worst of all, he had allowed weekend furloughs for prisoners in Massachusetts, one of whom—a black man named Willie Horton—had raped and assaulted a Maryland woman. "If I can make Willie Horton a household name," a Bush campaign media expert said, "we'll win the election." Done! Soon TV ads featured a threatening black man pushing through a revolving door as the voice-over talked about Dukakis's infamous behavior pampering criminals. Dukakis did not have a chance.

Immediately, Bush put his foreign policy expertise to work.

The pace of fast-breaking developments in Eastern Europe proved overwhelming. In November 1989, the unbelievable happened—the Berlin Wall came down, ripped apart stone by stone as East Berlin tasted freedom. Now, with Gorbachev's tacit consent, East Germany moved to reunite with West Germany. The Solidarity movement in Poland—led by shipyard worker Lech Walesa—surged forward creating an anti-Soviet political coalition that swept to victory in 1989. Free elections in Hungary deposed old-line Communists while in Wenceslas Square in Prague, hundreds of thousands of Czechoslovakian citizens took to the streets to celebrate the victory over oppression that had been denied them by Soviet troops in 1948 and 1968. In one of the most moving displays of genuine democracy ever seen, hordes of Prague citizens gathered each day in the public square of Old Town to debate the policies their country should follow—real democracy in a land now free. From the Balkans to the Baltic, winds of change reached a crescendo until finally, the event no one could have anticipated occurred—the Soviet Union itself collapsed, its creaky old structure of bureaucratic rigidity and party arteriosclerosis condemning it to disintegration.

During all of this, Bush responded with care, nuance, and patience. He never indulged in condescending glee at the enemy's destruction. Instead, he showed respect and deference, first to Gorbachev as he tried to navigate the disintegration of the Soviet bloc and then to Gorbachev's successor, Boris Yeltsin, who came to power after defying an attempted military coup against Gorbachev. Any ill-considered step by Bush could have created backlash. Instead, he permitted events to unfold at their own speed, in the meantime

By the end of the 1980s, the entire Communist monolith had started to crumble. In November 1989, the Berlin Wall came crashing down, and two years later, the Soviet Union itself crumbled. Here the Berlin Wall is depicted.

Credit: © Robert Maass/CORBIS

putting in place the pieces of a new coalition that might replace the rigid bipolar division of the world into communism and democracy.

Unbeknownst to Bush at the time, he soon would have the chance to prove what a new multilateral alliance could achieve for the cause of world peace and stability. The site was the Persian Gulf, the enemy Saddam Hussein's Iraq, the issue Hussein's sudden invasion of oil-rich Kuwait. In many respects the circumstances were bizarre. America had been Iraq's steady ally all during the 1980s. During that country's protracted war of attrition with Iran, American had provided weaponry, intelligence aid, and extraordinary financial support to Hussein. Secretary of Defense Donald Rumsfeld journeyed to Baghdad to embrace Saddam and pledge American assistance. The American ambassador to Iraq even suggested to the Iraqi dictator that the United States would not look aversely toward Iraqi occupation of Kuwait. But Bush, who had been intimately involved in America's courtship of Saddam all during the 1980s, now perceived his invasion of Kuwait as an act of blatant aggression that profoundly unsettled stability in the region. Putting the Iraqi dictator on notice, Bush consulted with all of America's traditional allies—Britain, France, Germany, Spain, Italy—but also reached out to Yeltsin in Russia, to the Chinese, the Japanese, and other Eastern bloc nations.

Using the United Nations as the rallying point to impose international sanctions, Bush succeeded in getting a unanimous Security Council vote— including Syria—to impose sanctions on Iraq and to demand Iraqi withdrawal from Kuwait, with the threat of military force if Iraq did not comply. In the meantime, under the leadership of General Colin Powell—and using what came to be known as the "Powell Doctrine," or overwhelming military force—the United States brought together more than three hundred thousand allied troops in the Persian Gulf. Despite deep divisions at home over whether sanctions were enough—the vote to authorize military force was 52–48 in the U.S. Senate—Bush now moved to war, using lightning speed and a devastating military attack to decimate the Iraqi army and send it fleeing back toward Baghdad. With more than three hundred Iraqi deaths for every allied fatality, the three-day war turned into a rout. Consistent with his mandate under a UN resolution, Bush and his generals declined to pursue the Iraqis into their own country and depose Saddam Hussein—a decision with consequences that would come back to haunt future generations. Still, they had done their job, proving the efficacy and strategic brilliance of pursuing a multilateral coalition under UN auspices and demonstrating how peace might be maintained in a world where international order reigned. Within days, Bush's popularity rating soared to 91 percent.

But foreign policy successes alone could not sustain the Bush presidency, particularly at a time when the economy was slowing, the deficit growing, and jobs continued to leave the country. Foolishly, Bush had finished his acceptance speech at the Republican convention in 1988 by announcing, **"READ MY LIPS! NO NEW TAXES."** To Bush's credit, once he occupied the Oval Office he recognized the folly of accelerating the country's indebtedness. As a result, he endorsed a bipartisan plan to reduce government spending and increase taxes—quantitatively (though not in percentages) the largest tax increase in history. (Headlines in the *New York Post* read, "Read my lips: I lied.") But the corrective action may have been too late. The nation entered a prolonged recession, and Bush did little to respond except to reiterate his plea for a "kinder, gentler" America that would help poor people through voluntary activity, creating "a thousand points of light." Bush's inaction did not mean he was indifferent to human suffering, but the distinction was lost on the American people. He did not *seem* to care, nor did his administration. "I don't think it's the end of the world even if we have a recession," his treasury secretary declared. "We'll pull out of it again. No big deal." It was one more example of the major critique made of Bush throughout his administration. "Where was the guiding concept," one of his aides said. "There was none." The president was not big on "the vision thing" and was content to believe that he could ride the tide of the Persian Gulf victory to a second term. Yet eight months after the war had ended, fewer than 40 percent of the American people expressed satisfaction with the direction the country was taking.

II. THE 1992 ELECTION

That set the stage for the 1992 election—one that many Democratic candidates had decided was hopeless just eighteen months earlier because of Bush's popularity after Iraq's defeat. But not Bill Clinton. A wunderkind, Clinton had taken the political world by storm after an extraordinary childhood, adolescence, and college/graduate school experience that had helped shape the patterns—and pathologies—of his life.

Born in Arkansas three months after his natural father had died in an auto crash, Clinton grew up with multiple parent figures and role models. He was initially raised primarily by his grandparents (his mother, Virginia, went to New Orleans for nurse's training), who ran a store with many black customers. From his earliest days, Clinton felt at home in the black community, playing with black schoolmates, learning black culture. Later, that ease would help explain why Toni Morrison, the African American novelist, called him "our first black president." Then there was his mother, Virginia—flirtatious, passionate, dramatic in her self-presentation, with a white streak down the middle of her black hair and a fondness for partying and ribaldry. Finally, there was his stepfather, Roger, whom Virginia had married not knowing that he had been wed before and been accused of wife-beating. (Her first husband had also been married before without her knowing it). He was also an alcoholic. Soon Bill Clinton became the "rescuer," stepping between his stepfather and his mother as Roger started to beat her, warning him never "to lay a hand on my mother again." It was not a simple life, but it set Clinton up to enact what one expert on children of alcoholics called the role of "Family Hero.... As redeemer [of the family name, he] is dispatched into the world to excel and to return with praise and rewards that will make the entire [family] unit feel worthy." By winning the friendship and praise of everyone, Clinton could thus save the family, cast his reflected glory on them, and simultaneously erase the family's shame.

From that point forward, Clinton lived what he later called in his autobiography "parallel lives." One of those lives started when as a member of Boys Nation, an American Legion version of the Boy Scouts, he rose to statewide prominence, then went to a national conference, where he defended integration at a time when the South was still fighting civil rights, and also had his picture taken standing next to President John. F. Kennedy. A star in high school, he went to Georgetown University rather than attend the University of Arkansas and was elected class president. After working in the office of Senator J. William Fulbright, the superachiever became a Rhodes Scholar and journeyed to Oxford University in England, where he struggled with what to do about the draft and his opposition to the Vietnam War. In a classic demonstration of manipulation as well honest self-disclosure, Clinton told the commander of the ROTC program in Arkansas (where he had signed up to avoid the draft) that he really was against the war but now felt—in good conscience—that he had to make himself available to the draft lest he harm his future political career by appearing to have tried to escape it. With a new lottery system just in effect, he drew a low number and managed to avoid army service anyway, so now he returned to Yale, where he attended Yale Law School, met Hillary Rodham, a classmate, and prepared to enter Arkansas politics, where, at the age of thirty-two, he was elected governor of the state.

The other side of Clinton's parallel lives concerned his "secrets," rooted in his stepfather's alcoholism and abuse but extending also to other, less attractive sides of his personality. A magnetic presence with friends of both sexes, Clinton attracted a following of young women, many of whom he courted but none of whom he told the truth about his early life. Nor did he acknowledge his tendency to see more than one woman at a time, even when he was theoretically in a committed relationship. Thus, when Hillary Rodham came to Arkansas during Clinton's first state campaign, thinking she was entering a permanent romantic relationship after a brilliant law career and a summer in Washington working on John Doar's Watergate committee, she found that Clinton's aides were ushering one girlfriend out of the back door while she came in the front. After marrying Hillary and throughout his governorship, Clinton engaged in multiple affairs, seemingly guilty of what he once described as an "addiction to sex," all the while protesting his devotion to family and his love for Hillary and their daughter, Chelsea.

The two lives converged during the 1992 presidential campaign when Clinton, enormously popular on the stump and waging a brilliant campaign as a moderate concerned with the real issues in people's lives—"It's The Economy, Stupid" was the sign in his campaign headquarters—suddenly faced a charge by Gennifer Flowers that for twelve years Clinton had been carrying on a love affair with her. Struck in his most vulnerable spot, Clinton—and Hillary—responded by going on the CBS show *60 Minutes* and baring their souls. Yes, they had experienced serious marital problems, but so had most Americans and now they had worked them out. "Listen to what I've said," Clinton told the huge audience. "I've acknowledged causing pain in my marriage. I have said things to you tonight...that no American politician ever has [said]. I think most Americans...[will] know what we're saying. They'll get it, and they'll feel that we have been more than candid."

It worked. Overnight, the polls started to change. The "comeback kid" had done it again. Recovering momentum, Clinton went on to win the Democratic nomination, giving a starry-eyed acceptance speech about his journey from being born in a town called "Hope" to running for the presidency of the United States. Then, in a campaign distorted by the third-party candidacy of Ross Perot—a maverick who seized on the discontent of millions of Americans fed up with jobs going south to Mexico and a sense that their country had lost its sense of purpose—Clinton went to the heart of Bush's weakness, attacking him for his lack of vision, his indifference to the suffering of the American people in an economy gone awry, and his failure to have a plan to deal with America's growing crisis in health care and the demoralization of the middle class. As one national magazine noted, this was a victory for youth, energy, and purpose. "What excites most people about Clinton is precisely the degree to which he speaks to their hunger for meaning and purpose, their half-conscious and often inchoate desire to transcend the selfishness and meaninglessness of a materialistic and narcissistic society." Clinton, another writer said, was "our generation's second chance." And Clinton agreed. "Today," he said in his inaugural address, "we celebrate the mystery of American renewal.... This is our time. Let us embrace it."

III. THE CLINTON YEARS—THE FIRST ADMINISTRATION

In the weeks before his inauguration, Clinton displayed the brilliance that so many policy "wonks" craved and had counted on. Convening streams of experts in Little Rock, he showed his intellectual mastery of the political landscape, bantering with environmentalists about global warming, with civil rights advocates about how best to promote equality, with educators about the critical importance of "emotional intelligence" and early childhood training. Nowhere were his skills better displayed than in the economic summit he chaired. CEOs, economists from the biggest banks and universities— all were bowled over by Clinton's command of complex economic models, his ability to master both fiscal and monetary issues, and his understanding of the relationship between deficit reduction and investor confidence. It all seemed a blur to the American people, but as Clinton prepared to move to Washington, in a populist bus tour that dramatically symbolized his ascendancy to the presidency, the mood was buoyant with expectations of a new dynamism in government. "Let us resolve to make our government a place for what Franklin Roosevelt called 'bold, persistent experimentation'," he told his inaugural audience, "a government of our tomorrows, not our yesterdays."

Yet for someone seemingly so well prepared—he had, after all, been governor of Arkansas for twelve years—Clinton entered the White House in an atmosphere more characterized by chaos than by clarity or discipline. When he had first become governor, Clinton could not figure out how to organize his staff or prioritize his objectives, with the result that he appeared confused and purposeless and lost his first reelection bid. Now he repeated all those errors, as though he had learned nothing. Instead of a chief of staff like James Baker or Sherman Adams, everything in the Clinton White House had to be cleared by three people—a virtual troika—with no decision implemented until Al Gore, Hillary Clinton, and the president all had signed off on it. Aides who had served well in Arkansas were bewildered by the intricacy and sophistication of Washington's atmosphere.

In the campaign, everyone had understood the importance of focus—"It's the economy, stupid!" But now, energies were fragmented and no one seemed in charge of prioritizing objectives. In a classic example of deflecting attention from national health insurance—the goal everyone expected Clinton to zero in on—Clinton allowed his presidency to be defined in the first weeks by his call for an end to discrimination against gays in the military. Not only had he not done his homework—General Colin Powell, chair of the Joint Chiefs of Staff, opposed the policy as did Senator Sam Nunn, chair of the Senate Armed Services Committee—but in addition, he allowed his presidency to be identified with an issue that polarized the populace rather than one that brought people together in a forward-looking coalition for change. It was a self-inflicted wound, soon followed by many others. Clinton's first two nominees for attorney general—both women—were forced to withdraw their candidacies because they had broken IRS and immigration laws in their hiring of household help. His third choice, Janet Reno, signed off on a raid by federal officials on a religious renegade fortress led by David Koresh in Waco, Texas, that led to the deaths of seventy people, including twenty-one children. The White House looked like a sailboat buffeted by crosswinds with no one at the helm. It was an "amateur presidency," political reporter Joe Klein observed, plagued by indecisiveness and the air of being lost.

Clinton finally found his sea legs when he began to zero in on the issue of deficit reduction. The president had been convinced that bringing the budget under control was pivotal to long-term economic growth. As a result, in one of his first assertions of bold leadership, he gave up the middle-class tax cut he had promised during the campaign and instead developed proposals that would raise taxes on the rich, limit domestic expenditures, and reduce the deficit by half. With no Republican support and in the face of several Democratic defections, Clinton nevertheless stuck to his guns and by a margin of one vote succeeded in getting his legislation approved. Whether by serendipity or as an act of economic genius, the deficit reduction package turned out to be one of the most important achievements of the Clinton years. It inaugurated the longest economic boom of the twentieth century, provided aid to the poor through an Earned Income Tax Credit, helped create conditions that caused investors to flood the market—raising the Dow Jones from under 3,000 to more than 11,000—and together with technological wizardry, fueled the dot.com revolution of the 1990s. By the end of the decade, the deficit was not only under control. The government had started to run surpluses of $200–$300 billion per year.

Yet from day one of the Clinton presidency, everyone understood that his success or failure would be determined ultimately by the fate of his proposal to guarantee health insurance to every American citizen. It had been the central initiative proposed by his campaign. Health care costs were skyrocketing, eating up 14–15 percent of the gross national product (double that of any other industrialized nation), growing at two to three times the rate of inflation, threatening to bankrupt if not destroy the nearly forty million Americans who had no coverage whatsoever. Virtually every European industrial democracy had enacted national health care at a cost less than half of that being paid in the United States. Prior to 1990, any effort to create a similar entitlement in the United States had fallen victim to the politics of anticommunism. Harry Truman's plea for national health care in 1947 had been shot down by Republicans insisting that it amounted to "socialized medicine" and would lead America down the path of Communist infiltration and victory. But now the Cold War was over. Health care had come back as a viable political issue. Harris Wofford had made it the basis for his successful race for the Senate from Pennsylvania in 1990, and now Bill Clinton hoped to make it the cornerstone of his presidency, an even larger contribution to his political legacy than Social Security had turned out to be for Franklin Roosevelt a half century earlier. A majority of the American people supported the idea. Now Clinton simply had to close the deal.

But as in everything political, the devil was in the details, and once more, Bill Clinton became a victim of his own past practices. Clinton's first error was to place his wife Hillary in charge of health care. As governor of Arkansas, he had defined education reform as his top priority and to achieve his objectives had appointed Hillary to chair a task force of experts to come forward with recommendations. He reasoned then that she was the most talented person in the state to master such a critically important initiative. Now, using almost the same words he used then, he asked her to take command of a national task force on health care because "she cared enough about it, had enough talent, and had enough understanding that if anybody had a chance to do it, she had the best chance." Appointing his old Rhodes Scholar classmate Ira Magaziner as her chief of staff—the ultimate "policy wonk," one reporter described him—Clinton expected the task force to cover all the complex issues and come forward with specific, detailed responses. They did so, recruiting more than six hundred experts in thirty-four different areas, with days of meetings around the country. Yet all the deliberations were secret, and public input was limited. Clinton became hostage to the process he had established. He was so close to his wife that he was immediately identified with whatever she proposed, unable to distance himself from her or take an alternative position. She, in turn, went into the process with a reputation for holding strong opinions and dismissing dissenting views. Thus the process itself—secret, complicated, unfolding over months of time, and headed by someone too close to the president—contained the seeds of disaster.

Most important, the process involved no consultation with those who would eventually have to enact the legislation. The chairs of the House and Senate committees that would hold hearings on health care and make recommendations to Congress were excluded from task force deliberations. Instead of debating a general policy and massaging the details in the age-old process by which lawmakers shape specific legislation, the Clinton approach envisioned a complete package written by "experts" and without congressional give-and-take. Even cabinet members with intimate knowledge of the issue were left out—Donna Shalala, secretary of health and human service, or former senator Lloyd Bentsen, now secretary of the treasury, who had vast experience handling related legislation. In this instance, Clinton discarded all his political instincts and acted in the stewardship mold of Jimmy Carter, telling Congress what to do as if he and he alone knew the wisest course to follow. Not surprisingly, when Congress finally received the 1,350-page bill produced by Hillary Clinton's task force, the response was less than exultant. One Republican denounced it as "incredibly bloated, complex, unresponsible [and] incomprehensible," while even the theoretically friendly American Association of Retired People complained about its "complexity." "If you're explaining it," one lobbyist said, "people's eyes glaze over."

Compounding the difficulties posed by each of these issues was the degree to which Bill and Hillary Clinton had become the focal point for conservative animus. In the best of worlds, the approach of using a secret task force on health care and not consulting congressional leaders might have spelled disaster. But these ventures were associated with a First Lady perceived by many right-wingers as a radical feminist who was brazenly seeking power in her own right, married to a president who seemed oblivious to breaking the rules of both personal morality and official propriety. The First Lady's feistiness as well as her well-known impatience with opinions contrary to her own helped fuel a conservative caricature of her as a power-hungry, arrogant woman—whom talk-radio celebrity Rush Limbaugh loved to depict as a "feminazi." Meanwhile, her husband, Bill, attracted the sobriquet "slick Willy" because of the ease with which he apparently circumvented difficult moral and political dilemmas.

It was the degree to which the Clintons came personally to symbolize all the satanic attributes conservatives hated that eventually helped doom prospects for health care reform. For a period, prospects for success brightened. Clinton made a powerful speech to Congress and the nation in September 1993 about the urgent need for health care reform. Even one Republican senator called it "comprehensive [and] brilliantly presented," while public approval of the speech was 2–1. But there was no follow-up. It took another two months for Hillary's task force to send to Congress its 1,350-page bill. In the interim, other issues took center stage—NAFTA (the agreement to reduce tariffs across North America and propel free trade) and a disastrous encounter of American troops with insurgent rebels in Mogadishu, Somalia, where eighteen Americans were killed, including one who was dragged through the streets by his murderers. As momentum on behalf of health care diminished, enemies of the Clintons generated enormous public controversy over their participation in Whitewater, a real estate scheme in Arkansas that they had invested in, where critics claimed the Clintons had used inappropriate influence to protect their investment. In the meantime, Republicans brilliantly orchestrated a media campaign that depicted the Clinton health care proposal as a monstrosity that was not only incomprehensible but also would allow the government to choose a citizen's personal physician and dictate a treatment plan. "There must be a better way," exclaimed Harry and Louise in a series of TV ads as they sat around a kitchen table bemoaning how big government was taking over their personal lives.

The "perfect storm" came to a conclusion in the spring of 1994, with the Clintons at the center of the political hurricane. Although Hillary Clinton proved an effective witness before congressional committees, her bill was attacked as too cumbersome, unwieldy, and expensive. In the meantime, scandals involving the Clintons seemed to crop up like spring flowers. Former Arkansas state troopers were quoted as saying they had been used to procure women for Clinton while he was governor, and one former state employee, Paula Jones, went public with a claim that Clinton had tried to seduce her. Between the Paula Jones exposé and Whitewater, news coverage of the Clintons' personal problems dwarfed media attention to health care or other Clinton initiatives. Then presidential counselor Vincent Foster— longtime law partner and close friend of both Hillary and Bill—took his own life, protesting in a suicide note that "getting people" had become a sport in the nation's capital. It was overwhelming. Rush Limbaugh insisted that Vince Foster had been murdered in a Clinton plot while telling his audiences that "Whitewater is about health care." Bumper stickers on automobiles asked, "Where is Lee Harvey Oswald now that we need him?" Everything became conflated—politics, personality, suicide, sexual promiscuity, feminism, health care—and it all spelled doom for Clinton's most prized domestic initiative.

Clinton's inability to integrate the "parallel lives" he had lived for so long played a critical role in the ensuing debacle. The president and First Lady had always fought with each other. Frequently, their spats occurred in the presence of staff. Each was a powerful personality, and they seemed to thrive on engaging in contentious debate—except when Bill Clinton was accused of sexual infidelity. Then he became submissive, deferential, even obsequious, trying to get back into his wife's good graces.

In two critical moments, the Paula Jones story helped shape the fate of the Clinton presidency. The first came when the *Washington Post* requested access to the full White House records on Whitewater. Led by David Gergen, most presidential aides favored releasing the documents to the *Post*, reasoning that if the Clintons had done nothing wrong, the *Post*'s examination of the record would exonerate them. Bill Clinton agreed, but he said that his wife must sign off on releasing the material. She refused to do so, arguing that from a litigator's point of view, one never gave away evidence to a potential enemy.

She would not even meet with Gergen to hear his arguments. Instead, a letter went to the *Post* denying the request. If the documents had been released, Clinton would never have had to agree to the appointment of a special prosecutor on Whitewater—which he did later that year—and there never would have been an impeachment. But when the request came—at the time of the Paula Jones headlines—he was in no position to stand up to his wife and overrule her.

The second critical moment came when moderate Republicans and Democrats in the Senate proposed a partial compromise on health care. By the spring, it was clear that the Clinton plan as drawn up by the task force would never secure a majority in either the House or Senate. But people like Lincoln Chaffee, John Breaux, and Daniel Patrick Moynihan were prepared to go part of the way—pass a bill that would be "half a loaf" and represent at least a start to health care reform. Once again, the president was willing to accept compromise. Hillary Clinton was not. Hence, the last chance Clinton had to become the FDR of his generation was allowed to pass. As David Gergen later wrote, "He was in no mood—and no position—to challenge her on anything....Might Clinton have passed a bipartisan [health care] reform if the shadow of the past had not hung over his relationship with his wife?" To Gergen the answer seemed clear. Thus in two pivotal instances, the dynamics of Clinton's personal history—and in particular his relationship with his wife—shaped the fate of his presidency. It would not be the last time.

During Clinton's first two years in office there had been moments of triumph. NAFTA had passed, largely due to Clinton's leadership. A pathbreaking deficit-reduction bill was enacted, laying the foundation for a decade of prosperity. Clinton created a national service program (Americorps), succeeded in getting the Brady bill passed (named after Reagan Press Secretary James Brady, who had been critically wounded in the Reagan assassination attempt), which for the first time imposed controls on the sale of handguns, and Congress enacted an expanded voter registration bill. Yet all of that faded in the face of Whitewater, Paula Jones, the "Harry and Louise" ads, and the demise of health care reform. Bill Clinton was on the ropes; moreover, he had helped provide Republicans with the boxing gloves they used to pummel him.

IV. THE REPUBLICAN ASCENDANCY

And pummel him they did. Newt Gingrich, the Republican minority leader, understood that a Clinton victory on health care would solidify voters' ties to Democrats for a generation. For that reason, he called it the Democrats' "Stalingrad, their Gettysburg, their Waterloo." Also for that reason, he refused to give an inch, defying at every turn efforts to forge a bipartisan coalition. Gingrich attacked Clinton with the ferocity of a hungry tiger, always coming down on the side of polarization rather than compromise and recognizing that the best way to regain power was to magnify the differences between the parties. Using health care as his wedge, Gingrich caricatured Clinton as the Genghis Khan of big government, committed to taking over the private lives and liberties of the American people.

Instead, Gingrich proposed his own "Contract with America"—a ten-point platform that would slash taxes, dismantle the welfare state, cut the size of government, and end welfare as the nation had known it. Leading the equivalent of a religious crusade, Gingrich and his conservative backers lambasted the Democrats with a vigor and freshness that had not been seen in more than a decade. And the voters responded. Although only 38 percent of the electorate went to the polls, the Democrats were decimated. The day before the election, Democrats ruled the House 258–176 and the Senate 57–43. Unimaginably—and in the biggest voter turnaround in an off-year election since 1946—the Republicans won 54 seats in the House and 9 in the Senate. Now they were in control. "The New Deal era is over....The nails are in the coffin," one Democratic leader said. Another echoed him. "The president is done," he said. "He's finished. He's like that old...cartoon where the guy has just had his head sliced off in a fencing match. He just hasn't noticed it yet, but as soon as he tries to turn or stand up, his head's going to topple right off his neck."

But it was one thing to crow about a humiliating defeat for Bill Clinton and another to bring a new regime to successful fruition in Washington. Clinton was depressed, felt repudiated, and initially at least, acted helpless. But this was the "comeback kid," the same person who roared back to the State House in Little Rock after being defeated in his first reelection bid for governor and who recovered from a plunge into the single digits in New Hampshire after the Gennifer Flowers affair to finish a respectable second in the presidential primary there. Now, as he watched the Republicans enact, with iron discipline, one after another of their Contract with America proposals, Clinton started to piece together his counterattack. First, it became clear that however drastically the Republicans wished to cut back government, the American people were not ready to see programs that they had come to depend on simply vanish into thin air. "Do the designers of the post-government age know what they're doing?" *New York Times* humorist Russell Baker asked. "In a matter of days they have been dismantling...structures that took years to put up....Who really has the vaguest idea what the results will be?" Clinton seized the opportunity to play on that fear, and within nine months after the new Congress took office, 58 percent of the American people expressed disapproval of the job it was doing.

Second, Clinton embarked on his own recovery plan, using carefully refined polls conducted by Dick Morris, a shrewd politico, to define reforms, small and large, that would appeal to specific segments of the American electorate. Launching his new initiatives, Clinton declared in the spring of 1995 that "we need a dynamic center," one that would focus on a "middle-class bill of rights." Among his proposals were selective tax cuts aimed at the middle class, an education credit targeted for younger people going to college,

After Bill Clinton failed to secure passage of national health care in 1993, the Republican Party won a decisive victory in the 1994 congressional elections. Their triumph was based upon the Republican Party's proposed "Contract with America," designed to reduce the role of the federal government. Gingrich was elected Speaker of the House.

Credit: © Wally McNamee/CORBIS

and support for stronger measures to combat crime and welfare. On each of these issues, Clinton effectively preempted Republican positions, depriving his foes of issues they otherwise might have used to attack him while making himself the hero of middle America. Thus he lobbied Congress to put one hundred thousand new police on the streets, supported giving three-time felons life sentences, and embraced a plan to limit welfare recipients to two years of public relief while supporting a jobs program to slash welfare rolls. Throughout, he sought to place himself above the polarizing politics of Republicans. Americans should move to a "leaner" government, he said, but not a "meaner" one. On affirmative action, he declared, "Let's mend it, not end it."

In the meantime, Republicans walked into the trap Clinton was setting. In a classic faux pas, House Speaker Newt Gingrich proposed cutting Medicare by nearly three hundred billion dollars over five years—an assault on the most cherished entitlement program in the country. To make matters worse, at the same time the Republicans proposed a tax cut for the wealthiest Americans that would put in the pockets of the rich almost exactly what they proposed to cut from Medicare. Gingrich even uttered the politically explosive prediction that Medicare would eventually "wither on the vine," thereby appearing to confirm Clinton's claim that the Republicans were out to dismantle the New Deal. By contrast, the "dynamic center" that Clinton had carved out for himself seemed a moderate's dream. In effect, Clinton had painted the Republicans into their own extremist corner, with the tables now turned and the same "Harry and Louise" line—"Isn't there a better way"— that had been invoked to kill Clinton's health care reform package now being used to decimate the Republican Contract with America.

Central to this entire recovery was Clinton's role as national healer—and leader. When terrorists bombed the federal office building in Oklahoma City in the spring of 1995, Clinton was on the scene immediately to offer solace and inspiration. A truck full of explosives had detonated in the garage of the building, destroying a child-care center and shattering federal offices. Nearly one hundred people were killed, many of them children. Americans had experienced a harbinger of this attack when Islamic revolutionaries set off a bomb at the World Trade Center in 1993, killing six and injuring one thousand. This time, the terrorists were domestic right-wingers seeking to avenge the attack on David Koresh and his Branch Davidians a year earlier. But the horror was no less. Responding immediately, Clinton flew to the city, spoke to the families of victims, and ministered to grieving parents. His instincts were exactly right. He said the right things, did the right things, and provided the balm—and strength—people looked to in a national leader. After months of being attacked as "slick Willy," consumed by partisan ambitions, and subject to a humiliating defeat in 2004, Bill Clinton now once again resumed his role as leader of all the people.

Using Oklahoma City as a vehicle for reasserting an image of national strength and the programs of the "dynamic center" as his political message, Bill Clinton had proven once again that he was the "comeback kid." No longer were Democrats convinced that New Deal liberalism had been "dead and buried." Instead, Clinton was forging a coalition intent on reclaiming the political momentum that had propelled him into power in 1992. It might not produce a system of national health insurance, but there appeared at least the possibility that Clinton could become one of the most successful presidents of the late twentieth century.

V. FROM TRIUMPH TO IMPEACHMENT: CLINTON'S SECOND TERM

The election of 1996 appeared to signal the completion of Clinton's redemption. Brilliant in his political instincts, sure-footed in his handling of policy issues, Clinton entered the race blessed with myriad "pluses." Although Senator Robert Dole, his Republican foe, was widely respected, he lacked dynamism, charisma, and an enthusiastic base. The New Right—especially evangelical fundamentalists—distrusted Dole's commitment on issues like abortion and gay rights. Clinton, meanwhile, continued to preempt Republican issues. "The era of big government is over," he had declared in his 1996 State of the Union address. By his support of welfare reform, his dedication to deficit reduction, a tough anticrime program, and a family leave act, he seemed to embody mainstream positions that Republicans once called their own. Although Republicans retained control of the House and Senate, Clinton had done something that Republicans had long feared: he reclaimed the loyalty of those "Reagan Democrats" who had moved into the Republican camp in 1980. Catholics came back. So too did labor and more and more of those in the affluent suburbs. And women voted for Clinton over Dole by 59 to 35 percent. The future looked rosy.

Yet within two years, Clinton's bubble had burst. It was almost as if every time Clinton stood on the brink of fulfilling his potential, something inside of him acted to block the final step. As had happened so often in the past, it was Clinton's "parallel lives" that got him in trouble. Even in the White House, surrounded by staff, Secret Service, and 24/7 surveillance, Bill Clinton could not discipline his sexual appetites. In his autobiography, he would subsequently speculate that "everyone" had addictions. Clearly, for Bill Clinton, the addiction was young women.

It had all started before the reelection campaign when, in a tense fight with Republicans over appropriations, the government "shut down" pending a continuing resolution by Congress to keep federal offices open. White House staffers worked around the clock, and one of the interns, Monica Lewinsky, brought pizza to the president. Long infatuated with Clinton, she succeeded in seducing him in a small room next to the Oval Office. Although the two never engaged in sexual intercourse, repeated instances of oral sex occurred, one of them resulting in a semen stain on Lewinsky's blue dress. The affair went on for more than a year. Eventually, staffers who feared what might be going on succeeded in getting Lewinsky reassigned, and Clinton broke off the relationship. But phone calls continued, as did the exchange of gifts.

More important, Lewinsky started to talk, telling a woman who became her confidante about her secret relationship with Bill Clinton. Linda Tripp, a former White House staffer herself, was a Republican who detested the president. Unbeknownst to Lewinsky, Tripp secretly tape-recorded their conversations. She then shared these with Kenneth Starr, the special prosecutor who had been appointed to investigate Whitewater. Starr—himself a consultant to Paula Jones's legal team before he became special prosecutor—immediately secured authorization to include the Lewinsky matter within his purview. The president of the United States had testified under oath in the Paula Jones lawsuit that he had never had sex with a woman named Monica Lewinsky. He had lied. Perjury was a felony. Having found nothing else that would provide grounds for indicting Bill Clinton, Starr now believed he had discovered evidence that could lead to impeachment.

In January 1998, the world learned of the Lewinsky allegations. Just one year after he had been sworn in for his second term, Bill Clinton started the fight of his life, this time not for health care but for the survival of his presidency. Had Clinton confessed his guilt, pleaded for forgiveness, and acknowledged his sinfulness, he might have recovered quickly. Most Americans loved him. They believed in him. They would have responded to his human weakness. But instead Clinton stonewalled. Rather than accept responsibility for the affair, he took the opposite tack. "There *is* no sexual relationship," he declared to a national audience. "I never had sex with *that* woman." To everyone, including Hillary and his daughter, Chelsea, Clinton proclaimed his innocence, digging himself deeper and deeper. Hillary went on national television to declare that the whole scandal was a "right-wing conspiracy"

President Bill Clinton was known for his womanizing prior to entering the White House. Once there, he had an eleven-month affair with a White House intern named Monica Lewinsky, which started when she brought him a pizza one night in the midst of a budget stantoff with Congress. Clinton denied the affair under oath and here does the same to the general public. Eventually, the House impeached him for committing perjury, though he was acquitted by the Senate.

Credit: Associated Press

and identified totally with her husband. She was correct. There was, and had been, a conspiracy of right-wing foundations to smear Clinton with any and every innuendo imaginable. But Clinton was guilty of the specific charge, and the truth would eventually come out. DNA tests on the dress, the tape recordings of Lewinsky and Tripp, all of it multiplied until in the summer of 1998, Clinton was forced to tell a federal grand jury, and the nation, that "I did have a relationship with Ms. Lewinsky that was not appropriate." Even then, a contrite president might have won the hearts of many. But instead, Clinton truculently denounced the special prosecutor, placed the blame on others, and seemed intent on not acknowledging his "parallel lives."

Eventually, impeachment proceedings were launched. The Republican Congress displayed a mania to "get" Clinton. Most of the rest of the world could not believe an entire presidency could be endangered by what, to their eyes, seemed a sexual peccadillo. But the killer instinct had been let loose, and by a strictly partisan vote, Congress voted articles of impeachment against Clinton in the late fall of 1998. Conviction of the president—and his removal from office—required a two-thirds vote of the United States Senate. A different body from the House, there never was a possibility that two-thirds of the senators would agree that Clinton's misbehavior amounted to the "high crimes and misdemeanors" described in the Constitution as the basis for removing a president from office. In the end, the Senate acquitted Clinton, and for the last twenty months of his presidency, Clinton was once more a "free" man. But only in the narrowest, most technical sense. Bill Clinton had disgraced his office, had committed perjury, and had betrayed all those closest to him, no one more than his wife and daughter.

The tragedy, of course, was that so much more might have been possible. Clinton had helped spark unprecedented prosperity in America. His economic policies led not only to elimination of the deficit, but also the beginning of a long-projected series of surpluses. Murder and crime rates plummeted. Eventually, Clinton signed—and took credit for—a welfare reform act that succeeded in reducing dramatically the number of people on the welfare rolls, although some saw the bill as a cruel evisceration of fundamental relief measures for mothers of dependent children. From the Family and Medical Leave Act to the Brady bill outlawing the easy availability of assault weapons, Clinton could claim significant progress. And in foreign affairs he finally found his footing. Under his leadership—and with the superb mediation skills of former senator George Mitchell—he helped restore peace to Northern Ireland. Clinton achieved a temporary halt in North Korean nuclear aspirations, belatedly (but crucially) found the courage to stop Serbian genocide in Kosovo, and with energies far surpassing those of any predecessor came within an inch of forging peace in the Middle East between Palestine and Israel through his ceaseless intervention. It was a record that suggested how much more might have been accomplished had Clinton not engaged in such self-destructive behavior. Yet in the end, he failed woefully to integrate his parallel lives with the result that the bright sun of his extraordinary talent could never escape the shadow of his personal weaknesses.

VI. THE RISE OF TERRORISM

To the detriment of the country, Clinton was devoting all his energies to the desperate attempt to salvage his presidency at the very time when his leadership skills were most needed to address a new threat that soon would preoccupy both America and the world at large. For more than a decade, American intelligence leaders and a variety of intellectuals had pondered the growing ascendancy of Islamic fundamentalism in the Arab world. The core of the jihadist movement emerged among middle- and upper-class Muslims distraught at the rapidly expanding cultural hegemony of American values, with their focus on consumerism and sensuality. Osama Bin Laden, child of a billionaire Saudi construction executive, typified the growing rebellion. Intent on preserving the purity of Muslim religious traditions and the sanctity of Islamic culture, Bin Laden and his allies saw the contemporary world almost as a reenactment of the Crusades, where Christian hordes from the West threatened to annihilate everything good about Islamic civilization. When Iraq invaded Kuwait in 1991, Bin Laden—who had been deeply involved in the insurgent movement to liberate Afghanistan from Soviet occupation in the 1980s—volunteered to lead an Islamic force to liberate Kuwait. Instead, the Saudi royal family turned to America, provided permanent bases in the Middle East for American forces, and in Bin Laden's eyes, sacrificed the purity of Islamic culture to the voracious appetite of Western capitalism and military aggression. In response, Bin Laden rallied thousands of followers to his Al Qaeda movement, dedicated to expelling the poison of alien armies and values.

American intelligence services soon realized the power and pervasiveness of Bin Laden's movement. Some American intellectuals hypothesized that a "clash of civilizations" was about to consume the world, a confrontation fully as dangerous as that precipitated by Nazism in the 1930s and potentially more far-reaching because of its religious implications. Samuel Huntington predicted the equivalent of a worldwide tsunami of sectarian violence, with those supporting Western, capitalist, and Judeo-Christian values on the one side and Islamic jihadists dedicated to preserving strict Muslim values on the other. As Huntington saw it—with many intelligence officials agreeing with him—the results would determine the fate of civilization in the coming millennium.

The bomb attack on the World Trade Center in February 1993 represented the first tangible evidence of terrorist aspirations. An Islamic religious leader based in New Jersey was later convicted of having plotted the attack, which killed six and injured one thousand. The Oklahoma City explosion occurred a year later and initially was attributed to foreign agents until Timothy McVeigh was arrested. A bomb at the Atlanta Summer Olympics of 1996 also turned out to be the work of a domestic terrorist, like McVeigh angry at governmental support of abortion and suppression of evangelical dogmatists. But then in 1998 Al Qaeda reared its head again, blowing up the U.S. embassies in Tanzania and Kenya in nearly simultaneous explosions that killed hundreds of Africans. The final blow of the Clinton years occurred when a gunboat loaded with explosives and piloted by Al Qaeda insurgents rammed the USS *Cole* in a Yemen harbor, killing scores and blowing a huge hole in the side of the ship. By that time, American intelligence agencies had concluded that Al Qaeda represented the nation's number-one enemy. Former senators Gary Hart and Warren Rudman, as well as Secretary of Defense William Cohen, publicly warned that the United States would suffer direct and substantial attacks in the imminent future from Al Qaeda forces.

Clinton viewed the threat as grave and immediate. He signed a presidential directive authorizing the assassination of Osama Bin Laden, launched a missile attack on Bin Laden's headquarters in the hills of Afghanistan that evidently struck only an hour after Bin Laden had left the location, and ordered other military attacks on suspected terrorist armories. Yet Clinton was so immersed in trying to survive the scandals surrounding him that his Republican opponents accused him of simply using such attacks to deflect attention from his own troubles. Others subsequently wondered whether the degree to which Clinton was distracted prevented him from zeroing in on the terrorist threat as much as he might have. In truth, the degree to which Clinton had always compartmentalized his life made those allegations less than convincing. The degree to which he exhausted himself trying to wring a peace settlement in the Middle East out of the Palestinians and Israelis testified to his ability to focus on issues he cared about. Whatever the final verdict, it seemed clear that the aftermath of victory in the Cold War was not necessarily a safer or more stable world. Just the opposite. It now seemed that the world faced an unseen enemy, unidentified with any particular sovereign nation, that threatened to wreak havoc on the globe for generations to come.

VII. AMERICAN SOCIETY AND CULTURE

If instability characterized both domestic politics and the world at large, the state of American society and culture suggested a degree of fragmentation, tension, and volatility that in some ways even exceeded the polarized conflicts of the 1960s. A wave of immigration threatened the old WASP-dominated social order. Race once again showed itself to be the underlying issue of division within the country. The bifurcation of the rich and the poor accelerated day by day, with fewer and fewer people able to imagine a path out of poverty into the middle class. Family life underwent profound transformations, literally reversing some of the entrenched patterns of just forty years earlier. And the culture/religious wars inside the United States between the New Right on the one hand and secular humanists on the other at times seemed as intense as the "clash of civilizations" that Samuel Huntington talked about between Islam and Christianity.

The addition of more than one million immigrants a year to the United States during the 1990s represented a dramatic break with the past. All during the 1930s, 1940s, and 1950s, less than one-tenth that number had entered the country each year. Then the numbers started to skyrocket—to 4.5 million per decade in the 1970s, then 7.3 million in the 1980s. Now, just two decades after the 1970s, the figures had more than doubled, and that did not count the 350,000 newcomers each year who were illegal and undocumented. Most of these new immigrants were Hispanic or Asian. Hispanic immigration alone grew more than 300 percent between 1970 and 2000, accounting for one-third of the populations of Los Angeles and Miami. In New York City, officials estimated that 4 out of 10 children over the age of five did not speak English in their homes. Although "Anglos" were still in charge, it was clear that by 2050 the country would have a nonwhite majority—a prospect that appeared to terrify many. California approved Proposition 63 in 1986 mandating English as the official language of the state. More and more people wondered where people would derive a shared picture of their communal identity in the face of such heterogeneity. The "clash of civilizations" political scientist Samuel Huntington pointedly asked, "Will the new immigrants be assimilated into the hitherto European culture of the United States, and if they are not...will it survive as a liberal democracy?"

In the years after the civil rights movement, many white Americans concluded that race had ceased to be a major source of conflict in America. More than a third of African Americans had entered the middle class; education levels had increased; business, political, and entertainment leaders celebrated their commitment to racial diversity. Even Ronald Reagan, despite crude remarks about "welfare queens driving Cadillacs," denied he had a racist bone in his body and insisted that Martin Luther King, Jr.'s, dream of a society where people would be judged by the "content of their character rather than the color of their skin" had been achieved. But now that state of complacency was shattered, with two notorious California episodes highlighting the ongoing abrasive presence of racial division. Rodney King, a black motorist in California, was stopped for speeding by highway patrolmen. When he protested, he was thrown to the ground and stomped upon—repeatedly—by white police with their guns drawn. The episode might have been ignored except that an observer videotaped the entire scene. Yet when the police who had brutalized King were put on trial in Simi Valley, California, before an all-white jury, they were acquitted. To blacks in Los Angeles, it seemed all too similar to the behavior of white juries in the racist South when perpetrators of lynching were put on trial. This time, they rebelled with a race riot in South Central Los Angeles that dwarfed in size and damages even the Watts Riot of 1964.

The second episode was even more revealing. O. J. Simpson, the star football running back who had become a hero to millions during his college and national football league years and who had subsequently become a national sports broadcaster and the primary advertising voice of Hertz rental cars, was arrested for having brutally murdered his former wife and a male friend outside her apartment. Simpson's wife was beautiful and blonde. She had repeatedly complained to police that Simpson abused her. DNA evidence

Rodney King, a black man, was stopped by California police, all white, for a traffic violation. There ensued a brutal altercation where King was thrown to the ground and pummeled repeatedly. An observer videotaped the beating, which led to a trial where, despite the documentary footage, an all-white jury acquitted the officers. King's trial—and beating—suggested the degree to which race remained a pivotal element in American life. "Can't we just all get along?" King asked.

Credit: Associated Press

linked Simpson to the crime scene. The trial was broadcast on national TV, preoccupying millions. Los Angeles police had a well-deserved reputation for racism, and Simpson's lawyers alleged that they had planted evidence against their client. Significantly, more than three-fourths of all whites believed Simpson was guilty, whereas three-fourths of African Americans believed him to be innocent. Simpson's lawyer, Johnnie Cochran, brilliantly played on the racial sympathies of the predominantly black jury. After a year of testimony, and just three hours after getting the case, the jury returned a verdict of innocent. Once again, the racial divide was laid bare.

If race (and ethnicity) continued to be a fundamental axis of division in American society, class differences became an ever more glaring—and related—source of conflict. For all the advances that had come with the civil rights movement, the women's movement, and the war on poverty, poor people remained a seemingly intractable presence in the country, with their ability to escape the chains of poverty ever more compromised by structural changes in the economy and the persistence of prejudice based on race and sex. As more and more manufacturing jobs fled the country, it became increasingly difficult for aspiring victims of poverty, however keenly motivated, to get jobs that paid more than a minimum wage. Service industries generated most new employment; those unable to secure a high school or community college diploma had little chance for white-collar work; and to a degree more striking than ever before, the rich got richer and the poor poorer. More than a third of blacks lived in poverty, there were as many black males between eighteen and twenty-two years old in jail as in college, and those caught in the inner city saw little possibility of escape. At the same time, the richest 5 percent in America saw their share of the national wealth grow ever larger, CEOs of the nation's largest corporations went from earning forty-eight times as much as their lowest-paid workers to receiving one thousand times as much, and the middle class was ever more challenged to hold on to its role as the center of American community life.

At least in part, the issue of poverty related to dramatic changes occurring in the American family. By 2000, the number of female-headed households with children had dramatically increased to 22 percent of all families with children under eighteen. In the meantime, the number of families headed by intact married couples had fallen to 53 percent. Nearly one-quarter of all adults had never married. By the dawn of the new millennium, more than half of all children born in America had no father—they were born out of wedlock—while married couples rearing children now represented less than 25 percent of all households. Fifty years earlier, 70 percent of all households consisted of a father who worked and a mother who stayed at home to take care of children. Now that figure had fallen to less than 30 percent. Those who did marry wed at a later age, on average had two or fewer children, and bore them at a later age. The consequences of these changes for poverty were striking. A child born into a female-headed household, now a majority of the new born, had a 1 in 3 chance of being poor. Under such circumstances, it became increasingly difficult to speak of the "average" family or the "average" child—even to think in terms of a society that shared a common set of values, norms, and expectations. Fragmentation, not consensus, seemed the word of the day.

All these conflicts became crystallized in the 1990s version of the "culture wars." In some ways it was like the 1920s all over again when Prohibitionists,

Ku Klux Klanners, rural fundamentalists, and antievolutionists, on the one hand, and city dwellers, Catholics, immigrants, Jews, and flappers, on the other, fought over issues like teaching Darwin in the schools, having the freedom to buy a drink, and who would be allowed entry into the United States. Many of the issues were the same—the battle over teaching creationism, for example, the attempt to mandate English as a state language, the struggle between "pro-choice" and "pro-life" advocates and between those who wished to order prayer in the schools versus those who insisted on taking religion out of the classroom. Intellectuals joined the battle, their views reflected in the titles of their books: Robert Bork's *Modern Liberalism and American Decline*; James Davison Hunter's *The Culture Wars*; Allan Bloom's *The Closing of the American Mind*; Gertrude Himmelfarb's *One Nation: Two Cultures*. Community was breaking down, these authors declared. People were "bowling alone," to use one intellectual's metaphor, rather than having a sense of identity with a larger community. "[A] massive collapse...of almost all established values," Zbigniew Brzezinski wrote in 1993, threatened to undermine American civilization.

The religious battle between New Right evangelicals and "secular humanists" continued to provide the primary fuel for these culture wars. Pat Robertson's Christian Coalition claimed a membership of more than 150,000 and through its televangelism outreach came each day into the homes of 50 million Americans with a message preaching that supporters of abortion were murderers, that homosexuality was the devil's effort to corrupt the young, and that only the acceptance of fundamentalist notions of family and morality could save the nation. On the other side were gay rights advocates, feminists, supporters of multiculturalism, and critics of moral absolutism. The immensely popular Jerry Seinfeld show each week brought the acerbic humor of secular humanism to the nation's TV screens, making fun of all moral certitudes and devoting an entire episode to how long characters in the comedy could desist from masturbating. On the other side, meanwhile, Bill O'Reilly on TV and Rush Limbaugh on radio excoriated the shameful moral relativism of "liberals" who defended as basic American liberties the right of people to read pornographic magazines and enter into same-sex marriages. (It did not help the Right when a number of conservatives who denounced infidelity and homosexuality were themselves found to be gay or to have had adulterous affairs). Interestingly, Bill Clinton came to be the personal symbol of these cultural battles. Like a magnet, he attracted to himself all the volatility, emotional intensity, and love/hate responses that surrounded America's effort to define its sense of community in a time of unprecedented change.

Ironically, America in the 1990s encapsulated the Dickensian paradox: it enjoyed the best of times yet also experienced the worst of times. Unprecedented prosperity brought a standard of living to millions unheard of in prior generations. The stock market soared above eleven thousand; high-tech start-ups soon sold for billions of dollars; and for countless people, there seemed no limit to the potential for growth, happiness, and fulfillment. Yet for countless others, it was a time of coming apart. Life got worse, not better.

Jobs fled the country. Families seemed to be falling to pieces. Children grew up knowing only one parent. Worst of all, there seemed no common vision holding the country together, no glue that cemented people of different religious persuasions and cultural values. And in the middle of it all stood Bill Clinton, himself the embodiment of twoness—one of the brightest, most charismatic, most talented persons ever to occupy the Oval Office, yet simultaneously, a person possessed of demons that hurled him back into defeat at precisely the moments when he was ready to score his greatest victories.

VIII. CONCLUSION

It was somehow fitting that the years during which Bill Clinton was president were a time of such bifurcation, change, and conflict. Clinton could not choose between his parallel lives or integrate them into each other. He remained a creature of paradox, one of "the biggest, most talented, articulate, intelligent open [and] colorful characters ever to inhabit the [White House]," *New York Times* reporter Todd Purdum said, but also "an undisciplined, fumbling, obtuse, defensive [and] self-justifying rogue." The two sides of Clinton seemed so foreign and hostile to each other yet flowed from the same source. "In a real sense," Purdum said, "his strengths are his weaknesses, his enthusiasms are his undoing, and most of the traits that make him appealing can make him appalling in the flash of an eye." At his best, as in his speech to Congress on health care reform, or in his gentle, powerful leadership after the Oklahoma City bombing, Clinton showed the nation a vision of how it might come together and be a better place and promised to provide the leadership to take it there. But at his worst, he dashed those hopes, succumbed to his own baser instincts, and plunged into personal and political disaster. Perhaps David Gergen identified the problem most acutely. Clinton's Achilles' heel, he declared, was "the lack of an inner compass....He has 360 degree vision, but no true north."

There was a direct connection between Clinton, the man, and America, the country—between a president divided against himself and unable to discover the path of integration and a country torn between conflicting sets of values, struggling to find a common purpose, a bond that would tie together those of different backgrounds, beliefs, and aspirations into a community of mutual respect and caring. In some ways, Clinton's health care plan might have provided part of the answer. Had he been successful, health care for all Americans would have reinforced the idea of everyone enjoying similar rights and being part of the same society. A national health care system might have strengthened people's sense of connectedness to each other and to the government as their representative. Instead, the failure of Clinton's initiative rejuvenated the centrifugal forces at work in America. People divided into opposing factions behind slogans that caricatured each side. Values conflicts over religion, reproductive rights, sexuality, affirmative action, and the meaning of human freedom took on their own transcendent power, tearing apart a body politic that otherwise might have been able to rediscover a foundation of togetherness. These conflicts, in turn, seemed to reflect deeper structural flaws that drove people apart into richer and poorer, those with exciting, fulfilling positions and those consigned to service jobs with no future. Clinton tried, often with success, to preach his doctrine that Americans must celebrate their commitment to opportunity, responsibility, and community. But with the failure of his health care package and his continued proclivity to self-destructive behavior, his message failed to take root on a sustained, ongoing basis.

In the end, the 1990s represented a tragic lost opportunity to rediscover a sense of common purpose. Although full of exciting progress for some, it was a decade of disappointment and disillusionment for others. Once again the fate of politics and that of society were linked, symbiotically, and in a mutually reinforcing way. How to find that sense of shared community—and how to make it a reality—would be the challenge of the new century.

13

The End of the American Century?
The First Decade of the New Millennium

The day dawned bright and clear. From northern Maine to southern Virginia, the skies were a crystalline blue. The air carried a slight hint of fall. As people in Boston, New York, and Washington rose from their beds, they greeted a day that seemed almost conceived in perfection. It was September 11, 2001.

That morning, Mohammed Atta took a commuter plane from Portland, Maine, to Boston. He and his traveling companions barely made their connection to first-class seats on American Airlines Flight 11, nonstop from Boston to Los Angeles. Within minutes, fifteen other men boarded three other flights—United Airlines Flight 77 from Boston, American Airlines Flight 77 from Washington, and United Airlines Flight 93 from Newark. All four flights were airborne by shortly after 8:00 a.m.

Within less than two hours, each plane had been hijacked. Immediately, they became missiles of airborne terrorism. At 8:48 a.m. American Airlines 11 flew into the North Tower of the World Trade Center in New York City. At 9:03, United Airlines 75 slammed into the South Tower. Shortly thereafter, American Airlines 77 exploded into the Pentagon in northern Virginia. Only United Airlines 93 was still aloft. Flying over eastern Pennsylvania, it had turned back to Washington headed toward the White House when a band of passengers, having learned from their cell phones about the other attacks, heroically rushed the cockpit, overwhelmed the hijackers, and crashed their plane into a field just outside of Pittsburgh.

At 9:59—just fifty-six minutes after AA 11 slammed into its superstructure—the North Tower of the World Trade Center collapsed to the ground. Thirty minutes later, the South Tower did the same. The horror was unspeakable. Countless people leapt, hand in hand, from the upper stories of the Towers, preferring to die by falling to being burned to death by the flames engulfing their offices. "There were bodies, luggage, torsos [everywhere]," one survivor reported. Hundreds of firefighters died climbing the stairwells to rescue those still alive, unaware that their commanders had ordered them to evacuate because the Towers were crumbling. Miraculously, the vast majority of the people in the World Trade Center and in the Pentagon escaped alive. But nearly three thousand people died that day, and millions of people watched as, hour after hour, television rebroadcast pictures of the second plane crashing into the South Tower, people hurtling to their deaths, and the largest buildings in the world—the symbols of American wealth and power—dissolving into heaps of dust.

On September 11, 2001, four jetliners flying coast to coast were hijacked by Al Qaeda terrorists under the command of Osama Bin Laden. Two of them crashed into the Twin Towers of New York's World Trade Center. Within an hour, the Towers crumbled to the ground, with nearly three thousand people killed. This launched the beginning of America's war on terror.

Credit: © Matt McDermott/Corbis Sygma

It was a day that would transform the world and shape the history of at least a generation to come.

I. THE PRELUDE TO TERRORISM

On the face of it, the president who would face the crushing blow of 9/11 was supposed to have been Al Gore. Vice president during the eight years of Bill Clinton's presidency, Gore had been intimately involved with all policy matters, especially those relating to the environment and economy. No vice president before him had ever played such a critical role in the White House. Moreover, notwithstanding Clinton's sexual indiscretions, he retained enormous popularity among the American people. When he left office, Clinton had a 65 percent approval rating. Surely, the person who had been at his side during all the successes of the administration should have been expected to benefit from the popularity of the administration.

But as the six years preceding the election of 2000 (and the six years following) would show, nothing in politics is predictable. Gore entered the presidential race with a substantial lead in public opinion polls. Despite being a policy "wonk," he surely displayed the "gravitas" expected of a president and boasted twenty-two years of experience in shaping the politics of the nation, both as a member of Congress and as vice president. Having survived a brief but tough primary challenge from Senator Bill Bradley (a former Princeton and New York Knicks basketball star), Gore easily won the Democratic nomination and was expected to triumph in the general election.

His opponent was George W. Bush, governor of Texas and son of George H. W. Bush, the former president. A former oil executive and owner of the Texas Rangers baseball team, Bush had at best an uneven record. His business ventures largely failed, and although his governorship was marked by charm and effective coalition-building with Texas Democrats, he had no foreign policy experience (he had been abroad only twice). He had vetoed a patient's bill of rights law and boasted no outstanding legislative achievements. Bush's major opponent in the primaries was John McCain, the former prisoner of war in Vietnam whose courage and independence won him the enthusiastic support of New Hampshire's voters in the first primary. But McCain then floundered, largely due to a vicious campaign of rumors emanating from a skilled Bush political team led by strategist Karl Rove. As a result, Bush soon surged ahead to win the nomination. Still, it looked like a contest where all the advantages were on the side of Vice President Gore.

Except. The first problem Gore faced was his own (and his wife's) ambivalence about Bill Clinton. Surely one tack Gore could have taken would be to identify his campaign as the best means to continue Bill Clinton's legacy. Yet Gore felt personally betrayed by Clinton. Repeatedly, he had stood solidly behind the president, imploring people to believe Clinton's denial that he had engaged in a sexual relationship with Monica Lewinsky. Clinton's belated confession of infidelity left Gore dismayed and angry. But his reaction was nothing compared with that of his wife, Tipper. Deeply religious and known for her commitment to conveying messages of moral integrity to the young (she had testified against sexually suggestive music at a congressional hearing), she abhorred Clinton's insensitivity to ethical issues. Hence, Gore sought to put as much distance as he possibly could between himself and Clinton. It may have been a fatal mistake.

Second, Gore seemed genetically incapable of finding his own personality in the campaign. He waffled between condescending affability toward Bush and scathing condemnation. Clearly more skilled in domestic policy and foreign affairs than his opponent, he committed the terrible error of seeming either smug or pedantic. Moreover, he committed the cardinal political sin of exaggerating his achievements, suggesting in an offhand remark at one point that he had "invented" the Internet—he *had* done more than most to facilitate information technology, but that was different from creating it. No one ever felt that they were dealing with the "real" Al Gore, a person of integrity, consistency, and intellectual depth.

In the end, therefore, the election turned into a contest not over who demonstrated the greatest mastery of complicated public policy questions but over who proved to be the more likeable personality. Bush was Gore's polar opposite. Whereas the vice president was pedantic and "schoolmarmish," Bush was gregarious, direct, gracious, and more often than not, "natural." He seemed more authentic, less scripted, less a puppet than Gore. Hence, style rather than substance proved decisive. A disbelieving political columnist wrote that "the wasting of Gore has been a stunning and quite unexpected phenomenon."

Nevertheless, on election night it still appeared that Gore had won. More than half a million votes ahead of Bush in the popular count, three networks declared him the winner in the crucial state of Florida based on early exit polls, only to withdraw their decision a few hours later. As it turned out, Gore lost two states he surely would have won had Clinton played a larger role—Tennessee (his home state) and Arkansas (Clinton's). That made everything turn on Florida. There, in the middle of the night, the networks reversed themselves and called the state for Bush. But just as Gore was on his way to make a concession statement, aides persuaded him that Florida was a kaleidoscope of contrasting trends, some favoring Bush, some favoring Gore. In Palm Beach County, a "butterfly ballot" confused countless voters by placing two candidates' names across from each other so that it was not clear whom one was voting for. (As a result, Independent Pat Buchanan received 3,407 votes there, 1600 percent more than his average in other counties). "It was the kind of week," a *New Yorker* writer observed, "when the free world contemplated the interesting possibility that the identity of its...leader would be determined by the fact that a couple of thousand sweet little old Jewish ladies...accidentally voted for a Holocaust denier." The picture got even more complicated as stories surfaced of how black votes had been suppressed. As it turned out, ballots in predominantly black precincts were invalidated at four times the rate they were thrown out in white precincts. Finally, there were the "hanging chads"—thousands of ballots where voters appeared to have chosen one candidate, but the punch hole had not gone all the way through due to ancient voting machines; as a result, the "chads" did not completely separate from the ballot, so the votes were not counted.

All of this resulted in a political dispute not seen in the country since the election of 1876 when Florida had also played a pivotal role in the election battle between Samuel Tilden, Democrat, and Rutherford B. Hayes, Republican. Initially, Gore chose not to seek a recount in all parts of the state, focusing only on the three most populous counties in the Miami/West Palm Beach area. Although one county failed to complete its recount in the time set by the courts, Bush's margin of victory had fallen to under 400 votes. The Florida Supreme Court then ordered a recount in all the counties, with Gore now confident that he would win. Except that the United States Supreme Court then intervened. Although most experts presumed the Court would let the state decisions stand—*Newsweek* noted that "federal courts generally do not like to second-guess state courts on election matters like ballot counts"—this Court determined by a 5–4 vote that no further vote counting should occur (the Bush margin was now 154 votes). The decision meant that Bush was declared the winner in Florida, and, in turn, the country at large.

Ironically, the Court used the equal protection clause of the Fourteenth Amendment to justify its decision. Originally enacted to protect the rights of black citizens recently freed from enslavement, the Court used the clause in this instance to argue that by initially separating out just three counties for a recount, the Florida courts had denied all voters the chance to be treated "equally." (At the same time, the Court ignored the degree to which black votes had been suppressed at a far higher level than white votes, an area where the equal protection clause might better have been applicable). The four judges who disagreed used language rarely heard in the halls of justice. The decision, Justice John Paul Stevens declared, "can only lend credence to the most cynical appraisal of the work of judges throughout the land." Justice Stephen Breyer agreed, calling the ruling a "self-inflicted wound...that may harm not just the Court, but the Nation." "There is no justification," Justice David Souter asserted, "for denying the State the opportunity to try to count all the disputed ballots now." The decision, the dissenting judges declared, violated "the basic principle, inherent in our Constitution...that every legal vote be counted." However much he might have agreed with those in dissent, Al Gore accepted the Court's decision with grace, perhaps understanding the degree to which his own errors had led to this result, and on January 20, George W. Bush became the forty-third president of the United States.

II. THE EARLY MONTHS

For the first eight months of his administration, George W. Bush pursued two themes that were an exercise in contradiction. Rhetorically, he celebrated the politics of inclusion and coalition. Bush's inaugural address highlighted his campaign's focus on "compassionate conservatism," pledging to address the "deep, persistent poverty [that] is unworthy of our nation's promise" and promising to include Americans of all backgrounds in his administration—a commitment he fulfilled by naming more Latinos, women, and African Americans to high positions than any of his predecessors. It was "by far the best [inaugural] in forty years," one pundit commented.

Despite his rhetoric, on the other hand, Bush pursued policies that catered exclusively to the right-wing base of his constituency. Whereas Reagan had often given lip service to antiabortion views, Bush delivered deeds. His first step as president was to terminate U.S. aid to international family planning groups. Bush lambasted the idea of gay marriage; replaced a policy of emphasizing condom use to combat AIDS—a practice that had proven very successful—with a new policy emphasizing abstinence; nominated federal judges with a "pro-life" record; and embraced a series of "faith-based" initiatives that placed the church front and center in helping the less well-off. The New Right could not have been happier. Finally, they had a man in the White House who would "walk the walk" as well as "talk the talk."

On economic issues, Bush also set new standards. Making Ronald Reagan look like a moderate, he proposed—and passed—a tax cut that slashed the taxes of the nation's richest citizens, with the top 1 percent of all taxpayers receiving 43 percent of the tax break of $1.3 billion enacted by Congress at

Bush's urging. At the same time, Bush took the axe to countless measures Clinton had sponsored on the environment. He countermanded Clinton's executive orders prohibiting logging in western forests and lowering the level of arsenic permitted in water supplies; reversed Clinton's decisions outlawing snowmobiles in national parks; and proposed a series of energy initiatives that seemed designed by big oil producers and that would sanction drilling in the Arctic National Wildlife Refuge, an area viewed as "untouchable" by most environmentalists. Indeed, on virtually every major issue, Bush's policies seemed guided by an almost instinctive desire to turn upside down Clinton's practices. Whatever Clinton might have done, Bush chose to do the exact opposite.

But nowhere was this more evident than in foreign policy. Rather than pursue the multilateralism of Clinton (and his father, George Herbert Walker Bush), Bush from day one of his presidency signaled to the world that America was going to define its own priorities and objectives regardless of what others (perhaps including his father) thought. Bush revived the long-dormant Reagan proposal to build a star wars system of antimissile missiles, abrogated the decades old ABM (Anti-Ballistic Missile) treaty that Richard Nixon had negotiated with the Soviet Union, and announced that America would have nothing to do with the Kyoto Global Warming Treaty that Gore had negotiated. As if that were not enough, Bush announced that the United States would say no to a treaty banning land mines, withdraw support for a Comprehensive Nuclear Test Ban Treaty, and not participate in or acknowledge the authority of the World Court to try war crimes. In what seemed another reflexive anti-Clinton move, Bush also abandoned efforts, supported by South Korea, to seek rapprochement with the North Koreans. America's allies were not pleased. As one British newspaper (usually pro-American) noted, "Mr. Bush's America seems in danger of convincing itself that it can force everybody to make concessions, while itself remaining impervious to change." Nothing spoke more powerfully to long-term issues of America's posture in the world than these early signs of unilateral assertiveness. On questions both domestic and international, Bush seemed intent on breaking with most of the precedents established during the New Deal and Cold War.

III. 9/11 AND THEREAFTER

On September 11, 2001, the nation was stunned as it had not been since Pearl Harbor. What had once seemed unthinkable had now happened. Certainly there had been harbingers—the truck bomb attack at the World Trade Center in 1993, the Oklahoma City bombing of 1995 (this time by a right-wing American terrorist), the assault on U.S. embassies in Nairobi and Dar es Salaam in 1998, the attack on the USS *Cole* in Yemen in 2000. But somehow these seemed far removed both in time and dimension from what occurred on 9/11. Although intelligence operatives were frighteningly aware of the threat—on August 6, 2001, the president's intelligence summary headlined the possibility that airplanes might be hijacked and used as missiles against American cities—average citizens had no hint of their vulnerability to such an assault. Going about their business on a picture-perfect day, Americans instantaneously became aware that no longer was their nation—their home soil—a fortress, safe from any and all terrorist attacks.

The president was reading to a second-grade class in Florida on a trip designed to promote his education policy when an aide delivered the news to him. After continuing for a few minutes, he excused himself. The presidential party then flew around the nation on *Air Force One* until the military could determine the degree to which he personally might be a target (as it turned out, the White House had been an intended destination for one of the hijacked planes). In the meantime, the Capitol and executive offices were evacuated, while Vice President Richard Cheney authorized the air force to shoot down any hijacked commercial airliner that seemed headed toward Washington. (United Airline Flight 93 fit that category and would have been shot down had not its passengers sent it diving into the ground in their revolt against the hijackers.)

As the nation grieved in shock, the president moved quickly to be a voice of both reassurance and leadership. He visited Ground Zero in New York, wept with the firefighters, and addressed a national payer service in a voice

As President George W. Bush rallied the country in the aftermath of 9/11, he identified with the victims of the tragedy. Here he is shown holding the shield of a New York police officer who perished that day, saying he would carry the officer's badge as a reminder of the heroism of those who had died trying to save victims of the attack.

Credit: © Reuters/CORBIS

strong with compassion and courage. A few days later he went before Congress and spoke to the American people. Effectively, he described the war on terrorism as a new phenomenon. It would have no finite boundaries, he said, no moments of unconditional surrender, no definitive contest between rival armies such as occurred at Gettysburg or Iwo Jima. Instead, this was an enemy without a nation, "a radical network of terrorists" disseminated across many national boundaries, united by an ideology and a sense of religious fervor.

The public soon learned the name of their nemesis—Al Qaeda—and its leader—Osama Bin Laden. Heir of a billionaire Saudi Arabian family, Bin Laden had visited the West but quickly devoted his life energies to freeing Muslim nations from the yoke of outside domination. At first, he fought against the Soviet occupation of Afghanistan where he received aid from and was on the same side as the United States. But soon America became his Satan, and he dedicated himself, his fortune, and his growing army of believers to freeing the Arab world of U.S capitalist rule. Bin Laden mobilized scores of squadrons to carry out terrorist attacks, all with the aim of destroying both Israel and America. "To kill Americans and their allies," he declared in 1996, "is an individual duty of every Muslim...in any country where this is possible." Clearly, the United States fit that description, embodying all the evils that Bin Laden's jihad mission sought to annihilate. Hence, the targets of 9/11. "The attack," one reporter observed, "was not only against a nation or government, but against a symbol, the twin towers of Sodom and mammon."

President Bush immediately sought to define the battle in the simplest terms possible. In words reminiscent of Harry Truman's at the beginning of the Cold War, he described the fight as one between good and evil. Bush identified the enemy as not simply a "radical network of terrorists" but also "every government that supports them." In a critical sequence, he then reverted to a description of America's foes as nation-states, not a dispersed jihad. "Every nation in every region," he told Congress, "now has a decision to make. Either you are with us, or you are with the terrorists." Clearly, Bush's rhetorical ploy was designed to eliminate the possibility that any country could define itself as "neutral" in the new war, and there was an underlying moral logic to his demand. Yet in the war on terror, there was no Soviet Union, no single nation that embodied the threat. Nineteen of the 9/11 terrorists, for example, came from Saudi Arabia, yet the Saudis were America's allies. In fact, Al Qaeda consisted of "cell groups" located throughout the world—in Germany, Britain, Spain, a spate of Middle Eastern countries, and America (as the 9/11 terrorists demonstrated). Hence, this was a different kind of war, one that could not be localized to any nation-state or geographical entity. Unlike the Cold War, "containment" did not constitute a viable strategy. The question was whether America was prepared to wage a war different from any it had ever fought before—one rooted in culture, religion, and ideology rather than state boundaries.

As the Bush administration began to negotiate this ambiguous terrain, the United States had the sympathy of people from all over the world. "We are all Americans," the French newspaper *Le Monde* declared. Leaders from Russia, Egypt, China, India, and Pakistan all offered their support. Most seemed prepared to support military action aimed at the terrorists, with everyone agreeing that Afghanistan was the most likely target. The home of Bin Laden's operations, it also boasted an Islamic fundamentalist regime—the Taliban—which systematically resisted Western influences. Unpopular with virtually every nation, the Taliban offered little basis for sympathy from others. Indeed, within Afghanistan itself, a powerful civil insurgency called the Northern Alliance was already engaged in an effort to bring down the government.

It was no surprise, then, when nearly universal applause greeted America's decision to attack Afghanistan in October, just four weeks after 9/11. Starting with a sophisticated bombing assault that pinpointed Taliban targets with devastating effectiveness—nearly 60 percent of all sorties utilized laser targeting—ground troops soon finished the task of liberating the country from Taliban rule. A new government took power, led by a Western-educated president, Hamid Kharzai; schools and universities were reopened; women's rights were championed. There was even reason to hope that with the sophisticated bombing technology and growing popular support, it would be possible to hunt down Osama Bin Laden and his allies in their hideouts in the Tora Bora Mountains on the border between Pakistan and Afghanistan. Pressured by Secretary of State Colin Powell, Pakistani president General Pervez Musharraf had promised to support unconditionally the American effort to clean out terrorist pockets along the Pakistani border.

It was precisely at this moment, however, that the focus of American efforts radically changed. Just as American military officials were begging for the deployment of four thousand additional American troops into the caves of Tora Bora, where intelligence agents believed Osama Bin Laden was hiding, the Bush administration shifted its gaze to another battlefield. Soon Iraq became the focus of attention, with everything else taking a secondary position. The attack on terrorism that had begun so auspiciously in Afghanistan, with nearly unanimous support from the community of nations, was about to dissolve into a far more controversial decision to make Iraq the principal theater of war, with results that eventually would threaten not only international comity but also the ability of the United States to dominate the world.

IV. THE WAR IN IRAQ

The seeds of future polarization were present at the creation of Bush's Iraq policy. Though less visible than they would appear in retrospect, even observers at the time recognized a series of conflicts—over going it alone or seeking international support, over the soundness of intelligence findings used to justify an invasion, and over the degree to which any connection existed between Al Qaeda and Iraqi ruler Saddam Hussein. Although each of these was resolved, temporarily, in the direction that George W. Bush favored, they would come back to haunt the decision to invade Iraq, help fuel a growing domestic opposition to the war, and ultimately call into question the credibility of the administration and its entire rationale for the war.

At one level, the divisions over Iraq were personal and bureaucratic. On one side were the secretary of state, Colin Powell, and the institutional preference of the State Department for multilateralism, reliance on the United Nations, and careful planning for strategic outcomes. On the other side were Secretary of Defense Donald Rumsfeld and Vice President Richard Cheney, who believed a quick victory was possible with a minimal allocation of resources and could be achieved, if necessary, by United States action alone. Powell brought to the issue his rich experience as former head of the Joint Chiefs of Staff during the first Persian Gulf War under George Herbert Walker Bush in 1991. He believed fervently that the nation should not go to war unless two preconditions were met: maximum support from all potential allies and a degree of force on the ground that would be so overwhelming that victory was guaranteed, not only in the short run but in the long term as well. Both conditions had been met in the Gulf War, with more than two score nations (and the United Nations) contributing to the alliance and over 300,000 troops on the ground. But now, eleven years later, Rumsfeld and Cheney banked on acting quickly and decisively, using a lean strike force of under 175,000 soldiers and willing to act alone if necessary. When the army chief of staff insisted at a congressional hearing that more than twice that number of troops would be required, he was shunted into early retirement. Nothing would stop the Rumsfeld/Cheney juggernaut.

But an even deeper dynamic was also at work. Ever since the Congress had placed serious constraints on executive power after Nixon's abuse of the executive office during the Watergate era—including his secret bombing of Cambodia with no congressional consultation or approval—Richard Cheney had been obsessed with the urgency of reclaiming presidential power. As articulated in a minority report that he wrote during the Iran-Contra hearings while a member of Congress, Cheney believed that as commander in chief, the president had total power. Neither Congress, nor the State Department, nor generals themselves, could impede the president's authority to do whatever he deemed necessary to protect the American people. It was a concept that many saw as totally alien to the intention of the Founding Fathers, with their profound concern for "checks and balances" and a separation of powers; but it was also one that Cheney—and Bush—would use to justify excesses of power over the course of the Iraq War that stunned many in the Washington establishment, including conservative Republicans. The underlying constitutional issue rarely surfaced in the immediate debates over policies to be pursued, but the Cheney-driven quest for total executive freedom in matters of foreign policy and war was an ever-present dynamic, just below the surface.

Finally, of course, was the role of George W. Bush himself. Some claimed he was simply a puppet, manipulated by Cheney, Rumsfeld, and a cadre of neoconservatives. According to this interpretation, Bush was not intellectually capable of the strategic thinking that guided his policies. Rather, he was "duped" into following a course that others had charted. But this view vastly underestimated George W. Bush. Whatever his mixed record as a businessman, he had pursued with singular purpose—and intelligence—a political career that demonstrated shrewdness and insight. Karl Rove, his longtime advisor, might receive much of the credit for Bush's political success with the conservative Right, but Bush made the final calls. Furthermore, he had a gut instinct on political matters that made eminently clear that he was in charge. As he told one audience during his presidency, "I am the *decider*."

But more important than anything else was Bush's personal faith. A one-time alcoholic, he had experienced a religious conversion. Becoming a born-again Christian, he swore off alcohol, believed he had a personal mission as God's messenger to fulfill, and set out do what this mission required. God, he said, meant for freedom to be established around the world, and he, George W. Bush, meant to see that God's wishes became reality. As the story of the Iraq war unfolded, all these forces—the dispute between Powell, Rumsfeld, and Cheney; the vice president's passion for an imperial presidency, and George W. Bush's sense of personal mission—would play critical roles in determining the course of action the nation would follow.

As only became evident years later, the Bush team had in fact targeted regime change in Iraq long before 9/11. Cheney, Rumsfeld, and "Bush Two" all were furious that Saddam Hussein was still in power. Cheney and Rumsfeld had been part of the "Bush One" decision to not "go to Baghdad" during the Persian Gulf War (Cheney, prophetically, had said in 1991 that to do so might unleash civil war and create a quagmire for an American occupying force). Hussein's continued defiance, and the fact that he had plotted to assassinate Bush's father during a Middle Eastern trip, further animated the wish to topple the Iraqi tyrant. Conversations had already taken place about how and when to do this, but now 9/11 provided the perfect occasion to move to the front of the action agenda, a policy choice that hitherto had been only a topic of discussion. Within two hours after the attacks on the Pentagon, Secretary of Defense Donald Rumsfeld had begun to talk to his aides about going after Saddam Hussein as part of the response to Osama Bin Laden, as though the two were inextricably connected. Shortly thereafter, George W. Bush signed on to the same strategy.

The problem was how to make the connection. Saddam was a secular Muslim. He had defined himself as the archenemy of Islamic fundamentalism. Far from welcoming Al Qaeda or its representatives, the Hussein regime actively opposed any political influence for Bin Laden or his allies. Moreover, U.S. intelligence briefings mentioned no link between the two, and for the most part, left Iraq off the list of major terrorist threats to the United States.

The initial disputes within the Bush administration over Iraq thus began with conflicts over what constituted meaningful intelligence sufficient to link Saddam to terrorism. Ever since the Gulf War, America had used international sanctions and the creation of a fly-free zone over northern Iraq to pressure the Saddam Hussein regime to engage in political and economic reforms. Although the population suffered extreme hardship as a result of the sanctions, Hussein barely changed his bellicose rhetoric. In 1998, the United States Congress went on record unanimously supporting regime change in Baghdad. Throughout these years, various intelligence services—those of the United States and others—speculated about Saddam having weapons of mass destruction. He had already used biological and chemical weapons during the Iraq-Iran war as well as to suppress Kurdish dissidents, and although United Nations inspectors had found no evidence of WMDs, Hussein had expelled the inspectors in 1998.

Thus, the purported existence of WMDs inside Iraq became the first stake pounded into the ground by the Bush administration as justification for a possible war with Iraq. Although the United States had few agents inside Iraq, and its hard intelligence was dubious at best, Cheney and others pressured the CIA to come forward with reports that emphasized the probability that Iraq possessed WMDs. When Rumsfeld and his Assistant Secretary of Defense Paul Wolfowitz saw aerial photographs of new dump trucks purchased by Saddam, they concluded that they were intended to be used as launching ramps for rockets. "This is lunacy," Secretary of State Colin Powell responded. But Bush was already well embarked on making the case. He denied a military request for four thousand additional marines to go to Tora Bora to capture Osama and in November 2001 authorized Rumsfeld to have secret plans drawn up for invading Iraq.

In the meantime, Bush created the rhetorical and ideological stage for what was to come, telling Congress in his State of the Union message in January 2002 that the United States was threatened by an "axis of evil," three countries—Iran, Iraq, and North Korea—who were plotting to destroy American freedom. Further charting the road down which he intended to go, he also pronounced a new American doctrine of preemptive war. "We must take the battle to the enemy," he told a University of Michigan audience, "disrupt his plans and confront the worst threats before they emerge." For the first time in history, the United States was talking about initiating a war on its own—a "shift with profound implications," the *New York Times* editorialized—thereby laying the groundwork for attacking Iraq because it might share its WMDs (whose existence had still not been proven) with other terrorists.

At this point, Powell stepped in and sought to stop the Bush/Cheney/ Rumsfeld blitzkrieg. Asking for a rare private session with the president, Powell put the entire strength of his military and diplomatic expertise on the line. Invading Iraq, Powell told Bush, would alienate many American allies, inspire worldwide hatred from the Muslim world, and potentially endanger friendly governments like Saudi Arabia. Taking up the same theme that Cheney, ironically, had sounded eleven years earlier, the secretary of state told Bush that America would become an "occupier." "You will be the proud owner of twenty-five million people," he declared. Once an invasion occurred, there could be no guarantee of the outcome, especially if insufficient forces were used. "You break it, you own it," he warned Bush. Only if the president went to the United Nations and sought international approval for whatever steps were taken, Powell concluded, could America's self-interest *and* reputation be preserved.

For the moment at least, Bush appeared to concede. He would go to the United Nations, he told Powell, and make the case for collective, multilateral action against Saddam's "rogue," torture-ridden regime. Powell believed he had snatched victory out of the jaws of defeat.

In fact, what Powell had done was to ratchet up Cheney and Rumsfeld's determination to seal the case. With no evidence to confirm his allegations, Cheney announced that "there is no doubt that Saddam Hussein *now* has WMDs and that he is amassing them to use against our friends, our allies, and against us." Almost as if he were fulfilling all the conditions laid out in Bush's preemptive war speech, he then declared that leaving WMDs in the hands of a "murderous dictator" represented "as great a threat as can be imagined," making the "risks of inaction [far] greater than the risks of action." As if that were not enough, Cheney went on to suggest that Saddam was developing nuclear weapons. Using spotty intelligence that Iraq was buying aluminum tubes that might be used to enrich uranium (the intelligence was later shown to be false), Cheney and his allies created a scenario where the failure to act immediately could be seen as reckless and irresponsible. "We don't want the smoking gun [that proves Saddam's guilt] to be a mushroom cloud," Bush's national security advisor, Condoleezza Rice, told CNN.

In one last desperate move, Powell persuaded Bush to seek a UN resolution requiring Iraq to reopen its borders to UN inspectors and conform to all weapons restrictions. The United Nations agreed and dispatched a new team of inspectors to search out *any* evidence that Iraq held WMDs. Over the next months, the UN inspectors performed this task, with no prior notification of when and where they would conduct their inspections. They found no evidence of WMDs. Nevertheless, under the guise of strengthening the American case at the United Nations, Bush went to Congress and won its approval to use force if *he* found Iraq to have violated the UN resolution. He now charged that Saddam was "teaming up with Al Qaeda," that he "has weapons of mass destruction," and that he was trying to find plutonium to build a nuclear weapon. "Time frame would be six months" for an A-bomb, he said. (Even the most suspicious CIA agents estimated it would take five to seven years for Hussein to get a bomb). When Hans Blix, the chief UN inspector, declared in January 2003 that he had found no evidence of WMDs but needed more time given Saddam's obstructiveness, Bush decided not to play the UN card any longer. He would go to war.

In a tragic and ironic postscript to that decision, Bush asked Colin Powell to make the case for U.S. action before the United Nations. Only Powell had the credibility to do so. As the good soldier he had always been, Powell agreed. Yet when he read the speech that had been prepared for him, he was appalled. Faced with the claim of a connection between the 9/11 terrorists and Iraq, he told one reporter, "That was worse than ridiculous." Powell believed that Cheney had a "fever" for war and had taken intelligence and "converted uncertainty and ambiguity into fact." Going to CIA headquarters, Powell carefully questioned CIA director George Tenet and others about the arguments he was going to make and the evidence behind them. They backed up the charges in Powell's text. In a shameful act of deception, no CIA officer told Powell that the key piece of evidence in the indictment of Hussein for having WMDs came from a source in Germany known as "Curveball"; nor did they tell him that no CIA officer had ever questioned "Curveball" or that German intelligence officials had concluded that "Curveball" was a mental case who could not be trusted. Powell went on to give his speech. It was effective. When he later found out what had been kept from him, Powell said he was "devastated." What he did at the United Nations that day, he stated, was a permanent "blot" on his record. But he had done what Bush had asked and performed brilliantly.

Now, Bush proceeded to the final step. With his "coalition of the willing"— England, Spain, Poland, and Italy had agreed to commit a limited number of troops—Bush ordered the invasion of Iraq in March 2003. Once again, he put on the table all the cards he had brought to play: Iraq, he declared, "continues to possess and conceal some of the most lethal weapons ever devised"; it still schemed to secure nuclear bombs; the United States must avoid another 9/11. With that specter as his backdrop, Bush announced, "We choose to meet that threat now ... before it can appear suddenly in our skies and cities." Invading Iraq was the way to accomplish that end.

V. "YOU BREAK IT, YOU OWN IT"

The initial results from the Iraq invasion brought jubilation to Bush and all those who had supported the war effort. With the same precision bombing that had decimated Afghanistan, American planes splintered Iraqi defenses, paving the way for a lightning foray of U.S troops from Kuwait into Baghdad. Befuddled and overwhelmed, the Iraqi army—one-third smaller than it had been in 1992—disappeared into the countryside. World television screens soon featured scenes of joyous Iraqi citizens toppling a giant statue of Saddam in the nation's capital. Saddam himself had vanished, but for the moment it appeared that Bush's dream of liberating the Iraqi people from a cruel tyrant had come to a magnificent conclusion. Rumsfeld's tactics of "shock and awe" had devastated the Iraqi army, which seemed totally unprepared for the lean, superbly trained strike force that ripped through their ranks. In the euphoria of repeated scenes of exhilaration among freed Iraqis, the Bush team decided to celebrate. Less than two months after the invasion, George W. Bush donned a flight suit, piloted a fighter plane that landed on a U.S. aircraft carrier off the California coast, and with a huge banner declaring **"MISSION ACCOMPLISHED"** told the American people, "The tyrant has fallen and Iraq is free. In the image of falling statues, we have witnessed the arrival of a new era."

After American forces invaded Iraq in early 2003, President George W. Bush, a former National Guard pilot, landed a jet fighter on an aircraft carrier to declare "Mission Accomplished." Bush's announcement was premature. Civil war soon ensued in Iraq, and six years later, more than one hundred thousand American troops still remained in Iraq in a way that two-thirds of the American people now felt to be a mistake.

Credit: Associated Press

Tragically, it turned out that nothing could have been further from the truth. Omens of what was to come appeared almost immediately after Americans occupied Baghdad. With impunity, looters plundered Baghdad's museums, seizing invaluable artifacts and archaeological remains. No one interfered. The Iraqi police and army had been disbanded, and the Americans claimed that "pacification" and protection of resources had not been part of their "game plan." Meanwhile the infrastructure of the country crumbled. Electricity flickered, with no reliable source of power. Water proved difficult to obtain. There were no firefighters, garbage collectors, or relief workers. Worst of all, within weeks it became clear that an Iraqi insurgency had taken root, fueled initially by Saddam lieutenants who remained free to roam the countryside, then reinforced by sectarian forces who became involved in what looked to most observers, within a year of "liberation," like a full-scale civil war.

The problems were so myriad they defied description, but two or three immediate causes fueled their proliferation. First, as General Sinsheki had told Congress two years earlier, Americans could successfully occupy Iraq only if they had more than 300,000 troops on the ground. Rejecting that advice (and forcing the general into early retirement), Rumsfeld insisted that his lean strike force of 140,000 could do it all. He was wrong. There never were sufficient American troops in Iraq to do the job. Second—and almost inconceivable to most observers—there was *no plan* for the occupation. The State Department had drawn one up, complete with proposals for dealing with problems of food, oil production, social dislocation, and civil order. But the Pentagon rejected State's input, refusing even to have State Department representatives on the committee it belatedly established to pursue postwar strategies. (Powell told one reporter that he "wondered if things could [possibly] get weirder.") By the time the Pentagon working group got off the ground, the situation had already deteriorated into chaos. Third, the Americans made two critical decisions that in effect denuded Iraqi society of the only people in the country with the experience to hold things together. Americans first dissolved the Iraqi army, many of whose members were prepared (and able) to continue to provide order in Iraq under the command of Americans; and then they engaged in the "de-Baathification" of the Iraqi civil service. All bureaucrats who had been members of Saddam's Baath Party—and anyone who wanted a government job *had* to join the party—were automatically fired. Hence, there were no people with experience in government to help sustain public services to the people of the country.

Within months after the president had celebrated "Mission Accomplished," the American occupying force in Iraq seemed incapable of mastering a rapidly growing insurgency and an intractable set of obstacles to effective civil government. Although Saddam was captured nine months after the invasion, the forces of rebellion continued to grow. Shiite militias, totally oblivious to government control, waged guerilla war on Sunni communities while Sunni terrorists conducted suicide bombings against Shiite strongholds. The body counts of civilians killed in random shootings accelerated daily. So did the vulnerability of American forces. Two years after the invasion, monthly totals of wounded and dead soldiers had tripled while the estimated number of insurgents had grown sixfold. Instead of creating peace, freedom, and democracy, the American occupation seemed trapped in a quagmire, with chaos, a shattered infrastructure, and political sectarianism the dominant features of the Iraqi landscape. From the point of view of those critical of the invasion, America's presence in Iraq, far from quelling the forces of terrorism, had in fact multiplied terrorist ranks, serving as a primary recruitment mechanism for Islamic fundamentalism.

Worst of all from a Bush perspective, it now seemed that not a single argument used to justify the war had been valid. An extensive search for WMDs led to nothing. "We have not yet found stocks of weapons," U.S. arms inspector David Kay reported five months after launching his search—then a year later, his final report: "We were almost all wrong," he said. A national commission set up to assess the performance of U.S. intelligence agencies concluded not only that the intelligence apparatus of the country was weak and inefficient but also that the findings it had provided as the basis for going to war were "dead wrong." No evidence existed that Saddam was preparing to build nuclear weapons. And the 9/11 Commission, in addition to faulting the government for overlooking multiple warnings that a terrorist threat was

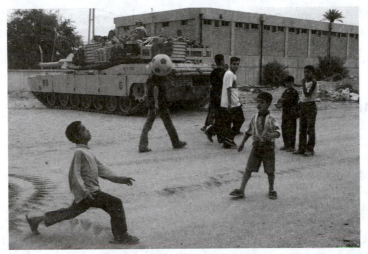

One of the worst problems American troops faced in Iraq (as they had in Vietnam) was not knowing how the local population viewed them. Were Americans alien intruders or welcome allies? In this picture, Iraqi children play soccer while U.S. soldiers and their tank search for weapons. But just as often, Iraqi dissidents planted IEDs (Improvised Explosive Devices) to ambush American troop convoys.

Credit: Associated Press

imminent, declared definitively that no connection had ever existed between Al Qaeda and Saddam Hussein.

By the time of the 2004 presidential elections, the Democrats hoped to make the poor performance of the Bush administration a basis for turning the Republicans out of office. Yet much of the information that discredited the war effort had not yet seeped in, and it was still possible—and profitable—for Republicans to attack Democratic critics of the war as "unpatriotic." John Kerry, the Democratic nominee, was a war hero in Vietnam, having won a Purple Heart and medals of bravery for rescuing his boatmates when they were under Viet Cong attack. The economy was bogged down, thousands of jobs had moved overseas, and more than 40 million people lacked health insurance. It seemed a logical year for Democrats to win. Yet Kerry let the war become his primary focus. That, in turn, played into a Republican strategy of defending the commander in chief in the midst of a foreign war. Scurrilous ads portrayed Kerry as having been a coward in Vietnam who had lied about his service and Kerry waited too long to respond. Instead of highlighting Bush's failure on the economy—he had created only 3 million jobs in contrast to the 22 million created during Clinton's administration—Kerry continued to pursue the war issue. In the end it all came down to one state, Ohio. There, Kerry should have had the advantage because no state more reflected the economic disarray of the country that this once industrial giant. But Ohio was also a place of conservative social values. Karl Rove and his White House political strategists masterfully mobilized the New Right constituencies of evangelical churches. These were God-fearing, patriotic "middle-Americans" who were appalled by Kerry's support of abortion and gay marriage as well as his willingness to attack the commander in chief. In an election most felt too close to call, Ohio weighed in on Bush's side, reelecting him to a second term.

VI. BACK AT HOME

Yet within months after Bush's second inaugural, the bottom fell out. All the bad news from Iraq finally took hold. As casualties continued to mount, so too did sectarian disarray. Sunnis refused to support a government of national unity or did so only occasionally; suicide bombing attacks multiplied; daily civilian deaths often mounted to 75 or 100. Donald Rumsfeld claimed that up to 150,000 Iraqi soldiers had been trained to take over peacekeeping responsibilities, but people on the ground estimated the real figure to be only 10,000. Electricity and oil production remained well below prewar levels. America's "coalition of the willing" began to fall apart as troops from Spain and Italy were withdrawn. A large majority of Brits deeply opposed Prime Minister Tony Blair's decision to stand by Bush while throughout Western Europe antiwar demonstrations multiplied. America stood almost alone, with millions of citizens among her once staunch allies convinced that Bush was a bully, pursuing unilateral policies totally at odds with the way America had proceeded in international affairs ever since World War II.

At home, meanwhile, Bush's effort to build a domestic policy legacy akin to that of Ronald Reagan also floundered. Having already passed a tax cut more radical than that of any of his twentieth-century predecessors, Bush now tackled the number-one symbol of the twentieth-century welfare state, Social Security. Arguing that the Social Security system was broken (in fact, experts said it was good through 2040 and could be sustained for far longer with only minor changes), Bush proposed that the system be "reformed" by having taxpayers invest some of their Social Security payments in private funds. The American people did not buy it. To them Social Security was sacrosanct. Moreover, those who studied the issue realized that the cost of the transition to a privatized system would be two trillion dollars, added to the national debt that was already growing out of control due to Iraq war expenditures and the tax cuts. Even Republicans in Congress shied away from Bush's initiative.

Nowhere did the competence of the administration come under greater attack, though, than in the aftermath of Hurricane Katrina. Hitting the coast of Louisiana and Mississippi less than one year after the 2004 elections, Katrina was a "perfect storm." With winds over 140 miles per hour and a flood surge that was unprecedented, Katrina devastated the city. The levee system, long criticized as totally inadequate, collapsed. Although the rich and middle class could escape the city in response to the mayor's mandatory evacuation order, thousands of the poor had no cars, squeezing into attics in the hope of averting the rising floodwaters or gathering in the downtown Superdome where there was no food, no water, and overflowing toilets. The streets of New Orleans were full of bloated bodies; raw sewage was everywhere; and the Federal Emergency Management Administration—which had been given full advance warning of the storm's severity —had only a few staff members on-site.

Indeed, FEMA's response—and that of the president—created mass incredulity. Bush, who had been given full advance warning of Katrina, stayed on vacation at his ranch for two days after the storm hit, then visited San Diego for a speech, taking notice of what had happened only on the fourth day as he flew back to Washington. "How could this be," *Newsweek* magazine asked, "how the president of the United States could have even less [awareness] than the average American about the worst natural disaster in a century.... [It is] a national disgrace." FEMA, meanwhile, acted as though everything were under control. When one TV anchorperson asked the FEMA director what he was doing about the thousands trapped in the Superdome with no food, water, or toilet facilities, he claimed to know nothing about the situation. "You mean you do not know about these people," she asked, "when their pictures have been on television for twenty-four hours." As one local official noted, "It's like FEMA has never been to a hurricane."

Nor did the performance of the government improve over time. Although Congress approved billions of dollars in aid to displaced home owners, three

When Hurricane Katrina hit the Gulf Coast in August 2005, it not only devastated New Orleans and surrounding areas but also highlighted the complete inadequacy of state and federal authorities to respond with effective, compassionate aid. Four years later, the poor, primarily black residents of New Orleans had still not reestablished a stable and safe living environment.

Credit: © Jason Reed/Reuters/Corbis

years after Katrina hit, hardly any of the money had reached New Orleans residents. Districts like the Ninth Ward, predominantly African American, looked like devastated war zones two years after the storm, weeds growing over streets and yards, mold covering the Sheetrock inside houses where the floodwaters had reached ceiling levels. Reflecting on what had occurred (or more accurately what had *not* occurred) in New Orleans, *New York Times* columnist David Brooks—a conservative—wrote, "The rich escaped while the poor were abandoned. Leaders spun while looters rampaged.... Leaving the poor in New Orleans was the moral equivalent of leaving the injured on the battlefield.... [The] national humiliation [of New Orleans] comes at the end of a string of confidence shaking institutional failures that have cumulatively changed the nation's psyche."

Brooks was not the first, or last, to see a link between the extraordinary failures of leadership in New Orleans and the downhill spiral occurring in Iraq. "The scrapbook of history," he wrote, "accords but a few pages to each decade, and it is already clear that the pages devoted to this one will be grisly. There will be pictures of bodies falling from the twin towers, beheaded kidnapping victims in Iraq, and corpses still floating in the waterways of New Orleans five days after the disaster that caused them." Thomas Friedman, Brooks's counterpart on the *Times* editorial page, echoed his more conservative colleague. "If 9/11 is one book-end of the Bush administration," he wrote, "Katrina may be the other." In addition to "ripping away the roofs of New Orleans," Friedman noted, "Katrina ripped away the argument that we can cut taxes, properly educate our kids, compete with India and China, succeed in Iraq...and take care of a catastrophic emergency...."

By the time the congressional elections of 2006 took place, disillusionment with the status quo had become widespread. Bush's popularity rating fell below 40 percent, 60 percent of the public disapproved of the president's handling of the war, and only 44 percent believed the United States had been right to take military action against Iraq. This time campaigning on the general theme that it was time for a change, Democrats won control of both houses of Congress.

In the meantime, events continued their downward trajectory in Iraq. Sunnis blew up Shiite mosques, Shiites retaliated, massive unrest proliferated, and millions of Iraqis tried to flee their homeland to find a chance for survival elsewhere. The Democratic Party became united in urging that America withdraw from Iraq. More and more Republican senators joined them. The president's popularity ranking fell below 30 percent—almost as low as that of Richard Nixon just before he resigned during Watergate—and a series of Democratic candidates for the presidency demanded that the United States leave Iraq. Bush's invasion had been the culmination of a commitment to transform the world in the name of democracy and freedom. It may also have been, in the words of one scholar at the Kennedy School at Harvard—soon echoed by Republican Senator Chuck Hagel—"the greatest strategic blunder in the history of U.S. foreign policy."

VII. ASSESSMENT

The first decade of the new millennium challenged as never before the dominant paradigms that had shaped America for the previous century. Throughout the years after 1900, the state had taken an ever more active role in regulating the economy; instituting reforms regarding wages and hours in the workplace; and promoting, however belatedly, the civil rights of African Americans and women. The New Deal represented one apex in that journey, the New Frontier and Great Society a second high point. But not even the most conservative Republican presidents in the postwar era—Richard Nixon and Ronald Reagan—had dared to question the fundamental tenets of the New Deal welfare state. Social Security was a topic never even considered to be on the table. The heart of both the "liberal consensus" and its barely different "conservative consensus" consisted of accepting a federal safety net under senior citizens, the unemployed, children, and the less well-off members of the society.

Now, George W. Bush had for the first time engaged frontally the fundamental cornerstones of the social welfare paradigm. Far more than the tax cuts advocated by Ronald Reagan, Bush enacted legislation that dramatically favored the richest members of society while doing barely anything for the bottom 20 percent or even for the middle class that had benefited so substantially from Clinton's economic policies. Whereas Clinton left office with a $200-billion-per-year surplus, Bush exploded the deficit. Whereas Clinton's Justice Department advocated strenuously for civil rights for women and blacks, Bush's department shifted its focus to advancing the civil rights of church-based endeavors. Ever since 1972, even if they opposed the principle of abortion rhetorically, presidents of both parties left standing protection of the *Roe v. Wade* decision. George W. Bush, by contrast, set out immediately to terminate, in action as well as rhetoric, any hint of government support for family-planning activities that countenanced the possibility of abortion. Bush appointees to the federal courts consistently ruled in opposition to pro-choice positions, and by the end of his administration, the president had successfully nominated to the Supreme Court two justices—Samuel Alito and John Roberts—who sought to reverse five decades of Supreme Court rulings involving race, opposing affirmative action and voluntary plans for desegregating schools, while also giving every indication of reconsidering the precedent of *Roe v. Wade*. Perhaps most dramatically, Bush even took on the sacred cow of the social welfare consensus, seeking to make privatization of Social Security a national option. With some policies such as taxation and court appointees, he succeeded beyond the wildest expectations of his conservative base. With others, like Social Security, he failed. The jury was still out on what might occur on issues of gay rights, abortion, and church/state relations, but there could be little question that this was the most radical presidency of the past one hundred years, seeking to undo much of what had been taken as a given over the last half of the twentieth century.

Yet it was in foreign policy that Bush's departure from past precedents was most striking. From the beginning, he and his chief allies—Vice President

Richard Cheney and Secretary of Defense Donald Rumsfeld—set out to dismantle America's commitment to multilateralism. In staccato-like fashion, the administration backed off from international treaties ranging from antiballistic missiles to the environment, from the abolition of land mines to international jurisdiction over war crimes. The Bush team came up with a new definition of national interest: the United States, by itself, would determine what the country needed to do to pursue its objectives abroad. If allies agreed, that would be wonderful. If they did not, Bush made clear that it did not matter. The United States would proceed on its own.

The horrors of 9/11 simply exacerbated the move toward unilateralism. Blessed with an outpouring of sympathy and support from almost all nations in the aftermath of the Twin Towers collapse, Bush nevertheless proceeded with his plans to invade Iraq in total disregard of the impact of such a strategy on America's international standing. So intent was the administration on pursuing its objectives that government intelligence agencies were pressured to come forward with "evidence" supporting Bush policies. Federal officials distorted or obscured intelligence that might call into question the validity of Bush policies. With what turned out to be a vastly inadequate army, Bush invaded Iraq. No systematic postwar plans existed to stabilize the conquered country. Those Iraqi institutions that might have restored order—the army and the Baath Party-controlled civil service—were disbanded. As sectarian violence accelerated in the newly liberated Iraq, there were neither adequate military personnel nor trained civilian bureaucrats to bring pacification.

Far from being a "Mission Accomplished," the Bush administration's Iraqi venture became a "Mission Imploding." As military and civilian casualties multiplied, the American people lost confidence in the competence of their leaders. Realization that there were *no* WMDs in Iraq, *no* nuclear weapon plans, *no* ties between Saddam and Al Qaeda further eroded that confidence. International opinion, meanwhile, turned stridently against U.S. policy in the Middle East. Instead of maximizing American power by pursuing a "go it alone" policy, Bush had created a situation where American power was less evident and more questioned than at any time in the post-World War II world. Instead of being at the center of every international issue, America found itself more and more viewed as occupying the margins, standing isolated while the rest of the world worked toward greater cooperation on issues like global warming, international security, and economic reform.

In part, all of this reflected the distinctive personalities of the president and his closest aides. They felt a mission, divinely inspired. Single-handedly, Bush, Cheney, and company set out to seize executive power without accountability to Congress or the courts, to redefine the country's domestic and international objectives, and to bring American power to a new ascendancy.

The Bush team believed that by pursuing with singular purpose these objectives they would revolutionize the country. The question that remained, after eight years of their efforts, was whether they had brought the American Century to a new level of dominance or whether they had inaugurated a new age of decline.

Epilogue

Whatever the ultimate fate of America's role in the world in the twenty-first century, the autumn of 2008 produced a moment of profound decision. Two events defined this moment as pivotal: first, the worst crash of the American economy since 1929; and second, the election of a new president.

Each event was totally wrapped up in the other. Bill Clinton had presided over eight years of unprecedented prosperity by raising taxes on the rich, reducing the deficit, creating new jobs (22 million of them), and generating confidence in the economic future through producing a budget surplus. George W. Bush pursued exactly the opposite policies. He cut taxes on the rich, hoping that prosperity would "trickle down" to the middle class; he initiated two wars without asking any financial sacrifice of the American people; and as a result, he sparked massive deficits while embracing systematic deregulation of the financial system.

In the Bush economy, every forward step for consumers and homeowners was based on credit. With banks subject to less regulation than at any time since the great Depression, sustained economic growth depended on solid loans, ongoing consumer confidence, and enough growth in jobs and consumer spending to keep the bubble from bursting.

In the summer and fall of 2008, it burst. With inadequate regulation, banks persistently made reckless loans, funding subprime mortgages that were sold to customers who were unprepared to pay. Once foreclosures started, they could not be stopped. Big banks folded, the credit market froze, consumers had *no* money to buy goods, and without customers, factories laid off workers or shut down. In an epidemic that literally became worldwide, monetary and fiscal systems collapsed, along with the stock market.

If George W. Bush's foreign policies caused America's reputation in the world to plummet to a new low, his economic policies had created an economic and monetary crisis without precedent–except for the crash of 1929. The parallels were eerie. As in the 1920s, the *appearance* of prosperity in the new century was based on "buy now, pay later." Such policies were inherently flawed, and once those flaws became manifest, chaos reigned and the entire economic structure imploded.

All of this occurred simultaneously with America's quadrennial presidential election. The 2008 election became *the* election of a generation because it offered the only opportunity the country would have to alter the policies that had caused the fall of America; and it involved two candidates who represented diametrically opposite approaches for how to deal with foreign and domestic crises.

A self-labeled "maverick," John McCain had opposed the way Bush implemented the Iraq war, criticized Bush administration policies on using torture to elicit information on terrorism, and, at least initially, opposed Bush's tax cuts.

Yet more than most, he championed deregulation of the banking industry (as well as all other business), voted with Bush 90 percent of the time, and not only eventually supported Bush's tax cuts, but proposed substantial further reductions for the wealthiest 5 percent of Americans. In foreign policy, McCain was a fervent nationalist, envisioning, a la George Bush, a world where America would continue to rule. "I want the twenty-first century to be the *American* century," he declared.

By contrast, Senator Barack Obama of Illinois personified dramatic change. In the words of former Secretary of State General Colin Powell, Obama represented a politics of "transformation." To begin with he was African-American. Even at the most optimistic moments of the civil rights struggle, barely anyone had envisioned a black president of the United States in their lifetime. In addition, Obama was an American born with an international perspective. With a Kenyan father and an American mother who worked in Indonesia, Obama brought to the election a perspective on people-to-people relations around the world vastly different than those offered by John McCain. Describing himself as a "citizen of the world," Obama reached out to other nations to work collaboratively on problems of climate change and nuclear proliferation. Perhaps most important, he championed policies on the environment, energy independence, health care reform, education, and government responsibility for managing economic issues that represented the opposite of those identified with McCain.

If anything dramatized the changed nature of America's power in the world, it was America's helplessness in the face of worldwide economic disaster. The 2008 "crash" focused the attention of America's voters on the fundamental issues dividing the two parties and candidates. Obama's approach recalled the experimental intervention of Franklin Roosevelt, championing a role for the federal government in regulating the economy and rebuilding the nation's infrastructure reminiscent of FDR's New Deal and Lyndon Johnson's Great Society. John McCain's top down tax cuts and continued support of deregulation, by contrast, evoked the era of Ronald Reagan—exuberant optimism and robust nationalism, but also a "trickle down" approach to economic issues, with government playing only a minor regulatory role.

The simultaneity of the crash and the election underlined how and why this moment represented a potential turning point for America in the twenty-first century—one as decisive for the nation's history in the new century as American intervention in World War II, and the American civil rights and women's movements had been for the twentieth century.

On November 4, 2008, the American people cast their ballots. They overwhelmingly elected Barack Obama. In so doing, they made a critical choice both for the nation's politics and its style of leadership. Their message, in effect, was that the time had come for a change, not just in economic policy, but in how America would present itself to the world. Whether Obama could achieve the "transformation" predicted by Colin Powell remained to be seen. But for the moment, it seemed, the question of whether America would rise or fall during the remainder of the twenty-first century had been put back into play, with a different vision of America's possibilities and a different captain at the helm.

INDEX

Page references in italics *refer to illustrations.*

311